W9-AVK-367

Invaders

INVADERS

*British and American Experience of
Seaborne Landings 1939-1945*

Colin John Bruce

CHATHAM PUBLISHING

LONDON

Copyright © Colin John Bruce 1999

First published in Great Britain in 1999 by Chatham Publishing,
61 Frith Street, London W1V 5TA

Chatham Publishing is an imprint of Gerald Duckworth & Co Ltd

British Library Cataloguing in Publication Data
A catalogue record for this book is available from the
British Library

ISBN 1 86176 045 0

All rights reserved. No part of this publication may be reproduced or transmitted in
any form or by any means, electronic or mechanical, including photocopying,
recording, or any information storage and retrieval system, without either prior
permission in writing from the publisher or a licence permitting restricted copying. The
right of Colin John Bruce to be identified as the author of this work has been asserted
by him in accordance with the Copyright, Designs and Patents Act 1988.

Typeset by Dorwyn Ltd, Rowlands Castle, Hants

Printed and bound in Great Britain by Bookcraft (Bath) Ltd

Contents

List of Plates

Foreword

by

The Honorable Raymond G H Seitz

US Ambassador in London 1991–1994

Few prospects on earth are more beautiful or serene than the convergence of the sea and the land. The sight of rhythmic waves lapping against a shoreline has inspired poets and painters for generations, and the sandy beaches of the world have become the postcard destinations for millions of travellers and holidaymakers throughout this century.

But in the Second World War a beach could be an ominous place of dread and sometimes horror. My father led an American regiment ashore on the OMAHA beaches in Normandy on D-Day, 6 June 1944. I returned there with him one fine Summer day some fifteen years later, and as cows grazed in the green meadows above the beach and gulls wheeled overhead in a blue sky, he wandered along the shore trying to pull back the memories of that fateful day. But he recognized nothing. He only remembered a nightmare of noise, chaos, confusion, fear and death, and these seemed unconnected to the dreamy, contented scenes around him.

In this book Colin John Bruce tells the story of amphibious warfare from 1939 to 1945. In those years of struggle, the Allied control of the sea was rarely in serious jeopardy. The real military challenge was to assemble forces capable of invading the European mainland and storming the fastness of the Japanese Empire. For these objectives, the Allies were initially ill-prepared, lacking both the equipment and the experience for such monumental tasks.

In the early days amphibious warfare amounted to little more than daring nighttime raids along the European or North African coasts. The largely Canadian attack on Dieppe in 1942 – the first operation of significant scale – ended in calamity, and military planners learned how complicated and perilous such an undertaking could be.

The skill of amphibious attack is to bring together all the different elements of military capability – inconveniently divided among the Army, Navy, Marines and Air Force – and to apply this power with sudden and overwhelming impact against an enemy in one place at one time. The orchestration of interservice logistics, intelligence and planning is alone a prodigious feat. But coordinating a seaborne attack that involves heavy naval and aerial bombardment, close artillery and air support, possible paratroop drops and the launch of thousands of infantry by small landing craft across choppy waters onto a remote and often hostile shore is a military wonder.

And yet the Allies carried off these combined operations time and again in the Second World War, working their way up the Italian coast until the ultimate invasion of France, and on the other side of the world, island-hopping their forces across the vast Pacific Ocean until Japan was finally defeated.

For all the military brilliance of combined operations, however, it was the valor of the individual Soldier, Sailor, Airman and Marine which made things happen. Colin John Bruce's story tells the tale of amphibious warfare from the water-level view of veterans who recount the ordinary details of their extraordinary times. This book is a tribute to their courage.

Raymond G H Seitz

Introduction

The ability to descend at will on an enemy's coastline has always
been one of the advantages which accrue from control of the sea,
and in 1939 both of the world's leading naval powers, Britain and
America, were aware of its potential. Yet when the Second World
War broke out neither had any idea how deeply they would soon
be enmeshed in the complexities of amphibious warfare. Young
officers in both countries had for many years been studying the
theoretical problems as part of their training, and both countries
had carried out small-scale landing exercises, but in essence
the techniques and equipment employed were those of an
earlier age.

Ray Tebble recalls them with some amusement.

Our 'landing craft' consisted of ships' 32ft cutters, propelled, of course, by oar
power. The method employed to insert us onto the beach was very basic. The
cutters were lowered and rowed by a couple of seamen to beneath a boom,
hoisted out at right angles to the upper deck. We would sling our rifles and
gingerly clamber out onto the boom – wearing studded ammunition boots
didn't enhance your surefootedness – and, clinging to the boom stay, we
would shuffle out sideways to a position above the cutter. Suspended from the
boom was a scrambling net. With one hand clinging to the boom stay – we
were about 30ft above the sea – the next move was to lower ourselves into the
net. Once this was accomplished, the climb down to the cutter below started.

This exercise was quite dicey; the net would swing furiously, and the cutter
would be heaving about with the motion of the sea. On reaching the
appropriate distance above the cutter you had to drop in, trying to avoid those
already embarked. There was no sympathy forthcoming if you landed flat
across the thwarts, just the usual ribald remarks from the 'old salts'.

When the Platoon was embarked it was organised into rowing positions, two
to a port oar, two to a starboard, four to a thwart. The non-rowing remainder
were packed all round. To say that this drill was awkward would be a major
understatement. We were all encumbered with equipment, packed in like
sardines and expected to row in unison.

Once cast off, with 'Jack' on the tiller, the Platoon Sergeant would call the
time. On nearing the shoreline, the command 'Toss oars!' would be given.
Each pair would then attempt to raise their oar to a vertical position. During
the execution of this movement, helmets would get elbowed over eyes and

many curses would be heard. The next order was 'Ship oars!'. This required the oarsmen to lay the oars fore-and-aft over the thwarts. At this stage of the proceedings the cutter was no place for the faint-hearted.

Once the cutter had grounded we were supposed to disembark, but usually this drill started off in waist-high water, as the cutter was never actually beached. I remember our officer, on one exercise, leaping over the bow with pistol aloft. He was about 6ft 2in, but virtually disappeared.

The traditional amphibious specialists in each country were the Marines, but the landing role was only one of many for them, and while the US Marine Corps at least set aside a permanent body of men – the Fleet Marine Force – for possible amphibious assaults, the Royal Marines were denied even that.

John Coke discovered how low amphibious warfare was on the list of priorities when he joined up.

I joined the Royal Marines as an officer in September 1935. It was the time when the Royal Navy – in fact all of the British services – were just beginning to expand, as the storm clouds gathered over Europe.

We started off at Deal for training, and then Portsmouth, where we did all the Naval courses. Because you see in those days the Marines were totally orientated towards service afloat, in the detachments carried aboard ships of the Fleet. So, since our job on board was to man some of the main and secondary armament, we had to do the same gunnery courses as the Navy people.

The only actual *military* force was the one I got involved with later on.

Was that by choice?

Well, not entirely. What happened was that I went first of all to the new cruiser HMS *Glasgow*. I joined her in 1937, and when I left her again in 1939 I was at Plymouth, waiting and wondering what I was going to do to specialise. Should I go into flying,[1] or physical training, or gunnery, or whatever. I couldn't make up my mind. Barracks life was very dull – I was second in command of a recruit company, where there was virtually no work left to do after 11.00am.

And then an opening came up for a searchlight course at Fort Cumberland, which was at Portsmouth. So I thought that might be quite amusing. Also, a friend of mine was getting married at Haslemere, and being a penniless subaltern in those days I thought well, Portsmouth's a lot closer to Haslemere than Plymouth is!

So I went up there, thinking it was for two weeks, and only when I got there did they tell me I was actually there for a two-year appointment. To train National Service people who'd been called up, which was just starting to happen.

---

1. Individual RM officers might choose to serve in Fleet Air Arm squadrons, but the Royal Marines did not have their own air units, as the US Marines did.

The first peacetime conscription in British history had been announced by Prime Minister Neville Chamberlain in April 1939, although it was July before the initial batch of youngsters were ordered to report for their six months' compulsory training. When the war broke out, additional legislation instantly extended their obligations and broadened the scope of the call-up.

So I thought oh well, there we are. One job's as good as another. And that was how I got into this force called the MNBDO – the Mobile Naval Base Defence Organisation. Which was designed to take over and run a base for the Navy, anywhere in the world. We would bring everything with us – searchlights, coast defence artillery, anti-aircraft artillery – the whole lot.

But the MNBDO wasn't like the Americans' Fleet Marine Force?

Oh no. The idea wasn't to use us to make an opposed landing. We were to go there after the Army had cleared the enemy away, to defend it. But we did get the first real landing craft when they started to appear. Which was largely due to our neighbours in Fort Cumberland, the Inter-Service Training and Development Centre, or ISTDC. They were the ones really thinking about future amphibious operations, and the kind of craft needed.

The ISTDC had been set up in 1938, bringing together represen-tatives from the Royal Navy, the Royal Marines, the Army and the Royal Air Force specifically to study amphibious warfare. On its recommendation, trials of a much-needed infantry landing craft to take the place of ships' boats had been carried out, resulting in the adoption of a standard design called the Landing Craft, Assault (LCA) in September 1939. An updated version of the earlier and slightly larger Landing Craft, Mechanised (LCM)[2] was also ordered. The LCM had been introduced in 1926, but there were still only a handful of them in existence when war came. Whereas the LCA was a personnel carrier, the LCM could carry a variety of cargoes, including a single tank.

Then the war started, in September 1939. And the C-in-C, Mediterranean decided he'd better move his base from Malta to Alexandria, because we didn't know what Italy was going to do. Malta was very vulnerable to Italian bombing, of course. And since Alexandria lacked defences, we were sent out there. Have you ever been to the Middle East?

Beirut a couple of times.

Ah, well, you'll know what I mean when I say Alexandria was a wonderful place. If you wanted to enjoy yourself with the real delights of life, Alex had it all. Our guns didn't arrive until November, so we were there doing absolutely

---

2. Prior to 1942, when the various designations were rationalised, the LCM was known as the MLC and the LCA as the ALC. To avoid confusion, only the final names have been used.

nothing, everybody getting grossly overdrawn at the bank, until our guns arrived.

Then eventually the Army sent out units to take over, and we came back home.

Similarly, when the Home Fleet wanted to use Scapa Flow in the Orkneys as its base, it found the defences unprepared. Honestly, I'll never understand how we won that war . . .

The gun sites on the main islands were to be done by contractors, but on the smaller islands of course nobody had any kit. We, with our landing craft, and our quickly-constructable piers and our strips of beach roadway, were the only people who had the expertise to do it, so those few who'd remained behind were already up there when I got back in January 1940. And we busied ourselves installing these guns all round the islands.

When you built one of these piers, you ran it out, hoping to get out to its limit at the moment of low water, building up the structure. And when the water came in again you had to stop working. Then you came back the next day and finished it. I've got a picture here of what they looked like. We had this special tubular steel [like scaffolding] made for us. Then you installed a crane on it. So we'd go to an island, put the guns in, then take the pier down again, and off to another one.

And we had beach roadways, which would get vehicles up from the landing craft.

When you say beach roadway, do you mean something which came in a roll?

No, no. Nothing like that in those days, my dear chap. These were solid steel, sort of interlocked.

More like the roadway of a temporary bridge?

That's right. Quite heavy steel stuff.

I loved doing all this. It really was rather fun. The weather up there at that time of year was appalling, but you see we lived in a BI [British India Steam Navigation Company] liner called the SS *Mashobra*, which had been taken over. She was still run by the Merchant Navy, with a Goanese crew, so when you came back freezing from work there'd be a steward there running the hot water for your bath, you know. Oh dear, it seems unbelievable now. Like Jules Verne.

Once we'd finished, and the guns were in place, the Fleet moved in, and the Germans started to bomb us. There'd be guns firing, and searchlights and things, and at a certain point all the guns would turn inwards and throw a terrific barrage over the Fleet. And when you saw this, it was a fireworks display to beat anything you'd ever seen.

Then the Norwegian campaign began, and it was decided that we'd go out there. My task was to help with the unloading of equipment for an airstrip at Skaanland, near Narvik. Some of the others went to the landings at Narvik itself, where all of their LCMs and new LCAs were lost. Even the *Mashobra* was bombed and abandoned. Like everybody else, we had a pretty terrible time.

ONE

Raiders: The Commandos 1940-1942

The Germans launched their invasion of neutral Norway on 9 April 1940. It was a bold move, made without having achieved superiority at sea and with no specialised amphibious shipping. The German planners believed, rightly, that paralysis on the part of the Norwegians plus their on rapid seizure and use of Norway's airfields would outweigh any disadvantages, and at the cost of a large part of their navy they succeeded in capturing a number of strategic points along the Norwegian coast.

The British and French, who had been considering plans of their own for violating Norwegian neutrality, hastily despatched their few available troops to oppose the German takeover. Most of the battleworthy British divisions were in France, however, and as a stop-gap it was decided to raise some guerrilla units from among the Territorial divisions still in the UK.

Harry Phillips had joined the Territorial Army at the age of sixteen and a half, and towards the end of 1939 had been posted to Ballykinler in Northern Ireland.

One day I was studying the noticeboard when I read that volunteers were needed to serve on a secret special mission. Headbanger that I was, I volunteered. Orders came through to pack equipment, and one night a party of us slipped out from the port of Larne to Stranraer in Scotland. We ended up sealed off in Fort William, only entry via an Army road barrier, and were told that our unit was to be called No 2 Independent Company.

Ten such units were being formed, each with an authorised strength of 21 officers and 268 other ranks. Only the first five, however, would see action in Norway.

Our equipment was changed to include yellow chamois mountain boots and grey woollen polo-necked jerseys, and we were instructed to scrub all blancoed equipment to white and not to polish any more brass. Using sand and bath-brick our equipment turned out snow white.

I was taught heliograph – sending of messages in Morse code by mirror – and how to blow up a 2ft section of railway line to sabotage it. And I was taught to load and fire a Bren gun blindfolded. I could assemble every part of it, which I still remember nearly sixty years on. Four groups – barrel, body, piston and butt groups. We also had to learn how to provide for ourselves off the land, so we lived rough and survived for days by shooting wild deer and blowing up salmon with guncotton in the Scottish lochs around Mallaig. Venison and salmon were both quite a novelty if you were from a poor family like me.

After two months' training we were packed into buses and travelled overnight by road to Aberdeen, where we boarded a Royal Navy sloop. On board we were given a large tot of Navy rum and told we were to set sail for northern Norway, to carry out sabotage.

We left on the morning tide and sailed via the Shetland Islands, being bombed by German Stukas [Junkers Ju87 dive bombers] when we got nearer Norway. I took a turn on the twin mounted Bren guns, to protect the sloop. There was no darkness to hide in, as it was May – 24 hours of light. Land of the Midnight Sun, you see. After about five days, zig-zagging to avoid German subs, we arrived at the coastal fishing town of Bodo, where we were billeted overnight.

Bodo was a town of about 5000 inhabitants, located south of the important port of Narvik, and just inside the Arctic Circle. The situation in Norway was an unhappy one. The Germans had complete air superiority and had already crushed the last opposition in the south of the country, where the majority of the population lived. In the wild, sparsely-populated north they so far held only the port of Narvik, now under siege by the remains of the Norwegian Army and by the French and British reinforcements, but they were gaining ground relentlessly.

Harry's unit was landed at Bodo to join Nos 1, 3, 4 and 5 Independent Companies, which were struggling to delay the German main body as it pushed north to break the siege.

Our CO remarked 'If I see one of my men ever give up, I will personally shoot him'. We never found out whether he meant it, but I think he did. As I could ride a motorcycle I was given a Royal Enfield and told to help a Lieutenant, who rode pillion and was to blow the vital bridges at the last moment.

We travelled south by ferry and road across fjords and snow belts, via Pothus and Mo-i-Rana. I suffered temporary snow blindness, and pains in the eyes and head, until I was issued with dark snow glasses.

Our No 2 Independent Company's job was to fight rearguard actions so as the troops further north could take Narvik, important for the export of iron ore to feed the munitions factories in Germany. After contacting hostile forces we were to conduct an orderly withdrawal, keeping in contact with the enemy.

We succeeded, fighting many battles, always withdrawing in an orderly fashion. We suffered a lot of casualties from frostbite due to inadequate clothing. Then, after numerous skirmishes, we were told to destroy all our equipment and to get back to Bodo, where we would be taken off. My motorcycle had to be abandoned as soon as it ran out of fuel.

On reaching one crossing we found the ferry'd been sunk by Nazi planes to cut off our retreat. She lay a little offshore, with her superstructure partly visible. The only alternative was to forced march 10 miles over mountainous snow.

We arrived back at our previous disembarkation point, Bodo, to find it had been incendiary bombed and razed to the ground, the inhabitants fleeing to the mountains. We spent a few nights in the burned-out timber buildings, living on the remains of Norwegian food found in the houses, hoping a naval vessel would evacuate us.

When one arrived she was a small Norwegian fishing boat. One hundred and twenty of us were packed like sardines into the fish holds, which were *stinking,* and battened down for the voyage back to Scotland. Sick and exhausted, we spent the whole trip, of many days, in total darkness being seasick over each other and having to go to the toilet where we lay.

We sailed all the way round to Glasgow, and then had to march the 8 miles to Kirkintilloch, where we were made welcome by the residents, who fed us, bathed us and gave us their beds until we could be billeted and regrouped in a local school.

Narvik had fallen the day before the evacuation from Bodo had begun, but it proved to be a hollow victory. With their position in France now also collapsing, the Allies simply destroyed the iron ore facilities and withdrew again, leaving the Germans to complete their delayed conquest of the North.

The events in France were far more alarming than the loss of Norway. After eight months of 'phoney war' the Germans had suddenly attacked on 10 May, their armour achieving a spectacular penetration which reached the Channel and cut off a large portion of the Allied forces. An improvised withdrawal by sea had managed to extricate many of the men, including most of the British, but their vehicles and equipment had been lost. On 21 June 1940 France surrendered, leaving the British without a foothold on the Continent except for the tiny enclave of Gibraltar, which guarded the entrance to the Mediterranean.

Despite this, the new British Prime Minister, Winston Churchill, was already looking for ways to maintain morale by hitting back at the enemy. An expansion of the Independent Companies seemed an obvious solution, and with Churchill's backing the Army began to raise new, larger units termed 'Commandos', after the South African Boer irregular formations which had made such effective adversaries in the first years of the century.

The British Army had always believed in aggressive patrolling. Raiding the coast of Occupied Europe was seen as simply an extension of that principle. In the longer term, though, the Army knew it would now have to prepare for a full-scale amphibious invasion – possibly several – if the war was to be carried to a successful conclusion.

In the meantime the vexed question of inter-service co-operation had to be addressed. The Norwegian campaign had again shown that rivalry – if not outright distrust – between the armed services was a serious problem. Churchill's char-acteristically radical solution was to create a completely new organisation, 'Combined Operations', to draw together the Commando units and the ships the Navy was assembling for their use.

Although this approach held an undeniable appeal in the desperate summer of 1940, it sowed the seeds of much subsequent confusion in the British command structure. There were constant arguments over exactly who was responsible for what – a situation which was not helped by Churchill's appointment of the abrasive Admiral of the Fleet Sir Roger Keyes to head the new organisation after its first month of existence.[1]

One of Keyes' first acts was to move Combined Operations Headquarters out of the Admiralty building and down Whitehall to its own premises at 1A Richmond Terrace. Regardless of the obvious symbolism, however, and regardless of the fact that it later had its own representative on the Chiefs of Staff Committee – giving Combined Operations in effect the status of a fourth service alongside the Royal Navy, the Army and the RAF – it was *not* a separate armed service. Personnel to man its ships, for example, were still recruited into the Royal Navy. Interestingly, when America entered the war it set up no equivalent organisation of its own, choosing merely to assign its units to an 'Amphibious Force' within each operational Fleet.

When Keyes took up his appointment on 17 July 1940 he had at his disposal the existing small force of LCMs and LCAs, with more on order, the ISTDC, the Commandos, and a number of passenger vessels undergoing conversion into Landing Ships, Infantry (LSIs). The LSIs, which carried landing craft in place of their normal lifeboats, were grouped according to their troop capacity and endurance, from the big ocean liners classified as

---

1. Succeeding Lieutenant General Alan Bourne, the Adjutant General of the Royal Marines, who had held the post since 14 June and now became Keyes' deputy.

Landing Ships, Infantry (Large) down to the shorter-range ferries classified as Landing Ships, Infantry (Medium) and (Small). In addition, a group of small vessels were given the designation Landing Ship, Infantry (Hand Hoisting) (LSI(H)), if their landing craft had to be hoisted aboard by hand. Some LSIs were commissioned into the Royal Navy as warships, and flew the White Ensign. Others simply retained their civilian crews and continued to fly the Red Ensign of the Merchant Navy.

Bill Miles was drafted to one of the latter. He cherishes few happy memories of his time in Combined Operations.

I was sent to Portsmouth for my initial seamanship and gunnery training, and after three months I was sent to Whale Island – the tough Gunnery School in Portsmouth – for more. The three weeks spent there were enough for me, and I was pleased when a draft came sending me to Hayling Island. It was only after I arrived that I found this was a Combined Operations training establishment. Up to then I'd believed that Combined Ops was a volunteer-only outfit.

At last the time came for testing and selection of landing craft crews. Myself and a few others went on draft to join an LCA Flotilla who were based at Inveraray, on Loch Fyne, Scotland.

Inveraray had become the site of the first Combined Training Centre, where landing craft crews and the Army could be trained together, in July 1940.

We were accommodated aboard an old paddle-steamer in the loch, where slung hammocks and poor food were the order of the day. It rained without stop, and the loch water was very cold. The troops, who were often up to their waists in water loaded down with rifles and equipment, at times needed help to get ashore. On top of this, live ammunition and blast grenades plus smoke mortars were being used to simulate battle conditions.

I wasn't sorry when a draft came for me to join a Landing Ship, Infantry – an LCA carrier ship – at Southampton Docks. Most of the way from Scotland on the train was spent standing in packed corridors, and by the time I reached the ship my legs had almost cried uncle. After reporting aboard I was shown down to a mess deck below the troop space at the very stern of the ship, where I was allocated a steel bunk and locker. I noticed that the bunk ran athwartships. All the better, fore-and-aft ones had been claimed. When the rest of the LCA crews came onto the mess deck I was given a large mug of strong sweet tea. They seemed a jolly likeable crowd, and I felt I was going to fit in OK. We were to join the small fleet of LSIs for sea manoeuvres, gunnery shoots and launching and recovery exercises.

The ship, an Irish Sea ferry, could make 17 knots and her somewhat sparse troop deck accommodated several hundred fully armed troops, with crude toilet arrangements. Hot water was supplied by a steam pipe in the well deck. She was a coal burner, and had extra bunkers to increase her steaming range. The worst thing about the ship was a heavy iron rubbing strake which went the length of the hull above the waterline. This constituted a life-threatening hazard to the landing craft and the men in them when hoisting or lowering, as the strake could crash down on them as the ship rolled. It could have been so easily removed during the ship's conversion – another cock-up by the armchair experts at the Admiralty. We felt we had enough to contend with without them helping the enemy. The ship had a Merchant Navy crew and RN gunners, but they kept themselves to themselves and we had little to do with them. They ran the ship, we manned the landing craft. The only connection was when they operated the hoisting and lowering gear, a task which I must say the Merchant Navy seamen became good at. Their officers left us alone and gave us no trouble. The ship had no doctor or medical staff.

Our LCAs were lowered into the water by heavy-duty power-operated davits, the troops and crew boarding the craft prior to lowering. The task of hooking on and casting off from the ship required a high degree of skill and seamanship from the coxswain and seamen. The snatch blocks used were very heavy steel, large and difficult to handle. One seaman stood on the stern deck by his block; the other was by the inboard bow block. The craft was dropped onto the top of a wave, and the blocks had to be released while there was slack in the falls. Failure to release together could mean a capsize and loss of life. The coxswain's job was to clear the ship before the rubbing strake could come down on him.

Hooking on was even worse. The coxswain had to manoeuvre his pitching craft alongside the ship under the davits, to where the seamen, bracing themselves on their unstable platform, could grab these bone-crushing blocks and hook on. Once again, failure to hook on together could spell disaster.

The seamen's duties, apart from what I've just described, were to be available to take over from the coxswain or stoker should they be killed or injured. On long trips they did relieve them. They also manned the machine gun, operated the signalling equipment and lowered and raised the bow ramp, plus operating the kedge anchor, if it was required. I once saw a seaman sitting on the bow of his boat preventing it from hitting a Teller mine which was attached to a beach obstacle. Every crewman was needed on an LCA.

What was the LCA herself like?

A strong, heavy wooden craft with armoured side panels and doors, and a ramp which was lowered to disembark troops. She lay low in the water and offered a poor target for the enemy, but this also made her less seaworthy. The power, which gave a speed of 10 knots, was supplied by two Ford V8 petrol engines controlled from a very small engine-room at the stern. The stoker received his instructions by telegraph and voice pipe from the coxswain in his armoured cockpit forward. Direct control of the engines would've been much preferred. The gun supplied was a Lewis machine gun with a rate of fire of 550 rounds a minute. This was a lightened version for easy handling, and if required could be fired from the hip. A mallet and a selection of round tapered wooden plugs came with each craft, and if the enemy shot nice round holes in the hull these could be very useful.

Very strong steel eyes were provided fore and aft for lifting and lowering. There was also a kedge anchor on the stern and a next-to-useless hand bilge pump.

These craft carried thirty-five soldiers plus a four-man crew. Our LCA ship's company consisted of thirty-six seamen and stokers, four maintenance ratings – an electrician, two shipwrights and an ERA [engine room artificer] – one seaman petty officer and five RNVR officers. The CO was a Lieutenant and the three deck officers and the engineer officer were Sub-Lieutenants.

The CO dished out punishment like he was Captain Bligh of the *Bounty*. He was disliked, and his ability to command wasn't respected. The engineer officer was a likeable man, who went about his business with quiet efficiency. Of the three deck officers, two were OK and one was very popular, and like Mr Christian of the *Bounty* stood up to the CO and complained of the excessive punishment being dished out. He was soon posted, but before he left the ship shook hands with all of us. We presented him with a cigarette lighter inscribed 'To an officer and a gentleman ... '. He went down the gangway with tears in his eyes, and we never saw him again. Shortly after, the CO put me on a charge for dumb insolence, which means he didn't like the way I looked at him. In this case the charge was correct, and at the time I felt the look was worth the five days of punishment I received.

If you ask me did I *like* Combined Operations, the answer is no.

If you ask me am I proud of being in Combined Operations, yes I am.

By contrast the Commandos, like the Independent Companies they replaced, were built up exclusively from volunteers. Commando officers were allowed to personally select the men under them.

Sapper *Alan Angus* was one of those who decided to apply.

On 18 July Captain Emmett and Lieutenant Banks visited the unit to interview the volunteers. They questioned our motives for volunteering, but were chiefly interested in our physical fitness and swimming ability. Of the thirty or so candidates interviewed they selected seven, including my friend Bruce Cowper and myself. The following afternoon the seven of us were sent off with all our kit to join our new unit at Bovington Camp. On arrival we were paraded with about forty men from various regiments, and told that we were to be known as 'C' Troop, No 4 Commando. Our Troop officers were Captain Emmett, Lieutenant Banks and Lieutenant Gardner, and a Sergeant White from the East Yorkshire Regiment was to be our Troop Sergeant Major.

We spent only a couple of days at Bovington, the time being occupied mainly in swimming, PT [Physical Training] and cross-country running. Further recruits were arriving to bring the Commando up to its projected strength of 500 men.

On Sunday 21 July we were all transported to Weymouth in a fleet of coaches, where we learned that our Headquarters was to be in the Pavilion by the pier. It was here that we first saw our new commanding officer, Lieutenant Colonel Legard, a very smart figure in the uniform of the 5th Royal Inniskilling Dragoon Guards. We were dismissed with instructions to find ourselves billets in the town, for which we were to be given an allowance of six shillings and eightpence per day, and to return to the Pavilion in the afternoon for a lecture from the Colonel.

The main theme of the Colonel's lecture on the Sunday afternoon was that as picked men we should have many privileges, but these privileges were not to be abused. He would demand the highest standards of discipline and training, and anyone who failed to come up to the required standards would be returned to his former unit. By intensive training and the rejection of any who proved to be unsuitable he was determined to make No 4 Commando a unit second to none. As a member of this select band one would normally have the privilege of living in civilian billets; there would be no unnecessary fatigue duties, and there would be no punishments – other than RTU, or return to unit.

The next three weeks were spent in hard but generally interesting training. First parade each morning was at 7.00am on the pier, and took the form of a swim followed by PT. Bruce and I were taken before the Colonel and threatened with RTU after only two days because we were a couple of minutes late for this parade, but after a severe talking-to we were given a second chance. We were lucky, because in those early days an RTU was liable to follow the slightest misdemeanour. We bought ourselves an alarm clock and managed to keep out of further trouble.

We used to return to our billets at about 8.00am for breakfast, and parade at the Pavilion again at 9.15am. For this second parade we had to be spotlessly turned out, and we usually had an hour's squad drill. Squad drill initially caused a great deal of trouble in the Commandos, because every regiment seemed to have its own peculiar way of giving the orders and performing the movements laid down in the drill book. It took some time to arrive at an acceptable compromise. The rest of the morning would be spent in lectures or weapons training until we were dismissed at 12.30pm for lunch. Bruce and I generally went with one or two others to the White Ensign Club. In the afternoon we used to go onto the beach for PT and instruction in unarmed combat, followed by a swim. Twice a week we would go on a 3-mile cross-country run, and at least once a week there would be a night scheme [exercise].

At that time No 4 Commando didn't go in for the long route marches which seemed to figure largely in the training of some other Commandos; the CO was more insistent that we should be able to cover distances of up to 12 miles in darkness at high speed and with little sound, and be sure of reaching our objective fit for action. He considered that any raid on enemy-occupied territory at that time would be on a small scale, the troops being landed and taken off again the same night. The objectives would therefore necessarily be near the coast, and the time allowed for the operation couldn't amount to more than a few hours.

After a short time it was decided that all the Sapper – Royal Engineers – members of the Commando should be formed into one Troop, which would specialise in the use of explosives. We seven former members of the 232nd Field Company, RE were consequently transferred to 'H' Troop, under the command of Captain Aylwin. The other officers were Lieutenant Tracy, a happy-go-lucky type who tended to treat explosives as toys and generally had a few detonators in his cap, and Lieutenant Lewis, a young infantry officer from the Dorsetshire Regiment. The Troop Sergeant Major was a Scotsman named McKay, a Regular of the best type. On parade he was very much 'on parade', but off parade he was a good friend to us all. He always seemed to enjoy life, and had a dry wit which could be relied upon to raise a smile even under the most trying conditions.

Training in 'H' Troop was largely concerned with explosives, although we also took part in the swimming, PT, night schemes and other activities. We became familiar with many different gadgets for detonating explosive charges, and we also visited the local gas works and other establishments to learn the most efficient ways of putting the plant out of action.

On 13 October, No 4 Commando entrained at short notice for Glasgow.

We arrived in Glasgow early on Monday morning, and were taken down to the quayside where we had our first view of HMS *Glengyle*, a converted merchant ship fitted out with landing craft which we were soon to know very well. Our accommodation was reached by a steep companionway leading down into what'd formerly been the ship's hold, but which was now divided into mess decks furnished with tables and forms [benches], and with space for slinging hammocks.

We spent two weeks on board the *Glengyle*, only going ashore for exercises with the landing craft and occasional route marches. The exercises were largely for the benefit of the Navy, whose main concern was to 'drop the kedge' at the critical moment as we approached the shore, so that the landing craft could be winched off the beach again when required. In the meantime the troops crouched uncomfortably in rows, feeling cold and seasick, weapons in hand, waiting for the moment when the ramp would be lowered for them to leap out onto the beach. On Tuesday 29 October we went ashore, supposedly to go to Oban, but there was a last-minute change of plan and we spent the night in camp at Inveraray. The next morning we were roused at 4.00am to march the 16 miles to the railway station at Dalmally. It was pouring with rain, so that we reached the station absolutely soaked, and then had to hang about for ages waiting for the train. After a very slow and seemingly roundabout journey we eventually ended up at Troon.

On Sunday 1 December we were given a few days' leave – embarkation leave we thought, as rumours were rife that a major operation was planned for the near future. We were back in Troon by the following weekend, but hardly had time to unpack before we were off again. We had a terrible rush to get ready, and after missing the bus which we intended to get, had to walk the mile or so to Troon at full speed carrying all our kit in order to be on parade on time.

Having travelled by train from Troon to Gourock, we embarked once more on the *Glengyle* and sailed down the Firth of Clyde to the Isle of Arran. All the signs were there that something big was about to happen – two more Glen ships, the *Glenroy* and the *Glenearn* [both White Ensign LSI(L)s like the *Glengyle*] were anchored in Lamlash Bay, and were being loaded up with stores of all kinds brought out by lighters.

During the next few days we took part in several exercises in which we made landings around Brodick, Whiting Bay, and on Holy Island. Other Commandos also took part, including No 7, who had solved the problem of headgear by wearing cap comforters, and No 11, known as the Scottish Commando, who wore balmorals with black hackles. These two Commandos seemed to specialise in going on long route marches round the island, or climbing Goat Fell. There was also No 8 Commando, known to us as the 'blue blood' Commando, among whose officers were such well known personalities as Randolph Churchill [the Prime Minister's son] and Evelyn Waugh [the novelist], and whose Troop commanders all seemed to be titled. Before the middle of December it was announced that the operation for which we'd been training – rumoured to be a landing on the island of Pantelleria in the Mediterranean – had had to be postponed; the required conditions of moon and tide wouldn't occur again for another month, and in the meantime, for the sake of security, we were to remain on the Isle of Arran and to have no communication of any kind with the mainland.

Early in January [1941] we were told that the operation had been cancelled. We went back on board the *Glengyle*, where Sir Roger Keyes, the head of Combined Operations, made a rousing speech in which he said that although this scheme had had to be cancelled, he had no intention of allowing 'this bright sword to rust in the Highlands'. We were then sent on two weeks' leave.

On returning from leave on 28 January 1941 we embarked once more on the *Glengyle* and sailed back to Lamlash Bay. A letter written the next day says 'I expect this will be my last chance of sending you a letter for some time, at any rate an uncensored one, as we are supposed to be sailing in a day or two. I won't be able to go ashore again, but I am hoping to find someone who is staying behind to post it on the mainland. We are anchored off Arran just now . . . The last shore party is leaving now I think so I will finish this'. This doesn't mention the fact that some members of No 4 Commando, including myself, had voluntarily transferred to No 7 in order to bring it up to full strength before sailing for the Middle East. The three Glen ships were to go, taking Nos 7, 8 and 11 Commandos, while No 4 was to remain behind.

The *Glengyle* and her sister-ships sailed from Lamlash Bay on 31 January, bound for the Middle East via the Cape.

When we'd sailed for the Middle East at the beginning of February 1941 the idea had been that the Commandos and the Glen ships should take part in an assault on the Italian-occupied island of Rhodes.[2] At the time the news from the Middle East was good; the British Army was advancing rapidly in the Western Desert, and by the end of the first week in February had taken Benghazi. A day or so later advance units reached El Agheila, and there seemed every prospect that Tripoli might soon fall. The Italian Army had been largely destroyed – one of the first sights that impressed us when we arrived at Geneifa [near the Suez canal] were the huge prisoner of war cages in which many thousands of Italian prisoners were confined. However, by this time the situation had changed completely. Commonwealth troops had had to be withdrawn from the Western Desert to meet the threatened German invasion of Greece, while at the same time German units were arriving in Tripoli to stiffen up the Italians.

Although we carried out some training at Geneifa in preparation for the attack on Rhodes, it soon became apparent that it was unlikely to take place. A powerful German force had been rapidly built up in the Desert, and by 11 April had driven the depleted British Army back to the Egyptian frontier, although Tobruk, completely surrounded, still held out. The threatened invasion of Greece had also taken place, and the situation there was rapidly deteriorating. We played no part in any of this, and in fact apart from a few route marches and PT to toughen us up after the voyage, we had a fairly easy time.

We left Geneifa suddenly in the middle of April, travelling by train to Port Said, where we embarked once more on the *Glengyle* and sailed for Alexandria. The harbour at Alexandria was a scene of great activity, with vessels of all sorts coming and going continuously in their efforts to keep the troops in Greece supplied. We watched all this with interest, as did the 'matelots' on the French ships impounded there, and we saw Colonel Laycock [commander of the Middle East Commando force] make several trips by motor boat to HMS *Warspite,* the flagship of Admiral Cunningham, Commander-in-Chief of the Mediterranean Fleet. We wondered what was being planned for us.

We didn't have long to wait. We sailed from Alexandria on 19 April, escorted by an anti-aircraft cruiser and three destroyers. Our Troop commander, Captain Nicholls, told us that we were to carry out a raid on the enemy-held port of Bardia, about 275 miles west of Alexandria, and about 20 miles from Sollum. The coast from Sollum [on the Egyptian side of the border] to Bardia [on the Libyan side] runs in a north-north-westerly direction, with small rocky beaches backed by cliffs 300ft high. Landings were to be made on four separate beaches designated A, B, C and D, of which D, the most southerly, was allocated to our Troop. Our objective was to destroy a coastal defence battery on the cliff top.

---

2. The occupation of the island by the Italians dated back to 1912, when they had seized it from the Turks.

It was dark when the *Glengyle* took up position 3 or 4 miles off Bardia at about 10.30pm, and our LCA was lowered into the water. There was an unfortunate delay because the supposedly quick-release device on one of the other craft failed to function, and we had to circle round for some time. Although there was only a slight swell a few of the men became seasick. We eventually set off for the shore about half an hour late. As we approached the coast we could see the high cliffs we'd have to climb, and below them we could see the waves breaking on the rocky foreshore. Fortunately the crew were able to bring the landing craft into an inlet where the rocks formed a natural landing place, and most of us were able to get ashore almost dry-shod. Our chief worry at the time was that the crew were shouting to one another as they fended the craft off the rocks, and I fully expected to hear shots from the shore as we headed for the cliffs. However, there was no sign of any opposition, and we were soon struggling up a steep path towards the top. Corporal Burford and I were both carrying packs filled with gelignite, and also fuses and detonators, as well as ammunition in our ammunition pouches. We were both armed with rifles, and, loaded as we were, it was hard going until we finally reached the top. We then followed the edge of the cliff northwards, and hadn't gone very far when Burford and I were ordered to stop and wait while the rest of the Troop went forward to attack and overwhelm the gun crews. We only seemed to wait a minute or two before a runner came back to tell us we were wanted. We were surprised there'd been no sound, but it soon became clear that there were no gun crews to worry about.

We found four guns arranged in two pairs in concrete emplacements, but they were rusty and uncared for and obviously hadn't been fired for some time. Burford and I nevertheless set about fixing explosive charges around the breech blocks of the guns, each of us working on one pair. Captain Nicholls stayed with us, but as time was getting short he ordered the rest of the Troop to head back to the beach. When the charges were ready we lit short lengths of safety fuse and took cover in a concrete dugout. After a minute there was a loud explosion as the charges on the first two guns went off, but although we waited another minute, no second explosion followed. The charges fixed by Corporal Burford had failed to detonate, and he was anxious to go out immediately to find out why. Captain Nicholls made him wait a little longer to be sure that it was safe before allowing him to go and fix another fuse, and this time it was successful. We paused long enough to make certain that all four guns had been definitely put out of action before heading back along the cliff top towards the beach. As we clambered down the steep cliff the rest of the Troop, most of whom were already in the landing craft, were shouting to us to hurry, as the *Glengyle* had to sail well before dawn if the danger of enemy air attack was to be avoided, and we'd taken more than our allotted time. As soon as we were aboard the landing craft we set out to sea again, and on reaching the *Glengyle* found that we were among the first to get back. There was a period of waiting during which most of the landing craft returned safely, but there were still two missing when it was decided that we could wait no longer and the ship set sail for Alexandria.

The raid can't be regarded as a success, although reports published later claimed that it'd served its main purpose by relieving enemy pressure at Sollum, and a certain amount of damage had been done to stores and installations in Bardia. The landings had been unopposed and the town unoccupied, yet one officer had been killed – accidentally shot by one of his own men – and more than sixty men who failed to re-embark had been taken prisoner; though one of the missing landing craft with its complement of men did reach Tobruk a day or so later.

On 20 May we heard the news that the invasion of Crete by German airborne forces had begun. We were about to start training with the Navy on some newly-arrived 'Eureka' landing craft [Landing Craft, Personnel (Large) – American craft comparable in size to an LCA but without the benefit of a ramp], and on the evening of 22 May our Troop marched to Aboukir Bay for this purpose. We'd hardly settled down for the night when an urgent message was received, recalling us as quickly as possible. We marched back in the early hours of the morning, to find on our arrival that everyone was packing up to go to Crete.

In the afternoon we marched from the camp, loaded up with as much equipment as we could carry, and boarded a train at the nearby station. After waiting for a short time we were ordered off the train again and marched back to camp. It was only a short distance, but the amount of kit we had to carry in the hot sun made it an exhausting journey, and tempers were becoming frayed. Back at camp, Colonel Laycock explained that it'd been intended to send us to Crete in the Glen ships, but the intensity of the enemy air attacks on shipping had forced a change in plan. Later the same day, however, an advance party moved out, leaving the rest of us on standby.

The next morning, Saturday 24 May, the move was on again. We piled into buses whose Arab drivers had obviously been told to get us to the docks at Alexandria as quickly as possible. Four destroyers were waiting for us alongside the quay, and as soon as one had taken on board her quota of troops she cast off and headed out to sea. The whole operation was carried out so hurriedly that Major Wylie was left standing helplessly on the quay as the last destroyer pulled out.

We travelled all day at high speed through a rough sea. The decks were constantly awash, and we heard that a man had been washed overboard. Certainly a ship's boat was lost from one of the destroyers. As darkness fell we were approaching the south western corner of Crete, and down on the mess decks we were listening to radio broadcasts giving the latest news – how the next few hours could prove decisive, and that reinforcements were on their way. In the meantime we were preparing to go ashore.

For some time we sat in full marching order. Captain Nicholls told us that we were to be landed in the south-west corner of the island, march about 40 miles over the mountains, and make a counterattack on the enemy-held aerodrome at Maleme the next day. It sounded a formidable enterprise, and as we waited expectantly, rifles in hand, we pondered silently about the possible outcome. The next news came as an anticlimax – it was impossible to put us ashore in the prevailing conditions, and we were heading back to Alexandria. The return journey was again carried out at speed, and by the evening of 25 May we were back in harbour.

We'd no sooner tied up alongside than we were ordered to transfer from the destroyers to the minelaying cruiser HMS *Abdiel* – the fastest ship in the Navy, as we were informed by her crew. A few hours were spent loading food and ammunition, but early in the morning of 26 May we were at sea and heading for Crete once more. The journey was uneventful, and we came within sight of the island while it was still daylight. It was a beautiful evening, with the sun glinting on the blue sea, and everything seemed quiet and peaceful. For a few minutes we watched an aeroplane in the distance, but it appeared to take no notice of us, and continued on its unhurried way to the east. It was hard to believe that a bloody battle was being fought only a short distance away.

Our destination on this occasion was Suda Bay, and this entailed passing round the eastern end of the island before turning westwards to travel along the northern coast for approximately 120 miles. The night was dark when we eventually dropped anchor in Suda Bay shortly before midnight. A landing craft came alongside to take us ashore, but first, we were somewhat taken aback to learn, it had to discharge a large party of men who were being evacuated. When we finally landed we had to wait on the stone jetty while the Troop commanders went off to get their orders. Captain Nicholls soon returned to tell us that we were to dump all our kit except our weapons and ammunition, that we were to fight a rearguard action across the island, and that our chances of evacuation were slim. Before we'd had time to digest this information we were being led out of the town and up into the hills immediately to the south-west, our packs abandoned on the quay.

When daylight came we found ourselves among the vines and olive trees on a hillside overlooking the main road from Suda to the west. We had a good view of Suda Bay and the Akrotiri peninsula beyond. In the bay were numerous vessels, many of them little more than smoking hulks. Among them was the cruiser HMS *York*, which we learnt had been seriously damaged some weeks earlier, and was now beached. She continued to be used as an anti-aircraft battery, and was a regular target for the German bombers. From our position on the hillside we were often looking down on the enemy planes as they came in almost unopposed. The few anti-aircraft guns still in action were subject to such merciless dive-bombing that it seemed incredible that the gunners could survive. One battery in particular, on the Akrotiri peninsula, was the target for a succession of Stukas throughout the morning, but the guns continued to fire. In addition to the dive bombers there were Messerschmitt fighters strafing anything that moved on the roads or in the olive groves, and there was a steady procession of Ju52 transport planes overhead.

We spent most of Tuesday 27 May in this position. We could hear the sounds of battle to the west, and knew that it wasn't far away, but we couldn't tell how it was going. Later in the afternoon, when the enemy air activity had diminished, we moved down to the main road near Suda, beside an old walled cemetery. A stream of stragglers was making its way eastwards along the road. Word had got around that the Army was to be evacuated from Sphakia on the south coast, and these men, the remnants of units that'd disintegrated under the savage air attacks of the past few days, were making for the beaches. Some were still armed, but many were not, and it was obvious that most of them were past fighting. As we watched them a Messerschmitt suddenly appeared, flying low above the road; there was an immediate dive for cover, but presumably the pilot had no ammunition left, for he didn't open fire. As he passed we were close enough to see him give a cheery wave, and we replied with a few ineffectual rifle shots.

In the evening we took up a defensive position astride the main road. We'd been told that all the forward troops were to be withdrawn during the night, and that we would be left holding the front line. It was dark before the first organised units appeared, but even in the darkness it was heartening to hear the sound of marching feet, and to sense that these were men who still had some fight left in them. They were far from being the disorganised rabble that we'd seen earlier, and in spite of all they'd been through they seemed cheery and confident. They were mostly New Zealanders, and we were particularly impressed by the bearing of the Maori Battalion; as they marched past we caught glimpses of men with captured enemy weapons slung over their shoulders, or with picks and shovels strapped to their packs. Every man seemed to be carrying far more than his normal equipment.

Eventually we were told that no more British troops were expected, and that anyone else approaching our line was likely to be German. All remained quiet, however, and shortly before dawn on 28 May we were ordered to withdraw. We followed the road along the side of Suda Bay as the sun came up and darkness gave way to daylight. On our right the hills rose steeply and appeared to be impassable, but after a couple of miles we reached a point where the coast road had been blown up, and another road turned inland. We followed this road up onto a ridge overlooking the bay, and soon we were greeted by another unit, who'd taken up a defensive position in the hills and now formed the rearguard.

We continued down the other side of the ridge into a broad fertile valley, under the impression that for the time being at least we were comparatively safe. To the south we could see in the distance the snow-capped White Mountains, beyond which lay Sphakia.

We had barely reached the valley bottom when we were startled by the sound of machine gun fire, and realised we were being fired on. We hastily took cover among the olive trees at the left-hand side of the road. On the other side of the road were some low hills covered with rocks and scrub, and it became clear that enemy machine guns were established on one of these. While the officers had a brief conference we discovered that the olive trees concealed a ration dump, and I took the opportunity to help myself to a tin of fruit – the first food I'd had since leaving HMS *Abdiel.* A few minutes later

Captain Nicholls returned to tell us that the Troop had been ordered to attack the German positions.

We were in dead ground as we approached the hill, and soon we were making our way up the slope. As we neared the summit we were ordered to fix bayonets, and a few moments later, as we came over the brow of the hill, to charge. We let out a yell and rushed forward. The enemy, unseen until then, suddenly appeared almost beneath our feet. One man sprang up from behind a rock only 2 or 3 yards in front of me, and as he turned and ran he threw a stick grenade in my direction. The grenade landed within a few feet of me, and I saw it explode, but miraculously felt nothing. In the meantime other Germans appeared, dodging from rock to rock in their efforts to escape. They presented only momentary targets, and although I fired off several rounds I don't know whether any of them found their mark.

I suddenly became aware that I was ahead of the rest of the Troop, and looking over my shoulder I saw our Bren gunner a few yards behind me and to my right. He was advancing with the Bren gun, which he was brandishing from side to side and firing from the hip. He looked as though he was watering the garden with a hose, and just as I was thinking he'd hit me if he wasn't careful, I received an awful blow in the backside. It felt as though someone had given me an almighty kick, but I could feel blood running down between my legs, and I knew I'd been shot. Corporal Crooke attempted to bandage me up with a field dressing while assuring me that no serious damage had been done, and he joked with me about the indignity of being wounded in such a place.

By this time we'd cleared the hill of Germans, and we were told to make our way down to the road again. I was relieved to find that I could walk without too much difficulty, although I was stiff and sore. I soon learnt that I wasn't the only casualty; my friend Bruce Cowper, who'd been with me since the outbreak of war in 1939, had been killed. And Troop Sergeant Major Dargue, although still on his feet, had been shot in the abdomen and was obviously seriously wounded. The only other member of the Troop to suffer injury was Corporal Johnson, who had splinters in his arm. Exactly how much damage had been inflicted on the enemy was uncertain, but for the time being at least they'd been driven from their position overlooking the road, and we felt confident that their casualties had been much heavier than ours.

We soon reached a village – which I learnt much later was Stilos – where we stopped under the trees to take stock of our position and to drink at the well. There were quite a number of British troops about, but few in organised units. I remember speaking to one Australian soldier who was lying among the trees with a Bren gun; he intended to stay there until he'd killed a few more Germans. We spotted a lorry about to set off with a load of wounded, and helped TSM Dargue into the seat beside the driver. That was the last we saw of him, and it's doubtful whether he survived the journey. Somebody suggested that Johnson and I should seek medical attention. I had mixed feelings about this, and in many ways would've preferred to stay with the Troop. I didn't think that my wound was serious, and apart from any considerations of duty or loyalty, I thought that our best chance of reaching safety lay in sticking together. Already the Germans had brought up mortars and were directing their fire on the village, and it seemed highly probable that the road to the south was already blocked. Captain Nicholls decided the issue for us by saying that we'd only hinder the rest of the Troop, and that it would be best for us to go.

After wishing the Troop good luck, Johnson and I went off to a nearby first aid post, where we found that the last transport was just leaving. We clambered aboard the crowded 15cwt truck, from which a small Red Cross flag was flying, and immediately set off. The road twisted and turned as it climbed high into the mountains to the south. There wasn't much room in the truck, and I had to adopt a squatting position over one of the sideboards; I couldn't bear to let my wounded behind touch anything, and so had to take my weight on my hands and hang on grimly as we swung round the bends in the road. At one point an enemy plane was sighted, and there was an immediate outcry that because we were under the protection of the Red Cross no weapons should be carried. My rifle, which I'd kept with me until then, was thrown overboard. Although there was nothing I could do about it, this made me feel that I was no longer a fighting soldier, and not much better than the stragglers I'd watched with something approaching contempt the previous afternoon. The journey can't have been more than 25 miles, but to me it seemed interminable.

Eventually, however, we reached an upland valley where a field hospital had been set up, and the driver stopped to allow the more seriously wounded to be taken off. He was prepared to take those of us who could walk a little further on our way, but warned us that we'd have to complete the journey on foot. He finally deposited us at a point where the road was blocked by burnt-out and shattered vehicles. There were bodies among the wreckage, and at the side of the road was the torn body of a mule. A rough track forked off to our left, leading down into a deep gorge between the mountains, and in the distance far below us we could at last see the sea.

It was a great relief to be off the truck, and I felt much more cheerful as I set off down the track with Johnson. The sun was shining in a blue sky, and everything seemed remarkably peaceful. Apart from a few men who got out of the truck with us, we saw little sign of life as we followed the track down through the gorge towards the sea. Between the mountains and the sea there was a more level expanse of stony ground split by occasional gullies, and when we eventually reached this we began to come across groups of men hiding among the rocks. We were told that the officer in charge of the evacuation had his headquarters in a cave in one of the gullies, and we were advised to report to him. We found the cave and spoke to a naval officer who informed us that walking wounded would be taken off that night; in the meantime we should make ourselves as inconspicuous as possible and wait for nightfall, when we should join the queue for the boats.

I wasn't sorry to have a rest. I hadn't experienced any difficulty in walking, but I'd been losing blood steadily all day, and was beginning to feel the effects.

The fact that we'd had practically nothing to eat and not much to drink during the last two days didn't help. I was still uncertain about the extent of my wound. When I was first hit I thought I'd been shot from behind, and half suspected that one of my own Troop was responsible. Closer examination suggested that the bullet had been fired from a position to my right and slightly ahead of me, for it had entered my right thigh, passed clean through my right buttock, and ploughed a deep furrow across the top of my left leg. Not surprisingly, Corporal Crooke's efforts with the field dressing hadn't been entirely successful, and my trousers were soaked with blood. Johnson was still in fairly good shape, although he'd lost the use of his arm.

As soon as darkness fell men began to appear from their hiding places, and a long queue formed on the track leading to Sphakia. We took our places, but we seemed a long way from the front. For a long time the queue didn't move, and I was feeling so weak that I had to get down on the ground. It seemed that I was no sooner down than the queue moved forward a yard or two, forcing me to struggle to my feet in order to keep my place. This procedure was repeated over and over again, until I almost felt that I couldn't keep it up any longer. I hadn't realised that the cave in the gully was so far from the village of Sphakia, and we'd spent several hours in the queue, gradually working our way forward, before at long last we came within sight of the little harbour and its shingle beach. We could see the men at the head of the queue getting into boats and being taken off to the waiting destroyers, and thought that in a few minutes our turn would come. Then, when we were no more than 20 yards from the water's edge, there was a shout. 'No more boats tonight – get away from the beach'.

We were bitterly disappointed, and I hardly had the strength to drag myself back up the track away from the village. We only went about 100 yards before we found a hiding place in a shallow gully alongside the track. The rocks in the bottom of the gully afforded concealment and protection, and we settled down for a long wait. I suppose I must've slept for a few hours before I heard the sound of aircraft overhead. We could only lie and listen as the dive bombers screamed down to release their bombs on Sphakia. Several times the explosions were near enough for us to be showered with debris, and I was thankful for the protection of the rocks. Wave after wave of planes continued the bombardment, and it was a long time before they finally departed. After they'd gone we could hear men shouting to one another as they checked that their friends were safe. Gradually they began to venture out to look for water. We were extremely thirsty after lying in the sun all day, and were glad to find a well near at hand. I was feeling very weak, as well as being stiff and sore, so that when a medical orderly offered his assistance and undertook to see me onto the boats that night I was grateful for his help.

At last the sun went down, and a queue began to form once more on the track leading to the harbour. I didn't feel strong enough to stand for long, and although we were close to the beach I thought we might have difficulty in keeping our place in the queue when the time came. Quite suddenly the ships seemed to materialise out of the darkness. I could see destroyers and cruisers lying just outside the harbour, and I also recognised the distinctive shape of HMS *Glengyle*. Soon the ships' boats and the *Glengyle*'s landing craft were picking up men from the beach and ferrying them out to the ships, and I was relieved to see our friend the medical orderly appear. He spoke briefly to the officer in charge of one of the boats, and the next thing I knew I was being helped by strong arms across the beach and into the boat. I saw that Johnson was following me, and it was with feelings of profound relief that we clambered aboard the destroyer HMS *Jervis* a few minutes later. I took one last look at the little harbour with its backcloth of mountains before being taken down below.

I completed the journey back to Alexandria in the comparative comfort of a bunk in the forward mess deck. There was one scare when the ship was shaken by a loud explosion, and I thought we'd been hit by a bomb, but a reassuring voice over the loudspeaker informed us that it was only the ship's guns being fired. When we docked at Alexandria late that night I was carried off the ship on a stretcher and taken into a transit shed where there were already long lines of stretcher cases to be seen. Further along the dockside lay the cruiser HMS *Orion*, badly damaged by air attacks during the voyage back to Egypt after evacuating troops from Heraklion. Dead and wounded were still being brought out from the wreckage.

After only two days in Alexandria I was taken by hospital train to the Canal Zone.

> Meanwhile at home the coastline of German-occupied Europe was being subjected to regular harassment, sometimes with far-reaching results.
>
> *John May* went on such a raid, still regarded as possibly the most audacious, and the most successful, of the war.

They called us all together for a briefing – all the officers, that is – and showed us this model. They still didn't give us a name. But I recognised it at once – I'd sailed right past it. And I whispered to my Skipper 'I know where that is. It's the *Normandie* Dock at St Nazaire'. I said 'It's 5 miles up the river . . . I don't think we're coming back'.

> The huge 1148ft dry dock at St Nazaire, built before the war for the liner *Normandie*, had assumed a new significance as the only facility on the Atlantic coastline large enough to accommodate the 43,000-ton German battleship *Tirpitz*.
>
> To discourage the Germans from moving the new ship to France, where she could menace their vital transatlantic convoys, the British decided to target the *Normandie* Dock for destruction.

How did you know what St Nazaire looked like?

Because I'd been there when I was sixteen and a half. I went to sea for a time when I was young. My mother was Danish, though she had a British passport because she was born within the 3-mile limit of British Honduras. My father was born on the Isle of Man, of Scottish descent. My Danish grandfather was a Sea Captain, so perhaps I picked something up from him.

I thought it would be fun to go to sea. And actually that voyage *was* fun.

But he decided not to follow the sea as a career and went instead into journalism, working at the London office of the US newspaper *The Christian Science Monitor*. When the war broke out he volunteered for the Navy.

I was sent to HMS *King Alfred* [the training establishment for prospective RNVR officers, at Hove].

Was that quite an intensive course? Turning you into an officer?

Yes, it was. But I passed out fairly well all the same, and found I was a Temporary Sub-Lieutenant, Royal Naval Volunteer Reserve.

Were you given a choice of what you wanted to do?

Yes, apparently if you passed fairly high on the list, you know, they would give you a choice. So they asked me, and I said I'd like to join Coastal Forces.

I was told that the new 20th Flotilla was being formed, and I was to be First Lieutenant of *ML 446*.

ML 446 was one of the Fairmile Type 'B' motor launches used by Coastal Forces. Built of mahogany and displacing 65 tons, they carried a crew of two officers and fourteen men.

What was your first impression of the 446?

Oh, they seemed a good crew. Very fine Skipper – Lieutenant H G R Falconar, RNVR. And we were given a third officer, who was supposed to be an expert in gunnery. He confessed to me he'd never seen a gun in his life! Sub-Lieutenant Hugh Arnold, RNVR. Anyway, we were then sent to Brixham to have additional fuel tanks put on our decks, and new guns fitted – Oerlikons.

So you knew something was up, then?

Yes, they issued us with tropical gear, giving us the impression we were going to Africa or somewhere. But other than that they didn't tell us anything.

We did one or two trips in formation. We'd never sailed in close formation before. And we did a mock night attack on Devonport. That was all to give us some practice. Some commandos had meantime arrived, and were being accommodated on board a Landing Ship, Infantry (Small) called HMS *Prinses Josephine Charlotte*.

But, as I say, it wasn't until they called us together and showed us this model of a dock that I knew where we were going.

It seemed madness.

And that's all we knew. We didn't understand the role of HMS *Campbeltown* virtually until the day we sailed.

In fact this old destroyer, specially lightened to accompany the MLs over the shoals of the River Loire, had had three tons of high explosive packed into her bows. The intention was to smash her into the gate of the dry dock, where her crew would then activate a delayed-action device before making their escape in the MLs. Both the *Campbeltown* and the MLs also carried commandos, whose job was to fan out ashore and cause as much damage as possible.

Anyway, we set off in the afternoon of 26 March 1942.

It's a long way to go, isn't it?

Oh yes, it is. In MLs we were never at sea for very long, until the St Nazaire raid. We'd certainly never been several *days* at sea. Because we would escort a convoy perhaps from Lundy Island round, you know, to Cornwall; or perhaps on to Portsmouth. A little air-sea rescue; anti-submarine patrols, or something. Just coastal work. As an officer I don't think I'd ever been out of sight of land before!

And we went further than it would have been in a direct line, because we went down as if we were on our way to Gibraltar.

In case you were observed.

That's right. And we *were* observed. There was a submarine, which we tried to sink, on the way. But we didn't catch her, and she got back a message saying that we were heading for Gibraltar.

We turned for St Nazaire just as darkness fell on 27 March. At that moment one of the MLs broke down – *ML 341* – with engine failure. And we were ordered to take her commandos and their ammunition aboard. Up to this point we'd just been a spare ML. I think there were two spare vessels in case this sort of thing happened; we were one of the two. So we came up alongside the *341* and took the commandos aboard.

I filled the deck tanks with water – we'd used them first, of course – while we were waiting. By the time we'd got them on board, everybody else had disappeared into the darkness. So we set off on what I *hoped* was the right course.

The submarine HMS *Sturgeon* was going to act as a buoy. She was going to flash the letter 'M' if she was on her position, or the letter 'U' if she was uncertain, but by the time we got there they'd turned the light out. We saw her on the surface, so the Skipper said 'We'll go and ask!'. So we went to ask, and to our extreme annoyance the *Sturgeon* went under. Pretty quickly.

Anyway, we assumed that the Royal Navy, you know, would be pretty accurate, so we ploughed on. And just as they were entering the estuary we caught up with the rest. We were even in our correct column. The port column. I was rather proud of that!

Then the searchlights came on from the shore, and there was a bit of firing. But *Campbeltown* had aboard her somebody who could speak German, and who flashed a signal that we were proceeding into harbour in pursuance of orders. Most of the searchlights went out, and we gained a bit more time.

A commando gave me a machine gun – by this time I was down on the forecastle.

Then suddenly firing began from *everywhere*. Of every kind. There was coloured tracer going all over the place, so I rather lost track of what was going on. We passed close by a ship . . . we didn't know what her purpose was [in fact she was a flak ship], so we fired into her as we went past.

We were meant to go and capture the Old Mole, or rather this other vessel – the ML we were replacing – had been, I should say. I knew there was a searchlight on it. But when I looked around, having been doing a bit of firing myself, I saw that we'd passed it. In all the firing we'd overshot it. So the Skipper began to turn the ship round, but things were in a hell of a mess.

The ship just ahead of us caught fire. Another one exploded almost beside us. Another one came out astern, and they shouted across 'You'll never get in!'. So, we didn't quite know what to do. The Skipper asked if there was anywhere else we could get ashore, but in that area . . . the reason the Mole is there is that there's no landing place.

So then we thought we'd better go up to the Old Entrance, where the starboard column had gone. Our commando officer had been shot in the head. His Sergeant and several of his men were wounded, and one or two of our crew.

We saw some vessels obviously retiring, so we thought perhaps we'd better make smoke in defence of them. That brought extra fire onto us, and our third officer was wounded. Luckily we had an Army surgeon on board, an Army doctor, so they could be looked after.

After all this everybody who was left seemed to be withdrawing, so we went out ourselves. We almost blundered into five German destroyers [which had just overwhelmed *ML 306* up ahead], but we picked up a signal from HMS *Tynedale* to HMS *Atherstone* about them in time. *Atherstone* and *Tynedale* were two of own destroyers, which had been outside the estuary, waiting for us. And they began to fire at these German destroyers, so we crept away, and got round them.

When it got a bit more light we found there were three others that'd got out.

These were the *ML 156, ML 270* and *MGB 314,* the raid leader. The *156* was so badly damaged that she was immediately abandoned. Shortly afterwards she was sunk by a German bomber.

When the two destroyers, *Atherstone* and *Tynedale,* appeared we transferred our wounded to the *Atherstone* and tried to make it home under our own power. But we couldn't. The ship wasn't really in a condition to.

Under repeated air attack, and with the speed of the three small craft dropping, the decision was taken to sink them.

When two more destroyers arrived that'd been sent out to help, we were taken off and the ship was scuttled.

The Captain of the destroyer gave me his sea cabin to sleep in. Of course I couldn't sleep. Every signal that went up to the bridge came past my ear! And we were attacked by aircraft, but not severely.

Then I think I *did* go to sleep, because the next thing I knew we were getting up towards the coast of England.

Was your Skipper wounded?

No, he was all right. But our Sub-Lieutenant was quite badly wounded.

And yourself?

Oh, I got a slight scratch, that was all. A little discomfort in the eye. But no, I was very lucky.

It's extraordinary that anybody came back at all.

Yes. When we got back, actually, the Skipper didn't . . . he felt that he hadn't done his job. That he'd failed. And so he handed all the things over to me. So I had to get things done, and had to make a report, you know, all that sort of thing.

So not getting the commandos ashore weighed pretty heavily on him.

Yes, it did. In fact so heavily that he never told his wife.

He never told her about the raid?

Never told her about the raid. Because when he died a few years ago we went to his funeral . . . Hugh Arnold, who was our Sub-Lieutenant, he and I went to the funeral . . . and spoke to his widow. And she was amazed. She'd never heard the story.

But as I understand it, most of the MLs had difficulty. It could be argued that the job they'd been given to do was impossible.

That's right, yes, it was. It's very sad.

When did you tell your wife about the raid?

When I had survivors' leave.

Despite the chaos which had engulfed the unprotected small craft, the raid on the *Normandie* Dock had been a complete success. The detonation of the *Campbeltown*'s explosives, together with additional damage caused by the commandos, kept the dock out of commission for the rest of the war. Indeed, the damage took so long to repair after the end of hostilities that some local inhabitants grew to resent the raid.

The majority, though, continued to sympathise with its aims.

I went to a ceremony on the 40th Anniversary, 1982, at the war cemetery at Escoublac-la-Baule [8 miles from St Nazaire]. And this old retired dock worker came up to me, and speaking very slowly and loudly – as we might to a foreigner . . . although I speak quite good French he didn't know that – he asked me if I would do him the honour of going to his house and taking a glass of wine with him.

And he said 'Before you came that night we thought we would never be rescued from the most appalling oppression. But after that night, we knew you'd come back. Thank you, thank you'. And he took my right hand in both of his, and pumped it up and down. And there were tears in both our eyes.

A good memory to take away with you.

Yes. Oh, yes. A very good memory.

While the Army commandos were building up a reputation for aggressiveness and daring, the Royal Marines were realising that they had missed their chance to fill this niche themselves.

So much of their manpower was tied up at sea, in the two Mobile Naval Base Defence Organisations – the second of which had been formed in 1941 – and in the belated attempt to form a Royal Marine Division from scratch that it was not until February 1942 that they raised the first commando unit of their own.

Joe Humphrey was a career Marine who seized the opportunity immediately. He had joined the Marines at the age of 17 in 1937, and had served aboard the battleship HMS *Ramillies,* first in the Mediterranean and then in the Atlantic.

At this time on the Atlantic run our newspapers were few and far between, and sometimes two or three weeks adrift. But I'd been reading about the Army Commandos and the wonderful work they were doing, raiding the European coast, the Lofoten Islands and the Channel Islands.

It was at this time that it came on Fleet Orders asking for volunteers to help form the new Royal Marine Commando, as it was called then. And I volunteered, and was accepted.

I left the ship in Liverpool and went down to Deal to become a founder member of what would eventually become No 40 (Royal Marine) Commando. I was promoted to Corporal, and was Section commander of No 1 Section, No 1 Platoon, 'A' Company.

After we'd handed in our blue uniforms and got kitted out, we went up to Scotland, to Oban. We got on board a boat there, and on her we went up to Tobermory in Mull, where we picked up our first landing craft and went across the Sound of Mull to Glenborrodale. And then we started some of the hardest training I ever came across. This was organised by the Royal Marines themselves. And we did forced marches, up roads, tracks, over mountains; they really pushed us. And I still say to this day that one of the toughest exercises I ever did was when we landed on the west coast of Scotland and we were to attack a target at Alness over on the east coast. The whole of Scottish Command – that was British Army units, Norwegians, everyone – they were all out to get us. Assisted by RAF spotter planes.

So we travelled the roads and through the woods and gulleys and things like that in the dark. During the day we slept up in the woods, where the trees would give us cover from these spotter aircraft. And eventually 200, over 200, of the 410-strong Commando got through.

After that we went to the Commando Depot [opened in February 1942 to standardise all Commando training] at Achnacarry – again, a very tough course. But by then we were toughened up to it. And we did a three-week course there. There was no such thing as Saturday or Sunday, it was just a solid three weeks' training. We did things like the cat walk – that's going across a single rope with full equipment, you know; you pulled yourself along with one leg hanging down. To get across rivers and things like that. And the death slide, where a rope was tied to the top of a tree on one side of a river, and near the bottom of one on the other side. And you soaked your toggle rope – we'd been issued with these – well in water, and swung that over, and slid right across to the other side. Sounds dangerous, but as long as you were careful it was OK.

After that we moved down to the Isle of Wight, where we were billeted in Sandown, Shanklin and Ventnor. The idea was that we would use the cliffs there for training. And we were also handy for the Portsmouth dockyard.

To cut a long story short, the whole thing amounted to the fact that they were preparing us for the Dieppe raid.

This, we were told, was to prove whether or not a seaport could be taken by a frontal assault from the sea, a perimeter formed, held for a while, and then an orderly withdrawal made. But even a young junior NCO like me thought they could've picked a better place than Dieppe. Because Dieppe had very heavy shingle, which went up at a steep angle. And it was overlooked by cliffs from 200 to 300ft high . . .

The shingle was to prove a serious problem for the raid's armoured vehicles, which were embarked in examples of the new Landing Craft, Tank – or LCT.

Designed to sail independently rather than be carried to the landing area, and with many times the capacity of the little LCM, the LCT marked a great leap forward in the provision of armoured support for the assaulting infantry.

The first example had been delivered for trials in November 1940. An improved version, the LCT Mk2, had been ordered the following month, and in May 1941 this design had been 'stretched' to produce the LCT Mk3, which by the time of Dieppe had become the workhorse of the rapidly expanding LCT fleet.

The raid was carried out mainly by the 2nd Canadian Division. But we went over first. No 3 Commando, under Lieutenant Colonel Durnford-Slater, went across in landing craft and unfortunately ran into a German convoy. Most of their landing craft were scattered, but Major Peter Young and about twenty men got ashore, and they still went up the beach, and climbed the barbed-wire defended cliff, up onto the guns on the top, and kept them busy.

No 4 Commando, they went in on the right under the command of Lord Lovat, and knocked out the guns there. One of their young officers – Pat Porteous – got the Victoria Cross.

In the meantime we had crossed on the gunboat HMS *Locust* from Portsmouth. Our orders were to go into the harbour, right along the dockside, go down jacob's ladders, and to smash up all the harbour installations. There was a crowd of German invasion barges there, in the harbour, and we were to either sink them or tow them back to England.

However, that wasn't to be, because when we came in to enter, between the wave traps, the German guns and mortars and everything opened fire and we had casualties all around us. And in the end the Captain of the ship I think must've realised the whole thing was hopeless, and he came out again. All the time under this heavy gunfire. So we went back and joined the command ship [the 'Hunt class' destroyer HMS *Calpe*, pressed into service in the absence of anything more suitable], and we were held in reserve.

In the meantime the Canadians – I can't remember all their regimental names, but there was the Essex Scottish, there was the Royal Hamilton Light Infantry, and the Fusiliers Mont-Royal – they were all going ashore on their different beaches. And they were being absolutely *massacred*. Mowed down in hundreds. Not dozens, in *hundreds*.

About 9.00am we were ordered to go in again. There weren't any LCAs left by then, there were only LCTs – great big boxes of things, that held several tanks.

The RAF went down, and they laid a smoke screen on the water's edge. And we came in line abreast.

But when we came clear of the smoke screen, though, instead of being on the beach, we were still 500 or 600 yards off it. And of course the German guns opened fire again. Our Colonel realised the whole thing was impossible, and he climbed up onto the gunwhales of his landing craft to give us the signal to retreat, to get out of it. And unfortunately he was killed. Some of the craft were so far in they couldn't get turned round, they had to go on. 'A' Company, the craft I was in, we were lucky. I think we must've just about touched the shingle when our young Lieutenant managed to slew the craft right round, and we came right out of it again. And eventually finished up with the *Locust*.

But while we were getting out of it we could see what was going on on the beaches, and it was *terrible*. There were hundreds of bodies all over the place . . . men calling out . . . there were tanks that'd sunk into the shingle – it was too soft . . . there were landing craft up on the beach and burning, on fire . . . all over the place.

However, we got back to the *Locust*, and then eventually back to England.

Of course when we got back to the Isle of Wight those landladies who'd lost their men were in an awful state [voice breaks] . . . And it was big headlines in the papers. And the Germans, they don't miss a trick, you know. Thousands of propaganda leaflets were dropped on Portsmouth, Plymouth and Weymouth. And right across the front page was this great big 'Dieppe' all in wiggly lines, making it look sinister. And pictures of the tanks sunk in the shingle, the landing craft all on fire, the hundreds of bodies. And dozens of men who'd been taken prisoner. All that sort of thing. And of course this was wonderful propaganda for the Germans.

Losses among the troops of the landing force in the single day's fighting reached an astonishing 59.5 per cent. Indeed, in many of the Canadian units the figures were even higher. The worst case was that of the Essex Scottish, which went to Dieppe with 553 men and came back with just 51, 28 of them wounded.

In the aftermath of the disaster numerous failings were identified, and a shopping list of new prerequisites for an opposed landing were drawn up, including better air and gunfire support and specially-adapted armoured vehicles to overcome natural and man-made obstacles. All of these would save lives later.

The Dieppe raid of 19 August 1942 was the largest the British would ever attempt. Raids by themselves were not capable of winning the war, and although they continued to play a role in overall strategy, attention was increasingly shifting to the next problem – that of mounting a full scale invasion.

TWO

Learning the Basics: the Invasion of North Africa 1942

The fall of France in June 1940 presented her overseas possessions with a stark choice – either to join the Free French, under the maverick Army officer Charles de Gaulle, or to obey the new Vichy administration at home. The majority followed the latter course, and since this made them little better than German puppets in British eyes, the Royal Navy was ordered to neutralise any warships based in their ports. In the ugliest incident, the French battleship *Bretagne* was blown to pieces in Mers-el-Kebir harbour with the loss of over 970 lives.

Relations between Vichy and London were irretrievably soured, but in spite of this in August the British and Free French still believed that a small show of force would be sufficient to rally Vichy-controlled Senegal, in West Africa, to their cause. Keen to control the strategic Senegalese port of Dakar, the British agreed to back a Free French expedition.

Two battalions of de Gaulle's men were quickly embarked in the Dutch liners *Westernland* and *Pennland*, while the British provided the four battalions of Royal Marines with which they were about to form the Royal Marine Division. The Marines were carried in four of the newly-converted Landing Ships, Infantry (Large) – the British *Kenya*, *Karanja* and *Ettrick* and the Polish *Sobieski*. Too few LCAs were available to outfit the landing ships properly, so ships' boats had to make up the difference.

After several brushes with Vichy French warships, however, the British and Free French arrived off Senegal on 23 September 1940 to discover that the garrison of Dakar was far from eager to switch sides. Shots were traded with the defenders for three days before the invasion force, unwilling to initiate serious bloodshed, admitted defeat and withdrew. The Dakar fiasco was an embarrassing start to British attempts at planning and executing an invasion, but loss of life had at least been kept to a minimum, and several useful lessons had been learned. Among these were the need for some kind of truly ocean-going vessel to land tanks, as well as the need for a dedicated headquarters ship for the assault force commander and his staff, equipped to handle the huge volume of signals traffic generated by a battle. At Dakar the cruiser HMS *Devonshire* had been earmarked as a command ship, only to be called away to face some Vichy cruisers when the force was off the African coast.

Not until the Spring of 1942 did the British again have to mount an invasion, and by that time they were much better prepared. The war had also been transformed. The Japanese attack on Pearl Harbor on 7 December 1941, which brought the United States into the war as a full partner of the British, had opened up an entirely new theatre of operations on the other side of the world. So rapid and so widespread were the Japanese advances that by March 1942 there was thought to be a real possibility of them gaining a foothold on Madagascar, the Vichy-controlled island off the south-east coast of Africa. Given that the French authorities were unlikely to refuse any Japanese demand for air and naval bases on the island, the British decided they had no choice but to launch a pre-emptive invasion of their own. Madagascar lay firmly astride their vital convoy routes, and could not be allowed to fall without a fight.

The Americans concurred, and lent their political support to the operation. They also despatched reinforcements, including the aircraft carrier USS *Wasp* and the brand new battleship USS *Washington*, to Scapa Flow to replace the British ships withdrawn for the invasion. Tuesday 5 May 1942 was selected as 'D-Day'.[1]

Jack Mansell was a Sergeant at the Headquarters of the recently-formed Royal Marine Division, whose CO would be given command of the landing force.

The Royal Marine Division was at that time dispersed around the Border country, with HQ situated at Priorwood House, Melrose.

The GOC [General Officer Commanding], Major General Robert Sturges, RM, and his senior staff officers were suddenly called away to London, and didn't return until a few days later, on 17 March.

We didn't know anything, but over the next two days we had to crate up all our office equipment and replenish stocks of stationery. Then a movement instruction was received, telling us we were leaving Melrose in two days' time, but giving no destination.

---

1. It was usual for the start date of a military operation to be given a code designation, meaningless in itself, in order to provide a point of reference from which all other dates could be reckoned. D+1, for example, would be the day after D-Day, or the second day of the operation. This allowed all aspects of the plan to be worked out in advance, even though the actual date of D-Day might remain to be decided.

There were four assault ships assembled, and we all cheered when we found we were assigned to the *Winchester Castle*, for she was the best by far. I'd previously been on three others for exercises. She had cabins for three or four, and this was pure luxury. In addition food was served individually from a large counter, instead of having a mess system.

> The *Winchester Castle*, still flying the Red Ensign, was also the biggest of the four Landing Ships, Infantry (Large). At 20,012 tons she was almost twice the size of the Polish *Sobieski*, which was also civilian-manned, and the two White Ensign LSI(L)s HMS *Keren* and HMS *Karanja*. The *Sobieski*, *Keren* and *Karanja* had all been at Dakar, the *Keren* under her original, pre-Royal Navy, name of *Kenya*. A fifth assault ship, the 3244-ton LSI(H) HMS *Royal Ulsterman*, would join the force later in its journey.

At 9.30pm on 23 March we slipped out of the Clyde, knowing nothing except that we were going somewhere hot. We were in a military convoy [WS 17, one of the regular troop convoys to the Middle East], and we felt powerful and protected.

At last, two days out, we began to find things out. We found we were now HQ 'Force 121', and instead of commanding the RM Division, General Sturges had the 29th Independent Brigade Group[2] as his invading force, plus the 17th Brigade Group [from the British 5th Division] in support. How did this come about? Well, the RM Division scattered around the Borders when the emergency button was pressed. But the 29th Brigade was embarked for an exercise, and the 17th Brigade was all ready to go to India. The RM Division HQ was an established entity experienced in the planning of an amphibious landing. So they simply stuck the head on to the body.

> A second brigade from the 5th Division was added later. Both 5th Division units, which travelled in ordinary troopships rather than LSIs, were to regard their new destination as merely a stopover on their way to India. The 29th also received No 5 Commando as an additional reinforcement.

On Easter Monday, now in tropical gear, we reached Freetown, but weren't allowed ashore. Off we went again, and now we were told our next destination was ten days' sailing time away. By now the experts had worked out that we would next call at Durban, and indeed we now started to type out orders where Durban was mentioned, though our destination was left blank.

Things began to quicken up admin wise, but then we reached Durban and paradise, or so it seemed to us. The Force had to stay at Durban for a week.

---

2. A British Brigade Group was the equivalent of an American Regimental Combat
   Team.

The few tanks had to be waterpoofed, as did the other vehicles. All kinds of supplies – food, water, ammunition, petrol, medical supplies – had to be restowed.

> Stowing supplies in a 'combat loaded' condition, ready for an amphibious landing, was a different art from stowing them using normal 'transport loading'. Combat loading involved ensuring that supplies of all kinds were available for rapid unloading in the order, and quantity, that the units ashore would need. It therefore made less efficient use of shipboard space than transport loading, under which supplies could be stored with little regard for their order.

Although we were still preparing landing tables and operation orders we worked in shifts, and so had a few hours ashore every day. At 9.00pm we'd be walking down brilliantly lit streets, with shops full of things we could no longer buy in England. Every South African knew where we were headed – Madagascar – and they entertained us royally.

Then it was all over. The GOC now transferred to the battleship HMS *Ramillies*, and his HQ transferred from the *Winchester Castle* to HMS *Keren*, which didn't have the comforts of our previous ship.

The heat was really on now. One day we received a signal from London which caused us to work in stifling heat through the night and all next morning on new operation and admin orders, only to get another signal cancelling the previous message.

On Sunday 3 May we held an impressive Drumhead Service, and for a few it was the last one they attended.

Because of the long journeys which the landing craft had to make from the parent ships to the landing beaches [designated Red North, Red Centre, Red South, Blue, White and Green] in Courrier and Ambararata Bays, breakfast was at midnight of 4/5 May. By this time everyone knew we were to land at the two bays and seek to capture the town of Antsirane on the opposite side of the tip of Madagascar, thus ensuring the use of the great natural harbour of Diego Suarez.

> Madagascar is the fourth largest island in the world, and is considerably bigger than Metropolitan France. So a division-sized force, only the lead brigade of which was trained for amphibious operations, was clearly insufficient to overrun it in the face of real opposition. The British therefore limited their objectives to securing its valuable northern tip – Diego Suarez, Antsirane and the nearby French air base.

Nobody could sleep between supper and midnight because it was so noisy. The landing craft were being made ready for the landing, and all kinds of stores were being manhandled onto the deck. Then there were the constant tannoy announcements. Some men read, some just talked, but the majority played cards.

In the early hours of Tuesday 5 May 1942 the assault troops gathered at the respective sally ports and clambered into the LCAs. The sound of electric motors filled the air, the LCAs were lowered and met the sea with a loud splash. People shouted their goodbyes, then the craft sped away into the darkness. They landed with little or no opposition, achieving complete surprise, as the French were confident no one could navigate through the reefs and rocks in the dark. The local commander woke up to find British troops in his bedroom, and was taken prisoner!

As to my involvement, Force HQ had a large room by the Captain's cabin on HMS *Keren*. At first, signals from ashore came in trickles, but then the battle message board we set up had to be abandoned due to the sheer volume of incoming and outgoing signals.

Steady progress inland was made until French defensive positions, excellently supported by their 75mm guns – there were no bombers to take them out – proved a very hard nut to crack. So on 6 May Force HQ was ordered by the GOC to go ashore and make its way inland so that the situation could be more accurately assessed.

We were issued with a 48-hour ration pack, which contained such things as hard biscuits, sweet biscuits, boiled sweets, cheese, dripping spread, tea, sugar and milk mixture in a tin, and even a tiny box of matches. Personally I found this pack adequate for the purpose.

Believe it or not, our new HQ was in a tin shack bearing an elaborate sign saying 'Robinson's Hotel'. It was the only building, if you could call it that, for many miles, and was owned by a Chinese from Malaysia who had fantasies about the Raffles Hotel in Singapore, but no money! It only served cups of coffee. As I say, it was the only building, so the French artillery were ranging on it. I was crouched down taking a message from the GSO1 [General Staff Officer Grade 1, in other words Sturges' Chief of Staff, Lieutenant Colonel J L Moulton, RM] as the barrage crept nearer and nearer. When a near miss caused all the dust and muck from the wooden rafters to come down on us, he said we'd better move and we did, jumping down a nearby gulley right on top of a dead Senegalese sniper. There were a lot of them about, but they were lacking in subtlety, as they'd pull branches aside to get clearer vision, and were obvious.

Then we moved forward a little and it all quietened down. We'd lost half our tanks, but it was decided to launch a powerful night attack on the pillboxes strung out across the approach road to Antsirane. At the same time fifty Royal Marines from HMS *Ramillies* would dash through the entrance to the harbour and land at the quayside.

Just after dawn we heard Antsirane had fallen, and we moved forward. On our way we passed two or three of our burned-out tanks, one with a dead crew member still hanging half-way out. Then we came to the pillbox area. French soldiers and British lay around, some gazing sightlessly to the sky, some looking as if they were sleeping.

It was now 7 May, and we moved into the Mairie, the Town Hall, from where we were to govern Antsirane for the next few months.

In addition to the LSIs, the expedition had been given the first of two new types of landing ship to try out. The RFA *Derwentdale* was a fleet oiler which had been fitted to carry fifteen LCMs in place of some of her fuel oil. Redesignated a Landing Ship, Gantry – or LSG – after the gantry cranes used to handle the LCMs, she was the first of three such conversions. The other new ship was HMS *Bachaquero*, formerly a shallow draught tanker designed for Lake Maracaibo in Venezuela, which had undergone a much more radical transformation. The interior of the ship had been completely gutted to provide a tank deck for carrying wheeled and tracked vehicles. Her bows had been replaced by two hinged doors, and an elaborate extending ramp had been fitted, to allow the vehicles to drive ashore. Designated a Landing Ship, Tank – or LST – she was thus the first of the landing ships to be able to deliver her cargo directly onto the beach, rather than having to ferry it ashore in smaller craft.

For *Derrick Cook*, however, the strategic potential of the *Bachaquero* was overshadowed by rather more mundane matters.

We left Durban for Madagascar in an oil tanker named *Bachaquero* which had been converted into a landing ship, with a large hinged ramp at the front. After two or three days at sea the refrigeration plant went wrong, spoiling all the meat and perishables and leaving us with just the usual hard tack. And the bread was so infested with weevils that we refused to eat it, so of course we finished up on biscuits.

At the time I was a Gunner in 'A' Troop, 19 Battery, 9th Field Regiment, Royal Artillery. Our job was to support the infantry with our 25-pounder field guns.

Our first landing was anything but perfect. The ship let down her ramp about 25ft from the beach, and one of her officers went down the ramp with his dipstick and said '2ft deep'. So off went the first gun and limber, with the Quad towing vehicle. They disappeared beneath the waves. The driver came bubbling up to the surface, muttering 'Stupid bastard . . . .'.

The ship pulled off the beach and had another go. This time the ramp landed on the sand, so we unloaded OK. While we were with No 5 Commando, unloading under fire, an officer with red tabs was wandering around, and we thought he was with the Beach Party. Turned out he was a senior French officer, and was waiting to give himself up. When they found out they surrounded the poor chap with commandos, and marched him off.

We now had to rescue our vehicle, gun and limber from the sea, so we had to dive down to attach ropes with which to winch them out. Eventually we had to leave the Quad, but saved the gun and limber.

The *Bachaquero* was supposed to have landed them much further south, but inadequate reconnaissance had failed to reveal the presence of a reef just offshore. She instead unloaded, after considerable delay, at Red Centre Beach, only to find that there were no tracks linking that area with Antsirane. This left Derrick's battery effectively marooned, far from the main action.

We set off for the Andrakaka Peninsula, jutting out into Diego Suarez Bay, but on the opposite side from the town of Antsirane. The peninsula was a few miles long, and as we entered it in darkness, with water either side, all of a sudden we were hit by a huge blue searchlight. Then 5.5in shells began screaming over our heads, so we dashed to the shelter of a small hillock. We had a Navy liaison officer with us, and as I was a signaller I went with him to the top of this hill with my signal lamp. He said the ship shooting at us was one of ours, so I'd just started sending the signal to stop firing when a shell landed below the top of the hill, smashing my lamp. We were lucky to get away safely. In fact she was a French sloop, the *D'Entrecasteaux*.

We pulled out from the hill and engaged her over open sights with our 25-pounders. A lucky shot hit her magazine and she blew up, sending the rear half up the beach. I believe we had a small brass cannon and her battle ensign as souvenirs.

We finally reached our gun position and in daylight [on 6 May, D+1] fired across the water into Antsirane, with instructions not to hit the water tower or the radio aerial. That evening the Marines came up the harbour in a destroyer and landed, finally capturing the town.

I forgot to mention that after we'd wrecked the *D'Entrecasteaux* the Royal Navy complained to us that they could've captured her, and anyhow she was no danger to us as she couldn't lower her guns enough to hit us! All I can say is they weren't there!

All the British objectives had been secured by D+3, and negotiations were opened with the Vichy French Governor regarding the rest of the island.

Over the succeeding months, however, it became clear that although no real resistance was likely, neither was there any prospect of the French surrendering. Despite the fact that further action in Madagascar formed an unwelcome distraction from the new, much bigger operation the British were discussing with their American allies, it was felt by August that the impasse needed to be resolved.

The renewed operations would again be spearheaded by the 29th Independent Brigade Group, the only unit trained in amphibious warfare. This would land first at Majunga on the west coast, then hand the area over to the follow-up force of infantry and immediately re-embark. After a trip around the island, it would then conduct a landing at Tamatave on the east coast as well. Both forces would subsequently converge on the capital, Tananarive.

Walter Grainger enjoyed a bird's eye view of both landings.

At the time of the military operation to take control of Madagascar I was officers' chef aboard the destroyer HMS *Arrow*, which took part.

Being well known to the officers I was allowed a few privileges, so took several photos, which I still have – some of the ships in convoy and some of the attack we made on Tamatave, when we dashed in to land a contingent of No 5 Commando. I went up in the crow's nest with my rifle and a camera while the commandos were jumping from our ship onto the jetty. All I shot was photos!

First, though, was our landing on the west coast.

We'd been detailed to lead the convoy and guide the assault craft to their landing place north of Majunga. This landing [on Thursday 10 September 1942] was made in darkness, so no photos, but our job was to navigate about eight LCAs full of troops from their parent ship to a certain spot where they could make a fairly safe landing with not too many obstacles to overcome. This was done in the dead of night with no one allowed to talk above a whisper, and engines just turning over. Once the troops were safely ashore we got one flashing light signal, and *Arrow* withdrew to about a mile offshore to give any protective cover, if needed, with her 4.7in guns.

All was successfully done without any casualties to troops or ship's company. We could hear firing from the landing force, and not many hours afterwards Majunga was taken, by all accounts by surprise.

The next place for landing was at Tamatave, which was to be in daylight. We lay offshore [on Friday 18 September] and an ultimatum was signalled for them to surrender or put up with the consequences. A fast motor launch was sent in with a white flag flying for their answer, but a few hundred yards from shore the launch was fired on with machine gun fire.

Then all hell was let loose, as the order was given for a 3-minute bombardment. Every ship tried to get as many rounds off as possible, and by the end of the 3 minutes white flags were appearing along the shoreline. Now was the time for No 5 Commando to go in.

We had to cut through a chain to get in to the quayside, then with me in the crow's nest to snipe or take pictures, the commandos swarmed ashore and soon had the situation under control, as had the troops who'd landed from landing craft.

That was our mission fulfilled as regards Madagascar.

Two further small landings were made in the south of the island, but its conquest was delayed more by the onset of the rainy season than by actual fighting, and casualties were light.

By the time the French Governor finally capitulated on 6 November the assault convoys for another, infinitely more ambitious, operation were already at sea.

The American President, Franklin Delano Roosevelt, was firmly committed to a 'Germany First' policy, reasoning that Germany, which had declared war on the United States on 11 December 1941, was the most dangerous enemy and should therefore be tackled first. But many of his countrymen were bewildered by the decision to contain Japan, the aggressor which had attacked Pearl Harbor, with minimal forces while concentrating on the defeat of Hitler. Mindful of this opposition, Roosevelt was determined to have American troops actively fighting the Germans by the Autumn.

The preference of the American Chiefs of Staff was for a direct assault on Occupied France, but their British opposite numbers were equally convinced that this was beyond their present capabilities. Both were worried, however, about how long the Soviet Union could continue to tie down the bulk of the German Army, and so in July 1942 a compromise plan was agreed.

The first Anglo-American invasion of the war would be directed at French North Africa, where the arrival of an overwhelming force might persuade the Vichy garrisons to give up without a fight. The assault units, coalescing as the British First Army, would then push rapidly eastwards to menace the rear of the Germans and Italians facing the British Eighth Army in the Desert.

In order to put ashore sufficient manpower to overawe the French, three separate task forces would be needed, each of them considerably bigger than the ones the British had assembled for Dakar or Madagascar. The Western Naval Task Force, for which the US Navy had to provide the ships, would carry the US Army's 3rd Infantry Division, most of the US 9th Infantry Division and part of the US 2nd Armored Division all the way from the eastern seaboard of America to the Atlantic coast of Morocco, where they would execute three widely-separated landings at Safi, Fedala and Mehdia.

The Centre Naval Task Force, for which the Royal Navy had to furnish almost all of the ships, would carry the US 1st Infantry Division and part of the US 1st Armored Division, plus a force of US Army Rangers[3] from the UK to Oran in Algeria.

Finally, the Eastern Naval Task Force, in which the majority of the ships would again be British, would carry the remainder of the US 9th Infantry Division, part of the US 34th Infantry Division and most of the British 78th Division, plus a mixed force of Commandos and Rangers, from the UK to Algiers. A small force

---

3. American commandos, the first unit of which had been raised earlier in the year.

of American paratroopers would be dropped near Oran to assist the landings there.

Because American troops were much more likely to be welcomed by the Vichy French than British ones, every effort was made to play down the British involvement. The Commander-in-Chief of all the invasion forces would be an American, Lieutenant General Dwight D Eisenhower. So would his deputy, and the commanders of all three of the landing forces.

Jack Hillier was one of many British soldiers who chafed at the orders to keep a low profile.

I was called up in early 1940 to join the Somerset Light Infantry, but not liking all the bull, I volunteered for what were then known as the Independent Companies. This was more to my liking – civvy billets, and six shillings and eightpence extra a day to cover the cost. Training was tough, but the esprit de corps was great.

We made quite a few landings – nuisance raids; quick in and out. Got the Jerries on edge, not knowing if it was a full invasion. So much so that Hitler ordered all commandos to be shot if captured [the infamous 'Commando Order' of October 1942]. At that time I was a Sergeant in No 1 Commando, under Lieutenant Colonel Tom Trevor.

Before the North African landings we trained up in Scotland with American troops from the 168th Regimental Combat Team [with whom No 1 Commando would be landing]. Some of them were supposed to be attached to us for the assault, but the CO rejected them, and they were replaced by a small detachment from a US Army Ranger Battalion.

In addition to training together, we handed in our rifles and were issued the Yanks' Garand instead. We also wore American helmets. Just before the landing we were asked to sew an American flag on our sleeves, but the lads refused.

Later we learned the newspapers were full of the 'all American' operation. Of course, it was all politics.

What did you think of the Garand?

A vast improvement. The Garand was a semi-automatic, not a bolt action like the Lee Enfield. It was simple to strip and clean, and the ammo came in clips of eight. On the last shot the clip was discarded and left the breech open. You then reloaded with a new clip of eight.

No 1 Commando, together with No 6, formed part of the assault force for Algiers.

Individual beaches were again given colour designations, but because of the increased size of the operation they were now grouped into distinct 'Sectors'. At Algiers there were three of these – Apples, Beer and Charlie. The first two lay to the west of the city, the third to the east.

Jack landed at Beer Green, the westernmost of the beaches in Beer Sector, when the attack began on Sunday 8 November 1942.

We made the beach, carrying bangalore torpedoes [long tubes filled with explosive] to blow a gap through the barbed wire. They weren't needed – there was no barbed wire, and up to now no opposition. For all the world it was like landing on the beach at Weston-super-Mare.

Our first target was a Foreign Legion-type fort [Fort Sidi Ferruch] a short distance on our right. Our luck held, and they surrendered without a fight.

By daylight the beach was crowded with craft.

Unfortunately many of them were delivering their loads to the wrong beaches, so there was considerable confusion. The 168th RCT was put ashore badly jumbled, and took some time to organise itself for the march on Algiers.

Eventually the Yanks moved off to their targets.

One amusing incident. I noticed the houses were all boarded up and all looked deserted. However, a Frenchman appeared, and on learning we were British he informed the other residents, who had gone to ground. In no time hundreds of peaceful French civvies appeared. They told us they'd thought we were Germans because of our Yankee helmets.

By now, dogfights and the bombing of transports were going on off the coast.

Air cover for the landings could initially be supplied only by the Navy's carriers, and since these would be no match for a sustained air offensive by the Germans, land-based air power needed to be established as quickly as possible.

Ron Bainbridge was one of the RAF men ready to move into the airfield at Maison Blanche, just south east of Algiers.

I'd joined up as a wireless operator/air gunner. But after I was trained on the wireless, and whilst waiting for my gunnery course, a priority signal came through asking for volunteers for Combined Operations training.

I was posted to HMS *Dundonald,* near Troon in Ayrshire, and put on a commando course. This consisted of advanced communications along with fitness and dummy beach landings. Then when I left *Dundonald* I went straight to Liverpool to board the merchantman *Dempo* for the North African landings.

On reporting to *Dundonald* we'd exchanged our Air Force blue for khaki battledress. The only difference between us and the Army was that we retained our RAF forage cap and greatcoat. Oh, and our RAF badges, of course. In the Med our tropical kit was RAF issue, not Army.

On the way out there was a fatal accident aboard the *Dempo* when an airman was killed whilst cleaning a Sten gun. Not one of our party, but it upset us nevertheless.

Ron's ship was bound for Charlie Sector, the closest to Maison Blanche. As at all the other sectors, things did not go entirely to plan.

After a rum ration we went down scrambling nets into landing craft. It was 2.00am, and although we were 8 miles out to sea, we could smell the land.

In the delays and confusion we were the first away, ahead of the American Rangers. It was pitch black, with a heavy surf running, and this tended to throw the landing craft all over the beach. Most of us were up to our necks in water getting ashore.

Our radio equipment and transport – two 30cwt lorries – landed at a beach further along the coast, from a different ship. The beaches were treacherous, with deep, soft sand. Everything was getting bogged down. We had some visits from Ju88s [twin-engined German bombers] based in Sicily, but no casualties.

After meeting the transport we were kept on the beach until the following day, 9 November.

We then moved inland to Maison Blanche, where three squadrons of RAF fighters had arrived from the base at Gibraltar. We reached it in the late afternoon, to find a squadron of Spitfires circling ready to land.

The Spitfires had just escorted in the bomber carrying Eisenhower's deputy, Major General Mark Clark, who was on his way to negotiate an end to the fighting with the Vichy French.

They were still overhead when the aerodrome was suddenly attacked by a wave of eight or nine Ju88s. An air battle [soon joined by the other two RAF fighter squadrons and by further waves of German bombers] ensued, in which all the Germans were shot down or chased off, with no friendly casualties [although two Spitfires were written off trying to land in the gathering dusk]. It was great!

Did you have any contact with the French Air Force?

No, we didn't really see them. Their planes were parked at the other side of the base. We were just housed in tents, and were self-contained. In fact we didn't get any real impression of Maison Blanche at all – we always seemed to be either sleeping or working.

Inadequate training among the landing craft crews contributed to delays and accidents in all three task forces, but was largely unavoidable. The demands of the operation had stretched both the Royal Navy and the US Navy to the limit, forcing them to use half-trained personnel in key roles.

Most of the carriers which escorted the Western Naval Task Force from America to Morocco had pilots so inexperienced that training flights during the transatlantic crossing were banned to preserve planes for combat.

In England, *Fred May* found himself plucked straight from a classroom at the Royal Navy Signal School.

Four of us were called to the Commander's office, including me. We were issued with webbing, revolver and ammo, travel warrants, meal tickets, et cetera, sworn to secrecy, told not to speak to anyone – even sailors dressed as we were – and then taken to the station to catch a train to Manchester. On arrival there we had to report to the RTO [Rail Transport Officer].

As expected the RTO didn't have a clue who we were, but he made a phone call and eventually an Army lorry turned up and took us to Salford Docks to various vessels, mine being the ss *Recorder*.

The visual signalling staff on board consisted of the Chief Yeoman of Signals, another signalman who'd been to sea before, and myself, who hadn't.

We were issued with tablets for water purification, and salt water soap. Fresh water was rationed, as the *Recorder* didn't have big enough evaporators for the boilers and the extra personnel she was carrying.

The crew were Indian, officers Merchant Navy, and there were RN seamen to man the landing craft. Also about fourteen Royal Engineers from a docks unit, and a fair number of US Army personnel – vehicle drivers and combat troops.

After passing through the Manchester Ship Canal we berthed to have the top part of the funnel and the top masts fitted back; also the triatic stay rigged and fitted.

What was the triatic stay?

On most merchant ships there are either no yards on the mast, or else the mast is too far forward of the bridge to hoist signals, so they're hoisted on the triatic stay.

The first bit of gloom came when all the beer was taken off. As we were carrying US personnel we had to stay 'dry' [as was customary in the US Navy].

After a couple of days we were ordered to the Tail o' the Bank [in the Firth of Clyde], where our convoy was forming. We joined the 'O' part of the convoy. The other part was 'A'. The Chief Yeoman hit the nail on the head when he said 'I expect "O" stands for Oran, and "A" for Algiers'. How right he was.

The invasion of North Africa saw the biggest assault convoys yet assembled. There were three task forces altogether, the wholly US one sailing direct from America. We formed up and sailed out into the Atlantic, with the luxury of having a little escort aircraft carrier and rescue tugs, et cetera. The weather was kind, which was better for all on board. We couldn't sling hammocks – there was no room – so we just spread them on the deck above the holds and under where the LCMs were. The heads were a long row of seats over like half of a big pipe, with water continually flowing along it. At the ship's side where it went overboard it was squeezed out through a thing like a large sieve using a heavy jet of sea water. Remembering that in those days there were no spy satellites, this was done to avoid leaving a trail which could be followed by a U-boat.

A weapons check was ordered as soon as we'd cleared land, and a few rounds were fired on safe bearings. On either wing of the bridge we had a FAM – a Fast Aerial Mine. These were rockets which when fired carried a parachute, a long length of wire and an explosive charge. The parachute opened and held up the wire with the explosive at the end, which was supposed to deter enemy bombers. We had a Leading Seaman DEMS [Defensively-Equipped Merchant Ship] gunner on board, who was incredibly accident-prone. This time he was checking one of the FAMs and pulled the lanyard, igniting the rocket, which couldn't rise because the lock was on. This started a fire and badly burnt his hand. We were all on the bridge waiting for the heat to detonate the mine. Luckily it didn't, and the panic subsided. We had a doctor on board, who dealt with the gunner. The Captain said to sling the FAM over the side, and to dismantle the one on the other wing as well. Then I spewed up. Bit of shock I suppose.

The ships kept station very well, but the odd signal would come from the Convoy Commodore like 'Stop making smoke!'. Difficult on a coal burner.

We all kept as clean and tidy as we could. One of the Indian crewmen was very good at cutting hair. He started off at threepence; towards the end of the journey it was ninepence!

The journey was really uneventful, and we passed through the Strait of Gibraltar OK in the dark. The U-boats were off attacking another convoy, so we had a safe passage.

The war against the U-boats was still in full swing, and even heavily escorted convoys could expect to be attacked, particularly if they had to pass through choke points like the Strait of Gibraltar.

Many feared that serious losses would be inflicted on the assault shipping, but in fact the luckless SL 125, a merchant convoy homeward bound from Sierra Leone, happened to attract most of the U-boats in their path.

Came time for landing. We were all on watch now, and had to look for a green light on a dan buoy for position. These had been placed by small vessels.

We found our light, the anchor was dropped, and unloading was commenced. We were off a place called Arzeu [in the Centre Naval Task force's Zebra Sector], a few miles east of Oran. It had a flat beach, and was a French seaplane base. It's now an oil and gas terminal. My son, who's an officer aboard Shell tankers, has loaded there. Small world!

The LCMs had to be hoisted by derrick into the water, and then the vehicles hoisted from the hold into the LCMs. This was in the dark with no lights, of course.

All was going well until the cable on one of the forward derricks slipped off the pulley wheel. There was a big shower of sparks, and everything came to a halt with an LCM hanging over the ship's side, out of the water. The First Mate reckoned he could get it into the water by dropping the jib of the derrick. This worked, and with the pulley and cable repaired, unloading proceeded.

Troops were ashore by now, and the LCMs started delivering their vehicles, including Honey tanks [the British name for the American Stuart light tank] and even a bulldozer. There didn't seem to be a lot of resistance, unlike when they got closer to Oran, where it was tough.

Work for us signalmen now began. All items which made it ashore belonged to a [pre-planned] 'serial', and these numbers [which determined the order of landing] were visually signalled to the Landing Ship, Headquarters (Large). This gave the info to the commanders about their available strength.

Having learned the lesson of Dakar, the British had provided the Centre and Eastern Naval Task Forces with specially-converted headquarters ships – HMS *Largs* for Oran and HMS *Bulolo* for Algiers. The Western Naval Task Force relied on the cruiser USS *Augusta,* only to find, as their allies had, that the roles of escort and floating headquarters were difficult to combine.

After the operation the Americans too began work on headquarters ships.

When we were fully unloaded all the landing craft were shore-sided, and I was sent from the *Recorder* to HMS *Queen Emma* to take passage to Algiers. The *Queen Emma* was a former Dutch vessel – her Dutch name was *Koningin Emma* – which had been converted into a Landing Ship, Infantry (Medium). She was a beautiful little ship, quite fast; and we made Algiers OK.

On arrival I had to report to the Naval office on the dockside. The next day – about 15 November – I was in a working party to help establish telephone communications from the harbour signal office to what was now being called Navy House.

Much to the relief of the Allies, the local French commanders had agreed to let them take over Morocco and Algeria without further resistance. The Germans, however, had taken advantage of French indecision in Tunisia to begin airlifting in their own units, which quickly seized control there.

As soon as their heavy equipment began to arrive by sea, the Germans in Tunisia deployed to block the eastward advance of the Allied landing force, now organised as the British First Army.

By this time Eisenhower's headquarters was a large hotel in Algiers called the Hotel St Georges. I joined a working party to go a few miles inland to a French

Army barracks, to help erect aerials for the radio station, which was operated by relay from the HQ at the St Georges. The lorry that we used was a confiscated Algerian one, fitted to run on gas.

After that job I was stationed at a fort to communicate with a cable-laying vessel called HMS *Lasso*. She was laying asdic loops – or sonar, as the Americans called it – in Algiers Bay. These loops were laid to a design, and any form of vessel crossing over them would be detected on the asdic equipment at the fort. The *Lasso* would transmit her position to me and this would be checked on the asdic receivers to line everything up.

Finally I was drafted back to sea again, and had to report to HMS *Misoa*. She of course was one of the first three LSTs – *Bachaquero, Misoa* and *Tasajera* – converted from oil tankers.

I went down to the docks and reported to her Officer of the Day, then sought out the Chief Yeoman of Signals. The visual signalling staff was the CYS and three signalmen, including myself. Also there were three telegraphists for the wireless.

She was part T124X manned.[4] The engine-room personnel were all Merchant Navy, as were the cooks, storekeepers, writers and stewards. The gunners, the communications ratings and most of the seamen were RN. All the officers except the Boatswain were Reservists. We also had a doctor.

I was told that my station for beaching and for entering harbour was on the after starboard pom-pom sponson. We had a large kedge-anchor, which was dropped at a set point when beaching, or in a harbour where coming alongside could be difficult. The after cable party was in telephone communication with the bridge, and when the order to drop the kedge was given it was passed on to the telephone number, who would yell 'Let go!'. I would be watching the starboard wing of the bridge, where the CYS had a small hand flag, and on the order of 'Let go!' he would drop his flag and I would raise mine and repeat the order. It was a good double check.

We had no radar or anything, and no gyrocompass.

We loaded troops and Bren carriers for Bone [230 miles east of Algiers], which at this time was the most forward decent harbour held by the First Army.

We were in a small convoy, covered by asdic trawlers and MLs between us and the coast, and a 'Hunt' class destroyer and an anti-aircraft cruiser on the seaward side. We discharged OK, but on the return journey our convoy was under attack most of the night. We had a stern wind, and the AA cruiser covered us with smoke, so we were creeping along in a man-made fog. We could feel depth charges exploding, but we made Algiers.

Also running the gauntlet of U-boats and bombers was *Geoff Southon*, whose ship was in one of the regular follow-up convoys bringing supplies and reinforcements for the First Army.

---

4. T124X Agreements, once signed, made the crewmen subject to Naval discipline and allowed them to stay on in their previous jobs when the ship was taken over by the Royal Navy.

I recall looking up at this 6000-ton tramp we were to go out on, the *Jean Jadot*, and thinking how big she looked – as high as a house. Of course, that was at the dockside in Birkenhead. Little did we realise that a 6000-tonner looks like a bloody rowing boat when you're in the Atlantic.

After loading we sailed and joined our convoy in the Clyde. The first day out into the Atlantic they opened up these boxes of fish, and found they were all rotten. The crew said 'Well, we can't throw it overboard for fear of it attracting U-boats', so it lay on the deck, stinking to high heaven. So, what with the motion of the ship and the smell of stinking fish, we spewed our guts up.

When we got further out a storm got up, which made it even worse. Because down below we were sleeping in hammocks, and of course the bloke next to you would throw up all over the place . . . You can imagine the fetid atmosphere. I found the conditions below unbearable, so I moved up on deck and made a bed on one of the hatch covers. I tied myself on, covered myself with a gas cape, and managed to get some sleep. The ship was still rolling so much that I looked out to sea once in the middle of the night, and there was nothing between my bed and the horizon!

But eventually the storm died down.

We realised we must be heading for North Africa, where landings had been made two months previously.

After some days we passed Tangier, with all its twinkling lights, and then Gibraltar. The sea was calm once we got into the Mediterranean, so we all did our washing and hung it up everywhere.

About 5.00pm on 20 January 1943, when we were just going to have tea, there was an almighty BANG. And the ship immediately started to tilt underneath us.

The *Jean Jadot* had fallen victim to the prowling *U-453*, which had fired a spread of four torpedoes at the convoy.

I was below decks when it happened, and I recall thinking that I *had* to get my kapok lifejacket. You just ignore other people. The ship was going down so fast that I was pushing through water up to my chest by the time I reached my stuff, but I grabbed the lifejacket and made it back up onto the deck. The ship's stern was well out of the water, and I wasn't going to jump that far, so I slid down the deck, hanging onto the rail, until I was only 5 or 6ft above the sea. Then I jumped over.

The lifejacket held me up, but God it was cold.

I found that I had to take my heavy Army boots off – no easy task – before I could swim. When I'd done that it was still hard to make progress, as the kapok lifejacket made it difficult to move through the water.

The ship went down in minutes. I could see someone hanging onto the propeller. He had no lifejacket.

Eventually I managed to get to a life raft, about 10ft square, which had been released from the ship before she sank. I can remember sitting on this raft, looking down and thinking 'They can't be *my* feet – they're blue!'. I mean literally blue. It was *so* cold. Everyone said 'Mediterranean? Bloody Arctic more like'. It was actually warmer in the water than on the raft, so we all took turns getting back in the water and just hanging onto the side of the raft.

I don't know how long we were in the water before one of our destroyers appeared – HMS *Verity*. She went round in circles and washed us all together, but she daren't stop until it was fully dark, because the sub would just get her too.

Then they picked us up. And I got the most wonderful sandwich and glass of rum I've ever tasted.

Next day we were landed safely at Algiers and taken to Maison Carree, which was a town just inland. We only had our wet clothes, and no equipment, not even 'eating irons'. To eat we had to get used bully beef tins, and using stones we bashed them into crude spoons and knives.

Of course, eventually we got properly re-equipped and went forward, eastwards towards Tunis. We drove through beautiful countryside – plenty of water; palm trees; rather like the southern part of France. Into Tunisia, to the Beja area to join the 128th Brigade.

That was the brigade your guns mainly worked with?

That's right. Three infantry brigades in a division, and three regiments of 25pdr field guns to support them. My Regiment – the 172nd Field Regiment, Royal Artillery – worked mainly with the 128th Brigade, which was all Hampshires – 1/4th Battalion, Hampshire Regiment; 2/4th Battalion, Hampshire Regiment; 5th Battalion, Hampshire Regiment. That was quite unusual, to have three battalions from the same regiment brigaded together.

The infantry had a hell of a life. They were up at the sharp end, and of course their casualty rates would be terribly high. Some of the time a battalion might lose a third of its strength in a single night. And they would just be replaced. When they had heavy casualties they'd pull the whole lot out, and send them to the rear. Give them a bath, clean them up, give them some decent food, and so on. And then fill up the gaps with replacements. Maybe a bit of training to weld them together, and then back into the line. So the faces in the infantry constantly changed.

In the artillery we had a relatively cushy life, so we stayed in the line most of the time. So when 'our' brigade, the 128th Brigade, came out for a rest, we simply supported someone else.

Our gun line would usually be several miles behind the front positions, because our standard range was 6000 to 8000 yards. That was the sort of distance we liked to fire at. We *could* fire up to 13,000 yards. And if the range started to get down to 2000 or 3000 yards we used to think 'Hm. Time to pull back, boys'. We didn't want to join *that* war! We were in the war which shot over the top!

Of course, the First Army was spread very thin, because it had to cover a vast area with relatively few divisions. And the Germans thought if they could break through, they'd be able to roll us up. And that would prolong the war in North Africa, which was what they wanted. Because we were pressing them from one side, and the Eighth Army from the other.

But for us the war seemed far away, and it wasn't until February 1943 that things started to liven up.

> The Germans and Italians attacked towards Kasserine, badly mauling the US 1st Armored Division. Then they turned their attention to Geoff's position, further north.

155 Battery had gone to Sidi Nsir, and the other two [153 and 154 Batteries, each of which had eight 25pdrs, for a total of twenty-four in the regiment] to Hunt's Gap, slightly to the south.

On the morning of 26 February the Jerries attacked the 5th Hampshires and 155 Battery at Sidi Nsir. This was out of range of the other batteries, so no gun support could be given. The Hamps and the guns fought all day, the 25pdrs firing over open sights. By darkness the position was overrun, the guns destroyed and many prisoners taken. Those who continued to supply the guns with ammo, up the single road to Sidi Nsir, deserve a mention, but in the end we lost a whole battery in our first day in action.

Over the following few days the other batteries were also fully employed, as Jerry continued to press on, trying to achieve a breakthrough which his tanks could exploit. But eventually we got the upper hand.

You know who won the war for us, don't you? General Motors! It was the sheer bulk of equipment, and the unlimited supply of ammunition, and of course petrol, that really tipped the balance. If you could get it there. Logistics – supply – is one of the real problems. If you're going to fire off 1000 rounds, some poor sucker's got to *carry* 1000 rounds.

One felt sympathy for the German commanders. They didn't have enough ammunition. They didn't have enough petrol. We were able to throw stuff away. 'Your tank's been knocked out? OK, here's another one . . .'. The Germans had to repair theirs.

When they finally surrendered in Tunisia on 13 May 1943 we took 250,000 German and Italian prisoners. The Germans marched in, singing their hearts out. They were quite happy. The war was over for them. Many of them had their own rations. They set up their own cookhouses, and all the rest of it. Got themselves inside the wire, and then organised concerts, with a bloody band, the lot! Very organised, you see.

I remember being in charge of a convoy of Italian prisoners. We stopped for what's now called a convenience stop, at the side of the road. Anyway, when we set off again a couple of the Eyeties came running after us! They said 'We don't want to get left behind!'. When you think about it, you see, they were out in the middle of nowhere. They *wanted* to stay prisoners of war. We didn't have to bloody *guard* them. Bluntly, they were only too happy to stay, and be fed, and looked after. If it'd been Europe, I suppose it might've been different. But here they were. In the middle of nowhere.

Even before the whole of North Africa had been secured, Churchill and Roosevelt had met in Morocco to lay out their general strategy for the rest of 1943.

Their Chiefs of Staff promptly renewed the argument of the previous year, but the British again got their way, and it was decided that after Tunisia the next step should be an invasion of Sicily, aimed at further weakening the already weary Italians. Capturing the Sicilian airfields would also greatly reduce the air threat to Allied ships using the Mediterranean.

No one doubted that Sicily would provide a much sterner test than either Madagascar or North Africa, but at least by the time such an invasion could be staged, the new purpose-built vessels beginning to flow from American shipyards would be arriving to strengthen the amphibious fleets.

THREE

New Men, New Ships: Building the Amphibious Fleet

By 1942 the Americans, like the British before them, were wrestling with the problems of how to raise, arm and train the huge forces necessary for a global war. The personnel strength of the US Navy, for example, virtually quadrupled during the course of the year. The British and American amphibious fleets were overwhelmingly manned by newcomers who had never considered a Navy career in peacetime, and who had no previous experience of the sea.

Dick Reiter was one of thousands of young men in this position who were nevertheless seen by the US Navy as potential officer material.

Back in 1941 it seemed to us that FDR could hardly wait to get into the war. Our aid to Britain was transparently non-neutral. Yet the Japs hit us first, while hiding behind their negotiators in Washington, DC.

Like most folks, I remember exactly where I was when some historic announcement was made. It's that way with the Japanese attacking Pearl Harbor. On December 7, 1941 I was at a cat show. Cleaning cages. And not the kind of cat show that sailors I told this to in later years brought to mind!

Enlisting in the US Navy was the natural thing to do. My folks never questioned my decision, and simply supported me throughout.

Coincidental to this, I'd met my future wife Lenore Lee Billeter in the Fall of 1941, as I swung a college chemical lab door back, almost hitting her. It's still easy in my mind's eye to see the frosted glass door, the radiator and cover behind it, and Lenore looking surprised.

I was called up in 1943, seven months after enlisting. I tried to get into Navy Aviation V-5, but the Navy had other plans. I ended up at Central Michigan College of Education in Mount Pleasant, in the V-12 program. This was a modified 'boot camp', as we continued college courses but were Apprentice Seamen, US Navy, and were put into better physical shape for Midshipmen's School to follow. V-12 in Michigan for three months taught us discipline and drill, and improved our endurance via endless soccer games and marching. Yet there was time off for studying, and travelling on weekends to visit Lenore in Illinois.

Midshipmen's School at Columbia University [in New York City; one of four – later six – such schools] took raw material, sailors and civilians, and in ninety days produced officers and gentlemen. We were called 'Ninety Day Wonders'.

The V-12 program had already instilled in us that as future officers swearing, getting drunk and smoking in public were just not done. So we didn't. No one wanted to give up the chance to be more than an Apprentice Seaman, that's for sure. The physical drills of V-12 now intensified, with a lot of marching. My boy scout days in High School may have gotten me the job of Platoon leader, calling cadence and sounding out marching orders. Crash courses all day, and evenings memorising nautical lore, Morse code, signal flags, aircraft recognition, Navy discipline, customs, knots, seamanship, et cetera.

We marched every Sunday evening through the quiet, dark streets of Upper Manhattan to Riverside Church. There we sang William Whiting's 'Eternal Father, strong to save', and heard the roll call of Navy men killed the past week. There was no joking during *that* Church service. 'Eternal Father' is a majestic hymn.

V-12 and Midshipmen's School taught us a lot, and a couple of things have stuck with me my entire life. One. Always leave a place cleaner than you found it. Since then, quite a few people using washrooms on commercial flights have benefited! Two. Standing to attention. You'll often see non-military men with hands in their pockets, grasped behind their backs, folded in front or some other self-conscious position. But once you learn to simply lightly press each thumb onto the forefinger and second finger at your side – as if there's a satin stripe going down the seam of your trousers – you'll look relaxed, and the appearance is that of nobleness rather than slouchiness.

The military service is no place for someone who cherishes his own image or worries about democracy in action. You have to salute superiors. That's just the way it is. Tough if you don't like it.

Getting used to *being* saluted was easy, however!

After these three months of training I was commissioned an Ensign – single stripe. We even got business cards ['Richard William Reiter. Ensign. United States Naval Reserve'], although I don't recall ever needing one.

John Towers volunteered for the Royal Navy, but as a rating rather than an officer.

I'd just turned sixteen in early 1942, and joined the Home Guard – originally named the LDV, or Local Defence Volunteers [Britain's last-ditch defence force, largely composed of the under- and over-aged]. People called it the Look, Duck and Vanish army! Our Sergeant, Mr Brady, had been in the First World War and was conversant with signalling procedures, and he thought I was a suitable candidate to learn Morse code and semaphore signalling. Being quite young I absorbed these procedures very easily, and could manage radio telegraphy and the use of lights and flags without much of a problem.

When I was seventeen, in early 1943, I wrote to the Admiralty offering my services. Of course they wouldn't accept me at that age, but said I *could* join at the age of seventeen and a half, and in due course I got my call-up papers to report to HMS *Raleigh* at Torpoint, in Cornwall.

On arrival at Torpoint in the early hours of the morning, hundreds of us from converging trains were met by a group of WVS [helpers from the Women's Voluntary Services] who plied us with sandwiches. We were all extremely hungry after our long journey, and wolfed the food down. I remember quite a lot of us had to drink our tea out of glass jam jars due to the shortage of cups.

Having arrived at HMS *Raleigh* we were allocated to our respective huts – mine being Hut 51, together with about fifty others. The hut leader and instructor was a fifty year-old ex-Chief Petty Officer brought out of retirement specifically for this purpose. At our age we looked upon him as a father figure, and we had to address him as 'Sir' at all times. No one seemed to have a problem with this.

From Day Two it was all go, starting with the issue of uniforms, some of which nearly fitted. We spent some time swopping various items of clothing with each other, until we all felt very proud and swaggered around as though we were old sailors with years of experience under our belts. I remember that we were all issued with a large multi-purpose knife, and a cut-throat razor to shave with. Of course most of us were too scared to try and shave with the razors, as we'd probably have cut ourselves to ribbons. I think they were just a legacy of the old-time Navy.

Our first and most important instruction was that we must at all times refer to the left side as the port side, and the right side as the starboard. The floor was never a floor, it was a deck. If you went into town – which we never did, as it was constant training – you were going ashore, and on your return you were coming on board! We were told off in no uncertain terms if we forgot. As with a normal ship we had to salute the quarterdeck.

A series of unpleasant inoculations was the next trial, which no one liked of course.

We did a lot of rifle drill and square-bashing. Here my training with the Home Guard helped me considerably, as I was acquainted with all the drill movements. One poor chap I remember just could *not* march; his left arm swung as his left foot did, most of the time. We all found it hilarious, but the poor victim didn't, especially when the drill officer had him running round the parade ground with his rifle above his head. He did eventually overcome this problem, but it took quite a long time. His whole coordination left a lot to be desired.

As I couldn't swim very well I too had my problems. The first exercise was to don our 'duck' suits [uniforms made from a heavy, white cloth] and jump in the swimming pool at the deep end, making our way to the shallow end. Half way there I submerged in a panic with the weight of the suit. Fortunately the pool was surrounded by PT instructors who grabbed you with a boat hook and pulled you safely to the side. Another test was to climb up a long ladder to the top of a huge tank filled with water, and to climb inside and descend to the bottom, climbing down another ladder situated inside the tank. The object was to reach the very bottom, banging the side with your fist to indicate your position. I never did get to the bottom, and by some crafty initiative on my part avoided a second attempt. I should add that before doing any of these exercises we had to line up in a row and someone with a large pair of scissors came along and cut our hair fringes to well above eyebrow level. It was a bit like sheep shearing.

My next port of call was HMS *Drake* at Devonport. Here I was informed that I was to become a member of Combined Operations [by now under the command of Vice-Admiral Lord Louis Mountbatten, who had replaced Sir Roger Keyes in October 1941]. I was then drafted to Dunoon in Scotland to join a Landing Craft, Tank as the only signalman on board.

How did you feel about going to an LCT?

As far as I can remember no one, including myself, objected to being drafted to Combined Operations; we just accepted instructions without question. I do recall, though, that a couple of lads at HMS *Raleigh* volunteered for service in submarines, which paid a little more per day. I made about twenty-one shillings a week, and I used to send home to my mother seven shillings of this.

As I was the only signalman on board the LCT, all my duties when at sea were spent on the bridge with the Captain or First Lieutenant, or both of them at times. So I got to know them much better than the rest of the crew. My signalling duties were to read and convey to the officer on watch any messages, mainly from our Flotilla leader. These would be sent in Morse code by Aldis lamp, or by signal flag. We had a small hardback book of flags and their meanings when hoisted by the leader – things like 'Keep closed up', 'Maintain station', and so on. In the main the LCTs only had to hoist one flag in reply – an affirmative or a negative flag. The flag locker and other signalling equipment was kept just aft of the bridge.

In addition to my signalling duties I had to keep a lookout for anything that might occur.

In Scotland we practised landing on beaches in Loch Fyne and Loch Alsh, and around Stranraer, Troon, Oban and other places. The large ramp at the bow had to be lowered and raised at the correct time. Dropping it too soon would flood the tank deck, so approaching and leaving the beaches had to be precise movements. I saw quite a few mishaps, and if it was the fault of the First Lieutenant, known fondly as 'Number One', or 'Jimmy the One', he got a good dressing down by the Captain.

On some occasions the kedge anchor positioned aft was ordered to be dropped some distance from the beach. This was used to help pull us off, as quite often it was difficult to get away by using the engines only.

Looking back, would you say you have favourable memories of the Royal Navy?

To be honest they're pretty negative ... Mainly I'm just glad I didn't go in the Army.

Except, I *do* feel I played my own little part in a war against a brutal enemy, and that's something to be proud of.

These increases in manpower were matched by a steady rise in the output of landing craft and ships, thanks to the harnessing of America's vast industrial capacity.

Prior to their entry into the war the Americans had built only modest numbers of the smaller landing craft, such as the LCM. Now their yards began to turn out the larger craft as well, including their first LCTs, built in three sections for shipment overseas. Since the latest version of the LCT in British service was the Mk4, the American design was officially referred to as the LCT Mk5. The first such craft was completed in June 1942.

This was followed in September by the first Landing Craft, Infantry (Large), or LCI(L), designed to carry 182 – later increased to 210 – troops and their personal equipment. The LCI(L) had originally been conceived as a large raiding craft, but by the time it entered service it was needed more for invasion work.

Another month later, in October 1942, the first American LST was completed. The British were simultaneously building a type known as the LST Mk1 to supplement their original trio of Maracaibo conversions, but the new British ships, though fast, proved to be too big and too difficult to mass produce. By contrast the American design, by naval architect John Niedermair of the Bureau of Ships, turned out to be a mass production classic. Designated the Landing Ship, Tank Mk2, the American LST quickly became the queen of the amphibious warfare ships, and the demand for them proved insatiable. Existing American shipyards rapidly expanded and new ones were opened, often on disused industrial sites.

One such yard was built on land occupied by a derelict asphalt plant in Perth Amboy, New Jersey. The New Jersey Shipbuilding Corporation demolished the existing plant, cleared and graded the 34-acre site, and laid out four parallel building ways – each capable of accommodating five LCI(L)s in various stages of fabrication – in just three months.

In March 1941 Congress had approved the Lend-Lease Act, which sanctioned the provision of military aid to countries deemed essential to US security. Since that time the planning of war production in Britain and the United States had become increasingly integrated, and, despite the demands of the US Navy, a substantial proportion of the new ships and craft were handed over to the British on completion.

One of the British sailors who came to the Perth Amboy yard to pick up an LCI(L) was *Jim Whent.*

On arrival in New York we were billeted with the US Navy in Brooklyn Barracks. We were poorly paid compared with the Americans, but they were very good to us. When we used to go ashore with them in small groups they'd insist on paying for most things, including taxis, meals, drinks, entertainment, and so on. It took us some time to get used to the decimal coinage – cents, nickels, dimes, quarters, et cetera [Britain at the time, of course, had a pound made up of twenty shillings, each of twelve pence]. We made lots of friends in the US Navy, and were also popular with the local girls. We were mostly teenagers at the time. I was just eighteen.

After about a fortnight in Brooklyn Barracks we were moved by bus across the Hudson River to New Jersey, and down the coast to a seaside resort called Asbury Park, where the Royal Navy had taken over two adjoining hotels – the Monterey and the Berkeley Carteret.

I was put in the latter, which was a multi-storey red brick building. I was on the sixth floor and had a room, with bathroom and toilet, overlooking the sea. There was even a telephone, but you had to go through the Reception switchboard for an outside number, and this was manned by Naval personnel.

We had the use of all the hotel's facilities, but had to parade for roll call every morning and then to breakfast, following which we were assigned certain duties, such as security of the building, cleaning rooms, cleaning corridors, and so on. Things were similar at the adjacent Monterey, which was smaller. There were no civilian staff.

Our landing craft – an LCI(L) – was being built up at Perth Amboy, New Jersey, and we watched her being finished. There seemed to be lots of women welders, women electricians, et cetera. I suppose all the men were in the armed forces. As soon as each one was ready, a crew of twenty-two would take her over and go to sea for trials, testing the engines and everything.

When we got aboard ours – *LCI(L) 245* – we had our kitbags and hammocks, but the hammocks weren't needed, as we all slept in bunks. Three-tier, foldaway, steel-framed canvas ones. The top of the large deep freeze also served as a table, where we had our meals, wrote letters or played cards. We had a tall, grey metal locker each, and there were fifteen of the crew on the mess deck. The officers and POs were elsewhere.

Once we had enough to make a Flotilla – twelve LCI(L)s – we sailed for the US Navy base at Norfolk, Virginia. Beaching exercises were very curtailed, as the top priority was to get across the Atlantic as soon as possible. The troop spaces [three forward, one aft] were then filled with tons of tinned foods, ranging from corned beef to evaporated milk. This was both to act as ballast and to top up food supplies back in the UK.

We sailed to Bermuda, where we took on water and diesel fuel, and then set out across the Atlantic, unescorted, in a convoy of twelve. It took us over a fortnight, mostly in heavy seas, but we arrived safely in the UK. Several similar convoys followed.

What were conditions like during the crossing?

Well, considering that even fully laden with tons of foodstuffs we only had a draught of a few feet – we were designed for beaching, after all – we were going at little more than a walking pace much of the time. The decks were constantly awash, and we had to rig life-lines criss-crossing the upper deck to prevent people getting washed overboard, especially at night in the pitch dark. No lights allowed.

With the constant buffeting anything not tied down was thrown all over the place, including plates of food on the table. The ship's cook, in his tiny galley, used to have the most difficult job keeping his feet, and frequently the galley deck was swimming with grease which had slopped over from chip pans, et cetera. The heat and fumes were nauseating. How he stuck it I'll never know.

The same with the engine-room. The heat was always 80 to 100 degrees Fahrenheit, and with the motion of the ship and the sickly smell of the diesel which always covered the deck. The roar of the engines made it impossible to talk. Everything was done by lip reading, or written notes. The engine room was very small and compact, with two large General Motors diesel engines [called Quad Units, because each consisted of four vehicle engines, linked together] on either side of a narrow gangway, driving two screws. There were also large generators each side, providing all the electricity for the ship. The engine-room staff had to take large salt tablets, the size of a penny piece, along with gallons of water, to compensate for the loss of salt and body fluids.

What was your own job on board?

I was the gunner on the port side stern Oerlikon, 20mm cannon. I'd be strapped into it around the shoulders, and I'd aim through a ring sight. There was also a loader, to take off the empty magazines and reload with full ones. Each magazine drum weighed about 25lbs, and was loaded with HE [high explosive], tracer, incendiary and armour-piercing shells, which made the Oerlikon very effective against low-flying aircraft, and even surface targets.

It was said that the LCI(L)s were the smallest Royal Navy craft ever to cross the Atlantic under their own power.

We zig-zagged every few miles and didn't encounter any U-boats, although there were wolf packs of up to eight or ten operating on known convoy routes.

New Zealander *Harry Elvey* remembers the anti-British sentiment which occasionally surfaced in the USA.

We travelled aboard the liner *Queen Mary*, on her first westward voyage after having sliced HMS *Curaçoa* [her escorting cruiser] in half. She docked in Boston, Massachusetts and went into dry dock there. She just towered above the surrounding streets, and when dried out the great damage from the collision with the *Curaçoa* was very obvious.

I'd been drafted to Boston to join the *LCI(L) 100*, and from the naval barracks we were in it was easy to visit the shipyards at Quincy where the craft were being built. Life was pleasant away from the war, and the coffee from the kiosk serving the shipyard workers was nothing short of magnificent! Boston was a lovely city, but in my naivete I wasn't prepared for the anti-British feeling which would be expressed as you passed someone in the street. Not very much, and it went over my head at the time, as I was so green that I didn't understand Boston was the most Irish of American cities.

We were finally commissioned, which wasn't without incident. The ship was crammed with stores in the troop spaces, and when they fuelled us there was a big balls up, and the cargo was soaked in diesel. However, we finally got away with fresh stores and set sail for Bermuda.

What did you think of the LCI(L)s?

I hated them. I felt they were the ugliest ships ever built, and I just couldn't feel any pride in them. They were just an ugly box with a great kedge anchor mounted on an unsightly bracket at the stern, so they could kedge themselves off again after beaching to disembark troops. They carried two ugly gangways, one on either side of the bows, which were lowered from sponsons to enable the unfortunate troops to disembark. They were like ferry boats below, with no sleeping room, just row upon row of wooden seats for the soldiers and their gear.

Eventually I was replaced aboard *LCI(L) 100* by an English rating, and took up new duties ashore. As a New Zealander who felt he'd joined the Navy by invitation, I'd steadfastly refused to do the officers' washing for them. No doubt feelers were out, and I was replaced by someone willing to do the washing as well as the wireless work!

Most of the officers were just as young as the ratings. *John Hiscock* was eighteen when he joined another LCI(L) as her First Lieutenant.

At the age of seventeen and a half I'd enlisted, along with other old school friends, under what was then known as the 'Y' Scheme entry to the RNVR. On passing the examination before a board of Naval officers this allowed entry to the Navy as a Cadet, with some recommendation to be considered for a commission in the future.

A week after my eighteenth birthday – which was on 7 June 1942 – I was called up to report to HMS *Ganges*, the training establishment [at Shotley] in Suffolk. Here a very intensive initial training was to be completed over a period of three months.

On completion of the *Ganges* course the Cadets who'd shown some proficiency were posted to the officer training establishment at Lochailort, in the Western Highlands of Scotland [newly opened in August 1942 to provide Seaman officers for Combined Operations, relieving some of the pressure on HMS *King Alfred*].

A large curriculum of subjects ensured fourteen hours a day of lectures, practical work and after-hours study to keep up with the pace. 'Recreational' activity was of a commando type, with hazardous mountain climbs and much cross-country running. There was no shore leave.

The pass rate was about 60 per cent, and I was one of the fortunates. At the passing out ceremony at the conclusion of the course most of us became

Temporary Acting Sub-Lieutenants, RNVR. However, those in my age bracket only became Midshipmen.

Just after Christmas 1942 many of us were posted to the USA.

We boarded the passenger liner *Empress of Scotland*, which had formerly been the *Empress of Japan*, and set sail from Glasgow bound for New York. During the ensuing days at sea most of the travelling officers were given lookout duties on watches at various vantage points on the ship as she steamed across the North Atlantic. My posting was as First Lieutenant aboard one of the many LCI(L)s being built in America.

On arrival in New York we were asked to report to the Royal Navy Staff Officer at the Barbizon Plaza Hotel on 58th Street, Manhattan – not far from Central Park. We were to reside at this hotel until receipt of orders to report to our allotted LCI(L).

Unlike the ratings' accommodation at Asbury Park, the Barbizon Plaza remained under civilian management, and the regime there was considerably less restrictive.

Other than the resident Naval Staff Officer, who regularly kept in touch with us, we were really on our own. I seem to recall that a daily contact each morning was required, but we did what we wanted to do, and were free to come and go as we pleased.

The Barbizon Plaza was, of course, still functioning as a civilian hotel. I met many of the people who were staying there, including a Cuban family I became quite friendly with. On reflection I think in uniform we were quite a novelty around the place, as people would often stop and talk to us. They'd also want to entertain us, which was all very pleasant. Sometimes we dined at the hotel, and sometimes we went out.

How were you paid?

The Naval Staff Officer had a small administrative staff, and included in this was a Paymaster. Officers were paid monthly, and crew members fortnightly.

I think I was there about four or five weeks before finally getting my drafting orders to the *LCI(L) 126*, which was lying alongside at Brooklyn Navy Yard. Brooklyn was a very gloomy place – typical of most waterfront areas where the docking, building and refitting of ships go on. Then it was a question of pulling out all the stops to prepare the ship for sea trials and the forthcoming transatlantic voyage.

The handing-over of the ship to the CO was coordinated by the Naval Staff Officer and the management of the shipyard. The paperwork was really only an inventory, which embraced the ship and all her contents. This was signed by the CO after a thorough check. Some of the equipment on board was regarded as expendable – for example ropes and cables – but everything else, as we were to find on returning the vessels to the USA in 1946, was accountable as per inventory.

Sea trials were undertaken in the open waters off New York, with shipyard staff on board. Any defects had to be made good. Our own engine-room staff had to familiarise themselves with the General Motors diesels, and with the two variable pitch screws, which I think were quite new to most of them.

As a general rule LCI(L)s were regarded as difficult craft to manoeuvre. This was due mainly to the relatively shallow draught. It wasn't so bad fully loaded with troops, or loaded with fuel and ballast, as was the case on the transatlantic crossing. But sailing 'light', an LCI(L) was rather like a cork. This was particularly noticeable when trying to berth alongside. A strong onshore or offshore wind would tend to take charge, and this made the ship difficult to control. As with most things, the more experience we had, the better ship handlers we became.

Did you practise beaching?

No, there was no beach training at all. It was just seaworthiness preparation, and trials to test mechanical efficiency. Other than play with the gangways whilst berthed alongside to see if they worked or not, there was no other activity. In fact the gangways were lashed down and greased thoroughly in readiness for the voyage.

We didn't experience the process of beaching at all until we arrived at Gibraltar, and then on a very minor scale. We'd nose into a suitable little cove nearby, drop our stern anchor just to get the feel of it all and to ensure the communications system to all parts of the ship was working satisfactorily. A simple but effective intercom system was fitted on the ship, which provided contact between the bridge and all the critical parts – the engine-room, the gangway winches, the stern anchor winch, et cetera.

Even on our 'mopping up' operations along the North African coast we were always able to berth alongside at the small ports we were operating from.

So when you did learn the process, what did it consist of?

Well, we'd approach the beach closed up at Action Stations, with everybody in life jackets, anti-flash gear, steel helmets and intercom phones. About 300 yards out you'd spot the Beach Party signal to come in. The troops would've already been alerted to assemble for disembarkation, and the CO'd be coordinating this with the Army officers responsible for the 'cargo', as it were. 250 yards out the CO would order 'Launch gangways!', and these would be extended like two horns, either side of the bow, in readiness to be lowered. 150 yards out he'd order 'Drop anchor!', and the stern anchor would be let go, so that we could kedge ourselves off the beach again. Then we'd continue, paying out anchor cable, until we hit the beach.

Then it was 'Stop together!' to stop the engines, and 'Let go gangways!'. If there was a heavy swell or surf running, you'd need to lift the gangways a little bit again with the order 'Lift gangways to water level!'. Otherwise the swell would take charge of them. Unfortunately this meant there was often a drop of 3 or 4ft from the end of the gangway to the sea bed, which was bad news for the troops. Particularly the short ones, who might be bowled over in the surf and find it hard to recover in full battle order.

When the gangways were OK he'd give the order 'Disembark!'. Once the last of the troops were ashore it'd be 'Up gangways. Up anchor!', and then, when we were clear of the beach, 'Gangways inboard!'.

And that's exactly how it was.

In some cases where we knew the beach was steep no stern anchor was necessary; we'd use our engines to keep the bow up on the beach, and just reverse off when disembarkation of the troops was completed.

Anyway, that maiden voyage from New York to Gibraltar in February 1943 was an experience I'll never forget. The route was via Bermuda and the Canary Islands, and there were three officers on board for the passage – Lieutenant Dickens the CO, me as First Lieutenant and an additional watchkeeping officer called Chapman.

From New York to Bermuda we were crossing the Gulf Stream, which made for a very rough trip, and not far out of New York I became seasick. I expected Lieutenant Dickens to show some compassion. I was horribly wrong. Sick or not, I was to keep my watch. ''Hang your arms over the binnacle of the compass and place a bucket between your feet', he said. Luckily after a period of feeling like death warmed up I came good, and was never sick again during my whole time in the Service.

More than twenty years later I returned to New York on business, and I decided to retrace my steps as an eighteen year-old, and visit the Barbizon Plaza. I caught a taxi, and yes, the hotel was still there in all its glory. I ventured through the big swinging glass doors to the entrance foyer. Things had changed. I didn't recognise some of the bars and lounges, as the hotel had obviously been given a facelift.

I eyed the Doorman – an aged gentleman in his brown and gold uniform. I asked him if he'd been at the Barbizon Plaza very long, and he replied 'Forty years, and I'm shortly due to retire'. I was quite excited. Here was my man! Yes, he remembered the British naval officers, the old bars, the lounges. And after finding a suitable substitute for himself, he took me on a conducted tour of the hotel, finishing up in the Manager's office to enjoy some celebratory drinks!

FOUR

Into the Lion's Den: The Invasion of Sicily

The plans for the invasion of Sicily were reworked several times, and the final version reflected very real fears about the safety of landing force. In particular, the air threat was expected to be far greater than anything previously encountered.

Peter Bayly-Jones served aboard one of the growing number of landing craft specially adapted for air defence.

In August 1942 I joined a number of other Lieutenants, RM at Eastney on a gunnery course specifically for the Landing Craft, Flak[1] – or LCF. Then in November I was posted to *LCF 7* as the second RM officer.

LCF 7 was a converted LCT Mk3, with a deck built over the tank space, and with eight 20mm Oerlikons and four 2pdr pom-poms fitted. She was crewed altogether by two RNVR officers, two Royal Marine officers, sixteen Naval ratings and forty-eight Marines. The Captain was Lieutenant Ken Lowten, RNVR; the Number One was Sub-Lieutenant John Ofield, RNVR, and the OCRM [Officer Commanding, Royal Marines] was Lieutenant 'Bunny' Stear, RM. They were all in their thirties, so I was very much the 'young Joe'.

She'd been built in London, and we joined her in the London Docks in very cold November weather – in the days when they still had London fogs!

What were the conditions like on board?

Better than an LCT. The Captain had a cabin to himself, and so did the Number One, who I think occupied the original cabin on the upper deck below the bridge which would've been the officers' quarters of the LCT Mk3 before conversion to an LCF. The two RM officers shared a cabin next to the wardroom. The Naval ratings' accommodation was aft in the original LCT mess deck, and the Marines were forward of the magazine.

Some attempt had been made to counter condensation from the deckheads by lining them with cork bits, but it wasn't very successful. Water dripped copiously off them, and I found it necessary to sleep under a waterproof cape!

We officers had bunks whereas the crew slept in hammocks. There was a shower, but it was seawater, and one never feels clean somehow after a seawater shower. The wardroom was roomy enough for four officers, but got a bit

---

1. Originally the German abbreviation for Flugabwehrkanone (anti-aircraft gun), 'Flak' had by this time come to be used by both sides as a shorthand term for anti-aircraft fire, or anti-aircraft weaponry.

cramped if we had visitors, which we often did in harbour, since for some reason the LCFs were allowed duty free booze but the LCTs weren't. You can imagine how popular we were!

Did you have stewards to look after you?

The RM officers had what were called Marine Officers' Attendants, or MOAs. In *LCF 7* my MOA was Marine Hamilton.

An LCF was of course unusual in that the Marines outnumbered the Royal Navy personnel, instead of the other way round. Did that result in any differences in how things were run?

No, I don't think so. The reason there were so many Marines was because they manned all the guns, except for the two aft pom-poms. They also formed the magazine and ammunition supply parties. When, much later, we handed her over to the US Navy the American crew were all Naval. No Marines.

My duties as the young Joe included supervising training and gun drills, kit inspections, helping the other officers to censor mail – a distasteful job – keeping the ship supplied with the right mix of ammunition, ordering clothing and stores for the detachment, and so on.

I was also in charge of the daily menu, and my greatest challenge was how to present corned beef in a different way each day. We did have some different types of tinned food, such as Spam – cold, fried in batter, diced . . . – tinned soya sausages and 'red lead' [tinned tomatoes], but it all got very repetitive. We did get a lot more butter, sugar, et cetera, than civilians in Britain, though.

At sea the two Naval officers took 'watch and watch' because the two RM officers weren't yet qualified, at that time, to take their own. Later on we got our watchkeeping certificates and were able to relieve the strain. In these craft very few of the crew were Regular RN or RM. We were all Temporary, or 'Hostilities Only'. I think the Coxswain and possibly the Detachment Sergeant Major were Regulars.

Where was your Action Station?

The second RM officer's Action Station was on the upper deck supervising the ammo supply and keeping the guns firing. The OCRM's Action Station was on the bridge with the Skipper – though there wasn't much he could do except advise him about ranges, et cetera.

After commissioning we sailed round the coast to Portsmouth to carry out working-up exercises; getting to know each other and the ship. While in Portsmouth we also got to know some of the WRNS liberty boat crews, and some of the pubs! We were issued with 'Blues' for ceremonial wear, although there wasn't much of that, and mostly we wore blue battledress with the blue beret and the Combined Ops shoulder flash.

After a few weeks of trying to hit the drogue and not the towing aircraft we sailed to Plymouth and were issued with khaki shorts and shirts, which gave us a good indication of where we might be going.

Sure enough, we sailed in a convoy of LCTs in April 1943, bound for the Med. In heavy weather the craft used to pound viciously, the bows rising on the crest of a wave and coming down on the flat bottom with a crash and a tremendous shudder. From the bridge you could see the whole craft wagging, rather like a diving board after someone's dived from it.

The passage was uneventful, although we did hear that one LCT broke in half in the heavy seas. We often saw a German Condor reconnaissance aircraft, which circled the convoy for hours on end. It felt odd when he wasn't there. We had a spell of shore leave in Gib which included a salt water bath. Bunny and I were invited to give our reasons in writing to the Admiral as to why we weren't carrying our gas masks. He's still waiting!

Our next port of call was Oran, where we weren't allowed ashore – probably because the French were still a bit sore about things. We were, however, allowed ashore in Algiers. But as we were only there one night the three older officers decided that I was too young to go on an 'exhibish', and that therefore I should be duty officer whilst they sampled the delights of the Kasbah.

On to Djidjelli, where we stayed for some weeks, and where we first had to do anything about enemy aircraft. There were a number of Red Alerts at night – all the craft in harbour were linked by radio and were ordered to provide a cone of fire which it was hoped the enemy raiders wouldn't penetrate. The fire was augmented by dense smoke let off by each craft. It must've been fairly effective, because I can't recall any bombs actually falling.

When we were in North Africa Joe Loss and his band entertained the troops in our area, and the big hit was 'Blues in the night'. Talking of songs, many of them bring back memories of those times – in Portsmouth before we left we were hearing 'Dearly beloved' and 'Moonlight becomes you', and 'Deep in the heart of Texas' was very popular.

In June of 1943 we went round to Sousse, and here we topped up with ammunition and stores ready for the invasion of Pantelleria.

This was a small, fortified island lying roughly half way between the North African coast and Sicily, whose capture by British commandos had briefly been considered in 1940. Now its airfield was required for the invasion of Sicily, and most of the British 1st Division was sent to take possession on 11 June 1943. The Italian garrison, which had been repeatedly pounded from air and sea, quickly surrendered as soon as the landings began.

We went in in support of the LCTs, which was completely unnecessary as there were no enemy planes in sight. One LCF was hit by shore fire and beached, taking no further part in the operation – not that there *was* anything further. The most spectacular part was the saturation bombing of the island as we approached it.

Then, in July 1943, we took part in the landings on the south-east coast of Sicily.

D-Day was Saturday 10 July, and the assault was made simultaneously by eight divisions.

A largely American Western Naval Task Force landed the US 1st, 3rd and 45th Infantry Divisions and 2nd Armored Division, aided by Ranger battalions, at beaches along the south coast.

On their right, a largely British Eastern Naval Task Force landed the British 5th and 51st (Highland) Divisions, the 1st Canadian Division, most of the British 50th (Northumbrian) Division and units of Army and Royal Marine Commandos on either side of the Pachino peninsula. Each British and Canadian division had been reinforced with a regiment[2] of tanks, and the 51st had also received an extra infantry brigade group.

The British First Army had by now been disbanded and its troops absorbed into the Eighth, so the latter controlled the British and Canadian elements of the landing force. The American elements were controlled by the new US Seventh Army.

We lay off the coast at Action Stations as anti-aircraft protection for the landing force, and whilst we were standing guard, so to speak – I was on the upper deck and the gun crews were closed up – we saw a couple of aircraft approaching us from the direction of the shore at only about 500ft. None of us were sure what they were until they both turned lazily to fly towards our stern – at this point we all saw the German markings and all yelled 'Open fire!' together. However, despite eight Oerlikons and four pom-poms blazing away, the two aircraft turned tail and beat a hasty retreat apparently unharmed – much to our disappointment. We realised shortly afterwards that they were Focke-Wulf Fw190s – a relatively new aircraft to us.

We were determined not to be caught unawares again, and some days later when cruising up the coast of Sicily keeping pace with the land forces' advance, I was on the bridge when I heard the lookout shout 'Aircraft red nine zero. Angle of sight zero!'. Two aircraft were coming in fast at sea level. This was an aggressive act, and the quick response was to open fire first and ask questions afterwards. We did just that. This had a marked effect on the two aircraft, who immediately banked sharply and waggled their wings to show their true colours – Spitfires! Fortunately we didn't hit *them* either.

Arthur Cornish was aboard another of the LCFs, detailed to protect the westernmost of the American landings.

I'd joined the Royal Navy the previous year, in 1942. Although I'd been an apprentice mechanic I was taken on as an Ordinary Seaman, and went for basic training to HMS *Collingwood* at Fareham.

---

2. British and Canadian armoured regiments would have been described as battalions in the US Army.

After a few weeks a notice on the board invited people to take tests for various trades, of which motor mechanic was one. I took the test, passed, and was made a Leading Motor Mechanic. A three-week course at Chatham on LCTs in general and Paxman engines in particular, in a class of about twenty mechanics, completed my training.

I first boarded an LCT at Troon in Ayrshire, and stayed for perhaps two weeks. Everyone was given this chance on an operational craft to get the feel of things before taking on one of their own. The mess deck seemed very crowded – not just with the occupants but with odd pieces of machinery – and the smell of fuel oil seemed everywhere.

I next went to Glasgow to take over a brand new LCT which was just being completed. However, on arrival I was told she was to be converted into *LCF 15*; I was to stand by while this was being done, and would have to find digs in Glasgow, which I did.

Every working day I went to the shipyard to watch the conversion. The well deck which normally carried tanks was decked over to take the eight Oerlikons and four Vickers pom-pom guns, the bow ramp was removed and a more pointed fixed prow was fitted. This also meant, of course, more space below, therefore the mess decks were much better than in the original LCT.

There were four LCFs being built at the same time – *LCF 15, LCF 16, LCF 17* and *LCF 18*. When they were commissioned the Skipper of *LCF 16* was Peter Bull the actor, who wrote *To Sea in a Sieve*.[3]

Aside from the officers, an LCF ship's company was a coxswain, a motor mechanic, two stokers, two wiremen, two signalmen, a telegraphist, an ordnance artificer, a sick berth attendant and five seamen. Also forty-eight Royal Marines who formed the gun crews. In spite of the numbers it wasn't as crowded as an LCT, and it wasn't until we were transported in a troopship, much later on, that we realised just how much an LCF – or LCT – pitched and rolled.

I was responsible for the engines, generators, pumps and anything else even vaguely mechanical – watertight doors, for instance. Also the electrics; even things like light bulbs, fuses and charging the batteries. The two stokers helped out. In harbour the working day was taken up with maintaining the engines – changing oil, setting tappets, et cetera – and, of course, painting and polishing brass and copper fittings. There was always something that needed doing. At sea the engine room staff kept watches in the engine room, checking oil pressures, water temperatures and so on, also adjusting the engine speeds as signalled from the bridge. When entering or leaving harbour all three of us were in the engine room.

In April 1943 we were issued with khaki tropical kit, and sailed to North Africa via Gibraltar. Soon after arrival at the base at Djidjelli I was transferred to *LCF 5*. Some time later *LCF 15* struck a mine and sank during the invasion of Elba [17 June 1944]. *LCF 5* was older than *15*, and had been on the Dieppe

---

3. *To Sea in a Sieve* (London 1956).

raid in August 1942. Before the invasion of Sicily we and several other craft were loaned to the Americans, who had no flak ships of their own. And so it was with the Americans that we went to Sicily.

I remember there was a storm on the way over, but by the morning of D-Day it was calmer. Being in the engine room we didn't see any of the first hour or so, but once we'd anchored off the beach we were able to go up on deck.

> So long was the frontage of the assault that in addition to grouping beaches into sectors, as in North Africa, sectors were now grouped into 'Landing Areas'.
>
> The British Eighth Army had five such areas – codenamed ACID NORTH, ACID SOUTH, BARK EAST, BARK SOUTH and BARK WEST – and the US Seventh Army three – CENT, DIME and JOSS.
>
> Within each British area, sectors were again named after letters from the phonetic alphabet, and beaches after colours. The Americans used numbers for their sectors and colours for their beaches.
>
> Arthur's LCF was standing guard over the JOSS Landing Area, where the US 3rd Infantry Division and part of the US 2nd Armored Division were going ashore.

The beaches were close to Licata, and the LSTs were offloading tanks and trucks. One of them'd had a direct hit – bomb or shell I don't know – and was on fire. We ourselves had a near miss which bent a prop shaft, and this had to be replaced in dry dock in Algiers some time later.

> Further east, near Gela, *Don Hunt* had to battle the heavy swell just to reach land.

In June 1942, about six months after Pearl Harbor, I'd had to quit school and go to work. I decided that if I was old enough to work I was old enough to join the US Navy, so I doctored up my birth certificate, and on October 6, 1942 [aged only fifteen] I enlisted.

After a three-week boot camp at Great Lakes, Illinois I was selected to attend Primary Diesel School at the Navy Pier, Chicago. From there I went on to Advanced Diesel School in Cleveland, and then to Little Creek, Virginia for small boat training in 36ft LCVPs.

> The LCVP – Landing Craft, Vehicle and Personnel – was a development of the earlier LCP(L), and performed the same functions in the US Navy as the ubiquitous LCA did for the British. More responsive than the British craft, it had a full-width

ramp, which enabled it to carry small vehicles like the jeep. The LCA, of course, afforded its occupants better protection because of its armour.

My group was among the first to be trained at Little Creek, which at that time was very primitive, as the camp was still under construction. We slept in tents.

After a brief training period I was assigned to a new LST Mk2, and crossed the Atlantic via Bermuda. Once in North Africa I was attached to various landing craft and ships, and eventually ended up in Bizerta, Tunisia. Ours was the first LST to enter Lake Bizerta through the 7-mile canal. We needed to proceed with extreme caution, as the Germans had scuttled many craft in the canal in an attempt to block its use. With all ballast tanks [one of the key features of the LST Mk2, enabling the Captain to select a shallow draught while beaching but a deeper draught for stability and seakeeping at other times] empty, and drawing the least amount of water, we just managed to clear all the sunken ships with the exception of the last, which was a small passenger ship. We slid, scraped, and bumped our way over the hull, but damaged our screws in the effort. Navy divers were sent down and set charges to blow off enough of the sunken ship to allow the following LSTs clear passage through the channel.

Once in Bizerta we transferred to shore duty, and were housed in the barracks behind the aircraft hangars at the nearby air base, which had been abandoned by the Germans. The barracks were heavily booby-trapped and mined, and had to be cleared by Army Engineers before we could use them.

We were very close to the PT boats [Patrol Torpedo boats – the American equivalent of British MTBs] which went out each night for runs to Sicily, and returned each morning full of holes from fights with E-boats [their German opposite numbers].

Shortly afterwards we boarded the *LST 313* in preparation for the forthcoming invasion of Sicily. We were scheduled to land troops from the US 1st Infantry Division in the DIME Landing Area, near Gela. Our LCVP crew consisted of Howard Heuser the coxswain, Stanley Hickey, Jim McFadden and myself.

Some LSTs had been fitted with extra sets of davits prior to the operation, to enable them to carry six LCVPs. *LST 313* retained the standard complement of just two – Don's LCVP on the starboard side, and another on the port.

On the morning of July 10, in extremely heavy seas, our orders were to escort five of the brand new DUKWs [examples of the latest, amphibious, version of the CCKW, the standard General Motors 6x6 truck] to the beach. Everyone was sick from the violent storm which had engulfed us. We all felt that the invasion should be cancelled until the waves subsided, but unfortunately the

82nd Airborne Division's paratroopers had already been dropped behind the beaches, and had to be backed up with reinforcements if they weren't to be wiped out.

> Although the American airborne landing at Oran had not been a success, the Sicily invasion was given a much larger airborne component. The same high winds which had whipped up the waves offshore, however, conspired to scatter the 82nd's paratroopers far and wide. Worse still, they caused many of the troop-carrying gliders from the British 1st Airborne Division to come down in the sea, drowning the men inside.

The die was cast, and over the side we went. Somehow, with the help of God plus good luck, we managed to lower away from the davits and get away. Several huge waves nearly dashed us to bits as we hung from the davit cables. The Boatswain on the LST was shouting to us to release and get away from the ship.

The port side LCVP had trouble releasing from the davits but was finally successful in getting away. We then had to wait for the five DUKWs to waddle off the *313*'s bow ramp, where the waves lifted them and slapped them against the side walls of the ramp opening. One man broke his leg when his DUKW was thrown against the ship as it was coming off the ramp. The injured man was brought alongside of the ship and hoisted back aboard for emergency medical treatment.

The soldiers in the DUKWs were part of the 33rd Field Artillery Battalion, attached to the 26th Regimental Combat Team of the US 1st Infantry Division. Between them the DUKWs carried three 105mm howitzers, ammunition and fifty troops.

It was 2.00am and we were many miles from shore when our mission began. The only confirmation of direction we had was when large naval shells passed over us heading for the beach.

In one stream of light from a passing shell we could see that one of our DUKWs had been taken by the sea, and as it disappeared beneath the waves the soldiers were left bobbing. The remaining DUKWs were signalled to form a circling rendezvous while for the next several hours we attempted to rescue the soldiers from the raging sea. The rescue wasn't easy, as the men were lost in the darkness, with only sporadic light from the flying shells. And when you thought you had a soldier close enough to throw a life ring to, the waves would pick him up and toss him 30ft or more away.

Miraculously we managed to pull every man out, and again focused on our objective, the beach. But once under way a second waterlogged DUKW sank. Fortunately we successfully retrieved all the soldiers. Then a third DUKW sank. Howard Heuser our coxswain deserves credit for his excellent handling and maneuvering of the boat in such difficult seas. Without his ability and quick reactions, I doubt that we could've saved all that we did.

It was obvious that the remaining DUKWs were destined to sink as well, and we decided to prepare a safe evacuation for those on board. So we transferred all the soldiers into our LCVP, with the exception of one driver who was left in each DUKW. Then, with all the soldiers in our boat, we headed for the beach with the two DUKWs following.

Our boat at this time was severely overloaded and showing only about 6in of freeboard. In the meantime the engine in one DUKW stopped, so we circled around and threw him a tow rope, and started in again with him in tow.

I was sitting on the transom stern by the tow rope, and all of a sudden felt my feet in the ocean and a strange sensation of slipping off the transom. This was very alarming, because I could make no visual assessment of the problem; I had to depend on my senses of touch and hearing. But just then a shell passed overhead and I saw the DUKW in tow had sunk, pulling our stern down deeper into the water. We were close to swamping. Fortunately I was able to use my bayonet, which was always kept with a razor's edge, and I hacked through the taut tow rope. I was successful in releasing the sunken DUKW, which allowed our bow to come back down. We then circled around, fished out the driver, and continued on with the mission.

All our effort and time to this point had only brought us half way, and now we were forty-nine soldiers plus a four-man Navy small boat crew in a boat whose rated capacity was thirty-six men. Andrew Higgins, who built these LCVPs in New Orleans, should've been mighty proud of his boats.

All of the men, soldiers and sailors alike, were tired, wet and vomiting. Even those who'd nothing left to expel took to dry heaves. I was too scared to be sick, because I realized that our boat was sinking lower in the water . . . and I couldn't swim. Then someone yelled that the water was in the boat. The water was rising higher and higher, and as I looked over the side I realized our bilge pumps weren't pumping. I reached down to investigate why they quit working, and discovered the pump screens were plugged solid with vomit. I got two able soldiers down on their knees scraping it away, and with this clearing of the screens the pumps gradually lowered the bilge water and we eventually gained a little freeboard.

We had to travel slowly because we were so low and close to swamping, but with the soldiers keeping the screens clear we finally saw the beach through the morning haze.

As I think back, I'm sure that vomit might have been the cause for the sunken DUKWs. The men were certainly seasick, and witnessing how it plugged up the pumps in our boat, it would be a logical conclusion.

After what seemed like an eternity we approached the beach. We were unable to land, however, because it was completely jammed with overturned and broached craft. The Navy had tugs and LCMs pulling them off and away from the beach in an effort to allow us, and hundreds of other boats, room to beach and disembark.

We finally found a spot large enough to run in and beach. We dropped our ramp and got our soldiers off just as the incoming wave picked us up and threw our stern around, allowing the next one to roll us over onto our side.

One lone DUKW managed to successfully reach the beach with its 105mm howitzer, and our fifty soldiers were now expected to complete their mission.

They were lucky to be alive, and fortunate to land on a part of the beach which was secured. Apparently its Italian defenders had decided they didn't want any part of this, so retreated and left the beach pretty much uncontested.

Our biggest enemies were the weather and the constant strafing of the beach by low-flying fighters. While we waited for our LST to beach and retrieve us we helped unload and stack incoming supplies.

We were alerted to each attack by gunfire up the beach, as the fighters would come from behind Gela and run down the beach firing. I remember one incident where Heuser and myself, upon hearing the firing up the beach, ran and jumped behind a pile of supplies. After the attack we stood up and realized that we'd hidden behind a pile of 55-gallon drums of gasoline. We promptly scouted out a large pile of rations for our next shelter.

Late in the afternoon we noted the *LST 313* offshore, and she eventually beached alongside of *LST 311* and prepared to start unloading her vehicles. But as we started up the pontoon causeway [another innovation, floated into place to span the distance between the 'false' beaches known to lie off many of the landing areas – which would of course stop the LSTs short – and the real beaches] to rejoin the ship we heard anti-aircraft fire up the beach. Realizing that we were being subjected to another strafing attack, we had to make a quick decision. Should we run the 200ft length of the causeway and seek the safety of the ship's tank deck? Or should we run back to the beach and get behind our pile of rations? We chose the pile of rations.

Things appeared as if in slow motion, with a Messerschmitt Bf109 approaching so low and close that we all thought we could reach out and grab hold of his wings. Then we watched in horror as a 550lb bomb was released from his underside, expertly arching downward, straight through the upper deck of the *LST 313*.

The bomb exploded on our tank deck with a huge flash. It ignited the ammo and gas in the vehicles on the tank deck, and the jeeps, trucks and ambulances on the upper deck were blown up and off the ship like toys. Practically everyone on the tank deck and in the area of the open bow doors was killed. Men who'd been hailing us only moments earlier were gone. Needless to say, had we not made the decision to run back to the beach, we too would have been in that tremendous explosion.

LST 311, which was beached right next to *313*, used her stern anchor and engines to retract off the beach to escape the fire and explosions.

The *311*'s Captain, Lieutenant Robert Coleman, USNR, then placed the bow of his own ship against the stern of the stricken *313*, saving about eighty survivors trapped by the flames.

I understand that the *313* burned for several days. However, the hours immediately following the explosion were spent pulling burned survivors and dead soldiers from the surf, with their monument of war burning behind us.

The ship continued her furious burn, with sporadic explosions from stored ammo.

The bodies and survivors were mostly flash burned, making it very hard to handle them or provide any kind of comfort. They had the appearance of over-barbecued meat, with leathery surfaces and crackled edges. Uniforms were melted into the skin and hair. We worked as best we could, gathering the men, and finally huddling together on the beach for the night.

In addition to damaging air raids, DIME quickly gained the dubious distinction of being the only landing area where enemy counterattacks during D-Day and D+1 reached the expected level of ferocity. German tanks almost broke through to the beaches, and only the massed firepower of the ships offshore kept the situation under control. On the evening of D+1 an attempt to drop in more of the 82nd Airborne Division resulted in another tragedy, when the force was shot to pieces by friendly fire.

The British beaches also came in for unwelcome attention from the air. *Garry Burrows* was in one of the new Beach Groups trained to sort out the confusion and keep the men and supplies flowing ashore. Much larger than those used in Madagascar and North Africa, each of the new Groups, or 'Bricks' as they were sometimes known, consisted of a battalion of infantry or Marines, plus attached specialists of all kinds and small RN and RAF contingents.

I was in the fourth or fifth wave, and being Royal Navy reported to the Beachmaster – a Commander, RN – for orders.

How many people were working directly for the Beachmaster?

As I remember there were about twelve of us – ten seamen, a telegraphist, and myself a signalman. The only differences between Naval ratings and Army troops were the words 'Royal Navy' on the shoulders of our khaki battledress, and the fact that we still wore our white caps.

I had a pair of semaphore flags, and a TBS [Talk Between Ships – an early walkie talkie set] strapped on my back. One of the seamen carried my Aldis signal lamp and a battery for power.

The object was to bring in ships in order of priority, troops taking first place, then ammunition, et cetera.

We were having some difficulty communicating with a merchant ship lying a few miles out to sea, so the Beachmaster told me to go and find out what the problem was. I discovered she was a Liberty ship, mass produced by Henry Kaiser [the American industrialist, whose shipyards could turn out 'Liberties' at an unprecedented rate, thanks in part to prefabrication], loaded with explosives and high octane aircraft fuel.

Almost as soon as I was aboard, a lone German pilot came over the invasion fleet and scored direct hits on us with two bombs.

The unfortunate troops on board hadn't been instructed how to use their old-fashioned cork lifejackets, and the result when they hit the water was the cork at the front caught them under the chin, breaking their necks. Those poor lads lost their lives without even getting into action. It was a dreadful sight. Even today the scene comes back to me now and again.

For myself, I didn't try to swim; I knew help would soon be coming, so I just turned on my back and floated. I was picked up by motor boat.

When I reported back to the Beachmaster he just said 'Try and get a dry battledress, grab a cup of tea, and I'll expect you back here in fifteen minutes'.

The American beach organisation had developed along slightly different lines, with battalions from US Army Engineer Regiments taking the place of the British Beach Groups.

The efficient running of the beaches was more important in Sicily than in any previous operation, since the Seventh and Eighth Armies were being landed along a coastline with no major cargo-handling facilities. In North Africa the great port of Algiers had been taken by the evening of D-Day, followed by Oran on D+2 and Casablanca on D+3. By contrast both of Sicily's major ports, Messina and Palermo, were in the north of the island, furthest from the Allied landings. The Armies would have to be supplied through small harbours and over open beaches for an indefinite period, something which had never been attempted before.

One of the factors which made this possible was undoubtedly the DUKW, whose use greatly simplified the transfer of supplies from the ships to the Army supply dumps ashore. What the DUKW could not do, however, was eliminate confusion from the crowded anchorages.

As in Madagascar and North Africa, the landings in Sicily had begun under cover of darkness, which compounded the inevitable problems and delays.

Edward Brothers was an Eighth Army DUKW driver.

The situation on the beach in the early hours of D-Day was somewhat chaotic, with landing craft of all sorts fighting for space. Having reported to the Beachmaster, we were directed to go to individual, named, ships to take off supplies of all types and return as soon as possible for unloading.

There then ensued a right balls-up, with ninety DUKWs buzzing around in a bay containing over a hundred ships, each trying to find an individual ship, to receive their cargo in a pre-arranged order of priority. This of course was in blackout conditions. The language of some of the crews on board the ships when repeatedly asked if they were the ss *So-and-So* during the night was, to say the least, choice. It was quite impossible to find any particular ship, and after wasting a lot of time and petrol it was decided that the only solution was to spread out and go to any ship, taking whatever cargo was offered. This was then taken back to the beach and sorted into various dumps. As dawn broke it became obvious that a lot of time had been lost, and some craft were themselves running short of fuel. Luckily a fuel dump had been set up on shore, and the DUKWs were able to refuel with the petrol they'd taken ashore during the night.

Another picture I can recall quite vividly was of an old man with a donkey and cart offering his services to move supplies in the beachhead!

Did you experience any mechanical problems with the DUKWs?

Very few. The main problem which began to show after some time was broken or leaking flexible brake pipes – usually on the back wheels. With no spares it became necessary to cannibalise some to keep the others roadworthy.

But they really were remarkable craft. They were quite at home on land, sea, snow or ice, and no other wheeled vehicle could match them for getting out of difficult situations.

At sea with the engine running at full throttle the exhaust would get hot enough to boil a gallon of water in less than twenty minutes, by sitting a can a couple of inches from it. A mug of tea on a cold trip in wet conditions was a wonderful bonus. In fact you could see the exhaust manifolds glowing bright red when looking down through the clutch and brake pedal holes. That was a bit worrying when any petrol spillage had been left washing about in the bilges!

In addition to British and American units, Sicily saw the first employment of a full division of Canadian troops. The original plan had earmarked the British 3rd Division for one of the assaults, but the Canadians' desire to see their ground forces in action again in 1943 led to its replacement by the 1st Canadian Division.

Alf Fairhead had sailed with the Canadians on their long journey from Scotland to the BARK WEST landing area aboard the LSI (L) *Empire Pride*.

We hove-to off the coast of Sicily in the early hours of 10 July 1943. After a very early breakfast the 'B' Troop drivers, of which I was one, were loaded into a small landing craft – which had been carried on the *Empire Pride* – to go and unload our vehicles.

It was a very busy scene, with landing craft seemingly travelling in all directions, a lot of small arms fire on the coast, and Spitfires from Malta doing a lot of strafing. On arrival at the merchant ship the landing craft coxswain brought us in alongside, to the bottom of a huge scrambling net, and in no uncertain terms told us to get climbing. He was in no mood for hanging around, so as soon as the last one had his hands and feet on the net he was gone, and there we were; blue sea below, blue sky above, and a hell of a long way to that deck rail. We had on all our webbing kit, big pack, small pack, respirator, Tommy gun [American Thompson submachine gun] and ammo, and in all our training in the UK we'd never used scrambling nets.

On arriving on the deck we were met by a Sergeant in the Royal Engineers, who took us to the forward hold where our vehicles were stored. We were told to get down and get the vehicles started, and an LCT would be along in about an hour to take us ashore.

Now this is where things began to go wrong. We found that the vehicles, having been in this hold for several weeks, wouldn't start. The batteries were just about flat, and as everything was waterproofed we couldn't as much as take a plug out.

Those engines were really stubborn, and the sun got higher and the hold got hotter, and soon we were stripped down to just shorts and boots. This struggle went on all day, and at nightfall floodlights were switched on in the hold. Then the air raids started, and the lights were switched off, so we found our way to the ship's galley, where the cook, in spite of all the shooting and banging outside, was calmly baking bread. He gave us each some of it, and made us a bucket of tea – the first food and drink we'd had since leaving the *Empire Pride*. After the air raids finished we went back to the hold, and by daylight we'd persuaded all our reluctant charges to start.

While waiting for our LCT to come we had a look in the after hold, expecting to see our Bofors guns, but it was full to the top with jerricans of petrol. Our vehicles had been stored in the hold on top of wooden packing cases, and when we started to move the vehicles about, to get them onto the nets to be lifted out, some of the cases broke open. To our amazement they contained tinned rations. Twenty-four hours and no food, and we'd been walking about on hundreds of tons of it.

The vehicles were offloaded from the merchant ship by the ship's own cranes – a large net under the front wheels and the same under the rear, coupled to the hawser and hoisted up and over into the LCT. Each driver stayed in his cab so he could drive off the nets as he hit the bottom of the landing craft. As this was done one vehicle at a time, it took quite a while to offload.

Once aboard the LCT we were told to keep the engines running. When the ramp went down we were to select low gear, and when the Naval officer in charge gave the signal, it'd be foot flat down and go. First off would be a bulldozer belonging to the REs, and I'd be next.

On arrival our LCT could only get to about 75 to 100 yards from the shore. Down went the ramp and away went the bulldozer, and then I was on my way. But to my horror when the 'dozer hit the water it kept going down until it was completely under, and the driver had to stand up in his seat. Fortunately, as with all our vehicles, they'd extended the air intakes and exhausts, and before I could think much about it I was in the water as well. Although I was driving a Bedford QLB Bofors gun tractor, which was quite high, and had a waterproof groundsheet draped on the outside of the radiator grille to act as a form of bow, I soon had water round my feet and legs. But the engine kept going, and I arrived at the shore. Here we came under the control of a rather harassed looking Naval officer acting as Beachmaster, who told us to go as far as possible up the shore and to get the waterproofing off the vehicles. By now our engines were red hot and couldn't be touched for a while, so while waiting for them to cool off a bit we went and found the Beachmaster again, and asked him if he knew where our Bofors guns were. His answer was 'How the hell should *I* know? Get your waterproofing off and GO!'. When we said 'Go where?', he replied '*I* don't bloody well know!', and started to walk away. Then as sort of an afterthought he stopped, pointed down the coast and said 'Try that bloody way', and with that he was gone.

So there we were. Hopefully they'd landed our Bofors somewhere, but they couldn't be doing much with them, because we'd got all the ammo on our gun tractors. Before leaving the ship I'd slung a few cans of those rations into my truck, so we decided to try one, which contained about 7lbs of treacle pudding. We soon devoured it. No doubt it would've tasted better if we'd paused to cook it first.

I moved off about the middle of the afternoon, by which time a lot of Italian POWs were being marched along the water's edge, and found a track which went in the general direction the Beachmaster had pointed. I hadn't gone far along this when my engine stopped and couldn't be persuaded to start again.

A Royal Army Service Corps DUKW which appeared from the opposite direction towed me into a field, but they were the last people I saw that day. I tried and tried to get my engine to start, but it was having none of it, and as the battery was getting low I decided I'd sit it out and hope that somebody would find me.

After dark the air raids started again, and this time they hit what must've been an ammo ship. Such a tremendous explosion and flash, and I could hear debris falling near me.

As dawn broke I switched on my engine, swung the starting handle, and it burst into life! So I again headed along the track, and after a few miles I found the guns. They'd come ashore in shallower water, and had had to be manhandled, which was some task. By mid to late morning all of the vehicles, including the radio trucks, had arrived, so we moved inland a bit, covering the supply routes.

We'd actually landed close to Pachino, which is at the southern tip of Sicily. As we moved inland the first large house I saw was pink in colour, and somebody had painted on the wall in white paint 'SECOND FRONT STARTED HERE JULY 10TH 1943'. We were the first Allied troops back in Europe.

We stayed there, in a tomato field, covering the supply routes for three or four days. The Bofors were manned all day, and if an enemy aircraft came in sight the crews shot at it without having to wait for orders. During the hours of darkness a different method was used – the guns were set on fixed bearings and fixed elevations to give what was known as a 'box barrage'. The bearings and elevation angles were worked out at Battery HQ. Each Bofors was then left with a clip of ammo in, cocked and set on auto [the other option being single shots] with the safety catch off, and two of the crew at a time – including the driver – would be detailed to do sentry duty. This was known as 'being on stag'. If and when Number One gun opened up, those on stag had to get straight onto their own gun. One had to ram his foot hard on the firing pedal, while the other started heaving fresh clips of ammo. The object of the box barrage was to try and divert enemy aircraft from the shipping and beachheads. Each Troop of six guns formed its own barrage. There were three Troops to a Battery, and three Batteries in the Regiment.

It was all quite spectacular, because the Bofors shells were tracer, which meant that you could follow them. For safety they had a built-in self destruct, so if they hit nothing on the way up they'd go on to the end of their run and then explode. Believe me, when a Bofors gun was working on auto there was a hell of a racket going on. On top of that you had the empty cartridge cases being ejected from the front of the gun under the barrel. This wasn't too bad on fixed bearings because you knew where they were going; it was when the gun was being traversed that you'd to watch out. The best thing was to keep behind it. The shells had a contact fuze, which the gunners told me was so delicate that if it hit a rain drop absolutely square on it'd detonate. So you never went around dropping cases of Bofors ammo endways onto the floor!

We also carried AP [Armour Piercing] shells with us, because the Bofors could be used as an anti-tank gun without any alterations. Mind you, having met the German Tiger tank later on I don't think our 40mm AP shells would've caused it much distress.

Our next move was a few miles to a forward airstrip, which was basically a clearing in the olive trees. We arrived about mid day and dispersed our guns and trucks, and in the evening some Spitfires arrived. They parked one of the Spits in front of my truck, about 10 or 15 yards away. I never really gave this a second thought, and just before dark I pitched my mosquito net, crawled in and went to sleep. Of course we had to take anti-malaria precautions; each morning we were issued with a mepacrine tablet, which we had to take. We were also issued with anti-malaria cream, which after sundown we had to rub onto exposed parts of the body. Long trousers had to be worn, and shirts buttoned up to the neck and the wrists, so that meant going to sleep like that, with your face and hands liberally covered with this cream. At first light next morning I heard several voices outside my mossy net, had a look out, and saw it was the ground crew servicing the Spit. Fair enough, so I went back inside my net. Then they started the engine up with a roar, and of course the slipstream began blowing all the dust and debris over me! I scrambled out of my net and was met by the lot – dust, leaves, twigs, and anything loose.

I went to the Spit and told the crew I wasn't happy, but they thought it was all very funny. I suppose seeing me emerge from the cloud of dust looking rather like the Wild Man of Borneo, with debris stuck all over me – especially on my liberally creamed face – *was* funny, but I didn't see it quite that way. They were rolling about laughing, and of course the more I tried to rub stuff off my face the more it stuck on.

Unfortunately at that time we were on a strict water ration; the Troop water cart used to collect it from a water point, and it was then kept by Troop HQ, who divided the number of gallons in the tank by the number of personnel to be supplied. That would then have to last X days, and of course radiators had to be topped up from this ration, so for washing and shaving in the mornings we had 6in of water. All the other ranks would wash and shave in the same water – the officers had their own facilities – and it'd stay there for the rest of the day in case anyone needed another wash. So when I turned up that morning in my state I was far from popular.

Our Bofors were now relieved of their barrage duties at night, because the 3.7s [3.7in anti-aircraft guns, standard equipment of the British Heavy Anti-Aircraft Regiments] had now arrived. Unfortunately that night whoever'd worked out their barrage position had got it all wrong; it was slap overhead, and when they opened up all their shrapnel rained down on us. You could hear the nose caps, which contained the fuze and timing mechanism, coming down all the way, because they used to make a loud whistling noise. It wasn't a very pleasant night. In the morning a roll call was taken, and fortunately 'B' Troop had suffered no casualties.

What sort of food were you getting in Sicily?

The rations consisted mainly of tinned bacon slices, porridge oats, M&V [tinned meat and vegetable stew], tinned margarine, coarse marmalade, fig jam, hard tack biscuits, occasionally tinned soya links, corned beef, sometimes dehydrated vegetables – mainly potatoes and onions – and tea of course. The M&V was quite good, and was in tins roughly the size of a present day 420g fruit tin, one between two men. The hard tack biscuits were *really* hard. They were square and about the size of a present day cream cracker, and there was always an ample supply of them. I knew then why we'd had to have our teeth checked before we left home. We used to get them with each meal, though dinner wasn't too bad because you could puddle them about in your M&V. For our tea we'd perhaps get about half a dozen of them, spread with margarine and either marmalade or fig jam. Have you ever tried fig jam? If not, I wouldn't bother. It and the marmalade were reputed to be made in Cairo. The cooks sometimes used to stew up the biscuits and mix in some fig jam to make a sort of pudding. I won't say too much about that . . . I suppose they were doing their best. The soya links were a little longer than a sausage – which they replaced – triangular shaped, and packed six to a tin. They weren't very popular either.

Also issued with rations were salt tablets, as we were told that we were sweating such a lot that we were getting rid of more salt from our bodies than our diet was putting back. We had cigarettes too. I was a non-smoker, and still am, but the opinion of some of the lads that smoked them was that the tobacco was made from dried camel dung. And that's putting it politely.

Actually the rations got me indirectly involved in another little problem. Our two storemen – a red-faced Scots Lance Bombardier and a Gunner with a large walrus moustache – had each day to take the rations round to the six gun sites on a fairly large two wheeled trolley. It was quite a long, hard journey over rock-strewn ground, so they asked me one morning if I'd go along and help push the cart. I said yes. I was always willing to help, and of course you never knew what you might need to scrounge from the stores sometime.

Arriving at the first gun site we unloaded their due amount of stores, and the Sergeant asked us if we'd like a drink. Apparently they'd got themselves a barrel of red vino; about 10 gallons of it. They'd rigged up a tarpaulin as a canopy to give a bit of shade, and under this was the barrel. At that time red vino meant nothing to me, never having seen it before, and the Sergeant poured us each an Army mugful. We were thirsty, so that went straight down like drinking water. It tasted good, so the mugs were refilled and got the same treatment. How many mugfuls we poured down our throats I never did know, but it must've been a lot. Eventually the Lance Bombardier said we ought to go on to the next site. I remember walking out into the sun, and that was the last I knew for two days.

When I came to I was laid out in the back of my truck. It seems they'd had to bring the three of us back on the hand cart.

When the Troop Sergeant heard that I was back in the land of the living he came to see me. I wouldn't like to repeat his exact words, but I can assure you that he wasn't wishing me a speedy recovery. Nothing more was ever heard of this episode, though. Had a thing like that happened in the UK I dread to think of the consequences, as we were actually drunk on duty.

The next morning my mate Ernie suggested going for a swim in the sea, as we were fairly close to the shore. When we got there, though, we saw lots of bodies lying about, and a Padre and a group of soldiers were checking them. We asked the Padre what'd happened, and he told us that some gliders had landed in the sea. The gliders and bodies were now being washed ashore, and they were trying to identify them. I was twenty-two years old at the time, and I'd never seen a dead body before, let alone that many. I think that was when I realised what it was all about, and that it wasn't all a big game. Needless to say we didn't have our swim.

At a later date I met an Airborne Corporal in a transit camp in Italy, who was one of the survivors. He said their Brigade [1st Airlanding Brigade, from the British 1st Airborne Division] had left North Africa on the night of 9/10 July, towed by the Americans. Their objective was to secure a bridge on the coast road to Syracuse, but as the aircraft approached the coast the flak started to come up, and the inexperienced tug crews let loose the gliders too soon. He said only the gliders towed by the lead aircraft made it to the shore against the head wind, and he was in one of them. The rest just dropped into the sea. So many young lives thrown away for nothing.

One morning we were visited by a Bf109; he came in very low, and began strafing the airstrip. Our Bofors engaged him, and damaged him fairly badly, so he cleared off and left us alone. There were no casualties or damage on the airstrip. One of the Bofors had to depress so low to get on target that the muzzle blast blew the top off a low wall close to the site! Anyhow, at least 'B' Troop were earning their keep.

Another morning I'd been to the other side of the airstrip to see if there was any water in the well there – unfortunately it was dry – and as I was walking back I passed a group of officers sitting on the ground. Seeing all the red collar tabs I knew that they were all high-ranking, and when I got quite close I saw that one was wearing a black beret. It was none other than Montgomery [General Sir Bernard Montgomery, commander of the British Eighth Army] himself! The others were obviously his senior commanders. They had a large map spread on the ground, which they were studying intently. I, of course, kept on walking. I don't suppose they even noticed me, but at least I'd seen the boss man – not that it did me a lot of good!

The other minor incident I remember was when I got told off by the Troop commander. We'd been told that we could now send letters home, but our address was to be: Rank, Number, Name, Unit and 'CMF'. I'd written to my family, and said that I was now in Sicily. As all letters had to be censored at that time at Troop HQ, he'd seen this, and told me that I shouldn't have done such a thing, and that he'd cut that bit out. Of course I had to accept my reprimand, but for the life of me I couldn't believe the enemy intelligence organisation was that stupid that they couldn't work out that CMF stood for Central Mediterranean Force!

Later on we could draw an issue of green-coloured envelopes, the letters in which were only censored at random, away from your unit. We could also later get Air Mail Letter Cards, and things called Airgraphs, which were handed in to Troop HQ, who sent them on [to Algiers] to be filmed and then destroyed. The film [containing a large volume of photographically-reduced images] was then flown to the UK, where it was developed and enlarged and the letters sent to their respective addresses. This meant a lot of letters could be sent in a small space, and fairly quickly.

Our next move was to a larger airstrip. This could take Beaufighters and Dakotas, which were flying in supplies. It was here that us drivers started being loaned out to other units. We'd be detailed to report to such-and-such a unit, given a tin of M&V or corned beef and some tea, and off we'd go. The interesting thing here is that we were never given any maps, so we couldn't work to map references. It was a case of hope for the best. Sometimes all of us would go to the same unit, sometimes only one or two. It was a very busy time, and we handled everything under the sun – 25-pounders, medical supplies, ammo, rations . . . Fuel and oil were left in small dumps in fields by the roads and tracks, so if you were passing one of these dumps you just pulled in and took what you needed. Drivers were relied on to keep their tanks full.

Travelling about meant that we saw more of the Sicilians. The country dwellers didn't say a lot, and to a point didn't seem happy to see us. Still, I suppose if thousands of troops had landed in *our* country, with vehicles and tanks going across the crops in our fields, taking our precious water, destroying our houses and nicking everything else going, I don't think *we'd* have been too happy either. And after all, to them we were the enemy.

Were the locals ever a problem?

Only a traffic problem. They travelled to and from their fields in carts pulled by mules, and the carts had wide hubs on the wheels, which took up a lot of room on the narrow tracks. Of course the whole family'd be on the cart – mama, papa and loads of children, or so it seemed. Daytime wasn't too bad, but they'd work until dark, and then sleep on the cart going home. The mule would know the way, but he only knew the middle of the road, and no amount of shouting or horn blowing would do any good.

On the whole they seemed to be living in dire poverty.

> After their initial counterattacks had been beaten off, the Italian Army and the increasingly dominant Germans had been content to conduct a delaying action, falling back on Messina in a series of stages.

Crossing over the mountains was a new experience. They were very high and very rocky, and the roads wound up in a zig-zag manner, turning back on themselves several times a mile in sharp hairpin bends. Travelling these mountains we realised what a hell of a job the infantry faced. The enemy, being above them, always had the whip hand, and also had a lot of natural cover from the rocks. It wasn't tank country, and not very good artillery country either [because it was difficult to deploy the guns], so losses were high.

Crossing the mountains with our Bofors required a technique of its own. We found that if, on a tight left-hand corner, we kept the truck wheels right on the edge of the road we could get round in one go. On a right-hand corner the Sergeant riding in the passenger seat would have to guide you to the road edge. Of course there'd probably be just a low wall about 6in to 1ft high, and then a drop of hundreds of feet, so there could be no mistakes!

Our Bedford QLBs were based on the standard QL 3-ton truck, with a heavy winch added, plus a heavier body, but using the same engine. Then we had ammo, spare gun barrel, crew, kit, and all the bits and pieces that went with us, plus the gun in tow. So to face the mountains we used to engage first gear, and four-wheel drive, which also gave a reduction on the main gearbox, and set the hand throttle fully open. If we'd stopped I doubt if the clutch would've been man enough to move us again, as our all-up weight must've been something like 8 or 9 tons. These journeys would take sometimes three to four hours, and having reached the top we'd then have to go down again. So then it'd be hand throttle full closed and stand on the brake pedal, and the crew would help by operating the brakes on the rear wheels of the Bofors. We had to do one journey like that in the dark, and all I can say is that I'm damn glad I never had to do another.

We had to wait once for an RAF convoy to come down a mountain. They had two of their huge Queen Mary aircraft transporters with them, and to get those around the hairpin corners they had a crane with each. The crane had to lift the rear of the transporter round little by little on each corner, so it took ages for them to get down. And we thought *we* had problems!

When we were crossing the mountains our engines took a real bashing, but not once did they let us down. Not in 'B' Troop, anyhow. And of course the oil that we used in those days was far inferior to what we have today, so all credit to the people who built those engines in the UK.

There was quite a contrast in temperatures going over the mountains. At the bottom it'd be very hot, but at the top you'd need a coat on.

The way the REs could build Bailey bridges[4] over deep ravines was something that had to be seen to be believed. They were good, hardworking chaps.

As time went on we mixed more and more with the ex-Desert lads, and found from them that we lacked one essential piece of non-issue equipment – the 'brew can'. This was usually made from an empty margarine can, with a handle made from a piece of wire. It was filled with the necessary amount of water, placed on two rocks, stones or bricks, and an M&V tin full of sand with petrol poured over it was placed underneath and lit. When the water boiled the tea was added and brewed, and believe me it was the best tea you could ever wish for. Every vehicle had one, and in a way it was a kind of status symbol, because the blacker it was inside and out, the longer the time on active service. There was a well-known Eighth Army saying – 'When in doubt, brew up'.

We took 'B' Troop to Cassibile airfield, and soon after arrival we drivers were sent off to move a Troop from another Regiment to Catania [further north]. For most of the campaign there'd been a shortage of transport, and we were still regularly loaned out to other units, hauling all sorts of things. Travelling up the coast I saw many graves with either just a rifle and steel helmet or a plain wooden cross marking them. Some had German helmets. Catania hadn't fallen easily. Close to Catania was a large airfield, which had taken a lot of bombing and shelling and was very badly damaged. The bombs had broken through into the underground sulphur workings, and clouds of yellow sulphur were pouring out. Everywhere was covered in a thick coating of yellow dust, and the smell was awful. We had to go through Catania and deploy the guns on the northern perimeter, parking our vehicles in a quarry close to the sea.

While we were there, my mate Jimmy and I decided we needed a haircut, so we walked into Catania to find a barber. At that time the order was that if you left your camp you had to be armed, so we took our Tommy guns. Arriving in the centre, we found the townsfolk had a different outlook to the ones in the country, for outside the cafes and bars they'd already got notice boards chalked in English. They'd soon latched on to the fact that there was money

---

4. Temporary military bridges designed for speedy assembly, and named after their British creator, Sir Donald Bailey.

to be had. Jimmy and I eventually found a barber's shop. Before we went in, bearing in mind what we'd been told on the *Empire Pride* about Sicilians and knives, we worked out a plan. Jimmy would sit in the chair to have his cut first, and I would keep the barber covered with my Tommy gun. We'd change over when he was finished.

We went in, and the barber came through from the back; only a little chap, with black wavy hair. As he put the apron on Jimmy I cocked my Tommy gun noisily and deliberately so that he knew what was going on. Actually the poor little chap was terrified, and I think we were in more danger from his shaking hands than anything else.

I don't remember whether he ever charged us or not!

Two weeks into the campaign, on 25 July 1943, the beleaguered Italian dictator Benito Mussolini had been deposed and arrested in a palace coup. A senior Army officer, Marshal Pietro Badoglio, had been appointed head of the new government, and had begun quietly sounding out the Allies over the possibility of an Armistice.

After a day or so we had instructions to return to 'B' Troop at Cassibile. We then moved with them to an airstrip near Catania, occupied by the RAF with Baltimores and Bostons [twin-engined bombers, built by Martin and Douglas respectively]. The grapevine said that we were there because the King of Italy [the septuagenarian King Victor Emmanuel III] was being flown in to try and negotiate Armistice terms with the Allies, but he didn't come, so the grapevine had got it wrong for once. In actual fact the Armistice was signed at Cassibile at a later date – 3 September – and the King wasn't even there then. We didn't stay at that airstrip long, and from there we kept moving until we reached Messina.

So the Sicilian campaign was over, and we were a bit older . . . and a lot wiser.

The campaign came to an end on 17 August, after a textbook withdrawal to the mainland – complete with tanks and heavy equipment – by the defenders.

The contentious question of what to do after the fall of Sicily had been left open at Casablanca, and again at a conference in Washington during May. Once the fighting had actually begun, however, the poor performance of the Italian Army had led to Eisenhower being given approval to carry the war to the mainland if he so desired.

By the time Messina fell, his plans had crystallised into a two-pronged attack. First would come a landing on the 'toe' of Italy. Then, despite slim resources, a landing further north at a place called Salerno.

FIVE

Trial and Error: Salerno and Anzio

The first landings on the Italian mainland took place on Friday 3 September 1943, when most of the British 5th Division and part of the 1st Canadian Division were put ashore near Reggio di Calabria. A preliminary sea and air bombardment and massive support from the Eighth Army's own artillery swept away what little opposition was offered, and a shuttle service was quickly established to reinforce the beachhead from Sicily.

Not all the Allied divisions in Sicily were destined to make the crossing, however. Many of the more experienced ones had instead been earmarked for the long-awaited cross-Channel attack on France, now tentatively scheduled for 1 May 1944. Troops for Italy would thus be in short supply, as would amphibious shipping to carry them, since losses, essential maintenance and the demands of purely logistical tasks had conspired to reduce the number of divisions which could be landed simultaneously from the pre-Sicily peak of eight to something nearer five.

As soon as the Eighth Army was firmly established on the 'toe', therefore, many of its landing craft had to be diverted to help carry the US Fifth Army to Salerno. Although nominally an American army, the Fifth in fact contained as many British divisions as American. A few of its units were in Sicily, having formerly been part of the Eighth Army or the US Seventh Army,[1] but the majority – including its headquarters – needed to be brought over from North Africa.

For its initial landings, the Fifth Army had selected a force of Rangers and Commandos on the left; the British 46th and 56th (London) Divisions in the centre, and the US 36th Infantry Division on the right. Most of the US 45th Infantry Division would remain offshore in floating reserve, ready to land on D+1. D-Day was to be Thursday 9 September.

---

1. The Seventh was being allowed to languish in Sicily because its brilliant but mercurial commander, Lieutenant General George Patton, had displayed one outburst of temper too many.

Because there was no more shipping, the build-up in Italy was sure to be slow. This presented few problems for the Eighth Army, whose sea communications were short, and which faced only more delaying tactics of the kind experienced in Sicily. The implications were more worrying for the Fifth Army, whose sea communications were much longer, and whose landings, so close to the great port of Naples, were likely to provoke a violent response. The Naval Task Force which had landed the US Seventh Army in Sicily, reorganised to include a large British component, was responsible for the naval side of the Salerno operation.

As had been the practice in Sicily, the British assault divisions were accompanied by landing craft specially modified for the support role. *Jim Mitchell* commanded a gun crew aboard one of them.

We were what was called an LCG(L). A Landing Craft, Gun (Large). We were just an expendable link to get the troops ashore, really. Lessons learned from the Dieppe raid had brought Combined Operations to the realisation that more sophisticated craft were required for the future, so the LCG(L) was designed for inshore support.

The LCG(L) was a conversion of an ordinary LCT, in the same way that the Landing Craft, Flak was. The tank space was made into mess decks, magazines and a galley – you could put a shovel of coal on the galley stove and step back into the magazine! Regulations on explosives? – not in *this* Navy! Above was a hatch to feed the guns.

The bow ramp was welded up, and a washplace and toilets added. Not ideal at sea, because the bangs of the waves hitting the flat bow were like Dante's Inferno. However, we did get 'hard lying' money. They did a better job on Flaks, giving them a proper bow. The guns on Flaks, of course, consisted of pom-poms and Oerlikons, for high-angle work.

Our fore well deck was open to the sky, and a heavy sea could flood it, which caused the loss of *LCG(L) 15* and *LCG(L) 16* off the approaches to Milford Haven [in April 1943], with tragic loss of life.

Our two 4.7in guns were mounted on the upper deck, with shields and ready-use ammunition lockers. As in Flaks, the guns were manned by Royal Marines. Broadside shoots were the norm, to keep the blast away from the craft, and looking back I didn't find the vibration too bad when firing. Although everything was battened down, of course.

What did your job consist of?

I was the senior non-commissioned officer responsible for the Royal Marine detachment. So I had to look after the records, issue the rum ration, organise work details, that kind of thing. In action I was in charge of the forward gun. As the gun recoiled I'd work the breech mechanism to expel the brass shell casing, which'd be hot. They were kicked anywhere out of the way in action. They were separate, you see. So the shell had to be rammed home before the cartridge case went in and the breech was closed.

The 4.7in shell weighed 50lbs, and its brass cartridge case 30lbs.

Ammo records were all kept for reference, separate entries for the different types. We had three types of shell – high explosive, semi armour piercing and starshell. The starshell [used to illuminate an area or target at night] had a reduced charge, and you could tell it by its serrated rim in the dark.

How were the guns directed to a particular target?

At first verbal instructions gave us the targets, but later we had a control bridge behind the guns. This gave us the range and bearing. I could fire at any target on my own initiative if required. I remember on one occasion we spied a train, and hammered it with our third shot. It's funny – we never stopped to think it could've been a civilian train.

We were a mixed bunch on board – Royal Marines and Royal Navy; some Regulars, others Hostilities Only. We manned the guns and the ratings ran the craft. The average age was about eighteen. I was twenty-three, and being the senior NCO made me a bit of a father figure! The officers consisted of two from the RNVR and one from the Royal Marines, who was a former Colour Sergeant Gunnery Instructor – so we could shoot straight!

Our LCG(L) left in 1943 for Gibraltar, and as we headed out into the Atlantic to give the German bases in France a wide berth the weather deteriorated. Water found its way into everything, seasickness was rife, and little or no work was done except to lash everything down. Food of a sort was prepared – corned beef and boiled spuds – but there were few takers. Ten days later the Rock never looked so good. Their Flag Officer wasn't so impressed with *our* appearance, though, and we were glad when we left for our new base at Djidjelli in North Africa. In July 1943 we took part in the landings at Licata in Sicily [the American JOSS landing area], and then next came Salerno.

The news of Italy's surrender came as we were on our way there, and everyone cheered. Unfortunately we'd forgotten the German presence. Jerry let us know he hadn't gone away when a fighter zoomed in at masthead height, and then we knew we'd still a tough time ahead. In fact Salerno turned out to be the shakiest landing we did.

The British landing beaches received only a cursory bombardment before the first assault, and the American ones no preliminary bombardment at all, in the vain hope of achieving surprise. This was subsequently acknowledged to have been a mistake.

Such shortcomings were compounded by the fact that unlike Sicily, where Royal Navy LCG(L)s and LCFs had lent support off the American beaches as well as the British ones, at Salerno the US Navy had elected to rely only on their own, much smaller, design – the LCS(S), or Landing Craft, Support (Small). These little craft, armed with machine guns and 4.5in rockets, were carried aboard the larger vessels in place of some of their LCMs and LCVPs, and had only a fraction of the firepower of the bigger British craft.

The British landings were supported by nine LCG(L)s, seven LCFs and three examples of the new Landing Craft, Tank (Rocket), which were LCTs converted to accommodate banks of 5in rockets instead of a cargo.

Mac Court was an officer in one of the British assault divisions. Born in Chelsea Barracks, he had joined the Coldstream Guards as a drummer boy in 1928. After the outbreak of war he applied for a commission.

I eventually finished up on the Isle of Man, at 166 OCTU [Officer Cadet Training Unit]. I was there four months, and then I was commissioned into the Hampshire Regiment as an officer in November 1942.

I'd only just joined my new Battalion when one night I was Duty Officer, and this chap with red tabs came in at about 11.00pm. And while we were waiting for the Adjutant to come along and see him, we got talking.

Anyway, when the Adjutant arrived, this chap told him 'We want a draft immediately for Africa – 200 men, 5 officers'. The Adjutant said 'Well, we can supply the 200 men, but we've only got 2 or 3 officers'. So he said 'What about this one?', meaning me. The Adjutant said 'But he's only been commissioned a week or so!'. 'With his experience, quite suitable'.

So the Adjutant said to me 'No need to finish as Duty Officer, I'll do that. Go back to your billet and get your kit ready, and I'll have a form made out for you for a week's embarkation leave'.

When we assembled, I found that not only was I *on* the draft of 200 men, I was *in charge* of it. As the only Lieutenant I was senior officer, you see. There were some Second Lieutenants there who'd been commissioned two or three months, but that didn't matter. I was the only Lieutenant, so I was in charge.

You'd been made straight up to Lieutenant because of your experience in the ranks.

That's right.

We left from Greenock in December 1942, aboard the *Queen Mary*. We'd no escort, because she was so fast. She'd just come off a run from America to Britain with US troops, so she was well stocked with chocolate and other things it was hard to get at home. I've still got three sample menus from our time on board. [The first of the cream-coloured cards is for 'Thursday December 31, 1942. Officers' Luncheon: Minestrone Milanaise. Baked Haddock, Creole. Dry Curry and Rice. Buttered Cabbage. Baked Jacket and Saute Potatoes. To order from the Grill – Chopped Veal Steak and Onions. Cold Buffet – Braised Ham. Devon Sausage. Salad. Peach Pie. Biscuits. Cheese. Coffee'. The second is for 'Sunday January 3, 1943. Officers' Dinner: Consomme Julienne. Halibut Poche, Sauce Mousseline. Roast Cushion of Veal St Claire. Green Lima Beans. Boiled and Roast Potatoes. Long Island Duckling, Apple Sauce. Creme Caramel. Dessert. Coffee'. And the final one is for 'Tuesday January 5, 1943. Officers' Breakfast: Chilled Stewed Apples.

Compote of Figs. Rolled Oats. Post Toasties. Smoked Codling, Melted Butter. Frizzled Breakfast Bacon. Grilled Country Sausage. Rolls. Toast. Scones. Assorted Jams. Marmalade. Tea. Coffee. Cocoa'].

So, as you can see, we spent Christmas and New Year on board, and arrived in Port Taufiq [at the southern end of the Suez Canal] in January 1943. Then it was off to a camp under canvas at Geneifa. The troops were gradually parcelled out as replacements, and in May 1943 I was posted to the 2/5th Battalion, Queen's Royal Regiment (West Surrey). This was right at the end of the North African campaign.

After the surrender, our Company was put in charge of about 500 German prisoners. They sorted out their own toilets. They did their own cooking. All we had to do was furnish them with rations. Next door another Company had some Italians, and they were *completely* disorganised. The Germans organised everything. They put their latrines over by the Italians, actually! Because the prevailing wind blew that way!

Our Company commanders were sometimes Majors, sometimes Captains. And within each Company there were three Platoons, each with an officer in command. At least in most cases. Sometimes a Sergeant had to be in charge, if they hadn't enough officers.

So you were given your own Platoon.

I was given my own Platoon. Which in turn was split into three Sections, led by Corporals or Lance Corporals. And with you in the Platoon HQ you had a Platoon Sergeant, who was your second in command.

Did you find it easy to adjust to being an officer?

I found it a much easier life. Whereas as an NCO I'd had to do all sorts of jobs, or make sure they were done, as an officer I found that if I told my Platoon Sergeant I wanted something done, that was it. I didn't need to bother any further. But of course you were responsible for them, and if anything went wrong you were the one hauled over the coals.

Did the Battalion mind that you weren't one of its own?

During the war, if you got replacements, wherever they came from, you were pleased to see them. The draft that I took out, some were Hampshires, some were Royal Sussex Regiment, some Queen's Royal Regiment. But when they got to the Battalion they became absolutely Queen's Royal Regiment. With me, I was *attached* to the Queen's Royal Regiment, but I was still a Hampshire Regiment officer. And I kept the Hampshires' cap badge and everything.

Did you find any differences between a Guards battalion and a Line battalion?

There's definitely a difference, yes. In the Guards, right from the Depot you were taught that you obeyed an order whether it was right or wrong. The 2/5th Queen's had been a Territorial battalion, so there was a slightly different approach, I think. Things were a bit easier in some ways than the Guards. But I wouldn't compare them too much. They both worked.

Territorial units, like their National Guard counterparts in America, consisted of part-time soldiers from a specific geographical area, who had chosen to undergo basic military training in addition to their full-time civilian jobs. But while National Guard infantry regiments were entirely separate from the infantry regiments of the US Regular Army, British infantry regiments contained both Regular and Territorial battalions.

The Queen's Royal Regiment (West Surrey), for example, had entered the war with two battalions of Regulars – the 1st, then stationed in India, and the 2nd, stationed in Palestine – and six of Territorials – the 1/5th, the 2/5th, the 1/6th, the 2/6th, the 1/7th and the 2/7th. There was no standard size for a British infantry regiment, and even the numbering of the battalions differed from regiment to regiment. After the outbreak of hostilities, of course, the distinctions between the full-time and part-time units effectively disappeared.

We had a period after that of training, during which we practised landings between Sousse and Sfax. We'd get on board a landing craft, sail round to somewhere, nip off . . . inland a bit, dig trenches, stay there for the night. Next day pack up, and go back the other way.

Eventually, at the beginning of September 1943, we found ourselves on our way to Salerno. We'd already seen on sand table models the area we were going to, and could see there was a plain surrounded by hills, with an airfield as one of the main targets. But we were only told the location after we'd set sail. On the ship they made it pretty clear that it wasn't going to be easy. We couldn't expect much protection from the air [because the landing area was at the limit of fighter cover from Sicily], but considerable support would be given by the ships lying offshore.

Then, on D-1 [8 September], the day before we were going to land, it came over the radio that Italy'd surrendered! Well! Everybody thought things were going to be *a lot* easier.

The surrender, of course, had been signed five days previously, but had been kept secret to prevent the Germans from gaining a firm grip on Italy before the Allies could land in force. In some areas, for example at Taranto, where a force of cruisers ferried in British paratroopers in a hastily-improvised operation, the surrender enabled the Allies to seize vital points with a minimum of interference. But in others, where German troops were stationed, the surrender of the Italians made little practical difference.

When we approached in the morning we were the first people to be landed at our beach. We had to climb down the side of the ship on nets to the LCAs. Then enemy batteries opened up, and shells started to fall among the landing craft. There were some casualties before we hit the beach. So much for an easy landing. There were Germans in the area, and since our Commandos and the American Rangers had landed already, nearer to Naples [to secure the left flank, and capture the important passes through the mountains there], they knew something was up.

And of course as we went in, our own ships started firing. Including rockets. I'd never seen those before. What a noise they made! And I thought well, there can't be much left ashore.

Being the first wave of infantry we were lucky to have no trouble on the beach itself. It was still dark when we landed. We ran inland a little bit, and lay down. I looked around, and I could see what I thought was a blockhouse on the right. I should really have got somebody and said 'Go and see what that is', but instead of that I took a grenade out and went towards it myself. Only to find it was an old hut.

So we carried on. We found we'd been landed 500 yards to the right of where we should have been. So the company on our right, 'A' Company, found themselves wading up the River Tusciano! We had no problems except ditches and thorns and swampy ground. Later on when we had time to reorganise I sent for my runner to take a message, only to find that he'd found it so difficult on the way that he'd dumped the bicycle.

When it got light our company, 'D' Company, was placed in reserve. So we didn't do all that much. And then towards evening we were told that it was our turn to advance again. We were marching up this road, and it'd just got dusk, you know. We were following another platoon. And the Battalion CO came back to speak to me, and he said 'Ah, Court. I want you to take your Platoon back to that farmhouse back there', he said, 'because I think there are some Germans in it'.

They'd been bypassed as the Battalion pushed inland?

That's right. But all I knew was that when we got a bit closer we started coming under fire. So we took cover and fired back in the direction of the farmhouse. Then we worked our way forward in the dark, some to the right and some to the left. I was on the left. There was a ditch there, a concrete ditch, where we took shelter. By this time it was fully dark and you just couldn't see a thing. I've no idea what time it was, but it was pitch black. And so I thought well, until we can see something, better to stay here. So we waited through the night.

Came the morning, and it started to get light. And suddenly we could hear tank engines starting up. Only then did we realise that a group of German tanks were laagered around this farmhouse. We didn't have any rounds for our PIAT [the spring-loaded Projector, Infantry, Anti-Tank], so all we had to hold them off with was my revolver, a Bren gun and some rifles. I got wounded in the leg by a ricochet. So when they called on us to surrender we knew the game was up.

We got out of the ditch and just walked towards them. They gathered us together, and took us back to the farmhouse. Two or three of the Germans could speak reasonable English. One of them said to me 'Have you had anything to eat?'. I said no. So they gave us some apples and biscuits.

Mac's captors were from the 16th Panzer Division, one of whose battle groups was now thoroughly intermingled with the British infantry.

In the distance was Montecorvino airfield [one of the initial objectives, but not yet under Allied control]. When one of our planes came in to land they opened fire on it. Whether they hit anything I don't know, but they were firing at it. Then after a while they said 'We are moving. You will get on the tanks. Anybody tries to escape, we shoot'. Because they'd realised that they were now on our side of the lines.

And so we had to climb onto the outside of these tanks. We turned onto the road, and turned left, and after about 200 yards suddenly this tank that I was on was hit. I was wounded again – in the back and side – and it was such a shock to get all this stuff in me that I sort of tumbled over, off the tank; tumbled into the ditch at the side of the road and lay upside down.

The tank stopped, then went on again. And when they'd all gone past I thought right, let's see if I can walk. Just up the road I found the chap who'd been next to me, already dead, with part of his head blown off. So I made my way back to the farmhouse, and found that quite a number of our own people, wounded, were there. They'd been there all the time. So we'd been firing at this farmhouse and some of our own blokes had been in there, wounded. They were from the two companies which'd been leading the advance earlier on.

What happened to the tanks?

Further up the road they came across our Company Headquarters, and made quite a mess of it. Robin Fevez [the twenty-two year old Captain commanding 'D' Company] and several others were killed. Whether they were just shooting as they passed them I don't know. But they're now in the Salerno War Cemetery.

A few years ago I went over to Italy on holiday, and went to Sorrento and Rome; a week in each. And while I was in Sorrento the rep who had a day off took me along the coast to Salerno. I found where Robin Fevez is buried, and one or two others. I was very impressed with the cemetery. It was very well kept. Then we tried to find the farmhouse, but it was all built up, and nothing looked familiar. Whereas in 1943 it'd been all just fields on one side of the road, and the farmhouse stuck by itself, now it looked different. I'd imagined being able to find my revolver – because before we'd stood up I'd taken my revolver and stuck it under a brick – but I couldn't pick out the spot.

So I sat with the other wounded in the farmhouse until some of our own people came along and collected us in various vehicles, and took us down to the beach. We were attended to by different medical people for about five days, then put on a hospital ship back to Algiers.

George Green was also wounded at Salerno, aboard one of the British LCTs bringing in tanks on D+1.

At the time of Salerno I was serving aboard an LCT Mk 4, so we could deliver nine American Sherman tanks, or twelve loaded 3-ton trucks, or 350 tons of cargo.

> A total of 787 examples of the Mk4 were built during the war, making it the most widely-used British LCT design. Marginally shorter but considerably beamier than the preceding Mk3, the Mk4 was notorious for the relative flimsiness of its construction, which had been pushed to the limit to save weight and thus allow beaching in the shallowest possible water. One of George's previous LCTs had snapped in half in bad weather – a fate which was not uncommon among Mk4s.

This time we found that we'd been placed under the command of the Americans, and that the General in charge was to be Mark Clark [formerly Eisenhower's deputy, now given his own Army].

There'd been quite a big build up of landing vessels going on at Bizerta, chiefly American LSTs. And whilst we were there we were invited to a large open air concert given for the troops by the American USO [United Service Organizations]. The main attraction in a star-studded cast was Bob Hope, supported by Frances Langford the singer and others. This was the highlight of the visit, and the following day we started loading for the next operation.

We had an American radioman, as they called them, come aboard as liaison, and I remember a terrific argument between him and our Coxswain. Snowy, the American, had brought about a dozen hand grenades aboard with him; for what purpose, we'll never know. Anyway, when the Coxswain found out about the grenades a hell of a row broke out, and he made Snowy get rid of them. Snowy thought he was a law unto himself, being in the US Navy, and wanted to keep them. I remember the Coxswain's final words were 'Either they go overboard, or *you* do. Yank or not, we're not having those things in the mess with the rest of us'.

Did you have many eccentric shipmates during your time in LCTs?

We had some whose names gave us a laugh. In one there was an Able Seaman called D'Aeth. Naturally everybody called him Death, much to his annoyance, as he insisted we pronounce it 'Dee-Ath'. One day when we were proceeding in line ahead at sea, we started to veer slightly from the craft we were following. Straight away the Skipper was at the voice pipe on the bridge asking who was at the wheel. The helmsman was D'Aeth, but for once he agreed with our pronunciation and replied 'Death at the wheel'! I don't know if you remember the big road safety campaign with the caption 'Keep Death off the road . . . '. Another AB I felt sorry for was one called Smellie, because you can imagine the number of ways he was ragged about his surname. Naturally his nickname was 'Stinker'.

Eventually we got under way in a huge convoy for Salerno.

I was on watch in the early evening when the senior escort vessel flashed us with Morse lamp that the Italians had capitulated to the Allied Command, but that the present operation was to continue as planned. The news was received with great jubilation when it was relayed to the rest of the Flotilla, and you could see men waving their caps in delight. Most people thought that now the landings would be a mere formality. Little did we know.

We continued on our way, and the next afternoon, which was a brilliantly sunny one, we were just off the island of Capri. I remember the Skipper asked me to signal the next craft abeam 'I wonder if Gracie Fields[2] will send a deputation out to greet us?', when suddenly out of the sun six Fw190s dived on us, releasing their bombs. To my dismay one of them scored a direct hit on the landing craft on our starboard side.

After that we were bombed continually during the daylight hours. The Germans were only a few minutes away from their airfields, so could load up with bombs, come and drop them on us, and then back for some more. There was a lot of moaning about the 'bloody RAF'.

About ten Lockheed Lightnings [long range fighters] gave us a reprieve for a while, and we watched several aerial dogfights going on, but then they broke off and headed back to their base. I suppose they were running out of fuel and couldn't risk staying any longer. So once more came the complaints about the lack of air support.

Darkness came, and still the bombing continued. Several ships were alight, flares were continuously floating down, and the whole scene looked like a picture of Hell. I had to take shelter from the shrapnel raining down, and it took quite an effort of will to make myself take up my station on the bridge again.

Come our time to beach I was absolutely petrified at the shell and mortar fire which was going on around us. Thankfully we managed to unload our tanks without loss and left the beach as hurriedly as we could, only to have to go and unload the merchant ships and do it all over again.

We were at it continuously for three days. At one time the rumour was that we were about to pull out, and we were to stand by to take off the troops.

For once the rumour was correct. German strength was building up faster than that of the landing force, and in several places the Allies were being forced back towards the beaches.

The option of evacuation began to be seriously talked about by the Fifth Army, and at one point the landing of further supplies for the two American divisions was halted in anticipation of such an order.

Anyway this eventuality didn't occur, as large naval ships [including the battleships HMS *Valiant* and, before she was knocked out by German bombing, HMS *Warspite*] bombarded the German gun emplacements, helping the troops to hang on.

---

2. The popular British entertainer, who was married to an Italian and maintained a
   home on Capri.

On our third night we went out to sea, dropped anchor and all turned in for a well-earned rest. At dawn, whilst on duty keeping anchor watch, I saw an MTB approaching us with a senior officer on board. I shouted for the Skipper to come up on the bridge, and he'd just arrived when the Gold Braid started to bawl at us to get back to the beach unloading the merchantmen, and 'Be bloody quick about it!'.

A large number of casualties were waiting on the beach to be evacuated, and we were detailed to carry a load of wounded servicemen to a hospital ship. The tank hold was filled with stretcher cases, who were a pitiful sight. We delivered them to the hospital ship *Oxfordshire*, and then the next trip to the beach was to carry a load of petrol cans and compo rations – which were boxes of food, enough for fourteen men for one day – to the troops. On beaching, German prisoners were sent to unload us. The crew had a duty roster to stand guard over these prisoners armed with a rifle, and see that they got on with the job. When it was my turn to supervise them I wondered, if the situation had called for it, whether I could've shot them. Thankfully the occasion never arose.

On having a load finished by the POWs we were next ordered to a merchant ship for further offloading of some lorries. We'd just pulled off the beach, and I was standing on some steps between the bridge and the flag deck to signal the Liberty ship as to which hold we should go alongside, when there was a terrific explosion. I felt a searing pain in my shoulder, and was sent flying.

As I lay there on the deck I could hear more shells whining overhead and splashing in the sea all around us. I've never prayed so much. The Skipper was crouched behind the sandbagged bridge, and shouted to me that he was heading out to sea, out of range of the German guns. There's a saying that 'you never hear the one that hits you', and now I knew this to be true.

When we'd got out of range, some of the crew members came to attend to me. Dressings were applied, and I was carried into the Skipper's cabin, where I bled on his white blankets. Meanwhile an American destroyer, seeing us get hit, had signalled that she was coming alongside. On reaching us their doctor came aboard and immediately gave me a morphine injection to ease the pain I was in. There were two pieces of shrapnel in my back, a piece in my right leg and another two needle-like spikes sticking out of my throat. After inspection the doctor said I'd have to get to hospital right away.

As luck would have it the *Oxfordshire*, which we'd previously been taking casualties to, was still in the bay. I took my leave of the LCT on a stretcher, by means of a sally port in the side of the hospital ship. I was left for a while, whilst a nursing orderly went to see if a bed was available, and when he came back the effects of the morphine were making me feel quite drowsy. Anyway they'd found me a bed, and once I was placed in it a nurse came and asked if I'd like a hot drink. I drank it thirstily, and was immediately sick all over the clean sheets. I felt terrible at this, but the nurse was full of sympathy and told me not to worry, saying it was the shock of the previous events. I heard the ship's engines start up, and I thought 'Thank God I'm out of that'. It was only four days, but it seemed an eternity.

Next morning I woke to a beautiful sunny day, and the calm and peace felt wonderful. After breakfast an orderly came to wash and put clean dressings on my wounds. He told me we were heading for Tripoli, and any treatment I needed would be undertaken in hospital there. In the meanwhile I'd just have to avoid infection in the wounds and have periodic clean dressings. The pain had eased, and apart from a little soreness I felt OK.

We steamed on, and after another day and night the ship's Padre came to see me and asked if I'd attend the funeral at sea of a sailor who'd died in the night. There were only myself and another couple of Naval ratings fit enough to be taken on deck for the ceremony.

It was about 11.00am, and as I came up on deck I could see the surgeons operating on some of the injured from the Salerno landings. The operating theatres were on the upper deck, and their sides were open to the air, with just a wire mesh grille. We were just off the island of Pantelleria when the ship's engines were stopped and the body, sewn up in a canvas shroud, was placed on a tilting board and tipped overboard after the Padre had said the appropriate words.

When we docked at Tripoli we were told that ambulances would be there next morning to take us to various hospitals in the area. Next day, after breakfast and daily medication, we were told to return the pyjamas we were wearing to the orderlies, as they belonged to the ship and would be needed for the next operational trip.

'You can wear the khaki drill you came on board in', we were told.

When I protested that I'd nothing to wear, as I'd arrived aboard covered only by a blanket, the orderly said he'd see what he could do. He came back later with a small pair of buttonless shorts.

After being placed in an ambulance containing three other men besides myself, we set off for our designated hospital. This turned out to be a tented mobile hospital a few miles outside Tripoli. After arrival and inspection by the doctor I was allocated to a battle casualty ward. I'd thought they were all battle casualty wards, but was informed that several of the patients had been admitted suffering from 'battle fatigue', or what was called in the First World War 'shell shock', poor chaps.

My second day there I told one of the doctors my brother Frank was stationed in Tripoli with the Royal Marines. After I'd told him the address nearby he asked me if I'd like to go and see him, and I jumped at the chance. They placed me in an ambulance and the driver was instructed to take me to the address, which was only about ten minutes' drive away. When we reached the Royal Marines camp the driver went into the camp office to enquire after my brother. I was utterly crushed when he came back and told me that Frank had gone on draft to Sicily the day before. On returning to the ward I thought I'd write to Frank and let him know of my change of address, so I immediately wrote to him at the camp, knowing it'd be redirected to his new posting.

That evening a large concert was given for the hospital and all the troops in the locality. The big star was Noel Coward. I must say I was non-committal about Coward before the show, but after seeing his outdoor performance in front of those homesick troops I became a fan; I really enjoyed his show. Later on when he toured some of the wards I was pleased when he stopped and had a chat with me. He told me he had an affinity with the Navy, and talked about his friendship with Lord Louis Mountbatten.

> Coward had in fact just played his friend in the feature film *In which we serve*, a fictionalised account of Mountbatten's time as Captain (D) of the 5th Destroyer Flotilla.
>
> Mountbatten himself was shortly to step down as Chief of Combined Operations, having been appointed Supreme Commander, South East Asia. His successor as CCO, who took up his appointment on 22 October 1943, was the leader of the Commando units at Salerno – Major General Robert Laycock.

The next afternoon I was lying on my bed, idly swatting flies, when to my surprise I saw my brother walking down the ward towards me!

He explained that there'd been a mix-up in the office, and the day he'd received my letter he'd taken it to his CO, who'd given him permission to come and see me right away. During our conversation Frank told me that he'd been at the Noel Coward show, and I thought how strange that we'd both been at the same venue, each unaware of the other's presence.

A few weeks later an orderly came and told me my kit had been sent from the LCT, and would I go and check it. I wasn't too concerned that my gas mask was missing, as I thought I'd just be issued with another one. But after I was eventually discharged as fit for duty I was put on a charge for losing it! The fact that I'd 'lost' it while being carried off my landing craft on a stretcher cut no ice with the Royal Navy.

> *Jim Law* landed slightly behind the assault waves, as a member of the 56th (London) Divisional Signals. Like Mac Court he was a pre-war soldier, having served as a motorcycle despatch rider and as a member of the TA's motorcycle display team, appearing at the Royal Tournament at Olympia in 1937.

After the fighting in North Africa was over we had an easy time. Good food, and we could go swimming if we liked. Then we began practising how to get our vehicles on and off of LSTs. You had to go on backwards, you see. Then in these American-built LSTs you had traffic lights. Red, amber and green. Red was unhook – because your vehicles were all chained down for the sea passage. When amber came up, you started your engines. Then when green came up, of course, the bow doors opened and the ramp came down, and off you went.

We got used to all this business. Then came the time they loaded us on but we didn't get off again. We stayed in the harbour – this was in Tripoli. So we said 'Are we not getting off, then?'. But they just said 'No, not this morning'. Some people reckoned we were going home, but no one really knew. Then one day we shoved off. And off we chugged in a convoy of LSTs. From reading books we were at sea for three days, but it seemed an awful lot longer than three days at the time. It was lovely weather, so we were just lying about and talking to the tank boys, from the Royal Scots Greys.

Then, one day, all hands on deck. OC Troops [the officer commanding the embarked Army personnel] wants a chat. Bit of a showman, he was. He'd got a blackboard there, and he said 'Where are we going?'. So everyone said 'Home!'.

'Ho Ho Ho', he said, 'You ain't going 'ome!'. And he unrolled this map. He said 'You're going *there.* Just south of Naples. A place called Salerno'. Then he told us we were having the honour of helping invade the mainland of Europe. We were making history. Only thing was, there wasn't going to be much air cover, because we were too far away. But very soon, because we were going to capture Montecorvino airfield within a couple of hours, they'd fly in planes and we'd be all right.

Took them nearly two weeks in the end.

My job, I'd got a 3-ton truck with a charging plant. And my job was to charge the batteries for the infantry's wireless sets.

The other thing that put everybody off was the Eyeties giving in. The night before we landed, 8 September. We landed on 9 September. I was supposed to land at H+2.[3] So, the night before, it was 'What now?'. We didn't know whether there'd be any resistance or not.

Well, we found out when we were still 5 or 6 miles offshore. It was daylight by the time we got there; still lovely weather. And you could see there was big haze of gunfire and smoke. Somebody said 'Well what's all this for, if they've given in?'. Somebody else said 'Oh, pockets of resistance'.

Pockets of resistance my arse. The Germans were waiting for us.

When we got closer, shells started to drop around us, but luckily we weren't hit. The LST next to us was, though. Our bow doors opened, down went the ramp, and off we went. You can imagine, all these big LSTs disgorging trucks into a huge traffic jam. A signals truck about four in front of us took a direct hit, and jammed things up even worse.

Of course, we were now in a different world. There were trees, and green fields, and all sorts of things. Completely different to what we were used to, after a couple of years in the sand. So we headed inland, past a crossroads, and it got quieter and quieter. Everybody else had turned off, and we were going up this road all by ourselves, just one truck. I said to my driver 'I don't think this is right, do you, Stan?'. And just as I said it, out from a ditch jumped a Sergeant in the Royal Fusiliers and told us we were almost in the front line! Our truck went like that [made a three-point turn], and we went back the way we'd come, and found Div HQ.

---

3. Two hours after H-Hour, the time at which the first landing craft would touch down. H-Hour for Salerno was set at 3.30am, which was just over an hour before sunrise. Large vessels like LSTs, because they made such tempting targets, were not normally expected to beach until the landings were well under way.

It's a funny thing, Div HQ was just a field with trucks scattered round, but for some reason you always felt safer there. I always felt that. Well, Stan must've felt it too, because in his rush to get in there he turned in too soon and the back wheel went in the ditch, and broke the half shaft between the gearbox and the transmission. I found our blokes, but there was no LAD [Light Aid Detachment. A unit of the Royal Electrical and Mechanical Engineers equipped for recovery and repair on a limited scale]. Eventually an American workshop welded it for us, and made a wonderful job. So we were mobile again.

But then, of course, the Germans started gaining the upper hand. We had to get our guns out and go and hold a position beside a knocked out Scots Greys tank, in case the front line was overrun. I've seen it written that the Germans got within a mile of the beach. There was an awful lot of noise going on, and under those conditions, as an ordinary bloke, you don't know who's holding what. It was a most peculiar situation to be in, because you'd hear on the wireless, from London, that there was heavy fighting at Salerno, you know. We'd to listen to the BBC to find out what was going on!

Suddenly, after about a week, we broke out.

The Germans, having tried and failed to throw the Fifth Army back into the sea, began to disengage on D+7, and the Fifth and Eighth Armies were able to link up. British armour reached Naples on D+22, 1 October 1943.

The Germans were on the retreat. Their next defence line was going to employ the River Volturno, so they were pulling back, and we were pushing north after them. I pinched this flag [unwraps a package to reveal a beautiful Italian royal standard] off the Royal Palace at Caserta, October 1943. I've never seen another one like it. Here's the maker's address, look – Via Duomo 289, Napoli.

The line of the Volturno was forced in mid-October, and the Allies fought their way laboriously northwards until another strong position was reached, this time including the Rivers Garigliano and Rapido and the natural fortress of Monte Cassino.

The battle lines now stretched right across the Italian peninsula, with the US Fifth Army on the left and the British Eighth Army on the right. The Germans remained in control of Northern and Central Italy, including Rome, and clearly intended not to surrender any more territory.

We spent Christmas at a place called Sessa Aurunca. The weather was bad; it was snowing. We had Christmas, and then New Year, and then in the middle of January 1944 they sent us in against the Garigliano.

We managed to get a bridgehead on the German side, and that's what we were doing when we heard about another landing up towards Rome, at Anzio.

They said it was going well; that everything was going according to plan.

> Unfortunately the plan in question, under which the British 1st
> Division, the US 3rd Infantry Division, part of the US 82nd
> Airborne Division and a force of Commandos and Rangers had
> launched a surprise landing south of Rome on Saturday 22
> January, was an ill-judged one.
>
> The idea of a small amphibious 'end run' to outflank stubborn
> German defences – as had been done in the latter stages of the
> Sicily campaign, and during the Eighth Army's initial advance on
> the mainland – had evolved into an attack which tied up a
> substantial portion of the Fifth Army's strength, but which was too
> weak and too far from the battlefront to have a decisive effect.
>
> The advocates of the plan, Churchill among them, hoped that
> creating the new beachhead would immediately cause the
> Germans to fall back from their positions on the Garigliano. In
> fact the Germans kept their nerve and stood fast, while rushing in
> enough strength to imperil the Anzio landing force, which had to
> be urgently reinforced.

One day one of our trucks went past, heading south. In the back was a bloke
called Ted, who I knew. So I shouted 'Ted? Where you going?'. He shouted
back 'Home!'.

And then another one came past, another truck. 'Course, you wanted to
know what was going on. You wanted to know if Jerry was pushing, in case you
had to get out.

Then the Regimental Sergeant Major came up, and he said 'We're going
back to Naples. No convoy, just make your own way back. CMPs [Corps of
Military Police] will tell you where to go. But you've got to take that truck'.
This was a Humber wireless truck with a load of muck in the tank, which
meant it'd do about 10 miles, then stop. It had twin carburettors, which you
had to clean out, and then it'd do another 10 miles. Consequently we got to
Naples miles behind everybody else.

Still no one said where we were going, but either the next day or the day
after we had to go down to Pozzuoli, which is next to Naples, and get on some
more LSTs. The crews seemed genuinely pleased to see us. 'Black cat [the
Divisional sign of the 56th(London)] boys! Blimey, we want *you*. They ain't 'alf
making a balls up, up there'. We asked where. 'Anzio', they said, 'We go up
there every night'. And that's when we realised we were going to Anzio. I
thought Christ, not another one. I'll never be as lucky this time.

But you know the day we landed, in the little harbour of Anzio itself,
the birds were twittering, and not a gun was firing. We got off, and the CO's
driver came along. He'd been there a couple of days. I said to him 'Lovely
here, innit?'. 'God Almighty', he said, 'you wait till the night comes. You won't
think so'.

And he was right. That night we were shelled and shelled. Shelling, mortaring, bombing . . . The Anzio beachhead was the first place we'd ever been in where you had to sleep by yourself. It was usually two in a trench, but there it was only one, to keep the casualties down.

We had doors over the top, for cover. There wasn't a bloody door left in Anzio – no wardrobe doors, no nothing. Because you'd put 'em on top of your trench; put some earth on top of that – lovely.

Our Division hadn't had a real rest since Salerno. We'd been fighting more or less continuously since 9 September, and now we were into February. But we and the other reinforcements arrived just in time, because Jerry put in what was going to be his final counterattack [to crush the beachhead], and we only just managed to turn the tide. After that the Germans gave up, and trench warfare set in.

Eventually our place was taken by the British 5th Division in March, and again we thought we were going home. Because we knew the landings in France must be coming up soon.

But you didn't go home?

No. Bloody Egypt again. At least the weather was better, I suppose.

When we pulled in, alongside us was another troopship, with replacements straight from England. Of course, none of us were dressed the same, whereas they were all blancoed up, buttons polished . . .We looked at them . . . and they looked at us . . .

And some wag shouted out 'Are the buses still red?'.

The grim stalemates at Anzio and along the main front dragged on until May 1944, when the Allies finally broke through to relieve the beachhead.

The task of keeping the Anzio force supplied for four months had proved a heavy burden for the Allied Navies, much of whose strength had already moved from the Mediterranean to the UK.

The Allies, however, were not the only ones shifting supplies along the Italian coast. Between 12 and 18 per cent of their opponents' logistical requirements were being moved by sea in night-time convoys.

John Jones' LCG(L) was one of three tasked with disrupting these movements.

After the Salerno landing in the Autumn of 1943 the American Fifth Army advanced up the west coast of Italy, but after taking Naples they were soon held up at Monte Cassino. Here the Germans dug in on a hilltop in a very commanding position, where they could see every move the Allies made.

In January 1944 we did the Anzio landing, which should've cut off Monte Cassino but failed to do so, and we were pinned down in the beachhead with the Germans holding another commanding position in the foothills behind. In spite of our air supremacy, and attacks on all the bridges and road traffic on the main north-south roads, the Germans were still able to keep their troops well supplied at Monte Cassino and at Anzio.

One reason they were able to do this was that they ran convoys of F-lighters – very similar to our LCTs – down the coast from Genoa and La Spezia in the north, and landed their cargoes on beaches or in small harbours. The convoys kept very close to the coast, travelled only at night, and by day lay up in small bays, covered by camouflage netting. To seaward they were protected by minefields all the way south.

At Bastia on the north-eastern tip of Corsica [evacuated by the Germans, along with Sardinia] a Coastal Forces base had been established, with British Motor Torpedo Boats and Motor Gun Boats, and also American PT boats. A PT boat was about the same size as a British MTB, and her main armament was also torpedoes, but she had the major advantage that she was fitted with radar. The Coastal Forces boys were going out every night from Bastia and trying to catch the German convoys just north of the Piombino Channel, which is the narrow stretch of water between the eastern end of Elba and the Italian mainland. They didn't have much luck, because when they attacked F-lighters the torpedoes usually ran underneath them [being designed to run at a depth of at least 8ft, while the F-lighters drew only about 4–5ft]. MGBs could do a lot of damage with their guns, but had to get in very close to do so, and usually got badly shot up themselves.

It was vital these convoys were stopped, and someone suggested that LCG(L)s should be tried. With their shallow draught they could, in theory, get across the minefields, and their 4.7in guns could provide some real hitting power.

The three selected were *LCG(L) 14*, *LCG(L) 19* and *LCG(L) 20*. I was First Lieutenant in *Landing Craft, Gun (Large) 14*.

First of all, early in March 1944, not having any idea at the time what it was all about, we were sent to the base on the island of Maddalena, which lies between Sardinia and Corsica. There we landed all our full-flash cordite charges and took on flashless ones, and the officers of the three LCG(L)s were given a preliminary briefing. We weren't very happy! The plan was for the LCG(L)s to insert themselves between the convoy and its escorting destroyers, and, using flashless cordite and firing starshell, attack the convoy whilst the Coastal Forces boys distracted the destroyers.

When we got to Bastia they were horrified to find we'd never fired starshell, had no rangefinder or radar, and weren't very manoeuvrable. We were told to land every bit of gear we wouldn't need – confidential books, charts, et cetera – and the crews were told to write letters home. Brown paper and string were issued for us to parcel up any personal belongings which we wished to be sent home to our next of kin. Scuttling charges were put in the magazines and under the main engines.

On the operation we in *LCG(L) 14* were to fire starshell from our after gun, and keep the target illuminated. We would use our forward gun to engage the enemy. We held two night-time rehearsals, with some MGBs acting as the enemy. Starshells must burst well beyond the target. If they burst short of the target *you* become illuminated instead. The three RM Gunnery Officers did their best, but the first rehearsal was a complete shambles. However, the next night – the Gunnery Officers having redone their sums – things went much better.

The next day was 27 March. The three LCG(L)s were to sail at 2.30pm and were to meet the Coastal Forces boys off the island of Capraia at 7.00pm. As sailing time approached we noticed groups of officers and men from the base and other ships in harbour gathering on the quayside. As we cast off our lines they just stood there watching us, saying not a word. We'd not yet told our own crew what it was all about, although they guessed something pretty unusual was happening. One of my forecastle party said 'Fuck me, Sir, I feel as though I'm going to my own funeral'.

As soon as we were out of the harbour we 'Cleared Lower Deck'. As he always did before any operation, our Skipper Lieutenant Sam Armstrong, RNVR went down on the gun deck and told the lads all he knew about the coming operation, and rehearsed them in POW procedure – name, rank and number and nothing else. Leaving me in charge on the bridge he then turned in, after advising everyone not on watch to do the same.

We proceeded in line ahead, with *LCG(L) 19* following us, and *LCG(L) 20* bringing up the rear. After just over an hour I noticed that *19* was dropping astern, and I sent her a signal to regain station at once. She then signalled that she had a bad leak right aft, and her pump wasn't holding it. She requested permission to return to Bastia. Sam wasn't at all pleased when I asked him to come to the bridge. When he heard what was wrong he didn't know what to do, because of course we were keeping strict W/T silence and he couldn't call up Bastia for advice. In the end he had little choice but to let *19* go back to Bastia. With her departure we'd lost over a third of our firepower, as one of our guns was going to fire starshell only.

At 7.00pm we arrived just south of Capraia, and in a few minutes the Coastal Forces boats roared up. We now went to Action Stations, and with Commander Robert Allan, RNVR in overall command in *PT 218* we all turned east, straight across the minefields to a point some miles north and east of Elba, and quite close to the Italian mainland.

On the way two PT boats were sent off to patrol in the Vada Rocks area, well to the north. We then proceeded north very slowly.

In a few minutes one of the scouting PT boats reported an enemy convoy coming south – six F-lighters escorted by two destroyers. Commander Allan then took up position close on our port bow in his PT boat, and before long he too had the convoy on his radar.

There then followed a whole series of alterations of course and speed, until we'd all turned 180 degrees and were heading slowly south again. All, that is, except the MGBs and MTBs, which had been sent well out to the west. We slowed right down, so that the F-lighters were out on our port beam and the destroyers about a mile on our starboard beam. The main body of the Coastal Forces were out of sight beyond the destroyers.

When all was ready, Commander Allan began passing us ranges and bearings. Then he ordered the Coastal Forces boats to go in and attack the destroyers. As soon as they'd opened fire he ordered us to attack the convoy. The range for the starshell was 5000yds, and as they began bursting, there were the six F-lighters. We'd already arranged with *20* that we would attack the leading F-lighter and they'd take on the next two.

We opened fire with SAP [Semi Armour Piercing] and hit her with our first round. We then followed with HE, and in less than five minutes she blew up with a huge explosion and sank.

Meanwhile *20* had attacked the next two lighters, and they were on fire and sinking. We then took on the other three. In barely thirty minutes the whole convoy had been sunk.

Thanks to our flashless cordite I don't think they ever saw us. The F-lighters had been firing their 88mm guns and machine guns – full-flash – up in the air, evidently thinking it was an aerial attack.

We then looked the other way to see what the destroyers were doing, but to our amazement they'd gone. The Coastal Forces boys claimed to have hit one with a torpedo, but said that as soon as they'd seen the convoy sunk they'd turned tail, back towards Genoa. We were sorry to learn that one of our boats had been badly damaged, with one man killed and another seriously injured.

We stayed around in the area for a while but made on further contacts, so at 0.30am [on 28 March 1944] Commander Allan ordered all craft to return to Bastia, which we reached without further incident.

Of course everyone in Bastia was jubilant at our success, and we were ordered out again the next night to see if we could give a repeat performance. We cruised around in the Vada Rocks area all night, but saw nothing. We got back to Bastia as dawn was breaking; very, very tired. This was the end of that moonless period, so having re-embarked all the gear and personal effects we'd landed, we returned to Maddalena to await the next one.

On the night of 24/25 April the three LCG(L)s were at sea again.

We rendezvoused with a slightly bigger force of Coastal Forces boats just south of Capraia Island at 8.00pm, and set course eastwards over the minefields for a position north east of Elba. Commander Allan was again in overall command. Our Skipper Sam Armstrong was senior officer of the LCG(L)s, and *19* and *20* were with us as usual.

Very soon Commander Allan received reports that there was a convoy of five F-lighters and a tug coming south, and also an escort group of three converted F-lighters – each armed with at least two 88mm guns and several large calibre machine guns – coming north. We wanted to attack the southbound convoy first, as it would be loaded with supplies. However, we were on a collision course with the escort group, and if we stopped to let them pass we'd miss the convoy. Luckily at the very last moment the escort group altered course slightly, and we were able to slip past unseen. Of course it was pitch dark at the time, and the Germans had no radar.

As before, we finished up steering a southerly course parallel to the convoy, with the F-lighters on our port side. However, this time we were much closer to the Italian coast, which was heavily wooded and which rose up from the shore to quite high hills.

At 0.05am we opened fire. As our starshell burst, only two F-lighters were visible, and the three LCG(L)s quickly began to hit them. In a few minutes both exploded and sank. Commander Allan then ordered us to search left, and three more F-lighters and an oceangoing tug became visible. Meanwhile some of our starshell and 'overs' from our guns had dropped into the woods on shore and started what became a huge forest fire visible in Bastia, almost 50 miles away.

The tug and two of the F-lighters were soon on fire and eventually sank. The third F-lighter, which we were sure we'd hit, disappeared from view, but Commander Allan still had her on his radar plot, and sent a couple of MGBs after her. They found her aground on the shore, and shot her up until she too caught fire and exploded. Returning from this job the MGBs came across a group of twelve survivors swimming around. Taking them aboard they found six of them were Dutchmen from the tug – forced labour engineers the Germans were taking to Elba to do a salvage job there. Needless to say they were delighted to be picked up by the British.

By the time this first action was over, Commander Allan was in radar contact again with the escort group I mentioned earlier. We were ordered to steer north, and away from the coast.

After a short time we were ordered to fire starshell, and there they were. They immediately fired a red recognition signal and Commander Allan ordered us to cease fire, but we continued to close with them until we were less than a mile apart. We were then ordered to open fire with starshell again, followed by SAP and HE with all guns. The Germans returned fire very heavily, using tracer and full-flash cordite; we were still using flashless cordite, and didn't use our pom-poms because they were full-flash.

The Germans overestimated the range, because their shells and tracer were passing just overhead. Their 88mm guns could fire much faster than our 4.7in, but with Commander Allan giving us accurate range information we soon began to hit two of them frequently, and within about eight minutes they sank. A PT boat and several MTBs finished off the third.

At 1.20am the scouting force to the north reported targets 10 miles away. This was too far away for we three LCG(L)s to engage, and with our slow speed there was no hope of catching them. Commander Allan therefore told the PT boats of the scouting force to go in and attack. This they did, and found it was another German escort group of three. The Germans opened fire on the PT boats before they were in a position to fire their torpedoes, but they pressed home their attack and fired two each. One of the group was seen to blow up and sink, but the fire from the other two was so heavy that they had to retire at speed under smoke.

Commander Allan now ordered the whole force to return to Bastia. Units had become scattered, and apart from his own *PT 218* there were only two other PT boats with us. At 4.00am we were well on our way home when Bastia signalled that they had unidentified targets on their radar plot, 3 miles west of Capraia. Thinking they'd be E-boats, Commander Allan put the three LCG(L)s on lookout bearing starboard, and sent the two PT boats to attack.

When they were illuminated with starshell they realised the enemy were three destroyers! They came under very heavy fire, but fired their remaining torpedoes and then retired at speed. We in the LCG(L)s felt a heavy underwater explosion, but since the destroyers had been close to a recently-laid British minefield we were never sure whether it was a mine or the torpedoes exploding.

In fact the German destroyer *TA 23* – formerly the Italian Navy's *Impavido* – had struck one of the mines. She was subsequently sunk by her consorts.

We got back to Bastia with no damage or injuries to the LCG(L)s, and although the Coastal Forces had received damage and some casualties, no boats had been sunk. A truly hectic night!

A month later at the next moonless period we tried twice more, but made no contacts. However, by this time the Allies had broken out of the Anzio beachhead.

As the Allied armies pushed north, taking Rome on 4 June, preparations were made for the French 9th Colonial Infantry Division and some French commandos to storm the island of Elba.

Many people, of whom I'm one, think there was little need for this operation. By 17 June, D-Day for Elba, the Allies were advancing up the west coast of Italy and were already almost level with the island. There was a garrison of over 3000 Germans on Elba, and it was well fortified.

There was only one place on the island where a sizeable landing could take place, and that was the Golfo di Campo, on the south side. To the east of this was high ground rising straight out of the sea, and built into the hillside were about six large calibre guns, all controlled from an emplacement on top of the hill. The guns appeared to be in single emplacements, well concealed, one above the other up the hillside. It was the job of *LCG(L) 8* and *LCG(L) 14* to draw their fire and prevent them from attacking the invasion craft as they entered the gulf.

Our convoy sailed from Porto Vecchio in Corsica at 10.45am on D-1. At 8.45pm we were joined by a convoy from Bastia, and we all formed up in two columns in line ahead. The port column was led by [the US Navy] *LST 352*, with the senior officer Captain Errol Turner, RN on board. We in *LCG(L) 14* led the starboard column.

The area between Corsica and Elba was still very heavily mined, and the minesweepers had swept a channel a quarter of a mile wide for us – not a lot of width for two columns of ships travelling at night without lights.

All went well until just before 11.00pm on D-1. At that time we were approaching the point where we were to make a major turn to port. After checking with us as to our exact position and agreeing, *LST 352* gave the executive signal to turn. The weather was fine and the sea calm, but it was dark, and by the time we'd realised that the LST wasn't turning as quickly as we were, we'd hit her hard. At least it was well above the waterline.

Then, a few minutes later, there was a flash astern of us and a heavy explosion. *LCF 15*, the last craft in our column, had taken the turn a bit wide and hit a mine. We couldn't see her, but I understand she sank very quickly with the loss of about half her ship's company.

At about 2.05am on D-Day *LCG(L) 8* and *LCG(L) 14* left the convoy in company with an American PT boat, *PT 203*, which had our Flotilla Officer Lieutenant Commander Ian Ferguson, RNVR on board. The PT boat, with her radar, was to help with bearings and ranges. At 3.40am we reached our pre-arranged position to open fire. The PT boat gave us an opening range of 3800yds to the shore, and a bearing of Red 040. We could see the silhouette of the headland.

At 3.51am the LCT(R)s opened fire with their rockets, and at 3.53am *LCG(L) 8* and ourselves were ordered to shoot. Exactly as we did so the Germans opened fire on us, and managed to straddle us with their first salvo. Our course was 120 degrees and our speed 6 knots, but we soon increased that to 8 knots and then 10. The enemy frequently near-missed us and kept up a heavy rate of fire, but neither LCG(L) was actually hit. From time to time they illuminated us with starshells, and we had to take constant evasive action. At 4.25am the Germans ceased fire, so we did the same, and took the opportunity to make some adjustments to our guns. We had then fired 212 rounds. Our Flotilla Officer in the *PT 203* then carried out a close-in recce of the enemy batteries, and was promptly fired on, to which he replied.

At about 5.10am we were ordered to reopen the bombardment, and now in broad daylight made several passing runs at varying ranges. The enemy's fire was quite heavy again, and more accurate, and we were constantly near-missed and sometimes actually straddled. However, we were scoring hits in the target area, and gradually we began to slow the enemy rate of fire.

At 6.30am we had to break off the engagement. We'd expended 480 rounds, and only had 67 rounds of SAP remaining. Both guns were dangerously overheated – the last time we fired it, No 1 gun fired as soon as the breech was closed, of its own accord, due to the chamber being almost white hot. No 2 gun was the same, but in addition had a fault in the breech mechanism which prevented it closing properly. *LCG(L) 8* had been firing at a slower rate and was able to carry on in the action.

We got permission to withdraw to the waiting area, and we'd only been there a few minutes when through my glasses I saw an enemy gun fire again. A second later there was an explosion close alongside our bridge. I'd taken my tin hat off, and I felt a hot sensation across the top of my head. I thought, God, I've been hit. But when I put my hand up I found the top of my head was still there, and all I got was a handful of smouldering hair.

The Skipper had been standing behind me on the wooden grating at the compass binnacle. Luckily he hadn't taken *his* tin hat off, because when I looked round he was lying on the deck with a deep dent in the side of it and blood coming from a gash in his hand. The blow had knocked him out, but he soon recovered with some help from our SBA [Sick Berth Attendant] and told me to take the ship further out of range. The piece of shrapnel that'd near-missed me and hit him had ricocheted around inside the bridge without hitting anyone else, and had finished up on the chart table, where it'd burnt a hole in the chart.

At about 8.00am I was alone on the bridge when suddenly there was a heavy explosion on our gun deck. Showers of burning bits of cordite came down on the bridge, and I had a hectic minute or two stamping on them to put them out before they started a fire. However, down below, the gun deck was on fire and several bodies were lying around. We always kept the fire hoses rigged and the water turned on when we were at Action Stations, so the gun deck was quickly flooded and the fire put out. Of the people injured two were very serious, but the others were mainly suffering from severe shock.

What had happened was that our ordnance artificer Marine Moore and Marine Richardson had been trying for some time to repair the fault in No 2 gun's breech mechanism, and had done a trial loading. As Richardson tried to load the cordite charge, the heat in the breech chamber had set it off with the breech still partly open. The shell had travelled a short distance into the barrel and then stuck, and the brass case of the charge had split into several pieces. Moore and Richardson, being right behind the breech, had got the full force of the explosion.

We called for urgent medical help, and in a few minutes *MGB 655* came alongside and took off the casualties. She then transferred them to *LCI(L) 278*, which was acting as a hospital ship, and she took them to Bastia. I'm sorry to say that George Moore died of his injuries, but Richardson, although also seriously injured, did eventually recover and return to the UK.

After the Flotilla Officer had visited us he agreed there was nothing more we could do, and later that day we received orders to return to Maddalena. From there we were sent down to Malta. There both guns were condemned and we were fitted with new ones.

Elba was a nasty little operation. There's no question that the French troops fought with great courage and determination, and they eventually achieved their objective [securing the island on D+2, 19 June 1944]. However, when one considers the cost of the operation in casualties and material, and what was achieved, one asks was it worth it? The answer has got to be – no, it wasn't.

Many asked the same question of the Italian campaign as a whole. It was, however, instrumental in depriving Germany of a partner, and in tying down units which could otherwise have opposed the great landing in France, on which British and American hopes were now pinned.

SIX

Reaching the Peak: 6 June 1944

American troops intended for an invasion of France had begun arriving in the UK as early as January 1942, but not until the Washington Conference of May 1943 had a target date for the operation finally been agreed.

Thereafter the influx of Americans increased dramatically, and by May 1944 the US Army had amassed a staggering 1,526,965 men and 5,297,306 tons of supplies and equipment in the British Isles. The US Navy, too, had established a heavy presence. One of the many American servicemen who arrived before D-Day was *Dick Shreffler*, a young naval officer.

During the war we had several Midshipmen's Schools. I went to the one at Notre Dame University in Indiana, a major Roman Catholic university. There were six of these 'quickie' schools, and because we got our training in such a short period of time we were called 'Ninety Day Wonders'. Just imagine – I went through the course and emerged as a fully-fledged officer in the US Navy, without ever putting a foot on board a boat or a ship! I was then assigned to Gunnery School at Dam Neck, Virginia, to be trained as a Gunnery Officer.

One very dark night we were placed on a train to an unknown destination. It seemed to take us forever to get to wherever we were going, but around midnight we got off the train in a railroad switch yard. I never knew there could be so many railroad tracks to stumble over. Added to this we were all loaded down with heavy duffel bags.

Finally we came to some kind of ferry, and off we went across a body of water. After about 15 minutes we climbed on to a very high pier, which was very dimly lit but had a regiment of American Red Cross ladies to serve us doughnuts, coffee, hot chocolate, peanuts and candy bars, along with some dandy kits filled with razors, toothbrushes and toothpaste. When we asked where we were going they just said 'On board the ship'. 'Where?'. 'You're standing by it'.

On looking up we discovered that we were, indeed, standing by a great grey wall – the side of a massive liner. It was the *Queen Elizabeth*. On board I found that sixteen officers were to bunk together in a stateroom designed for two! There were a great number of us on board – thousands and thousands [incredibly, up to 15,000 on each trip]. I remember that our dining room was in what should've been a swimming pool. I remember, too, that the crossing was made in record time. To pass the journey there was a great deal of heavy gambling on board. The attitude seemed to be eat, drink and gamble, for tomorrow we die. The trip was, of course, from New York to the Firth of Clyde. This was in November 1943.

After we put in at Greenock we were sent across the Firth to Rosneath, where we were quartered within the stonework of the old castle. I remember that it was in very bad repair. After about three or four weeks we junior officers were moved to Quonset huts down on the base, so that senior officers could take our place. I was frankly quite glad, because the castle had rats as big as horses. The senior officers found that out!

How did you feel about serving in Europe?

I was delighted to be sent there rather than to the Pacific. The major reason was that the liberty in Britain was far, far better. The people spoke the same language as I did, and even during the war there were wonderful cultural things to see and do and hear.

Really, when I came to the ETO [European Theater of Operations] I didn't know where I was going. My destination could've just as easily been the Mediterranean.

Strange as it may seem, the war years were amongst the happiest of my life. I have so many vivid memories. One is of an early Sunday morning in Edinburgh. I was at the top of the Royal Mile, which begins at Edinburgh Castle and ends at the gates of the Palace of Holyroodhouse, a mile down the hill. While there are so many places to remember on that street – places like the Castle, the Cathedral and John Knox's House – there are three in particular that stick in my mind.

The first was an antique store on the right side of the street. In the window I saw a beautiful Paisley shawl, but of course being Sunday the store was closed. Fortunately a week or two later I was able to return to Edinburgh and purchase it. It's now on my sister's grand piano.

The second scene that I remember from that Sunday morning occurred about half way down the street. There was a tiny grocery store with lots of candy in the window – well, not lots, because it was wartime – but whatever, as I was turning to go away, a charming old lady came out of the shop and said to me 'Would you like some, Yank?'. I said I sure would, but I didn't have any ration coupons. 'Come in', she said, and she gave me some anyhow. This occurred in December of 1943. During the Summer of 1962 I passed by the same small store, and told a man of about my age the story. 'Ah', he said, 'that old lady would've been my granny'. He was pleased that I'd told the story, but he didn't give me any more candy!

The third thing I remember of that morning occurred at the foot of the hill, in front of the great gates of Holyroodhouse. There, at the gate house, stood a single bottle of milk. It seemed so wonderfully incongruous in front of such massiveness!

We were at Rosneath [which was, among other things, the home of a US Navy Gunfire Support School] to take over some British LCG(L)s, which our Navy didn't have. We were to use these to support the landings in France, and then hand them back again. The LCG(L) – or Landing Craft, Gun (Large) – was a twin-screw craft with two 4.7in guns for bombardment. The guns were real old, but effective. Sadly the Royal Navy hadn't given us enough basic necessities, like cutlery. We needed everything – knives, forks, spoons, mess trays, pots and pans, the works.

So, on one cold, rainy, foggy, absolutely miserable night our head cook Sills and I raided the US Navy base galley at Rosneath. For our stealing costumes we chose any garment that had lots of pockets. While Sills entered the galley area on the base and engaged the watchman in idle conversation, I was to enter the supply area in the back and steal as much as I could in ten minutes. There was quite a trick in doing this, because all of the equipment was metal, and would rattle. However, thanks to Sills' line of chatter I managed to collect quite a pile of gear before we met up again in a cluster of holly trees down by the main road. We were so proud of ourselves, and while each of us stuffed our pockets with the smaller items, we also filled two big bags with most of the larger utensils and mess trays.

All of a sudden from out of the fog a jeep came up behind us. Before I knew what was happening Sills had jumped into a clump of bushes with the bags of loot, while I was left to face the driver of the jeep.

Who should that be but Captain Sabin, our senior officer! When he saw me he said 'Jesus, Mr Shreffler, what are you doing out on a night like this? Hop in, and let me take you down to your ship!'. I said 'Oh no, Captain, I'm just out for a walk'. He must've thought I was out of my mind, but I knew I couldn't get into the jeep because of my pack horse condition, and so I said again 'Really, Sir, it's just nice to be walking by myself in the rain'. He drove on, and Sills came laughing out of the bushes. In fact, the two of us laughed all the way home.

During World War Two there was meant to be no fraternization between officers and men. However, I did so like orchestral music, and there was a symphony concert being performed in Glasgow. None of my fellow officers enjoyed such concerts, and I didn't wish to go alone. I knew that the radioman on board ship enjoyed music, and so I invited him. He was hesitant about going, but eventually agreed to join me.

We arranged to meet at the end of the pier and catch a train into the city. It turned out to be a great evening for the two of us, not only because of the music but because we enjoyed one another's company. However, on the way home we were confronted on the train by a real 'book-bound' officer from another craft in our Flotilla, and he gave us the word that he was going to report us for fraternizing. He made us feel that we were about to be court martialled! Fortunately, he never did report us. As an addendum to this story, the officer in question was a lowly Ensign in the US Navy. In fact his lowliness in rank was so intolerable to him that I found him one day soaking all of his brass buttons and insignias in salt water so he would have the appearance of being an old sea dog!

In late December of 1943 we sailed via Douglas on the Isle of Man to Salcombe in Devon. The little harbor of Salcombe [where a US base had opened in October] then became our home port until we returned the LCG(L) to the Royal Navy. Besides myself there were two other officers – the Skipper and the Exec [Executive Officer]. I was the Gunnery Officer, which was quite ironic really, because when we were kids my father wouldn't let us have anything to do with guns. They were forbidden on his property.

One of the things that had to be changed when the ship was commissioned into the US Navy was that bunks had to be installed. Hammocks weren't favored in the US Navy because the powers that be said they were hard on the kidneys.

Another difference that was noted was that the US Navy didn't allow any alcohol on board, except in the medicine chest. I did get some of the brandy from there once, however!

When the Royal Navy was training us in the use of the craft, there was a double crew on board during the day. At night the Royal Navy personnel would go ashore to sleeping quarters, and for their breakfast and evening meals. One day when both crews were below at noon day chow, I and the Royal Marine officer who was training me in gunnery were together topside having a leisurely chat. All of a sudden he asked me 'Mr Shreffler, are you a swimmer?'. I've always been quite a good swimmer, and so I was something of a bragger about my ability. With that he told me to go over the side, into the freezing Channel water! He then called to the conning tower that a man was overboard, and to cut the craft's speed to steerage way. At the same time the Man Overboard alarm was sounded.

Well, the crew was very slow at responding because they were eating, and by the time they got up topside no lifebuoy with a line attached could reach me; only a buoy without a line made it to me. Since no craft sailing in a Flotilla was allowed to turn about for a recovery, the next astern was signalled to make the rescue. Fortunately, that was able to save me. When I was pulled from the water you might say that I was cold! As a result, they broke out the brandy from the medicine chest. That was the only thing that made the crews envious of me! I was returned to my own LCG(L) that evening. After that, when a Man Overboard drill was held the men really turned to. It's not an experience I'll ever forget.

The cross-Channel invasion for which everyone was training, and whose site was still a closely-guarded secret, had meanwhile had to be put back from May to June in order to gain another month's production of landing craft.

As the target date approached, Dick's career of larceny con- tinued.

Just before the invasion we were told to collect all of our personal gear from ashore. I really had nothing other than my Navy topcoat. When I went to the base cleaners I was told to come back shortly after noon, when a final delivery would be made from Kingsbridge. As I was about to leave, I noticed a beautiful flat iron – beautiful because I knew that my crew wanted and needed such an item. So, when everyone had their backs turned, I stole it.

When I got to the small boat landing I had to make a jump for the boat that was to take me out to my LCG(L), which was anchored in the harbor. When I jumped, the great weight of the iron caused it to slip from my grasp, and it nearly went through the bottom of the boat! I received various kinds of looks!

After lunch I returned to the Naval cleaning establishment to collect my coat. As I waited my turn to be served, Mr Whaley, the base Engineering Officer, asked the attending Mates if they could arrange to have his dress blues pressed for an evening dinner. To this request one of them said 'I'm not sure that we can do that, because some God-damned son of a bitch stole our iron!'.

I do believe that that's the first and only time I've been called that – at least to my knowledge! Not at all a proper way for an enlisted man to describe an officer and a gentleman.

Only a few miles west of Salcombe, at Thurlestone, *John Good* was under training as a Second Lieutenant in the Royal Marines. The vast majority of those joining the British and American services during the war did so on a purely temporary basis, but John was one of the smaller number who signed on as Regulars.

At that time I hadn't the slightest idea what I wanted to do with my life. There was a war on, and I knew I should have to join up anyhow, so I said right, *that's* what I'll do. And I took a Regular commission in the Royal Marines. I think perhaps, looking back, that was a mistake – I should really have come out after the war. But, as things have worked out, it's been a pretty good life.

Where did you do your basic training?

Chatham, in Kent. The barracks was knocked down long ago, which is a pity. Not that I could say my first twelve weeks there was a bed of roses. Anything but. But I don't think your first experience of the services ever is. The system in the Royal Marines then was that you belonged to either Chatham, Portsmouth or Plymouth. I happened to be a Chatham officer, so after my overseas postings I always came back to Chatham. Our quarters were right on the road that ran past the barracks down to the dockyard. And every morning at the same time the dockyard rush would start – the day shift would be going down, and the night shift coming back up. Plus, late at night, sailors would be returning to their ships, slightly the worse for wear! But that was all par for the course. It was a good spot to be.

As a Regular officer, was your training any different from the training of your Hostilities Only colleagues?

Oh yes. It was very much longer. We took eighteen months, which was far *too* long, really. But I suppose we were certainly well trained at the end of it. The best part of the training by far was, I think, the five months we spent down at Thurlestone in Devon, where they trained Hostilities Only officers. We Regulars had a slot there, which was *wonderful.* An extremely good course, in a requisitioned hotel, and we never lacked for eggs and butter from the local farms.

Did they give you a mix of classroom and practical work?

There it was mainly classroom, but towards the end of our time we did something which I don't think any other course did – we were allowed to witness the dress rehearsal by one of the American assault divisions preparing for France. I've yet to meet another British serviceman who had our luck. How on earth we were allowed I don't know, but our Course Officer – an excellent chap, Major Jerram – somehow managed it.

And so we found ourselves standing on some high ground at the south end of Slapton Sands watching this invasion practice. It was absolutely amazing. I remember so clearly; all our diagrams, learned in the classroom, becoming reality. You looked down onto the bay, and there it all was, in front of your very eyes. Including the fire support – guns, rockets, the full works. And as it progressed we were able to watch the big LSTs coming in and beaching. I think I learned more from those few hours about an amphibious operation than any amount of classroom work could ever have taught me.

At that time the whole of that stretch of coast was a restricted area, and they'd evacuated all the local civilians from their homes so that they could conduct these big exercises.

Of course in one of the rehearsals [on the night of 27/28 April 1944] some German E-boats got in amongst them and torpedoed three of the Americans' LSTs.

> The heavily-laden *LST 507* and *LST 531* were sunk, but the *LST 289* managed to limp back to port. With grim irony, the losses were greater than the same force was to sustain in the real landings.

This was all kept quiet at the time, though.

I've often said that you don't realise it at the time, but looking back now you can see that you were living through history. They were stirring times. But you just took it all in your stride

Never mind. It's all gone, thank God.

> Not until the invasion forces had completed their rehearsals and been sealed off from the outside world were the details of their coming assaults revealed to them. The US First Army and the British Second Army were to be put ashore at five points along the coast of Normandy. The units landing on the first day would be the British 3rd and 50th (Northumbrian) Divisions, the 3rd Canadian Division, the US 1st and 4th Infantry Divisions, most of the US 29th Infantry Division and parts of the US 90th Infantry and British 51st (Highland) Divisions, heavily reinforced by tanks and supported by Commandos, Rangers, aerial bombardment and naval gunfire.

The British 6th Airborne Division would be landed by parachute and glider to secure the left flank, while the US 82nd and 101st Airborne Divisions secured the right.

In contrast to the landings in Madagascar, North Africa and Italy, the assaults this time would be conducted in daylight. Because of tidal factors, those in the two American landing areas – UTAH and OMAHA – would go in first; the British and Canadians would attack a little over an hour later at GOLD, JUNO and SWORD. D-Day was set for Monday 5 June 1944.

Patrick Wall was an officer in the Royal Marines who inveigled his way into the American assault at OMAHA.

In December 1943 I'd become Chief Gunnery Instructor at HMS *Turtle*, the Combined Operations training base at Poole in Dorset. So I trained the support craft – LCT(R)s and LCG(L)s – for all five landing areas, ready for Normandy. We used to go out every day and bombard the nearby Studland range, till there wasn't much of it left – much to the fury of the ecologists!

When we'd finished training all five forces I was told to take the School back to Wales, where it was to remain until we could begin preparing people for the Japanese war. However, I thought this was a rotten idea. So I persuaded the CO of the last of the forces to come through, Captain Lorenzo Sabin, USN [senior officer of the Close Gunfire Support Group destined for OMAHA] to take me with him. I said to him 'Don't you think, having trained all your people, I'd better come along as your Gunnery Officer?'. He said 'Very good idea. Come along'. So I did!

You obviously got on well with the Americans.

Very well indeed. I always have, actually. One thing that amused me about them, when they came along to Poole to train, was the way their young draftees used to slope about the deck smoking, and things like that, but as soon as they went to General Quarters they were first class at their jobs. My Gunnery Instructors were absolutely astonished. They did extremely well, I thought.

I kept in touch with Captain Sabin, and went over to the States to see him quite frequently until his death some years ago.

With American-crewed LCG(L)s, the guns were manned by Navy personnel rather than by Marines, as they were in British ones?

Yes, they were all-Navy crews. The predominant concern of the United States Marine Corps was of course the Pacific war. In fact, although small numbers did serve in Europe I don't think I saw an American Marine the whole time. Which was a great pity.

So you went to OMAHA aboard a US Navy craft?

Yes, an LCH – a Landing Craft, Headquarters. Which was an LCI(L) converted to accommodate a signals staff.

We sailed from Poole the first time, but then of course they had to halt this whole gigantic operation for a day because of the weather, so we had to go back. Not to Poole; to Salcombe, in Devon. So we really started D-Day from Salcombe.

> The convoys had been recalled because Eisenhower, who had been brought back from the Mediterranean to act as Supreme Commander, had felt compelled to put the invasion on hold for twenty-four hours to see whether the weather would clear.
>
> The Channel was still very rough when he came to make the final decision about launching or calling off the assaults, but bearing in mind the inevitable delays and the difficulty of maintaining security, he decided to proceed.
>
> D-Day was irrevocably fixed for Tuesday 6 June, and the convoys sailed again.

When we got across the Channel we were right in the front of it, of course, because the LCT(R)s we were with had only a short range. They made the Germans get their heads down pretty quickly! We had quite a lot of them, and they were all firing at the same time, which was a terrifying sight. They must've had a terrific effect on morale. My God, they frightened *me*! And then came the turn of the LCG(L)s. I'd given them targets, and then told them to fire on targets of opportunity, which they did.

How had you selected the initial targets?

We had wonderful maps, with all the defences marked in blue and purple. Absolutely detailed. Aerial reconnaissance and so on. We couldn't really be sure our 4.7in guns, two of which formed the main armament of each LCG(L), were going to penetrate some of these concrete emplacements, so we just had to fire on them and hope we were doing some good. Because the defenders were all dug in, of course, and prepared for this kind of stuff.

> The preliminary air strikes turned out to have been ineffective at OMAHA, and an attempt to ferry artillery pieces ashore in DUKWs, as in the rough seas off Sicily, quickly proved a disaster. Most of the new amphibious tanks were also swamped as they tried to make the shore, leaving the infantry to struggle on alone. Many who were wounded and unable to move drowned in the rising tide.

The assault waves had a hell of a time when they got to the beaches. The Germans gave them a pretty bad time of it, and it was touch and go for a while.

We knew there was a lot of trouble ashore – the troops were huddling under what cover they could find. There were a hell of a lot of dead on those beaches. And a hell of a lot of wrecked landing craft. But they got through, in the end.

UTAH, on our right, had much less trouble, although the Airborne were dropped in the wrong place – the usual thing with parachutists.

The confusion of the first terrible hours left unloading at OMAHA well behind schedule. Of 2400 tons of ammunition and supplies due to be landed there during D-Day, only about 100 tons actually made it.

Well, after three days, of course, they were out of range of us. The rockets were out of range after D-Day. The LCG(L)s went on popping away at various things, but even they were out of range after a few days.

And my Captain, Sabin, was sent ashore to speed up the unloading operation. So he took his Operations Officer and myself ashore with him as his staff. That was fun. Because I got to deliver very rude remarks from Captain Sabin to the US First Army, who wondered what in the world a British Marine was doing there!

Jim Van Orsdel had an even closer view of the carnage at OMAHA, after finding himself in the US Navy largely because of his prowess as a sportsman.

Five or six games into the [baseball] season I received word of my commission, and upon receipt and swearing in as an officer I had to depart Great Lakes and report to the Amphibious Force, Atlantic Fleet at Norfolk, Virginia.

When I came to the main gate of the United States Naval Base at Norfolk the Marine on duty had never heard of such an organization, and they had to call the main headquarters, who told them it was new and that the officer should report to the Admiral's yacht, based at Pier 4 on the Operating Base, for further instructions. The Commanding Officer of the Amphibious Force, Atlantic Fleet was Rear-Admiral H Kent Hewitt. My first night was spent lounging and sleeping on his rolling yacht – my first experience of sleeping on water!

I found that I was one of the original thirty-seven officers forming Rear-Admiral Hewitt's staff. We worked from a Quonset hut on the Operating Base until they finished our headquarters at the Nansemond Hotel in Ocean View, a few miles away. The Nansemond was a very nice pre-war hotel facing Chesapeake Bay, with ample space for our offices. We ate all our meals there, but we lived elsewhere – most of us in an area called Oakdale Farms. We were picked up each day by US Navy station wagons from the base, and taken in to work.

My direct boss from the day I reported to Norfolk was Rear-Admiral Hewitt's Operations Officer, Captain E A Mitchell. He was a terrific man. Very demanding, but once he gained confidence in you he'd discuss every detail of what we were working on. Commander Wellings [Commander T F Wellings, in charge of matters relating to Gunfire Support] worked in the next room from ours, and in the other rooms, all side by side, were Commander Woods [Commander R W D Woods, the Staff Air Officer], Commander Evans [Commander Donald S Evans, Communications] and Commander Bachman [Commander Leo A Bachman, Intelligence].

Our first assignment was to draw up operational plans to conduct an amphibious landing in Morocco in the late Summer or early Fall of 1942. It was a very busy time. Each outfit – Operations, Intelligence, and so on – had one or two junior officers, and we were a very close team, from top officers to Ensigns. I was Captain Mitchell's helper, and my work consisted of both desk work and travel. If there was a job to do he'd call out 'Van Orsdel!'. I carried more papers, more plans and more sailing orders up and down the East Coast than you could ever dream! I travelled by station wagon, with an enlisted man driver, to every nook and cranny where there were amphibious ships. Also Washington DC [where the Army's equivalent planning staff worked].

Along with this, it was all under our guidance that the Amphibious Landing Schools at bases like Little Creek, Virginia and Solomons, Maryland were built up. This was a terrifically large undertaking, and all the planning and scheduling came from our headquarters in Norfolk.

All practice was performed in Chesapeake Bay. The fire support ships poured practice rounds into targets on Bloodsworth Island, and landings by small craft with troops were made all along the unpopulated area of the Maryland coast. After the troops would make landings, they'd be returned to their various Army posts. You have to remember that these were dead-green youngsters, and so were all the men running the ships and the landing craft.

Finally, in late October, the powers that be felt that the armada was ready, and we left the eastern seaboard. The general rendezvous bringing all the ships together north-east of Bermuda was accomplished smoothly.

> Hewitt's command, designated the Western Naval Task Force as soon as it put to sea, had deliberately left in several groups with staggered sailing dates so as not to draw attention to itself. The whole force rendezvoused on 28 October 1942, when it was well out into the Atlantic. With it had sailed most of the Amphibious Force, Atlantic Fleet staff.

Our headquarters ship was the USS *Augusta*, an old-fashioned heavy cruiser, and the troops were carried in transport ships confiscated from passenger lines, operating principally from Atlantic ports. The landing craft were hung on the sides of these transports, in place of their lifeboats.

After the United States Army got their first foothold on North African soil we returned to Norfolk, Virginia, to our Nansemond Hotel headquarters. The trip back across the Atlantic was something else! We went through a tremendous hurricane, and the *Augusta*, along with about twenty transports, had to stop in Bermuda and have heavy welding repairs over the entire ship.

Meanwhile the training bases in the Chesapeake were being swamped with trainees, and new bases were being opened. The original landing craft [like LCP(L)s] were being replaced with vehicle-carrying LCVPs, and LSTs, 328ft long, were arriving. All these ships, with their personnel, had to be run through our Amphibious Force, Atlantic Fleet training bases, which were becoming enormous. There had to be schools of navigation, crews to run the landing craft, mechanics to handle the engines, communications personnel to handle messages, underwater demolition teams to clear channels, fire control teams to land and direct fire support . . . Our Headquarters, which started with thirty-seven officers, was mushrooming into the thousands.

In February 1943 Hewitt was succeeded as commander of the Amphibious Force, Atlantic Fleet by Rear-Admiral Alan Kirk.

Our next assignment was the landing in the underbelly of Europe – going into Sicily in the Summer of 1943.

The Amphibious Force, Atlantic Fleet was again to form the basis of an armada sailing from the eastern seaboard, but this time it was only one of several American forces, the others assembling in North Africa. Kirk's force consisted of the ships which would carry the US 45th Infantry Division across the Atlantic.

Our Sicilian invasion was to originate from Oran [where Kirk's force paused for a few days before setting out for the CENT landing area], and our actual assault came in early July. The British landed to the east of us. The only real hardship we had was a Mediterranean storm during the day prior to our landing. The troops, as well as many of our sailors, were all sick.

The landings were very successful, except the Germans conducted an air raid on the beaches just before our paratroop planes were coming in for a drop, and we shot down a large number of our own planes filled with paratroopers. It was a tremendous loss of lives right in front of our eyes. But our amphibious landings were highly successful, and the beachheads were established. We were able to pull out and head back to Oran three days after the landings.

We were ordered back to the United States, but our ship, the USS *Ancon* [the first of the US Navy's dedicated headquarters ships], was held in the Mediterranean, so we came back aboard various other ships. I chose to return in a destroyer, which was fine. However, duty on a destroyer at sea isn't for a weak stomach, or anyone subject to seasickness!

Ninety days or so passed, and then we were once again called to foreign duty. This time our orders were to report to New York for further assignment. From there we proceeded to London, England, to begin the planning of the Normandy invasion, as our boss, Rear-Admiral Alan G Kirk, USN, had been put in charge of the Western Naval Task Force.

This new, and again largely-American Western Naval Task Force would be responsible for landing the US First Army at UTAH and OMAHA, while the largely-British Eastern Naval Task Force landed the British Second Army at GOLD, JUNO and SWORD.

We had our Headquarters at 19 Grosvenor Square, near the United States Embassy in downtown London. Our planning staff lived in the Mount Royal Hotel Apartments, in the nearby Marble Arch area. I was again working under Captain E A Mitchell, getting the operational data and the plans ready for the Normandy invasion. This put together the largest group of ships ever assembled in history, and everything – ships, equipment, food – all had to be put into place. We worked fifteen hours at least a day. Sundays we were allowed off.

Three months before D-Day we moved to Plymouth, and started dry runs and training exercises in the English Channel. It was fun, but very, very hectic. The Germans knew we were coming, but how, where and when were the most terrific secrets.

Eventually everything was set. Then came the storm, and General Eisenhower pushed the start back a day, to June 6. If that date would not have been sea ready, a long postponement would've occurred. On June 5 about midnight we were under way. The sea was still very choppy, and remember, all the men on the ships had been kept aboard and had experienced a full day and a half of waiting.

Our headquarters ship [the cruiser USS *Augusta*, familiar to many of the staff from their time in North Africa] came into position off OMAHA around 3.30am. Paratroops were landing ahead of us, and the Air Forces were dropping their loads on the coast defenses. Their bombing attacks in the UTAH area were reasonably successful, but at OMAHA they missed their objectives [having had to bomb blind through the clouds], and the German gun emplacements and obstacles on the beach weren't destroyed. So the initial landings at OMAHA were very, very bloody.

In the smoke and confusion, few messages about the situation were being sent back to the headquarters ships. On board the *Augusta*, Jim was ordered to go ashore and check the progress of the unloading.

I received orders from Captain Mitchell to go ashore and check to see what the Naval Beachmaster might need in the immediate future. I was to report back to Captain Mitchell and Rear-Admiral Kirk.

From the bridge of our command ship, the Duty Officer signalled a passing LCVP to come alongside and take an officer ashore. This was accomplished, and I was bound for the Normandy shore – a lone coxswain running the boat and myself.

I was really shocked. The landings were all messed up. As I neared the shoreline I saw men drowned, a beach full of dead and wounded, and troops going around obstacles in the water and then crawling along the sand to the cliffs just off the waterline.

I directed the coxswain running my LCVP to drop anchor before we touched bottom, and the last words I gave him before we dropped the ramp were 'Don't let the boat touch bottom, and keep your engine running at a good speed'. This he did, and I stepped into about 4ft of water and moved toward shore. We'd underestimated the number of underwater obstacles planted by the Germans, some with barbed wire and other fence wire around them. Bodies were floating everywhere, and men shouting and screaming.

Every half minute or so a spray of water would kick up and pass down the beach. This, I realized, was machine gun fire from atop the hills, spraying the beachhead. I watched the men ahead of me dive out flat and wait for the spray to pass by.

Words will never cover the bravery and guts of those men that went ashore at OMAHA and cleared the way inland. I know, because I was there with them, and I'll never forget.

Thank God for them.

At the other four landing areas the situation was less critical.
Dudley Roessler's was one of the first craft to arrive off JUNO.

I'd done my basic training at HMS *Collingwood*, the training establishment for ratings at Fareham. From there I'd progressed to the Combined Operations officers' course at HMS *Lochailort*, opened in August 1942 to supplement the output of young officers from HMS *King Alfred*.

We did everything at *Lochailort*, in the Western Highlands of Scotland, that was necessary to equip us to take a landing craft to sea and get her back again. All spaced out by hideous bouts of physical training twice daily. Those who survived were commissioned as Temporary Midshipmen, RNVR, or Temporary Sub-Lieutenants if they were over nineteen and a half years of age.

A certain percentage who'd done best in navigation were retained for service in major landing craft – that's to say, landing craft that proceeded under their own power and weren't lifted in davits. I was one of those. We then received extra astro-navigation, signalling and meteorology, because from then on we were going to be little units under our own power. After leaving *Lochailort* we also did aircraft recognition at Fort William.

The first LCT I joined after all these courses, which lasted a couple of months, was a Mk3, *LCT 419*. I was then a Temporary Midshipman, RNVR. With mauve tabs [on the uniform collar]. Midshipmen, RN had white tabs, but we had mauve to distinguish us. No one knew what these things were. Some people thought you were an engineer, because mauve was also their branch colour. If you stood waiting to ask the porter something on the station you found yourself collecting tickets!

Then I joined a new Mk5 – *LCT 2435*. Believe it or not that was later my brother's landing craft in the Arakan. Though I was only aboard her for a short time before I was whipped away again. I had no idea why, except that the whole thing was in a state of frantic flux – remember it was getting on for D-Day. The Mk5s were specially designed to be mass-produced in three sections in America. So you had a stern bit, a middle bit and a bow bit. You brought these across in merchant ships, pushed them over the side, then you sent a chap down to join them up with bolts and a spanner.

Mk1s and 2s there were only very few of. The Mk3s and 4s were mostly built by boilermakers and platemakers and the like. They were trying to keep the work out of Naval yards.

The Mk3 was the most popular – very strong, solid, no-nonsense. The Mk4 had a much lighter construction, because Rowland Baker[1] was told to make some landing craft which would get us across the Channel. Nobody said 'with eventual Far East capability', or anything like that. So there was always one breaking her back. But the Mk3 you could take anywhere, especially once the open tank deck was sealed with a canvas cover. I survived a typhoon in one in the Malacca Strait.

You mentioned that your brother preceded you to the Far East.

My brother Paul, yes. He was a year and ten months younger than me. He was out in the Arakan shortly after D-Day. Of course I lost all touch with him. In late 1943 I'd met him in Portsmouth when he was a rating. And the next time I met him was a year and a half later – he turned up when I arrived for the invasion of Malaya [which took place in September 1945]. He came marching through the door and I thought he was an Indian Naval officer! He was a brown as a nut, like this table! That was Paul.

The landing craft herself was just something you had to learn about. One of the courses we had before being let loose on one was how to flood the double bottom – what the flooding plans were, and how to distribute it to alter the trim. LCTs had enormous double bottoms. You could carry at least 350 tons of water ballast [349 tons in seven double bottom and fourteen wing tanks for an LCT Mk5; 445 tons in seventeen double bottom and fourteen wing tanks for an LCT Mk3, and 729 tons in eighteen double bottom and twelve wing tanks for an LCT Mk4]. Very handy. You wanted a lot of weight down aft to get the screws to bite; on the other hand you knew you were going to have to bottom on fairly shallow beaches, so you couldn't have too much. It was a bit of a black art. There was a standard plan to help you – you just flooded down to Plan A for passage, and so forth. And when you had a cargo on board, you pumped a bit out.

LSTs travelled 'heavy' and then pumped out prior to beaching. Did you do that?

No, we travelled and landed on the same trim. Personally I didn't do much tank landing. I think I only did it twice. The rest of the time we were working with a regiment of DD [Duplex Drive] amphibious tanks. This was aboard a Mk4, *LCT 707*.

I did six months with them in Southampton, training them for D-Day. Night after night we'd be casting off about 11.00pm, 12.00pm at night. Down the Solent, over to Osborne Bay, lower the ramp, and swim the tanks off. My job as the First Lieutenant was to say 'Go!', because you'd get the stern of the vessel upwind, lower your ramp; the waves would be going like this, up and down the ramp. The tank would position itself. There were marks on the

---

1. The outstanding designer responsible for most of the British amphibious warfare vessels. Later Sir Rowland Baker.

chain [supporting the ramp], and when the wave reached a certain height you had to say 'Go!', and he had to go then. If he held back the tank would drop sharply off the end, and it would engulf his canvas flotation screen. If he went too soon he'd become seaborne and crunch on our ramp as she came up, and probably tear it away, so it had to be quite finely judged. Quite a lot of responsibility for a young Midshipman like me.

A bit hair-raising for the tank crews, as well.

They were as mad as hatters. Canadians. I was given a ride ashore once by one of their subalterns. Wonderful blokes – do anything.

Of course, they didn't blow up the compressed air tubes [to raise the flotation screen around the tank] until they were about to launch, and then it shot up. Just like inflating a modern survival raft. Then as soon as the tracks began to bite on the bottom [the term Duplex Drive referred to the fact that the tanks used both a propeller and their normal tracks to move through the water] they'd collapse it again, because of course up until that point the man driving it couldn't see.

Actually, the man we lost most in accidents was the driver. He didn't have much chance. We lost two or three drivers, until they hit upon the idea of giving them Davis escape apparatus.

Like submarine crews?

Exactly. So the driver had a chance of getting out. When they lost one, a diver would go down and pull a wire rope out to the submerged tank, attach it to it, and they'd have another tank drag it bodily up onto the beach. It was something I didn't want to know too much about. Bad enough having to launch them.

What were conditions like aboard an LCT?

The small wardroom was only about as wide as this dining table is long, and about three times the other way. And that was two bunks, a thin table in between. Just like in a yacht, really. But it was literally just a steel box, so the top used to attract moisture. It'd been sprinkled with cork granules to minimise this condensation, but I still had to sleep with a raincoat over me all night – drip, drip, drip. You got very close to people. The two officers shared a collapsible basin for washing. The crew were all down aft in a dungeon-like mess deck. They had some primitive heads and a galley, all crammed into this little space in the after section. The rest was tank. A Mk4 could hold almost 300 tons of tanks [up to a maximum of nine Shermans, or six of the heavier Churchills], or 350 tons of stacked cargo.

When my CO was sent to Poole to train with LCTs converted to fire rockets, I said I wanted to go too. So we went to see our Flotilla Officer, and he said he'd do what he could. But by the time I arrived my own CO, Jacko, had already started the course. They paired you off on arrival – 'You're the CO, you're the Number One'. The COs were mostly Lieutenants, or senior Sub-Lieutenants.

I was promoted to Temporary Sub-Lieutenant, RNVR in April 1944. You couldn't become a Lieutenant until you were twenty-two. Then you got your second ring. I know I was put up for a second ring three times before I was twenty-two, but had to wait. I eventually made it when I was in the Far East.

Everybody thought that this new type of rocket craft – the Landing Craft, Tank (Rocket), or LCT(R) – was pretty hot stuff. In particular, its reputation from Salerno was such that the Army said they wanted rocket craft for Normandy, and that was that. I think for the morale of the invading troops, as much as anything. The chaps in these little LCAs were enormously cheered seeing these rockets going over their heads, and the entire beach disappearing under friendly explosions. However good your training, it's still very hard when you know that you're going to be the first man ashore. The fact that there may be another thousand following on behind you isn't really very relevant.

It was intensive training – we had to learn the theory and the construction of the rocket. Obviously you can't handle over a thousand 5in rockets without knowing something about them. Talk about the Health and Safety at Work Act! With a full load we had 1080 loaded and 1080 reloads; we had hand grenades in boxes, Very lights, pistol ammunition, rifle ammunition, boxes and boxes and *boxes* of Oerlikon ammunition, all stuck in the same tank space.

The rockets were in racks. You manhandled them into the launchers and slid them down in. The forecast was we were going to lose a lot of these craft, 50 per cent losses on D-Day, so we were told to carry just one load. Then if we survived we'd come back and they'd put Royal Marines on to take the donkey work off the crew, and we'd be rearmed and turned around in twelve hours. Each rocket had to be lowered down with a sort of hooked stick. You were watching all the time, in case it hit the bottom and came straight out at you again. One did! Landed in the Mayor of Southampton's garden, I think. The rockets themselves weighed 56lbs. Half of that was cordite propellant, which was deemed to be pretty safe, and half of it was high explosive. You had a fuze on the front, which when it accelerated would arm itself. But before that you had to pull out the locking pin, so off the coast of Normandy you had to lug each rocket back up again, with your hooked stick, and take this arming pin out, and lower it gently back down again.

Who got the job of doing that?

Oh, you had the whole crew on it. They were taught the seriousness of the job, because you could upset quite a lot of people if you blew your craft to bits. Sympathetic detonation of fourteen tons of warhead wasn't very good news. The racks were only actually full on D-Day itself. When we did our trials firing, from Poole, we fired just a few.

As I say, they were in banks. You couldn't fire this whole bank off, and then that whole bank, because you'd start doing this [rocking]. So you fired a representative number from all over the vessel. When you pressed the firing switches it connected them up.

So there was a set sequence actually built into the firing circuits?

All hard-wired, that's right.

And you flicked these firing switches manually from the bridge?

Oh no, the bridge was untenable when the rockets were going off. The firing procedure was to go down below, everybody except the CO and the signalman. The radar operator would be calling the range – LCT(R)s were the only landing craft fitted with radar from the outset. We had to range by radar, you see. That was part of our training. The rockets fired a fixed distance ahead of us, because all 1080 of them were set at 45 degrees to the deck. And the interesting thing was that the mutual efflux somehow caused them to move apart, so the fall of shot was much bigger than the LCT(R). So when your radar picked up the beach you had to calculate the mean point of range – perhaps you were trying to hit a gun emplacement 100yds inland, so you had to run on that distance – then add corrections for wind, corrections for temperature, and so on. All done at the last moment.

So where was your Action Station?

I would be down in the wheelhouse with the helmsman. Where we had our beautiful big gyro compass. As opposed to the 4in boat's compass up top. So the helmsman could judge it perfectly, because of course the only way of aiming was to aim the whole craft.

So I'd be in the wheelhouse watching the helmsman, and making sure the radar operator was getting the right ranges in. He'd start off in 100yd steps, and then down to 50yd steps, and then when he reached the appropriate one – we'd tell him which one to emphasise – he would sing out.

By that time the CO would've instructed the signalman to get below. He'd disappear and join us. That would leave only the CO up top. Since the bridge was untenable while the rockets were being fired, there was an armoured box built there, with a voice pipe down to the radar operator, so the CO could hear the radar operator's voice. The CO would duck in at the last minute and slam the hatch, and when the radar operator said 'Fire!', he'd close the master switch. Until the CO's master switch went over, he had the power to arrest the firing. The Navy does cling to this idea that the Captain's the only one who knows what's going on.

After that we just fired blind, for however long it took – thirty salvoes of thirty-six rockets each. About three minutes. During which time our speed would decrease steadily – we'd be slowed down from 6 knots to about 1 or 2, by the efflux from all the rockets blasting away. We reckoned on 5 per cent of the rockets not firing. I think on D-Day our particular count was fourteen misfires.

What did you do with the duds?

Well, everybody stayed below deck for half an hour anyway. Only the CO and the signalman were allowed back on the bridge. You stooged around for these thirty minutes to let the deck cool down, because it got red hot. We were fitted with a sprinkler system, but immediately after firing the deck was so hot that the sprinklers didn't manage to get water onto it – it turned to steam before it touched the metal. So when you look at these pictures [shows me photographs] you think 'Look at all that cordite smoke!', but it's not, it's steam! After the half hour was up, the law said you could go on deck and have a look, and after an hour you could remove the misfires and chuck them over the side. So after the appropriate time had elapsed I despatched the two blokes who'd volunteered – you know, 'You and you'.

And then, of course, there's a sudden feeling of emptiness. Wondering what the hell to do next. The instructions were to turn round and make for a position out of the way. I'll never forget turning round and looking back out to sea again, at this *mass* of ships. We retreated over to a corner of JUNO – we were on JUNO for the bombardment – and then we threaded our way back, so we were in the Beaulieu River that night.

I've since sailed there, again in the Summer, and it still amazes me how we got that big LCT(R) – 'flat bottomed cows', we called them – up there. And with two right-turning screws, as well. Because in order to get LCTs into mass production they'd given them two identical 500bhp Paxman Ricardo diesels, 12 cylinder jobs. That meant two right-turning screws, which made manoeuvring very difficult. When you started up, for example, there was an immediate kick out to starboard by the stern. Going astern it moved to port. At least with out-turning or in-turning screws you're balanced. Incidentally, all LCTs rolled like cows. LCT(R)s, with their very high profile, not only rolled badly but also made 3 to 4 knots broadside-on downwind if the engines were stopped. The engines themselves were pretty good, but they had to have a major service after every 1000 hours. Whoever heard of a marine engine having to be serviced every 1000 hours?

So we went back to Beaulieu, and maybe a day, or two days later we were sent down to Portsmouth to reload. I remember complaining to this Royal Navy Captain that I'd yet to see any evidence that the Germans existed. 'Oh, don't worry about that', he said, 'I was in the Great War. I was at sea the whole time, and I only ever saw the enemy for eleven seconds!'.

Mick Goldsmith was the turret gunner in an armoured engineer vehicle on D-Day. Having served in a General Construction Company, Royal Engineers, in France in 1940, the return to France brought back troubling memories of the evacuation from Dunkirk.

Now my return to France was aboard an LCT, as a turret gunner with the 80th Assault Squadron, RE. After the very costly landings at Dieppe the British had decided to form units of 'funnies' [armoured vehicles specially adapted for specific roles in an assault]. I was posted to one, and did my special training in Suffolk, on all the open ground at Orford. This was together with Sherman Crab flail tanks [adapted for minefield clearance] and Churchill Crocodiles [for flamethrowing].

Mick's own training was in the use of another Churchill adaptation – the Armoured Vehicle, Royal Engineers.

Never having been a very good shot, I was of course told by the Army that from then on I was to be an AVRE turret gunner . . . My job was to maintain and fire the Petard, which was a very large spigot mortar that could hurl a 40lb bomb at the target. Bit of a hit or miss weapon, the Petard, but it was very effective against pillboxes. I remember later on in the Normandy campaign very successfully demolishing a farmhouse that had Jerry machine guns on each side. The Regiment de la Chaudiere [an infantry battalion of French-speaking Canadians, from the 3rd Canadian Division] were so pleased that they gave us some bottles of calvados – the local apple brandy – they'd 'liberated'. You couldn't aim so well after a few Army mugs of that stuff!

How many were in your crew?

A normal Churchill fighting tank had a crew of five, but in an AVRE you had six – commander, wireless operator, gunner, demolition NCO, driver and co-driver. The drivers came from the Royal Armoured Corps, and all the rest were Royal Engineers.

The bombs for the Petard mortar, which were cylindrical and looked much like calor gas bottles, were primed by screwing in a tail fin. This was done by our demolition NCO, normally a Corporal or Lance Corporal, who sat beside the co-driver, with the bombs stacked as close to the co-driver's hatch as possible. The normal hinged hatch had been replaced by a sliding one. To load the Petard I, as the turret gunner, traversed the turret so that the Petard was immediately above the co-driver's hatch. I watched a couple of chalk marks that told me when it was just right. The demolition NCO then slid back the co-driver's hatch and, reaching up, heaved the bomb up into the barrel and prepared the Petard for firing.

Inside the vehicle was a long metal lever that had to be pushed down with force, to hurl the bomb at the target. As you can imagine, the closer we were to the target, the more likely we were to score a hit [80yds was regarded as the maximum accurate range]. Gunners who got one hit out of two were thought to be pretty good.

We all entered the vehicle by climbing down through the turret hatch. There were pannier doors on either side of a Churchill, but these were very awkward to get through, especially in a hurry, so were only used in an extreme emergency.

What was your gunner's position like?

The seat – round, leather-covered, only just bum-sized – could be moved up or down to suit your height. You looked through a periscope, using your hands to control the turret traverse – there was both manual and power traverse – and to fire the Petard, though very often a good clout with your boot was as good as anything for firing. Unorthodox, but for little blokes like me quite effective. I also used a foot pedal to fire the Besa machine gun. This we were a bit wary of, because if the gun was cocked it was quite possible when getting back into the turret to step on it and fire a burst by accident. Anyone in front of the vehicle would be killed – and this did happen.

So, in the turret were me, the commander and the wireless operator. In the driving compartment were the demolition NCO, the driver and the co-driver. I was also the second wireless operator. For D-Day we had to be 'netted in' both to our command tank and also the supporting 22nd Dragoons, with their Sherman flails.

A few weeks before the invasion we were sent down to Gosport with our AVREs to waterproof them, so that if need be they could land in about 6ft to 8ft of water. This was a sealed camp, guarded so that none of us could get out and spill the beans. Our unit – 80th Assault Squadron, RE – together with 26th Assault Squadron, RE was to lead the attack of the 3rd Canadian Division.

> Each Assault Squadron was organised into four Troops, and had a total of twenty-six AVREs. The 3rd Canadian Division intended to land two Brigades side by side, with 80th Assault Squadron assisting the one on the left, and 26th Assault Squadron the one on the right. The Division's other Brigade would land later.

As you'll know, we spent twenty-four hours in very rough weather waiting for it to be calm enough to make a successful landing. Aboard our LCT were two flail tanks – Shermans, to de-mine the beach – followed by four AVREs. Frankly we all felt the weather was worse on 6 June, not better, and we were all *terribly* sick on the way over. Our AVREs were chained down, and we were all too ill to be interested in anything except getting on dry land as soon as possible.

We actually mounted up and got ready about 2 or 3 miles from shore, as we knew we'd be in action directly the LCT beached, and that our lives depended very much on each other, however ill we felt. When we grounded the first flail got off and started up the beach OK, but as the second one commenced to land, the third vehicle – one of our AVREs with a bangalore torpedo on the turret; that's like a long drainage tube packed with explosive – took a direct hit from German artillery. The AVRE commander was killed, as was the commander of the flail in front of him, and many from both crews were wounded. The rest of us were badly shaken. I should've said that this was about 7.55am, and the bangalore torpedo was to clear barbed wire entanglements that we expected to meet.

Because of the damaged vehicles we were completely unable to get off the LCT, and as others were waiting to come in behind us, we had to pull out and return to England again.

That night we were allowed out to the local pubs to celebrate being alive. While we were waiting to board at Portsmouth we'd been issued with condoms, and as we were all anticipating that we might have to swim for it, we'd used these to wrap up our watches and the new French Francs that we'd also been issued. When we got to the pub and searched our battledress pockets for English money, the landlord, seeing the french letters, said 'I thought you went over there to *fight* the Germans!'.

As soon as the locals learned where we'd been we all had several pints lined up in front of us, but we never got to finish them, because our Pay Corporal came and said anyone who wanted a seventy-two hour pass should get back to barracks, so that's where we went.

On arriving home, my dear old mum said 'Thank the Lord you weren't in those *landings*, son . . . '.

The LCG(L)s, LCT(R)s and other existing support craft were to have been joined in Normandy by another new type – the Landing Craft, Gun (Medium), or LCG(M). However, when it became clear that none of the new craft would be ready in time, a stop-gap measure was adopted to increase the volume of direct fire.

Ordinary LCTs were taken in hand and fitted with a platform from which two Centaur tanks, sitting side by side, could engage targets with their 95mm guns. The initial idea was that these should be permanent fixtures, with gun crews provided by the Royal Marines, but when the tanks were subsequently allowed freedom of movement the Marines found themselves organising the first true armoured units in their history. Each Troop of tanks consisted of four Centaurs plus a Sherman for the Troop officer.

The less successful feature of the conversion was that it involved crudely bolting armour plate to the LCTs to make each one into a Landing Craft, Tank (Armoured).

Tom Sutton's new Mk5, *LCT 2233*, was transformed into *LCT(A) 2233* by this rather brutal process.

The armour plating was added about three weeks before D-Day, at a local shipyard in Southampton. The 0.5in thick plates were just bolted on. I have a recollection of the large bolts and packing, covered by red oxide paint.

I was anxious about the weight of the armour on the thin steel of the craft, and this was confirmed by us having to keep the pumps working all the time to keep the water level down.

At 7.30pm on 5 June we left the Beaulieu River and, with the Flotilla, set course as ordered. The weather was very bad, and the craft could only just make the necessary speed against the wind and sea. Our load was one Sherman and two Centaur tanks, and a contingent of Royal Marines. The after part of the tank hold continually had 6 to 12in of water in it, making life difficult for the Marines. A number of craft failed to keep pace with the leaks and didn't reach the landing beaches – they filled with water and overturned on our passage across the Channel.

We arrived off the beach [Green Beach, in the Jig Sector of the GOLD Landing Area] while the naval bombardment was still in progress, and from 6.30am to 7.00am our engines were only run at slow ahead. We aimed to land to the east of the village of Le Hamel, at a spot about 50yds to the left of the wreck of an old fishing boat.

It took two attempts before we bounced up the shallow beach at 7.15am, and it was a relief to see the two Centaurs trundle off and up the beach. The Sherman was unable to start its engine, so I made a third landing at 8.12am when it was ready to go.

What had been the problem during the first attempt?

The weight of the tanks plus the armour plating and the extra sea water in the hold meant that the craft was further down at the stern than planned, and the bows were too high in the water to allow the tanks to be offloaded.

Opposition was light, but about fifteen shells burst near us as we kedged off to make the second run-in, the nearest being about 10yds off the starboard bow.

We unloaded the Sherman tank in the third landing, but hit an underwater obstruction – luckily without an explosive device attached to it. The engines and generator stopped running, and she settled onto the sand.

> In the neighbouring landing area, JUNO, only half a dozen of the 2nd RM Armoured Support Regiment's forty tanks made it safely ashore.
>
> *Jim Tuff* commanded one of them.

When the war broke out I was in the cruiser HMS *Kent*, as personal servant to the C-in-C China Station, Admiral Sir Percy Noble. Then, after the *Kent* was torpedoed in the Med and came home for repairs, they sent me on a coxswains' course, and then to the River Medway on landing craft. Then I went down to Dover to the Royal Marine Siege Regiment, to help crew one of their cross-Channel guns, a 13.5in rail gun. I was there until November 1943, and then on 30 November I was sent down to Devizes to join the 2nd Royal Marine Armoured Support Regiment, where I was introduced to the Centaur tank.

So you see I'd been in the *Kent*. I'd been in landing craft. Then on cross-Channel guns. Now I was in tanks. That's the thing about Marines – we're such a versatile lot. As we used to say about the difference between us and the Guards, 'Not so big, but twice as smart!'.

> The Centaur was a variant of the British Army's new 27-ton Cromwell, but with a less successful engine because of shortages of the Meteor, the tank version of the legendary Rolls Royce Merlin used in the Spitfire and Lancaster. Ironically it was this trouble with their engines which had led to the Centaurs being selected in the first place.

Originally they weren't even going to drive these tanks. What they were going to do was put a ramp on the front of an LCT and put two of these tanks side by side, to fire over the bows during the run-in to the beach. And then come back. But then they decided, well, that was a complete waste, you know, of a landing craft. So they'd leave the [tank] engines in, and let them go ashore.

So down we went to Salisbury Plain, and had marvellous fun. One Sherman per Troop, for the officer, and four Centaurs. And although we had Army driver/mechanics, we all learned to drive and do the mechanical stuff, so if the driver was pranged one of us could take over. The driver was an Army bloke; otherwise they were all Marines.

I remember they even built a wooden turret on Salisbury Plain, and they'd bring us tank commanders up one at a time, to train us. They'd say 'There's a target. I want you to engage it'. And you'd have to work out the deflection and everything. I passed it, anyhow. We had a South African officer in our Troop, a South African Lieutenant. He was in the Sherman, and then we had a Sergeant in charge of each Centaur.

The boffins came up with some good ideas. Like these tins of soup with heating elements in the centre. In the middle of the night, sitting there on watch, you'd have hot soup in seconds. They were wonderful.

Sometimes their ideas weren't so good. For example, because you could only carry so much ammunition inside, they decided to attach a steel sledge to be towed behind each tank. It was a flat, steel sledge, just sliding along the ground. Attached to the tank by two massive chains. When you were on the ramp, on the LCT, it was slid underneath. And as you moved off the chains tightened and you pulled it after you. Sealed and waterproof, and packed with ammunition. So in Normandy we started off, dragging these things behind us. It was all right on the sand, but then we got on the road, and you should've seen the sparks! These things were absolutely *hot*! So we just took as much into the tank as we could, and then dumped them. We were only supposed to help form a beachhead, and then go home. But in fact we were there much longer than planned.

Had you practised getting the tank on and off landing craft before D-Day?

No, we just drove down to Southampton and parked in the streets. Every street was lined with tanks. It was a sealed area – the civilians and everybody were sealed in. You parked your tanks in the various streets, and then you were put into an encampment. We were in with some French Canadians from the 3rd Canadian Division, because we were going to be landing with them. We were all writing letters, though none of them were posted. They just held them, for security. So the families got them all in one batch.

So the first time you drove on board an LCT was for real?

That's right. There were landing craft *everywhere*. Six deep. You'd go down the hard [prepared ramp, usually concrete, leading down to the water's edge], load up, and the landing craft'd be off, to let another one in.

There was a mate of mine on another one about two quays along, and so I said to my officer could I go and visit this bloke. He came from Norfolk, same as me. I was born in a little village there – beautiful country, away in the wilds, with pheasants running everywhere. My father worked on the land as a teamster – two horses, ploughing. With a single-furrow plough, not a multi-furrow one like they have now. All agricultural work round about was done with horses. Anyway, my officer said he'd have to come with me, so I never did go. The security was *so* tight.

So we sat aboard there, and of course then the bad weather came, and we were held up. We didn't know much about it, actually. But eventually off we went. It was still *very* choppy. One of our LCT(A)s capsized before we even got past the Isle of Wight. A lot of them didn't make it.

If you wanted to get out of the weather you had to get in your tank – there was no troop accommodation. My South African officer went down below, and I remember him coming back on deck, absolutely green with seasickness. 'I'm coming up on deck, Colours', he said – I was a Colour Sergeant – 'It's terrible down there'. Stuffy and claustrophobic. He looked absolutely awful.

Did you fire your 95mm on the run-in?

Oh yes. Then we came in, and the LCT broached-to [slewed broadside-on to the incoming waves]. By the time our Centaur went off it was pointing back almost to England! We went right under. A couple of waves came right over us. We were all waterproofed, except the top hatch just above my head, so the water was running down my neck. And I was ordering the driver 'Drive left . . . drive left . . . drive left . . . !'. He said all he could see was seaweed.

Then the main thing was to get off the beach. Once you got off that beach you weren't too bad. We'd been shown photographs of what was where – that's a fortified house, over there's a pillbox, that sort of thing. They said 'But they won't be there, because with the Air Forces and the shelling from the warships, they'll probably all be obliterated'. Well, they were still there, all right.

Those Beachmasters were terrific. Naval officers, shouting their lungs out. The organisation was just absolutely unbelievable. The stuff they had to think of. That's why it succeeded. We surprised them, and all the stuff kept coming in – the kit, the troops.

There are some things I wish I could just wipe out from my memory. Friendly tanks ran over some of our own people, I know. Because you had to get off that beach. Get off the beach. Never mind anything else, get off the beach. That'd been drummed into us. They wanted to get this beachhead formed. That was the only thing that mattered. Get us off the beach so they could bring in more behind us. This time they were going to pile the stuff in. Pile the stuff in. Mulbery Harbour. Pile the stuff in. That's why it succeeded.

SEVEN

Piling the Stuff In: Build-up and Break-out in Normandy

Normandy was the closest landing yet to the borders of the Reich, and the Germans, despite harassment from the air and by the Resistance movements, could be expected to assemble a counterattack force with lethal swiftness. To ensure they won the build-up race, the Allies had meticulously prepared for this, the largest amphibious operation of the war.

They planned to have the equivalent of over eleven divisions ashore by the end of D-Day, thirteen by D+1 and seventeen by D+4, when it was expected the three airborne divisions could be relieved. Thereafter the totals, excluding the airborne, would rise to twenty-one divisions by D+12, twenty-six by D+20, thirty-one by D+35 and, as the flow of fresh units continued to tail off, thirty-nine by D+90.

Large numbers of escorts were required to protect the build-up convoys from E-boats and submarines as they criss-crossed the English Channel. *Peter James* was in one of the many ships taken off normal convoy work to help out.

We sailed from Harwich at 8.00am on 6 June, with a convoy of various landing craft and ships. I was a telegraphist in HMS *Clematis*, a 'Flower' class corvette.

We arrived off the French coast at midnight. We saw fires burning ashore, and could hear machine gun fire. Then a German plane flew among the ships, only 20ft above the sea, firing its guns at them. We anchored in the particular spot assigned to us, and next morning at daylight the landing craft went ashore.

During the forenoon a few shells landed on the beach, but the large battleship near us directed a couple of salvoes of heavy shells ashore, and nothing more exploded on the beach. Later on, a nearby LCT(R) fired a few salvoes of rockets ashore – very noisy. Later still three large troopships drifted with the tide along the coast towards us, no doubt so as not to set off any [free-floating] mines.

After anchoring off Arromanches for a couple of days we sailed back to Portsmouth with a convoy of coasters. Next evening we escorted another convoy to France. As it got dark, a convoy ahead was being attacked by E-boats. Starshells were exploding in the sky, and there was much gunfire.

At midnight we were sent to Action Stations, as the radar had picked up two or three E-boats, a few miles away. My anti-E-boat Action Station was just under the bridge, at the ammo hatch. We'd gone to the head of the convoy, where I was watching a tug towing a Phoenix caisson [one of the huge, hollow, reinforced concrete structures designed to be floated across the Channel and sunk as breakwaters].

Suddenly a small coaster exploded with a giant flash, then HMS *Fernie*, a 'Hunt' class destroyer, switched on a searchlight, lighting up two E-boats passing ahead, right to left. Then it was all action – *Fernie* firing her guns, us opening fire, 'snowflake' [fired for illumination at night, like starshells] being sent up. On our starboard side, which I couldn't see, the frigate HMS *Halsted* was firing. Minutes later there was an explosion on that side, which turned out to be the *Halsted* having her bows blown off, stern half still floating. We picked four men out of the water, but one died later, and we buried him at sea. On our return to Portsmouth with a gathering of LSTs and cargo ships we were told to trans-ship the three survivors to an LST, as we taking the cargo ships up to the Thames.

Our usual routine after that was to sail from Sheerness in the afternoon to Southend Pier, where the convoy would be gathering, and leave with it at 2.00am in the morning.

The only excitement after the E-boat action was when about ten shells were fired at us by the German heavy guns at Calais – no hits – and a flying bomb crashed into the sea half a mile astern. We saw hundreds of these V1 rockets streaking towards land, and the sky would be black with shell bursts from Deal to Dungeness.

By nightfall on 18 June – D+12 – over 629,000 troops, 95,000 vehicles and 218,000 tons of supplies had been put ashore in Normandy.

In addition to amphibious shipping, which of course could unload directly onto the beaches, an average of nine troop transports, twenty-six Liberty ships and thirty-five coasters were arriving off the beachhead every day.

Reg Edwards was Skipper of one of the LCTs kept busy unloading them.

She was one of the new Mk5s, and had come across the Atlantic in three parts, then been bolted together. Previously I'd been First Lieutenant of a Mk4, *LCT 883*, but this new American one, *LCT 2436*, was much easier to handle. The Mk5s were shorter than the British LCTs, but similar in construction. The section beneath the wheelhouse and bridge formed our living quarters, with just a steel partition dividing the officers' and crew's quarters. As an LCT we were completely independent, but the washing and laundry facilities were very spartan.

The bridge was open. This was where I conned her from. Voice pipes led down to the wheelhouse. Whenever you opened the flap on the voice pipe you could tell they were smoking, because it would puff out! 'Cut it out, Cox'n'. 'No, Sir, we're not smoking, Sir!'.

I was lucky to have in my crew a young sailor who in civilian life had been trained as a baker, so prior to Normandy I made sure he had all the necessary supplies so we could bake our own bread and pastries – much to the envy of the rest of the Flotilla.

Did your wife know what life in landing craft was like?

I kept her in the picture, yes. I remember once we'd gone up on the slips at Millbrook Hard so they could work on the hull. And of course it's a bit muddy up there. They put the crew in barracks for a few days. I had my wife down, so we were in a hotel. And I took her up there to let her come on board, to see what it was like.

Our Flotilla Officer, an RNVR Lieutenant-Commander who'd survived Dieppe, was up there with the Engineer Officer of the Flotilla, to look over the craft. And as he came up, climbing up the old ladder onto the jetty, smothered in mud and everything, you know, he said 'What are you doing here, Edwards?'. I said 'I've just come to see how things are going, Sir. This is my wife'. And of course he shook hands with her. When he saw me later on, he said 'You rotten so-and-so! There's me looking like a tramp!'.

What did she think of the LCT?

She said 'You don't *live* on these, do you?'. She was never under any illusions after that.

When we joined the 106th LCT Flotilla we were told by this Flotilla Officer that we should expect 70 per cent casualties on D-Day. But luckily it wasn't as bad as that. I mean, it was pretty bad, but it could've been a *lot* worse. Look at OMAHA. There the troops had to hit the beach and then it was steep cliffs, you know. And nobody'd told them an extra German division had moved into the area. They really were dead unlucky.

Our Flotilla was the first in at JUNO in the initial assault – I carried an AVRE with a great bridge thing sticking up, to lay over obstacles, and a flail tank, for clearing mines. Once we were there we stayed on the French side, and didn't come back to England. Quite a few of the flotillas on the shuttle run from England to France had been in Sicily and Italy. But the Mk4s had a tendency to break their backs if they dried out [were left stranded on the beach by a falling tide], so we were used for that.

So your job was to unload freighters, and so on?

Yes, that's right. Once you got alongside, as long as the fenders were out, you were OK. They'd let down scrambling nets, and the Army'd be down in no time. It was only when they had to unload things using their cranes and winches that you were alongside for a while. Once we'd got the initial troops and their vehicles ashore, then our loads after that were sometimes foodstuffs and ammunition, and sometimes more troops.

But the practice for this beforehand had been incessant. When we'd joined the 106th LCT Flotilla we'd exercised down the coast at Studland Bay, and in some of the later exercises they'd had live firing by the LCT(R)s – which also gave us experience of the fact that six or so rockets from each LCT(R) would fall short, in amongst us!

The Army used to use live ammunition too. To get us used to all that nonsense. Because a lot of us were very new, you know. Not all of us, of course. I mean, in our Flotilla we had a survivor from the *Edinburgh* [the cruiser HMS *Edinburgh*, sunk on her way home from North Russia in May 1942]. But it's fair to say there were only a couple that'd been in right from the start.

On D-Day we were supposed to land in front of the beach obstacles, but either they'd messed the time up, or we were late, because the tide was higher than we expected. So when we got there, instead of seeing the obstacles clear of the water, we only saw half of them – they were partially immersed by the tide. Of course our orders were to land the Army at all costs, so we ran over the lot. Two or three of our LCTs – there were twelve in a Flotilla – got ramp doors blown off. That didn't really matter, but if they got it in the engine room, that was that.

So, as I say, we stayed off the beachhead and did the work there while the Mk3s and Mk4s shuttled back and forth across the Channel. An Army Major used to come down to the beach practically every day, and if we were stuck there at all, as sometimes we had to be – if the tide was falling rapidly and it was taking a long time to unload the stuff – he'd come down and keep us informed about what was happening inland.

We used to come ashore and see these German prisoners lined up. A lot of them were fairly young, but they were still arrogant buggers even then. I remember one of the Skippers I knew, who shuttled back and forth to England, had to take a load of them back with him, to get them out of the way. He got them in the tank deck, and they complained that they wanted seats. So he said they could bloody well sit on the metal deck, you know. And the German officer then said haughtily that *he* didn't expect to sit on the deck. But this chap said the beauty of it was, on the way back it got a bit rough, and it was shipping it over. He said by the time they got to England these Germans were half-drowned and soaked to the skin, so they were a bit more subdued!

One of the other amusing things was that after the first few nights, when everybody opened up with their Oerlikons when the Luftwaffe came over, the order came out that landing craft and other small vessels berthed or anchored in the area of the beachhead were *not* to open fire on enemy planes. They were more or less saying we were more of a danger to ourselves than the enemy!

Then of course the Germans started up with these human torpedoes, and their E-boats and things. They were mostly kept at bay by the Trout Line [a defensive line of support craft formed every night at the eastern end of the beachhead], but once these attacks started they got the wonderful idea that the battleships like *Nelson* and *Rodney*, the big ships, which were anchored off the beachhead at nighttime, they'd got to be protected. So after a day of constantly beaching and coming off, and all that sort of business, at night we had to go and moor around these battleships, three deep. In other words, if they were torpedoed, we got it first. We thought well, that's bloody nice, isn't it?

And the fact that the Regular Navy didn't appreciate us made it even worse. The Regulars always regarded us as something to be looked down on, a tin can Navy.

These are some photos taken of me. I grew that [a beard] in Normandy. Quite a difference. I look a bit tired there, too.

You seem to have grown up quite a bit.

Yes. Well, I'd grown up enough in the Navy before, but that finally did it. When I went through *King Alfred*, and went and picked up my first landing craft as First Lieutenant, I went up with a chap from Kilmarnock called George Guthrie. I joined *LCT 883* at Paisley, and he joined *LCT 884*. We were great pals. We trained up there, working with DD tanks, and then we were separated. You see, you did either three or six months as a First Lieutenant, and then you got your own command. We thought we'd both get our own LCTs at the same time, but he went first, while we were at Oban. And it wasn't till about two months later, after I'd come down with the Flotilla to Portland and Weymouth, that I went on *my* Commanding Officer's course. You went up to Troon to do that. I met him once in Southampton prior to D-day, and had a quick chat, and then I went to Normandy.

One day one of the other craft that'd been doing the run from England to France came in, and the Skipper was somebody I'd met through George. And he semaphored over to me 'George Guthrie's missing'. I didn't know any more until I came back to England, and saw another chap I knew who knew George, and he asked if I knew he'd been killed on D+1. There'd been some garbled yarn that he'd been in collision with a battleship, during the invasion. But in fact what had happened was he'd beached his Mk3, *LCT 427*, in the GOLD Landing Area, just a little bit along from us, and they were absolutely blown to bits. They never recovered his body.

We were just young Subbies then. And when you're that age you don't really think about dying. Or if you do, you think it'll be quick, like poor old George, and don't think any more about it.

The Channel weather had been a concern right from the start. But in the early hours of D+13 a north easterly gale of unusual severity began to get up, causing mayhem in the packed anchorages.

D-Day should have been 5 June, but it was too rough then. And the great thing was, it was so providential that Eisenhower decided to go sooner rather than later, because a fortnight later and we'd have been beaching in the middle of the great gale.

George Spratley, in *LCT 2241*, he and I used to anchor together at night. One night I'd drop my anchor and he'd be hooked to me, next night he'd drop his anchor. Of course, the night the gale broke out it was my anchor down, wasn't it.

We used to nip down below for a couple of hours' sleep, and I'd no sooner got down below when the Quartermaster rushed down and said 'The anchor cable's parted!'.

So old George floated off, and I had to stooge around.

After a while a landing barge came and bashed alongside us. Of course, I shouted over 'Get that so-and-so thing out of it!'. But they called back 'Can we hook alongside, Sir? Our Coxswain's broken his leg!'. They only had a crew of four on board. So they hooked alongside, you see, and I said 'Well, you'd better get him aboard'. The poor devil must've been in dreadful agony, because the gale was blowing, and our fenders were *thumping* against this barge. But they got him on board. I'd nothing for him, you know; so the only thing we could do was try to hail one of the motor boats that were floating around. We tried to make him as comfortable as possible.

But the strain on these bollards, with my ropes around, holding on to this thing . . . It looked as though they were going to be torn out. It was dreadful. So I said to the crew 'It's no good. You'll have to cut her adrift'. So they cut her loose, and she floated away. Then this motor boat came along and, struggling again, we got this poor coxswain on board. He was still in agony, but at least this thing took him to a hospital ship, anchored off the beachhead. So that was fair enough.

But the gale went on and on, and we were just being tossed around. So I said to my First Lieutenant, 'Bugger this', I said, 'I'm going in on the beach. I've had enough'. It was getting to the evening by then. So we headed for the beach, which was absolutely littered, as far as the eye could see, with landing craft and stuff that'd been pushed on.

I saw a gap, and we hit the beach. Where we landed up, on our starboard side was this barge, so we put the crew back on board. And on the port side was an LCT(R), whose Skipper turned out to be Ken Dunnett, who I'd been at *King Alfred* with. He'd gone into rocket craft. I said to him 'Here, you want to learn to fire those things properly!'. So there we were.

Then the Beachmaster sent his messenger down to say 'Get that landing craft off the beach!'. And of course I sent a message back with the messenger saying that if he wanted it off, he could come and do it himself. Of course, he comes storming down. Bearded. RN bloke. 'Where's this cocky so-and-so telling me what to do?'. So I had to get the gin bottle out, and managed to pacify him. I sent my Coxswain along the beach to find another anchor – there were plenty of them, stuck on the sand. And that's how I got an anchor back. Otherwise I'd have been charged for its value! That's how it was in those days.

Of course for flat-bottomed craft like us the sea state was completely hopeless. The beaches were just closed for the three or four days. Luckily I was able to get off early, because this Beachmaster came down with an Army Scammell [recovery vehicle] and helped push me off.

I'd been out in a hurricane when I was on the lower deck, going up to Scapa and that, and I mean that's terrifying enough. But that gale we had was the worst for about twenty years.

Storms were nothing new to *Charles Wales*, a driver in the Royal Army Service Corps, either.

633rd Company, RASC was a wartime unit, formed as a GT – General Transport – Company using 3-ton Bedford lorries. But in January 1944 we were ordered to carry out an intensive six weeks of training on DUKWs. On arrival at the training area there was a gale blowing, with 10ft breakers on the beach. But to my amazement out to sea we went, 'shipping it green', as they say. It gave me a lot of confidence in the seakeeping qualities of the vehicles!

So when I first drove a DUKW out to sea myself I'd no qualms, having been driven by an instructor during that gale. The procedure was to halt at the water's edge, engage the propeller, select second gear, and then apply full throttle. She'd shudder at the first few breakers, then lift and perform just like a motor boat. At the top speed of 6mph you'd use a gallon of petrol a mile. We also had to learn Morse, semaphore, tying knots, handling ropes, and about tides, winds and of course maintenance.

From there we went for further training on the Isle of Wight, and then on to Ipswich in Suffolk, where we were camped in a compound and issued with brand new DUKWs, awaiting D-Day.

What were they like to drive?

I found them extremely nice – very steady on the road, similar to a coach. Though the 6ft of bonnet in front took a little getting used to, and the gearbox was non-synchromesh. Driving on a soft sand beach was strange at first, but you were able to lower the pressures on all six wheels with a lever in the cab. Six-wheel drive with low transfer engaged – this reduced the ratio of the gearbox by 50 per cent – gave good traction, but changing gear on sand was awkward, as momentum was quickly lost once you depressed the clutch. So you had to be very fast.

DUKWs, being American, were left-hand drive. The maintenance on them was very high. In fact I saw in a magazine recently about three DUKWs still being run as pleasure craft in America, and it said it took four to five hours of maintenance a day to keep them in peak condition.

How did you get to Normandy?

On board an LST. We arrived off the beaches on the evening of D-Day, but remained on board the LST overnight. And then on the morning of D+1 we went ashore. I, being the last on the LST, was first off. On approaching the shore there was a Beachmaster equipped with a bat in each hand, signalling us to a position ashore between the underwater obstacles and some wrecked landing craft. All our DUKWs had been preloaded with cargoes before leaving England – I had flamethrower liquid, stored in cylinders. We'd be carrying supplies ashore, and then six stretcher casualties each from the Casualty Clearing Stations back to an LST offshore. An LST could accommodate three DUKWs inside, bow to stern. After unloading the stretcher cases we would back out and go to a designated ship to load up again, and back to the shore with more supplies.

How did you know which ship to go to?

Each ship was numbered, with a large board on the bridge side, and the number was given to you by Beach Control. As time went by unloading became more refined. For instance Coles mobile cranes were used to unload us, instead of POWs.

The storm, when it came, badly disrupted the unloading effort. The only respite from the weather was afforded by the lines of blockships sunk off the beaches for just this purpose, and by the special prefabricated harbours, called Mulberries, now in place in the GOLD and OMAHA landing areas. Inside the British one, off Arromanches, the DUKWs were able to maintain a limited service.

The shoreline was protected by blockships and Phoenix caissons, so inside of this man-made reef the water was just very choppy, while outside 15ft seas were running.

We were able to operate every day except one.

The American Mulberry off St Laurent was less fortunate, being smashed by a combination of wave action and numerous collisions with helpless craft.

But as the weather moderated again, the handling of supplies settled back into its rhythm.

We operated from Jig Sector of GOLD for 80 per cent of the time. There was a wide concrete slope from the road down to the beach, and Beach Control was at the foot of this slope. A nearby field was used like a taxi rank. You had to park around the perimeter, and as vehicles were called for by Beach Control we all moved around the field like taxis. Here was a chance to top up with petrol from jerricans on the stern deck, or have a cigarette.

Ships to be unloaded provided a spring line from bow to stern, with a steel hook adjacent to the hatches. Coming alongside we would connect the hook to the DUKW, turn the steering wheel away from the ship's side and open the hand throttle[1] to a fast tick-over, so holding the vehicle hard against the ship. A jacob's ladder was provided to allow the Pioneer Corps men to descend into the DUKW to unload. Supplies were loaded by rope nets, but large shells like 5.5in were loaded loose in wooden trays.

Even in wartime, pranksters abound. There was a centrifugal pump driven from the propeller shaft, whose intake was about 6in from the bottom of the bilges, and whose outlet was on the port catwalk. A driver would open the seacocks and let water into the bilges. Provided the engine only ticked over

---

1. On the instrument panel beside the ignition switch. It could be used in preference to the accelerator either to start the engine or to set a sustained speed.

slowly it woudn't pump. While waiting to go alongside a ship he would spy another DUKW also waiting, and would slowly move along her starboard side, keeping his port side close to her. And as he drew level he'd press the accelerator to the floor. The pump would pick up, throwing a column of water over the occupants and soaking them to the skin.

So, when waiting to load you kept a good lookout for DUKWs closing up on your starboard side!

What was your daily routine?

Up at 4.00am. Wash, shave and breakfast. Start up at 5.00am, drive to the Pioneer Corps camp, collect the men to unload the ships. Drive to Beach Control, receive the number of a ship, deliver the men to her, wait for a load, and then back to shore with it.

This would continue all day until 10.00pm. Then we'd collect the men from the ships, deliver them to their camp, and finally back to our own camp. Refill with petrol, check oil and water, have supper, another wash and get to bed around midnight.

Did you use lights when you were driving in darkness?

We had masked headlamps and sidelamps fitted, but in Normandy we never used lights at all, no.

And how about meals during the day?

Meals during the day were taken by dropping off my spare driver at a cookhouse marquee on the road to the unloading area, so he could collect his meal while I drove on to unload. Passing the cookhouse again on the way back to the beach I'd pick him up and he'd eat his meal either in the 'taxi rank' or finish it off on the way to a ship. This would be repeated on another trip for myself.

Our camp was in a field inland about 3 or 4 miles. We dug slit trenches around the perimeter the same size as the hold of one of our vehicles, because while operating the DUKWs we didn't require the canvas covers over their holds, or the U-shaped steel supports. So we dug the supports into the ground over our slit trenches, and covered them over with the vehicles' canvas covers to keep out the dew and rain. Four men to a trench. The cab of the DUKW also had a removable canvas canopy, which was seldom used. If the rain was heavy it might be rigged, but it'd be removed from the vehicle again as soon as possible. In the centre of the field tree trunks were erected, to stand upright supported by wire stays, and these were covered over with camouflage netting to make a garage we could drive in and out of.

My best job on the beaches was when I was told to report to the Naval HQ ashore. Here I reported to the Naval officer in charge of entertainment. My job was to take a concert party to the warships offshore for a show, and of course return them. Two different ships each day; one in the morning and one in the afternoon. The food and accommodation were very good, and I was rather sad when I had to return to my Company!

As I say, we mostly worked off Arromanches. But at one time we moved further east, to Queen Sector at Lion-sur-Mer [in the SWORD landing area]. Working here was dangerous, because we were shelled constantly, with some casualties. Luckily our stay was short – about a week – and then it was back to Arromanches.

But while we were there I was alongside an old tramp steamer which was well out of the water, showing she was nearly unloaded, when some shelling started. Suddenly the DUKW reared up and the tide seemed to be rushing past at a terrific rate. I jumped into the driving seat and glanced at the coast, which was rapidly moving backwards. Then there was a bang as the ring welded to the DUKW for mooring parted, and we were sliding down the ship's side. I realised that the ship was under way. As we swung backwards under the counter stern I saw this giant propeller turning half in and half out of the water, with us heading towards it to be chopped up. Fortunately the starboard corner of the DUKW hit the rudder post and deflected us away from the ship and out of danger.

That, I felt, was very close to a nasty accident. No one called over from the ship to tell us that the anchor was up and they were under way. I don't think they liked the shelling!

Could you swim?

The answer, I'm afraid to say, is no. When we were informed we were to become a DUKW Company, our officer noted the names of the men unable to swim. Later, batches of men were taken to the local Swimming Baths for lessons. In alphabetical order.

After about three weeks I was sent for an advanced driver's course, more difficult than the previous six-week one. On returning, I enquired about the swimming lessons and was told they'd finished. So I said 'But I still can't swim'.

They told me to wear a lifejacket.

Despite the need for urgency, the planners had erred on the side of caution when it came to handling the big LSTs. Worried that they might break their backs if they dried out on the beaches, orders had been issued for them to remain offshore and to discharge their cargoes into smaller vessels – particularly the rectangular, self-propelled pontoons called Rhino ferries, two of which could empty an LST.

Unfortunately, as *Ken Smith* discovered, the Rhino proved to be a ponderous beast.

I served in the Royal Engineers for four and a half years, and after initial training I was sent to the 961st IWT [Inland Water Transport] Operating Company, RE. We were stationed at Southampton prior to D-Day, engaged in various duties at Southampton Docks and at Marchwood, on the other side of the river.

We first got involved with the Rhino at the building stage. After assembling them we trained with these craft for three months before D-Day, operating with HMS *Tasajera*, which was one of the original three oil tankers converted into LSTs. We then had six weeks on the Isle of Wight before we left to board an American landing ship for the journey to France. Our Rhino ferries were towed behind to the beaches, where we began unloading tanks, trucks and guns.

We started to operate on 6 June, but bad weather held us up, making it very hard to get the Rhino under the ramp of an LST without causing damage to ourselves or the LST's bow doors. We managed to get our first load ashore at Arromanches, and we later operated in the Courseulles area [of JUNO].

After a few days it was decided the Rhino ferries were too slow, so they were used as floating pontoons on the beach.

Thereafter, in an effort to reduce the backlog of unloading, the LSTs were allowed to beach and dry out, which proved perfectly safe.

Could you describe a Rhino?
A Rhino was made up of smaller pontoon sections, made of steel, and bolted together. At the aft end there were two large outboard motors, which were also used to steer the craft, by turning them left or right as required. At the bow end were two wooden ramps, lowered or raised by simple ratchet gears and wire cables, to allow the vehicles to get off. The Americans also used them – their crews came from the Seabees [CBs – the US Navy's Construction Battalions].

They were very cumbersome in bad weather. Which of course we had off the beaches on D-Day. The engines proved to be underpowered for what we were trying to move; not surprising when you think of the weight of the Rhino plus maybe forty loaded trucks or tanks, motorcycles and armoured cars.

When under way and going in to the beach we were under the orders of the Beachmasters, who told us which one to use. But owing to the underpowered engines we sometimes couldn't make the right beach!

In training we hadn't had this problem, as we always seemed to practise in good weather. Off the Normandy beaches, though, the weather wasn't very kind.

Stan Leech was one of those who landed from a Rhino ferry – the one method he had never practised during his Combined Operations career.

On 9 April 1942 I'd been posted from the Headquarters of the 54th (East Anglian) Division to B10 Beach Signals, for Combined Operations training up in Scotland. B10 Beach Signals was one of the units formed specifically to provide communications in the early stages of a landing. The Beachmaster is in a sense just about the most important officer in the early stages, and we were his servants.

Everything was strange to us, because although we were Army, this place in Ayrshire where we were posted was a Naval shore establishment, HMS *Dundonald*. I remember when we first arrived we were going out on the town in the evening, all togged up; we were going out the main gate, and whatever bell it was they were striking I can remember a Chief Petty Officer shouting at us 'YOU! YOU LOT IN KHAKI! STAND *STILL*!'. But then gradually you got to know how things worked – going on parade with the Royal Marines in the morning, all this kind of thing.

We did countless wet landings while we were there, and we had to learn the Navy codes and everything. We even spent a few days at sea aboard the cruiser HMS *Orion*, when she returned from America after having her stern blown off at Crete. We went out to her in an LCA, and the sailors on deck looked rather apprehensive, because they obviously thought they were going off on a landing job. But it was just an exercise, mainly to help us learn their communications procedures. So now I'm a member of the HMS *Orion* Association, which I consider quite an honour – I'm only the fourth soldier to belong to them.

The Orion *hoisted you out of the water on her davits?*

Yes, we were picked up and hoisted on board. There was quite a lot of interest in these strange creatures in khaki. We were given an area on a mess deck, and shown how to sling a hammock, but like most soldiers found we couldn't sleep. We'd brought with us our light safari beds – aluminium framed and weighing only a few pounds – so I spent my nights aboard sleeping in the torpedo repair shop, my bed at right angles to a torpedo, which was just right as a pillow. I think the authorities thought 'Daft Army', and left us alone.

We went out past Ailsa Craig and into the Irish Sea, where we went on speed and gunnery trials. And fired all our guns at different points, you know. And then we finished up with a mock raid on Troon.

She was a sister ship to the *Ajax* and *Achilles*, from the Battle of the River Plate [against the pocket battleship *Admiral Graf Spee*, in December 1939]. Beautiful ships. And very fast. Strangely enough, the *Orion* finished up in the breaker's yard at Troon, when she was sold in 1949.

So the job you were being trained for was Beach Signals.

That's right. The Beach Section I was in was B10. B9 was before us – I don't know if there were ever any numbers before B9. If there were, we never knew of them. B11, though, they came at the same time as us, were considered to be a better group than us. Possibly, I think, because they had a good officer. They eventually got rid of our officer, and we got a new one, who wasn't a tough *looking* character, but was a real tough soldier. Super bloke. We had a great regard for him.

But I think had we been considered the best by Combined Operations Headquarters, then we might've been sent to Dieppe instead of B11 . . .

B9 went to the North African landings. And we of course went to Normandy.

Was all your training done at Troon?

No, we also spent some time at Inveraray, further north. That was a Combined Training Centre, preparing Army units *and* the Navy crews who would carry them. Various battalions of infantry came for landing exercises. The Royal Navy training mainly involved teaching coxswains how to land the

Army in various types of landing craft – not always successfully. We soon learned that Loch Fyne had a very steep beach or no beach at all, and outside Inveraray it was reputed to be 60 fathoms deep, 50ft out.

I remember being aboard an LCA early one morning doing practice landings. It was about 4.30am, still quite dark, and our craft grounded on barbed wire and debris. The coxswain pulled astern with the ramp still down, with no beach and many fathoms beneath us. A few words were said.

One of the curses of a signalman's life was called an 18 Set, Transmitter and Receiver [a portable radio set, carried on the back and weighing 32lbs]. Surely one of the most unreliable pieces of equipment in the Army. If a wall was in the way you couldn't get a couple of hundred yards out of it.

We were sent on an exercise in groups of about five to climb Ben Vorlich, The Cobbler, Ben Lomond or, for the old and infirm – in other words, anyone over twenty-five – a smaller hill just outside Inveraray. My mountain was Ben Vorlich, and I remember getting to the top and seeing the most beautiful scenery. We transmitted over 17 miles, which must be some kind of record for an 18 Set. Of course, there'd be no Ben Vorlichs on the beach in Normandy, but it was a lovely day, and lovely to be young and fit.

The prelude to D-Day began on 10 May 1944, when we moved to our marshalling area, where we were effectively imprisoned for over three weeks. We all relaxed in different ways. We had one character, Batty by name and nature, who spent hours throwing axes at a target.

How did you get to Normandy, when the time came?

Aboard an American LST. And then came off on a Rhino ferry, with some Priests – 105mm self-propelled guns.

There'd been a Church service on the Sunday before D-Day, held by a Naval Padre. We were all tied up together, and we heard the service through loudhailers. That was on the Sunday night.

Where were you tied up?

Gosport. Then it was marvellous going across, because the battleship HMS *Warspite* was lying off, maybe 3 or 4 miles, and as she was firing her broadsides, the flames from the big 15in guns were rolling over the sea, you know. It was quite an awesome sight.

Looking back on Normandy, the impression which remains is how *interesting* everything was, not how frightening. I'm no braver or more cowardly than anyone else, but I was so caught up in the excitement of it all. Everything was new.

B10 Beach Signals consisted of an officer and thirty-six of us. Six groups of operators, each group being a Corporal and three operators. That's twenty-four. Then there were six DRs [despatch riders]; that's thirty. Two cooks; thirty-two. Two electricians; thirty-four. And the Lance Sergeant, Sergeant and officer. That was B10 Beach Signals.

There was an advance party of three operating groups. The rest of us made up the main party, so they were well established when we got ashore.

Did everyone in B10 make it across safely?

Yes. One chap lost both his upper and lower dentures being seasick on the way over. He had a completely new set by D+5, better than his old ones. You may remember Winston complaining about things like Army Dental Corps units being landed so early. Thank goodness they were – Jim would've had a hard time with Army biscuits otherwise!

Where did you have orders to report to?

The Beachmaster's office. We knew that would be our focal point, you see.

Everything was *so* crowded. All the lateral roads and the approach roads were jammed with traffic. And there was an instruction from the Beachmaster that all unnecessary traffic was to keep off the roads, so that people could reach their objectives. So the first thing we did was dig in our radio sets. That was our first job on D-Day.

And then on D-Day evening – of course it was coming up to Midsummer, so it was light for quite a time – there was such a commotion. Everything started firing; people got their Stens out, and rifles, and everything. And two Junkers Ju88 bombers came over. They could only have been 40 or 50ft up, and both of them were on fire. The nearest one to me, I could see the pilot as clearly as I'm seeing you. And they swept over our heads, hit the sea and blew up.

Later the same evening there was another British glider landing [to bring in more of the 6th Airborne Division], and as they were coming back we saw a Stirling [four-engined British bomber, being used as a glider tug] had been hit.

It's a frightening sight, to see a big aircraft burning, you know, in the sky. And of course the whole little bay at Lion-sur-Mer and Ouistreham was absolutely packed with craft waiting to get in to SWORD, or lying off. And this Stirling, even though it was burning badly, was still manoeuvring so that it didn't hit anything . . . Then when it hit the sea there was an almighty explosion. You suddenly realised you were in a war then.

It's strange how detached you can remain. When you see a body in the water, you don't associate it with a human being; that it could've been you. I think there's some mechanism in us that helps. I'm certain that happens.

Previous to going to Normandy I'd been offered promotion if I went to B13. But I said to my officer 'Well, I've been with B10 since the beginning; I want to stay with you lot'. So he said that was all right. Well, the fellow who went in my place, he got a back full of shrapnel, and lost a leg. Their signal office took a direct hit. I think there were eighteen or nineteen killed and badly wounded.

I always thought be a good soldier, yes. But be a *lucky* soldier.

Our landing area, SWORD, used to get shelled every day. Mainly they were after the dumps on the beach, and the DUKWs coming in. But, of course, you couldn't worry about that *all* the time.

Like their British counterparts, many of the American units flooding into the beachhead had spent a long time preparing for combat.

National Guardsman *David Robertson*'s journey to Normandy had started in February.

In February 1944 the equipment was turned in, and we loaded onto a train and made a five day journey to Camp Kilmer.

Camp Kilmer, New Jersey, with a capacity of over 37,500 troops, was the largest of the staging areas serving the New York Port of Embarkation.

Here concluding arrangements for overseas shipment were carried out; shot records were brought up to date, all clothing and individual equipment was either combat ready or was replaced. Mail was censored and personnel were restricted to camp, except that one half were authorized to go off post every night provided they were back by midnight.

One morning I noticed one of the men off by himself quietly weeping, with no signs of stopping. A discreet enquiry to one of the Sergeants revealed that the young man's grandmother had just passed away. I took it on myself to try and console the young soldier, only to learn that his mother had died before he ever knew her, his grandmother had been the only mother he'd ever known, and he wanted to be at her funeral more than anything in the world. The regulations concerning this were very strict. In the event of the death of a spouse, an actual parent, or a child, the individual concerned would be transferred to a Replacement Company where leave would be granted, but he would never see his regular unit again. This was a real dilemma. If we prevailed on the authorities to give the man compassionate leave, we'd lose him from the Battery. Neither he nor I wanted that. It just wasn't fair. The Battalion had been stooging around Camp Kilmer for three weeks, and it looked as if it would be three more weeks before anything happened.

First Sergeant Ralph Miller and I came up with a solution. The soldier would surreptitiously leave the post, attend the funeral, and return as quickly as he could. To protect him from meandering Military Police, Sergeant Miller had some phoney leave orders counterfeited and given to him. He would give us a telephone number where he could be reached. If at any time while he was absent the unit was alerted [to move] he'd be telephoned to return at once. If he failed to return he'd be reported as a deserter.

The young man agreed, then plaintively said 'But I haven't any money for a railroad ticket'. Since I was in it up to my ears already, I fished out my last fifty dollars and gave them to him with the admonition that I was to get them back.

By dark he was gone. Thirty-six hours later he was back. This entire operation was known only to the soldier, Sergeant Miller, a few companions of the man, and myself. Several pay days later the young man returned the fifty dollars and then stated 'Thank you very much for everything you did'. It was never mentioned again. To this day I don't know if anyone really knew what happened. Sergeant Miller and I never talked about it. Captain Robert Strupp had done the same thing for his Chief of Detail several weeks earlier, but that was under somewhat different circumstances. Strupp's client was a Staff Sergeant, the Battalion wasn't in a staging area waiting for movement to a Port of Embarkation, and the Sergeant had his own money.

The long-awaited announcement of embarkation finally came, and one evening just at dark the Battalion loaded onto a train at Camp Kilmer. We were barely settled in our seats before we unloaded again from the train, onto the cinders between the tracks, and started hiking. We walked for ever, it seemed; loaded down with virtually everything we owned. Eventually we came to a ferry slip and were crowded onto a large ferry boat which promptly tooted her whistle and shoved off into the dark. When the ferry docked, we were herded off onto a concrete pier, in one door of a shed and out another, and then assembled alongside the biggest damn ship I'd ever seen. This was the moment of truth. A big military band was playing; troops were everywhere; officious little men carrying clipboards and wearing Transportation Corps armbands were darting from place to place. The ship was the Cunard White Star liner *Mauretania*.

The Batteries were lined up; the Sergeants in charge of boarding shouted out a last name, you replied with a first name, middle initial and serial number, and up the gangplank you went. As each man climbed up the gangplank one of the Red Cross ladies hung a small ditty bag with a drawstring top somewhere on his body or on his equipment. Believe me, with all the junk we were carrying there weren't any free hands to grab anything. At the top of the gangplank, ship's crew members led each string of troops into the bowels of the ship along passageways, through doors and down ladders, ending up in a compartment with a designation such as F4 or G2. The decks were lettered A through whatever, and compartments on each deck had a number.

The troop compartments were big open bays with a few tables and stools for messing. The troops slept in hammocks or on pads laid out on the table tops, while the officers were quartered in the cabins, two to ten in each cabin depending on the size.

Two meals were served each day. The officers ate in the passenger dining room, fully attended by ship's stewards. The food was terrible. The troops ate from their messkits in their compartments. Their food was terrible too.

The only rewarding things on this voyage were that it was the first time at sea for most of us, and the crossing was short.

The ship docked at Liverpool, we loaded onto railroad cars, and shriek shriek, we were on our way to Wimborne Minster, a small town in Dorset. European engines didn't have low pitched whistles as did American locomotives, but shrill screams like a Pekinese in agony.

For six weeks or so we stayed at this location, billeted in requisitioned houses, drawing all of our equipment from handkerchiefs to M4 Medium Tractors – which towed the guns and each carried eleven men and thirty rounds or so of ammunition, as well as all the guns' ancillary equipment. We also learned to drink warm English beer, and to drive on the left side of the road.

In April 1944 we motor marched north to Salisbury Plain, erected a pup tent camp, and made ready for combat. On one of our many exercises at this time, the Battery was making a night displacement and I was riding in the far right side of the fourth tractor. It was warm in the tractor, I was in my usual state of near exhaustion, and I'd unintentionally fallen asleep. I suddenly woke up to see the tail light on the muzzle end of the gun ahead of us looming larger and larger, and heading straight toward me. My immediate thought was that we'd stopped and the tractor and gun ahead of us were rolling backward, so I blindly leapt out of the tractor into the ditch. Luckily I wasn't hurt. What had actually happened was that the gun ahead of us had stopped, and the driver of my vehicle was slowly closing the gaps between the Sections when I awoke. Later I learned that the same set of circumstances had created the same fright in others on night marches. So far as I know, I was the only one to bail out into the ditch.

When D-Day came we were, in true 119th Field Artillery Group tradition, having an inspection in ranks by our beloved Group commander. But it wasn't too many days later that we got our orders, which were swift and direct: motor march to Southampton, move into the holding camp, and prepare for loading.

Arriving at Southampton, we found that the entire parade of units to be loaded onto landing craft was stalled in a column of vehicles many miles long. A terrible storm in the English Channel had suspended cross-Channel traffic, resulting in this long backup of military units. The authorities at the staging areas set up kitchens to feed the incoming troops along the route into the camps. We were stalled on the street in one place for almost thirty-six hours, which under normal circumstances would've meant four or five meals. Not our men. Since these kitchens were serving continuously, our troops ate continuously. Some of them must've eaten every two or three hours the entire time we waited. Eventually things started moving, and we were moved into the camp to await embarkation.

I'm not sure about the rest of the Battalion, but Battery 'B' – my Battery – had two guns and two tractors, the kitchen truck and trailer, the Battery Executive's truck and various other vehicles loaded onto a British LCT, while the remainder of the Battery was loaded onto an LST. The Battalion Headquarters was on a Greek Liberty ship, and the rest of the Battalion I just don't know. Once loaded, we all settled down for a long nap and hopefully a safe crossing of the English Channel.

When loading vehicles onto an LCT the vehicles and trailers must be backed in, as it's virtually impossible to turn around once inside, and all loading and unloading is done through the bow end. The ramp into the LCT involves going up a steep incline, over a hump, then down onto the deck of the vessel. Our training to perform this maneuver consisted of practices with concrete mock-up landing craft and their ramps. The drivers had no great difficulty mastering the skills to load the wheeled vehicles and their trailers. The guns and tractors were a different story; it was just impossible for a driver to back this combination onto the landing craft. The dilemma was solved, following a recommendation from one of the tractor drivers, by attaching a pintle to the *front* end of the tractor. 'Pintle' is the military term for the hook on a vehicle for towing a trailer or gun. The eye on the trailer or gun is called a 'lunette'.

This was all well and good until the night we loaded onto the landing craft, when a somewhat dim-witted one star [Brigadier] General interceded when he saw one of our guns being pushed up the ramp rather than following the conventional method of backing on. He threw a fit, and brought the entire loading to a stop. There didn't seem to be any way to counteract his interfering until some Transportation Corps Second Lieutenant told the General in no uncertain terms 'Go away and leave these people alone. They know what they're doing and you don't'. Bizarre as it may sound, the General departed and we never saw him again.

The crossing was safe and uneventful. Never having practiced a beach landing, we didn't know anything about water depth, incoming tide, outgoing tide, and the like. The day was June 24; the time was early afternoon; the weather was clear and warm. In short everything looked perfect. Ships were unloading. DUKWs were swimming ashore with their loads. Troops and vehicles were moving over the beach, up the bluffs, and away into inland France.

Our LCT stopped, the ramp was lowered, and the ships's officers indicated that we were to get off. I asked how deep the water was, and one of the officers poked a long stick over the side and said '3 ft'. Four jeeps belonging to the US 9th Infantry Division, in the bow end of the LCT, were to lead the drive through the surf and onto the beach. The drivers started their engines, roared down the ramp, and disappeared into an underwater bomb crater. The water was 10ft deep in front of the ramp.

The hapless men were fished out of the water, the LCT backed up, shifted to the side and went in for another try. The lead tractor, towing its gun, went down the ramp and promptly drowned out as soon as it hit the water. There we were, a dead tractor hanging out the front end, with a gun inside the landing craft firmly attached to it. What we didn't realize was that the tide was incoming, and the longer we spent unloading, the deeper the water.

A solution was suggested by the driver of the other tractor, the one that was still in the LCT. He proposed that he uncouple from his gun, connect to the tail end of the stuck gun and tractor, and pull them back into the landing craft. This was done. Then the functional tractor made a trip to the beach, towing his gun ashore; then two round trips through the surf to tow the other gun, and lastly the dead tractor. The other vehicles made dry land with no further trouble.

Too late, I realized that the LCT crew had done a job on us by not going hard aground, letting us drive onto dry ground, and then letting the incoming tide float the then lightened craft off the beach. When I explained this bit of news to the gun crewmen, one of them said 'Don't take it too hard, Lieutenant, we're even – we took all their rations and spare blankets ashore with us'. Believe me, the troops had gotten into the LCT's lockers and put everything that was loose into our vehicles. It wasn't a real coup in any case; the rations were British, typically kidney stew and the like, and the blankets were scratchy.

That night we occupied a position, got the guns laid and the ammunition unloaded, and were ready for bear. The Battalion Headquarters had gotten lost somewhere, so our Battery commander organized a provisional Battalion

Fire Direction Center and established communications with our new Group. The next day the Battery fired the first of many rounds in anger, and the war was on in earnest. Our new Group was the 228th.

The entry into combat was indeed thrilling. Nightly the sky was criss-crossed with tracers from automatic weapons, as the Luftwaffe flew overhead to bomb Allied units.

One of the problems affecting all military units in combat is the ability to determine who's an enemy and who's friendly. To make sure our ground troops wouldn't fire at them, all the Allied tactical aircraft had three white stripes painted around each wing. These were called 'invasion stripes', and remained on all the planes until the end of the war. The Allied vehicles and equipment on the ground weren't camouflage painted, as we would've preferred, but were left a solid olive drab color. The reason was that the Germans used pattern painting, and we didn't trust our own air arm to make a proper identification before firing at a target.

Back in the States, training the gun crews, the commands to the crews had been shouted out by the Battery Executive Officer in a very rigidly structured sequence. This was all well and good for training, when the guns were emplaced 15yds apart and there wasn't any interrupting noise such as the adjacent battery firing, low-flying aircraft, moving vehicles, et cetera. However, in combat the guns were anywhere from 30 to 50yds apart and there was lots and lots of noise. Furthermore, firing anywhere from 20 to 100 missions a day would totally destroy the Executive's voice in short order. To overcome these difficulties, a telephone wire was run from Executive Post to Gun Section in a continuous loop. This would permit the Executive, using a telephone, to issue the commands to the Section Chiefs in a normal speaking voice. That is, as normal as military commands ever get. Military personnel have a tendency to converse like gorillas discussing the banana crop failure.

The firing commands were computed in the Battalion Fire Direction Center – FDC – and telephoned to the Battery Recorder, who entered them on a recording sheet. The Executive was in telephone contact with the Section Chiefs; the Recorder was in telephone contact with the FDC. To get the commands to the gun crews the Executive read the commands from the recording sheet and transmitted them to the Section Chiefs, who in turn passed them on to the gun crews.

One thing we learned, and learned fast, was to sleep whenever and wherever we could, because there might be stretches of twenty-four to thirty-six hours of continuously standing at the piece ready to fire at a moment's notice. There were lots and lots of times when we all suffered from sleep starvation, to the extent that simple, normal undertakings could be done only with extreme concentration. I well remember that one morning, pulling on my socks and boots, I was *convinced* I'd lost a sock. I normally wore two pairs of socks with the boots. The next time I pulled them off, I found that I had three socks on one foot.

The Allied forces, prior to crossing the Channel, were quite concerned with the possibility that the Germans might use chemical weapons against us.

Everyone was real nervous about this threat. Then one night it happened; the gas alarm was sounded. Obviously this was no drill, since you don't fool around with things like that in combat. When any unit heard the gas alarm it immediately sounded *its* alarm, and soon the entire area, perhaps even the entire First Army, was in masks.

My problem was that I couldn't breathe when I put on my mask. Apparently the chemicals in the canister had gotten soaked with salt water during the beach landing and had solidified, so I was unable to pass any air through the filters. The signal for All Clear in a gas attack was to take off your mask so the others could see you breathe without it. I thought this was a genuine gas attack. I couldn't breathe with my mask on; if I took it off, others would follow suit and there would be more casualties than just me. So I cut the hose free from the canister, stuck the loose end in my shirt front and faked it.

A few minutes later, when I realized I wasn't dead, it became apparent that the gas attack was a false alarm.

> Although the Germans were still managing to contain the beachhead, the Allied build-up was fast outpacing them.
>
> Two further army headquarters – those of the US Third Army and the First Canadian Army – had been brought in to prepare for the coming breakout, which was to be initiated by the Americans.

As the US forces slowly pushed inland, we would make small displacements so as to provide deep artillery fire. Our 155mm guns were primarily counterbattery weapons, so were used most of the time against German artillery positions.

One day, shortly before the US breakout at St Lo, the Group's Protestant Chaplain came to conduct communion services at the Battery. Since the men couldn't leave the guns, the Chaplain agreed to lead a short service at each gun pit in addition to the general service for the other personnel in the Battery. The Chaplain, a good member of a fundamentalist faith, but away from his Church and any restraining influence, decided to conduct the communion with wine instead of grape juice. But, totally unenlightened on the subject of alcoholic beverages, was serving a shot of good French brandy along with the bread.

At the first Gun Section most of the men participated in the service. At the second Gun Section he got that Section plus some from the previous Section, and several men from other parts of the Battery. At the third Section his congregation was even larger. At the fourth and last Section he must've had 100 celebrants. When he left the Battery, his comment was 'It's certainly gratifying to know that there are so many serious, devoted Christian soldiers in this unit'.

Keeping the Battery resupplied with water, rations, ammunition and gasoline was a never-ending task. Every day trucks were dispatched to the supply dumps to be filled with what'd been used the day before, and sometimes additional stuff was picked up because resupply the next day might

British infantry practise an assault using LCAs. (Imperial War Museum: H20025)

LCA production at the Harris Lebus furniture factory in North London, one of many such sites. (Imperial War Museum: A9836)

British-manned LCI(L)s en route to the invasion of Sicily, July 1943. (Imperial War Museum: NA4028)

A DUKW, Sicily 1943. (Imperial War Museum: NA4798)

LSTs and a pontoon causeway, Sicily 1943. A Bofors gun is in the foreground. (Imperial War Museum: NA4378)

An LCT(R) firing her rockets. Note the clouds of steam from the deck cooling system. (Imperial War Museum: A27943)

(Left to right) An LST, an LCI and a merchantman high and dry on one of the Normandy beaches. The White Ensign of a Naval beach party is in the foreground. (Imperial War Museum: A24012)

Mulberry 'B' harbour, Normandy 1944. Floating roadways connect the Spud pierheads to the shore. On the right are the rectangular Phoenix caissons of the inner breakwater. (Imperial War Museum: C4626)

An LCG(M) sinking off Walcheren, 1945. (Imperial War Museum: A26236)

be impossible. Water and gasoline came forward in 5-gallon cans which looked almost exactly alike. The gasoline can had a screw top, to which a flexible nozzle was attached for pouring the gasoline into the vehicle fuel tanks. The water cans had a large flip top and no nozzle.

Occasionally some of the local farmers would provide us with eggs. One morning I was frying a pair of these wonderful French oeufs when I was called to the telephone. Sergeant Kerber volunteered to take over the cooking while I was engaged. The conversation finished, the telephone was put back into its case, and there were my beautifully fried eggs . . . adorned with the most dreaded lunch meat of all time – Spam. Kerber thought he was doing me a favor, when actually he came closer to losing his life than ever before or later.

Another of the culinary treats of these times was french-fried potatoes. The fields were literally alive with potato plants, and all we had to do was scrounge enough fat, while our mundane kitchen prepared their usual distasteful, dehydrated spuds.

When the Germans were driven out of St Lo, the race across France began. It wasn't unusual to have displacements of 25 to 50 miles, and eventually there was a displacement of over 100 miles. It was move, shoot, move, shoot and move again for several weeks.

When the Battalion moved it was customary that an advance party went ahead to find gun positions, in the case of a displacement to a new firing position, or to select a suitable bivouac area. When going to a new position, the advance party usually consisted of the Battery commander, an NCO from each Gun Section, the Executive or Assistant Executive, a small wire-laying crew, and the Battery Survey Party. On the occupation of a position, the NCO from each Gun Section would stake out the line of fire for his gun, and dig the spade holes. Then, when the guns arrived, this NCO would signal his tractor driver and lead the gun to the position. This procedure saved many minutes of precious time, and simplified what could be a terribly confusing operation.

When the 228th Field Artillery Group was moving, little paper arrows, 3x8in in size, were stapled or tacked to fence posts, trees, and the like along the route to be followed.

Our Battalion commander, having read an article somewhere pertaining to leadership, decided it would be best that the officers eat out of messkits as did the troops, and that we always eat last to ensure that all the troops would be fed. Now, this is all well and good in theory. It didn't bother me to eat out of a messkit, but it was rather irksome waiting for the last-ass straggler to chow down before I could eat. This was particularly bothersome when we were having our meals during lulls in the firing, or at other weird and inopportune times. I've often wondered if this ordeal was practiced at Battalion Headquarters, or was just an imposition on the poor dumb Firing Battery officers.

One of the more unpleasant, but not hazardous, duties to be performed was the censoring of outgoing mail. The rule was that letters written by the soldiers would be censored by one of the unit's officers. If the soldier wanted to say something he didn't want read by one of his own officers, he could mail the letter with the words 'Base Censor' written on the envelope. All of the officers' mail was handled by the base censors. In a Battery such as I was in there were only three officers, and one of them was generally at the Observation Post, so that left two of us to struggle through the mail. The rules were pretty simple. No precise place names – 'somewhere in France' was all right. No reports on combat actions until they were at least a week old. No casualty reporting until after the family had been officially notified. No codes and ciphers, or secret messages. The officer acting as censor couldn't mention anything he read in any of the letters. If there was any offending material in a letter, the writer could either rewrite the whole thing, or else the censor could cut or blot it out. The letters were deposited, unsealed, in the Battery mailbox, and then the reading started. After a month of this I was so thoroughly fed up reading 'How much I miss you . . . how much I love you . . . how hot it is . . . how cold it is . . . what we ate for breakfast . . . what we ate for dinner . . . what we ate for supper', and on and on, that I didn't want to write home myself.

Occasionally someone would write something really enlightening, really funny, or just original, but in keeping with the rules it couldn't be mentioned. One fine young soldier's wife had their first baby during this period, and I was able to gather from his letters to her that she'd chosen the names 'Malcum Duglas'. I *so* wanted to tell him 'I think it's wonderful that you have a son, but don't penalize the kid the rest of his life with this atrocious spelling. Please tell your wife it should be Malcolm Douglas!'.

One night about 10.00 or 11.00pm we heard an awful roar heading straight for us. My first impression was that it was a V1 – we'd seen and heard quite a few of them going over. Then I realized that it was something else. It had landing lights on, and was heading straight toward the Battery. The angle of approach was very slight, and the object's altitude was low enough to hit a tall tree, causing it to flip over and crash 150 yards in front of the guns.

Sergeant Gwisdala took a patrol out to the site of the crash, returning within an hour to report that it was a British Halifax [four-engined] bomber, apparently trying to do a wheels-down landing. Only two crew members were aboard at the time of the crash, and both had been killed.

Tactical air power had been an important factor in previous invasions, but in Normandy the ground troops enjoyed an unprecedented degree of support from the strategic bomber forces as well.

RAF Bomber Command and the US Eighth Air Force, with their long-range heavy bombers, normally fought their own war, quite distinct from the one being waged by the other services. But from April to September 1944 these two fiercely independent forces were used in direct support of the Normandy invasion and breakout.

Charles Sleigh joined a front line squadron in Bomber Command during the preparations for D-Day – 463 Squadron, Royal Australian Air Force.

The posting came through telling us to report to RAF Waddington, just outside of Lincoln. This was a pre-war station, so we were billeted in barrack blocks. None of your Nissen huts and pot-bellied stoves. The table service in the mess was very nice, and the bar excellent.

We expected to get straight onto ops, but not just yet. Instead we had a few more cross-countries and other exercises, which took another week or so. I told Liz, one of our WAAF drivers, that I felt like an impostor; here were all these aircrew types we were rubbing shoulders with going on ops every night, and us not yet 'baptised'.

Of course, eventually we were put on Battle Orders, as they say, and had to report for briefing. All the crews assembled in the briefing room at the appointed time, and all stood up when the CO entered the room. A large covered map of Europe was on the wall. The CO then started to address us, and on saying the target's name removed the cover to show the location. Tonight it was a German Army base at Mailly le Camp, in France. The Germans had thousands of troops there, with tanks, lorries and workshops.

As we taxied around the perimeter to the main runway, the WAAFs, airmen and others were there waving us off and wishing us good luck.

Off we went, thundering down the runway and away into the night. All of a sudden it seemed lonely and quiet, apart from the droning of the engines.

It was 3 May 1944, and a clear moonlit night – so clear, in fact, the moon cast shadows of the trees and hedgerows below. We arrived at the target at 00.05am, only to find there was a mess-up and the Master Bomber couldn't contact the other aircraft. We were ordered to orbit 8 miles north of the target. This created complete chaos, with dozens of aircraft flying round in circles. While all this was going on, Cheshire [Wing Commander Leonard Cheshire, Marker Leader for the raid] was going down to ground level ensuring the TIs [Target Indicators – brightly coloured pyrotechnics dropped by the marker aircraft for the main force to bomb on] were within the target area, minimising the risk of harming any French people. We were carrying a bomb load of 10,000lbs – one 4000lb 'cookie' and twelve 500lb high explosives.

We were ordered back to the target at 00.13am, and bombed at 6750ft, which is low for a Lancaster. Minute by minute, Mac the rear gunner was reporting to the navigator 'Aircraft going down on the port quarter' . . . 'Aircraft going down dead astern, Nav' . . . At each report the navigator would enter it in his log. These reports were so numerous that Frank, the navigator, asked us not to bother any more as he maintained they were special shells the Germans were sending up to try and demoralise us by looking like aircraft going down in flames. In actual fact they had no such things. It was incredible to see so many aircraft go down. As I watched, I thought 'God, I've got another twenty-nine of these to do'. The 8 minutes we were orbiting north of the target gave all the night fighters in that part of France time to get airborne, and they had a field day; we lost forty-two aircraft that night.

> 16 Mosquito and 346 Lancaster bombers took part in the raid, and 42 of the latter fell victim to flak or fighters. One of the other Australian squadrons, 460 from Binbrook, lost five of its seventeen Lancasters.
>
> Such loss rates were by no means unusual. Few crews made it through a full tour of thirty operational missions unscathed.

One naturally doesn't remember all the trips done in a tour, but there are some that stand out more than others. One, for instance, was Prouville. This was a flying bomb launch site. 'Just inside of France. Piece of cake', they told us. As we approached it we could see scores of searchlights sweeping the skies, and when we got nearer we could see aircraft being caught in their beams. Instantly a dozen to twenty more would latch on; we would see the bomber diving, twisting and turning trying to get free, then all of a sudden a line of tracer would streak across and the plane would either blow up or go down in flames.

Our turn came just as we were coming in on our bombing run, where we had to keep straight and level. Inside the plane it was like daylight, and all of a sudden I heard the sound of gunfire. I switched on my intercom and asked Mac if he'd opened up with his four Brownings in the rear – 'You're goddamn right!'. So I joined in the firing, up and down, round and round. Eventually I heard Bob, the bomb aimer, say 'Bombs gone!' and then scramble up into the nose turret to join Mac and me firing, as now we'd started twisting, diving and turning. We just couldn't get clear, until eventually we outflew them.

We did about half a dozen daylight trips in the tour, and I remember the first one and the last one in particular, as the same tragic thing happened on each occasion over the target area. A Lancaster released its bombs and cut the Lanc below clean in half. On the first occasion the front half went down as though in slow motion, turning in a clockwise way, while the rear portion went down changing direction and finishing as though it were a small aircraft, with the rear turret becoming the 'nose'. I watched it go down for as long as I dared, and I didn't see even one of the crew get out. Not one.

> The same day that Charles flew his final mission, Tuesday 15 August 1944, the US Seventh Army[2] was landed in the south eastern corner of France.

---

2. Now under a new commander, Patton having been given the chance to redeem himself in Normandy.

This additional landing was originally to have been conducted at the same time as the one in Normandy, but there proved to be too few amphibious vessels left in the Mediterranean for this to be practical.

By the time some of the shipping used in the cross-Channel invasion had been redeployed, the breakout was already in full swing. The new landing, which was also supported by many of the same bombardment ships which had seen action off Normandy, thus proved with hindsight to be superfluous, although it did serve to complete the German rout.

The initial landing force consisted of the US 3rd, 36th and 45th Infantry Divisions, part of the French 1st Armoured Division and French, American and Canadian Commandos. The equivalent of an airborne division, largely American but also containing a British contingent, was dropped behind the beaches.

In common with all fighting units, the assault divisions required a constant flow of trained replacements if they were to maintain their efficiency. *Hubert Ranger* was one such replacement, sent ashore in the wake of the 3rd Infantry Division.

How did I come to be in the Army? Well, I was a University student studying Chemistry, hoping for a career in Photographic Technology. At the end of my second year the Draft Board of my home town – Fairfield, Maine – sent me a postcard saying simply my classification had been changed, and I was now available for conscription. My choice was to volunteer, or to wait until I was in the middle of my course and suddenly be called up, so I decided to volunteer then. This was the beginning of my education on how the induction system worked.

The new recruit was first processed through an Induction Station, where he was assessed to see whether he was physically and mentally acceptable. Unless rejected at this stage he then passed on to a Reception Center where he was assessed again, this time to determine which branch of the Army – and consequently which Replacement Training Center, or RTC – he was destined for. The matching of recruits to jobs was hardly a scientific process, as Hubert discovered.

At the Reception Center at Fort Devens, Massachusetts I was interviewed by a non-commissioned officer who attempted to identify any special skills individuals had that might be of use to the Army. He learned that I played the trumpet, so he classified me as a potential bugler.

It was then decided to send me, along with a couple of hundred others, to Fort McClellan, Alabama for basic training. When I arrived at Fort McClellan I learned the Army no longer needed buglers, but the Personnel Officer offered to give me a choice of the Training Battalions they had at the post. I said I'd like to stay with the group I arrived with, since we'd become friends. That was acceptable, and I spent seventeen weeks [the standard training period; prior to the Summer of 1943 it had been thirteen] at the Infantry Replacement Training Center at Fort McClellan.

The RTCs sent groups of men where they were most needed at any given moment. The first group from my Company was sent to England, and became replacements for men lost in the Channel crossing of June 6, 1944. My group was directed to a troopship leaving Newport News, Virginia for Africa, where we were to become replacements, as needed, for whatever was developing there and in Italy. We sailed directly and unescorted from Newport News to Algiers, on a new troopship called the *General M C Meigs*, just after her trials, and with a Coast Guard, not a Navy crew. After a couple of other stops we finally landed in Naples, Italy.

The replacement system in the US Army was different from the British system. Up until we replacements were assigned to a specific unit we weren't really a part of anything. The US system assured a continuing supply of men who were trained at least in some degree, but they lacked the esprit de corps of the British system of assigning men to well known and proud regiments from the start.

Both systems had their strengths and weaknesses. The disadvantage of the British system was its inflexibility, and urgent necessity sometimes meant replacements from the 'wrong' regiment being accepted by a depleted unit. The US system was highly flexible, but left many of its men feeling like interchangeable components in a vast and soulless machine.

Hubert found himself in one of the replacement companies of the 2nd Replacement Depot, which was preparing to make good any losses suffered by the Seventh Army. Each of the assaulting divisions was to be followed ashore by a 600-strong replacement company to meet its immediate needs – the 379th Replacement Company in the case of the 3rd Infantry Division, the 380th Replacement Company for the 36th Infantry Division and the 381st Replacement Company for the 45th Infantry Division.

The US 3rd Infantry Division landed at the head of the St Tropez peninsula. We were close behind them.

The invasion of Southern France was and was not a piece of cake, depending on exactly where someone was at the time, and what happened to them. The weather was with us, the invaders. The broad view intelligence was complete. We had clear low altitude aerial photos, maps and descriptions of the whole coastline.

Fortunately, most of the defenders were unprepared and rapidly surrendered or retreated.

The weather was so gorgeous that by the afternoon of D-Day – August 15, 1944 – some of us were swimming in the warm waters of the Gulf of St Tropez. Others were trying to root out strongholds of resistance, and a few were killed or wounded in the process.

Another story was told by a paratrooper, who said the aircrew of one of the Dakotas signalled their planeload to jump while still over the ocean. This resulted in the loss of his Company Headquarters group, including the Company commander, First Sergeant and Communications Sergeant. He said he was dropped from another plane while the plane was above some clouds and while it was still dark. They were supposed to be below the clouds, so he thought they were water and started unbuckling his chute. Expecting to hit water, he instead passed through the layer of cloud with only one buckle still holding his chute on. He eventually landed on the ground unhurt, but never found any members of his Company until a day or two later, and then only about half of them. He was one of the lucky ones.

The invasion was overkill in other respects. Not a coastal building was untouched by naval gunfire.

Our group were there to replace the anticipated casualties the Division didn't experience in the landing. What they *did* experience was a flood of prisoners, who knew they were cannon fodder and wanted no part of it. The casualty replacements, such as my Company, became prison camp guards, and it was November or December before we could be relieved for combat.

We were guarding prisoners out of all proportion to our strength, but they wouldn't have tried to escape even if we'd insisted. The war was over for them, and they, at least, saw a chance of surviving it.

The fact is, we got so many prisoners after D-Day that no one knew at first what to do with them. Since the Germans had had the foresight to blow up the docks along the coast, supplies came in on freighters and were offloaded by cargo net onto DUKW amphibious trucks. These came up onto the easily-approached sandy beaches and the cargoes, still in their nets, were lifted onto the beach or into fields just inland by the A-cranes on the backs of some of the DUKWs. This is where the prisoners became useful. We had them sort out and stack the cargoes, which were mostly in wooden crates, according to the color on the corner of each crate – green for rations, red for ammunition, orange for medical supplies.

It was amazing how quickly the prisoners learned the color coding for quartermaster supplies, and dropped selected cases to split them open. We sometimes divided the loose cigarette and candy bar rations with them, and then told them to cut it out and get back to stacking cases by color code.

The follow-up forces consisted entirely of French divisions, which were given the task of clearing Toulon and Marseilles while the Americans pushed north to link up with the units fanning out from Normandy.

An American concession to the French was to allow their Army to take the major cities. As a result these hadn't witnessed the presence of much of the American Army, and when we did our initial explorations of them just to see what was there, little knots of people would gather around us. Their joy at liberation seemed to be exceeded only by their joy at the regeneration of a source of cigarettes.

There were some unnecessary tragedies during the invasion. I saw people hacking at high explosive shells with a bayonet, or a pick. The curious GIs were hungry for souvenirs, and the FFI – French Forces of the Interior – civilians from the Underground were hungry for weapons. I rescued three FFI men who'd tried to salvage German machine guns from a field that was mined. They set off a mine and were wounded.

I got them out and in the process set off another mine, and ended up in hospitals in Southern France for some weeks. I wasn't badly hurt, and thus had a lot of time to learn about what was happening in the area.

By the time I was well enough to be released the unit that needed replacements the most was the US 79th Infantry Division, so I joined them as a radio operator for Company 'A' of the 315th Infantry Regiment. By March 24, 1945 we were crossing the Rhine as part of the new US Ninth Army, which was under the British Field Marshal Sir Bernard Montgomery [in his capacity as commander of the Twenty-First Army Group. At the time of the Rhine crossing this consisted of the First Canadian Army on the left, the British Second Army in the centre and the US Ninth Army on the right]. We crossed at 3.00am in small boats, and were one of the northernmost American units at that time, the British being on our left, facing east. I was supposed to be in the first boat across since I was carrying the radio, but due to the usual mix-ups in combat I arrived in the second boat by a matter of minutes.

A particularly poignant part of the war was my experiences liberating slave labor camps in the Ruhr Valley. I talked with many of the inmates, and since I could speak German and French I learned a great deal.

I stayed with the 315th Infantry until the end of the war in Europe, eventually ending up in Czechoslovakia.

EIGHT

Seaward Flank: The Mulberry Harbours

One of the unique features of the Normandy operation was its use of the prefabricated Mulberry harbours, which had sprung from the concerns voiced early in the planning that such a large build-up could not be sustained over open beaches alone.

Events were to prove this an overly-pessimistic view, but the British in particular were not prepared to take that chance, and embarked on the task of designing and building both harbours – Mulberry 'A' for their American allies, and Mulberry 'B' for themselves.

Each consisted of an outer floating breakwater anchored to the seabed, then an inner breakwater of blockships and concrete Phoenix caissons, and finally the floating piers and pierheads.

One of the engineers overseeing the construction of the pier-head units was *Tom Coughtrie,* whose association with heavy industry had begun in his formative years. Forced to leave the Lanarkshire Steel Company steelworks because of ill-health, Tom quickly found himself in demand by the Government, as an inspector.

So how were you introduced to the Mulberry harbour project?

I was asked to a meeting one morning, at which plans of something new and secret were handed out. I wasn't a gaffer at that time, so I didn't get a set – only my new boss. I was going off to Dundee to do some transformer tests when the call came over the tannoy to report to his office. It was a great big room, but I couldn't get the door open because the whole of the floor was carpeted in these drawings! He couldn't make any sense of them.

It took me some time, too, walking round on top of these things. And then I suddenly realised that I'd actually seen one – the prototype, in fact. Some time before, my friend Bob Hynd had taken me to Napier & Miller's old yard on the Clyde, which had been pressed back into service again. Napier & Miller had gone out of business, because they'd built two ships for the British India trade and they'd turned out to draw too much water for the Suez Canal. So the yard closed, and was lying derelict until Alexander Findlay & Company took it over during the war.

Findlays weren't shipbuilders?

Oh no. Bridge builders. From my home town of Motherwell. But now, of course, they'd been made main contractor for the Mulberry pierhead units.

And that was what the strange structure I'd seen on their slipway had been – the prototype pierhead.

The design was derived from a dredger built by Lobnitz & Company in Renfrew. This Lobnitz dredger, fitted with a leg at each corner, had survived a storm off the Bahamas which had wrecked practically everything else. So the pierhead units were similar – 200ft long, 60ft broad and 11ft deep, with four independently-movable legs called 'spuds', each 89ft tall and 4ft by 4ft square, with big feet on the bottom to grip the seabed. The intention wasn't to lift the body clear of the water on these legs, just to allow it to rise and fall with the tide, securely anchored in place by them.

Three sites around the country were selected for pierhead fabrication yards. One, at Conwy, was in North Wales. The other two fell within Tom's area.

The two sites for pierhead construction I was concerned with were at Newhaven, on the east coast of Scotland near Edinburgh, and at Cairnryan, on the west coast just north of Stranraer. A third site, at Faslane, was where the pierheads would be 'spudded', or have their legs fitted. Newhaven was run by Findlays and had a civilian workforce, but the other two were in the hands of the Army.

Designated Military Port No 1 and Military Port No 2, Faslane and Cairnryan had in fact been built to replace cargo-handling capacity lost elsewhere. All the jobs of a normal port – stevedores, crane drivers, railwaymen – were done by Army personnel.

Time was desperately short. Every existing shipyard was working to the limit to replace the ships being lost to U-boats. There was no more skilled labour available; since the pierheads were welded, the shortage of welders was particularly bad. Yet the timetable allowed only eight weeks to equip the building yards at Newhaven and Cairnryan, and prepare the extra facilities at Faslane. And while the prototype had taken nearly four months to build, the building time for each pierhead was soon supposed to be four *weeks*.

Most of them were built at Newhaven, where there were four slipways. Cairnryan had only two [as had Conwy]. I think Newhaven built thirteen and Cairnryan four. Newhaven was also given orders for sixteen pontoons [to support the floating roadways which would link the pierheads to the shore]. Work went on seven days a week, though the power to the Newhaven yard was once cut off because of over-demand. You should've heard the language! The cranes at Newhaven were just old semi-derelict derricks, and they'd to handle not only the unloading of sub-assemblies arriving from all over the country, but also suspending the large prefabricated sections in mid-air while they were welded into place. Each pierhead was built parallel to the shore, ready to be launched sideways.

Inside, the pierheads were divided up into a succession of squarish compartments, each entered from the deck above through a rather small manhole with a tight cover. The area where the crew had to sleep – accommodation was provided for one officer, six NCOs and fifteen men – was criss-crossed by steel angle irons as stiffening, so to lie down a crew member had to slide his body under these things, which wasn't very popular.

Where cables passed through bulkheads they had to be glanded to preserve the watertight integrity, and these had to be rigorously inspected. They had a machine which forced the compound in with compressed air.

A lot of work down in the bowels of each unit had to be done using rather poor temporary lighting. The areas inside each compartment were masses of wires, cables and air hoses, and the atmosphere was choked with fumes from welding rods and acetylene torches, and the smoke from lamps.

Our first production pierhead was launched on 26 January 1944, with me on board. In fact I was on *every* pierhead unit at her launch. At my first launch I didn't stay on deck like all the other silly monkeys did; I went up on one of the bridges. They were all absolutely soaked!

As the output at Newhaven rose the units had to be launched as soon as the hulls were complete, and before the electrical and other work was finished. It was decided that this would be finished off by other electricians at Faslane, supervised by charge hands who could be spared from Newhaven. So that meant even more travelling for me, and I was now working seven days a week. The pierheads had to be towed right up and round the north of Scotland to get to Faslane, where they'd be 'spudded' and finished off.

The blokes at Cairnryan were getting contentious about never having any time off, because we were doing launches late at night, or whenever – to catch the tide, you see.

There was nowhere to take them in Cairnryan, but just up the coast was a beautiful wee village called Ballantrae. So we borrowed a vehicle, and we went to the bar in a small hotel there. Tragically there was no whisky to be had from the little white-haired old lady behind the bar, but during the course of the evening, which we spent talking about Scottish history, she gradually moved her chair up nearer and nearer to us. And when we went back a few weeks later, and I was telling the story of Robert the Bruce and the War of Independence against the English [1306 to 1328], she magically produced a bottle of Laphroaig. At first she took down only one glass for me as storyteller, but then she laughed and took down glasses for the others as well. And then of course it was story after story. The blokes couldn't wait for my next visit!

So that was our only entertainment. But it was enough. They were good men. They had a lot of difficulties – for example, they were paid by postal drafts, which were made out to the Postmaster in Glasgow. The small Sub Post Office in Cairnryan claimed they didn't have the authority to cash them, and passed the buck to Stranraer, which also refused them. So I scrawled across each one 'Pay at Stranraer. Signed, Michael Moose'. Nobody in the Post Office queried that they were signed by Mickey Mouse! The bureaucratic mind!

As the launches continued, the Army personnel at Cairnryan were gradually posted away to other jobs. In fact they so reduced the Army workforce that when it came to their last pierhead it was questioned that there'd be sufficient manpower left to do it. So they sent in some civilian workmen. Well, I was there, and to my certain knowledge the Army men wouldn't let the civilians lay a paw on her. She was *theirs*. And they wanted to finish her.

99 per cent of the time people – civilian and military – were doing a very good job. The only really obstructive ones were those right at the top. Towards the last of the pierheads I got a new boss, whose contribution was to constantly return reports so that a bit here or a bit there could be expressed a different way. But the people doing the work took a pride in their job. They were under enormous pressure, and had every opportunity to skimp, but I never came across one instance of that. And they finished the job in time for the Summer of 1944.

I think when you grasp the magnitude of it . . . They built two harbours, bigger than Dover, and took them with them. The sheer imagination of it. The beauty of it. The cleverness of it. Beyond measure.

And the secrecy was terrific. It really was. Only later did I discover that my fellow apprentice from before the war Jock Maxwell had been working on the blockships to be taken down and sunk as initial breakwaters. I'd seen him frequently, but I'd never told him what I was doing, and he'd never told me.

All the labour expended on the Mulberry harbours would have been wasted, however, had they been positioned incorrectly.

RNVR officer *Aubrey Waters* was one of those working to prevent avoidable errors off the beaches.

The Mulberry harbours took a lot of work to design and build, but the question was 'Where do we put them?'. That was the next thing. Where to position them. And when they *were* put into position, it had to be in exactly the right depth of water. Too deep and the hollow Phoenix units of the breakwaters would be drowned – the waves would just break straight over them, especially in bad weather, when the wave heights would be greater.

That's where we came in.

In 1943 I volunteered for a navigation course up in Scotland, and I did this course, which I enjoyed very much, at Tighnabruaich. I'd always been interested in navigation – it was *my* subject, really – and on completion of the course I was approached. They were looking for eight RNVR officers to form the new 712th LCP(SY) Flotilla, under the command of Lieutenant Frank Berncastle, a Regular RN hydrographic surveyor. I think I was one of the first to be recruited.

So from there on we started specialist training in Southampton Water, and the Solent. Where it was quiet, inside the booms. No enemy craft to interfere with us. Firstly in the daytime, because hydrographic surveying's a very specialised art, and none of us newcomers had any experience of it at all. We were good navigators, and we could handle the boats and all that, but hydrographic surveying was a bit different. So we practised in the daytime, surveying various small areas of the Solent – West Solent mainly – and then moved on to training in the dark.

Where was the Flotilla based?

At Warsash, on the Hamble River. A base called HMS *Tormentor.*

And what sort of craft were you using?

A Landing Craft, Personnel (Survey), or LCP(SY). An American LCP(L) – Landing Craft, Personnel (Large), like this [shows me a splendid waterline model] – but specially equipped. Crew of one officer and six men for survey work. Wooden hull. As we were concerned with pin-point navigation it was actually an advantage not to have too much metal close to our compasses, so a wooden hull was ideal. Wonderful seaboats, and very low in the water, as you can see from this model. The German radar almost always failed to detect us. Half the time the wave height was higher than the boat – we were hiding in the trough, so to speak. Very difficult to pick up. And we were doing our work at night, of course. Single petrol engine. The early American ones had Chrysler engines, but ours had Hall-Scotts.

Did you always work with the same crew?

Usually the same crewmen, yes.

And what was the special equipment you mentioned?

Well, the boats were specially fitted with an echo sounder, and taut wire measuring gear. Are you familiar with that? No? Well, taut wire measuring gear had a drum – it's not fitted on this model here – with 9 miles of piano wire on it, very thin wire. A cast iron sinker was tied on to the end of the wire, and dropped overboard. As the wire ran out it was measured, in feet, on a gauge inside here [the cockpit of the LCP(SY)]. You let it run for 100ft or so, little bit more, and then you started to measure from there. And that would give you a very accurate measurement of the distance you'd run. The depth was recorded on paper by the echo sounding gear, and every 100ft the taut wire operator would press a button to record that distance on the echo sounder trace. So then you had a line – a compass bearing line – with depths every 100ft along it.

Of course it's all very well to say 'Right, there's 6ft of water there'. Then you had to extrapolate from the tide tables, bearing in mind the time of day, and the date. All we could do was take it off the available tables for Cherbourg and Le Havre. Because there was no established tide table for the survey area, where there was no navigation. So that would give you an idea of what the tide level was for that day and hour. The format for this hydrographic surveying took quite a bit of working out. Done by Berncastle, of course. He was the brains behind it. Quiet chap, but very determined.

So once you'd established your starting point, everything followed from that.

Exactly. That's the difficult bit – establishing your starting point.

In addition to everything else on board we carried the forerunner of Decca [a navigational system using master and slave transmitters sited on land], which worked in the same way as Bomber Command's 'Gee' sets. But this had never been used before on such a low-profile boat, and what worked in a bomber didn't always work for us. These high-strength signals were being sent out from England, but with the curvature of the Earth and so on, it was only partially successful. Occasionally we'd get a good signal. We could often get one line, which was better than nothing. And we could use the echo sounder to give us an idea of where we were – we'd know, for example, that we were on the 6-fathom line, or whatever, from the echo sounder. But we couldn't always get a fix from the navigation system. So then we had to rely on observations of the shore.

In 1942 the authorities had appealed for photographs of the French coast – holiday snaps and things. Well, you may not know this, but the houses along the Normandy coast were very distinctive. Individual houses had a very distinctive outline. And of course the churches as well. So although it was dark, when we were right on shore we could see a church perhaps, or a distinctive house, and we'd take a bearing on it with our compass.

Actually the Decca set was so secret that a Sergeant from the Royal Engineers came on board one day and said 'I've got instructions to put a small charge on your boat'. And he fitted this explosive charge behind the Decca! 'You see these two buttons here?', he said, 'If you press 'em, it'll blow up the set'. And then he added 'It's only a small charge. It won't hurt you. Much'.

I didn't like that word 'much'! And neither did the crew. They used to sidle past these buttons very warily, in case they set them off by accident.

So I was expected to blow up the boat.

We were briefed on what to do if we were captured, and we each carried an escape kit, which wasn't much, really. Just basic rations, and so on. And I had a miniature compass hidden in my top button.

So what would an operational trip consist of?

We would start off from the Hamble River, down the East Solent, through the boom, pick up our escort of three MGBs there, and they'd tow us across to a point off the French coast. There they'd leave us, because they didn't want to be picked up on radar themselves. Then quietly, not at very high speed, we'd go in on our own to the survey area. We'd aim to arrive about midnight and leave again at 4.00am, so we'd usually get about four hours' work done. Pick up the MGBs, and be towed back. This was November [1943], you see, so there was quite a lengthy period of darkness to take advantage of.

How many craft did the Flotilla have working on this?

There were usually three craft working on each survey. Two would survey, and one would act as the marker. That's the point we were discussing earlier; we'd anchor one boat very carefully, and then use that as the starting point. For example, this is a copy of the survey we did off Arromanches [unrolls a chart].

This black circle on the chart is where the marker craft was anchored?

That's right. Then we'd run a line of soundings from that point inshore, as you can see. That was done at high water. The prom at Arromanches is just there. So we took soundings right up to the prom.

You must have virtually been able to step ashore!

Oh yes. On one occasion the crew did have to jump over the side and push the boat off. That was the night we were right on the beach at Arromanches and the engine suddenly stopped. And we couldn't get it started again. You can imagine the noise of a starter motor being constantly turned at the dead of night. Fortunately this was at Christmas time, and the Germans must've been asleep or still celebrating! After a while we managed to get it going, and we carried on. Then the engine stalled again. This must've happened, oh, a dozen times. There was clearly something wrong. The whole boat was shuddering when the engine was running, so there was obviously a problem with the propeller, or the shaft.

We managed to complete our survey, and crawled away in a northerly direction at a much reduced speed. By dawn we were still in sight of the French coast, and about an hour late for our rendezvous with our MGBs. Our low profile and grey camouflage enabled us to escape detection, and we located our escort at about 8.00am. Soon after this a lone Spitfire appeared, to report our impending return to the Naval authorities in Portsmouth.

An inspection of my boat's propeller revealed that several feet of measuring wire was bound tightly around the shaft, causing the previous night's problem. They had to chisel the stuff off.

On another trip we ran into thick fog close to the Normandy coast, and found ourselves in the middle of a German convoy heading for Cherbourg. We were without our escort at the time and were therefore defenceless. Fortunately the fog enabled us to escape their attention, but it also, of course, made surveying impossible.

The surveys continued on moonless nights until the end of December 1943. We also took samples of the bottom, as best we could.

How did you get those?

Oh, with a lead line, with tallow on the end of the lead weight. Not particularly satisfactory. The echo sounder would also give you a basic profile – if the bottom was mud it would show a blurred line; if it was rock it'd be a very hard line. So a trained operator could tell. It's only a rough guide, mind you. In fact it's a sandy bottom all over here [indicates the area where the British Mulberry harbour was to be positioned].

The French hydrographic charts weren't very good, because of course this wasn't a navigational area for ships. So the French hadn't taken much interest in it.

One of the problems of creating a harbour where none existed before.

Exactly. Back in May 1994 I attended a lecture on the Mulberry harbours hosted by the Royal Engineers at Chatham. There were lots of people there, including engineers who'd built them. And I got into a bit of a discussion – well, *more* than a discussion! – because they alleged that the survey we did wasn't accurate enough. They were a bit critical of it. Not *very* critical, but a bit.

But the British harbour arrived, and they built it where we'd surveyed with no great upsets. To them our job seemed simple, but it wasn't!

Anyway, the survey was completed and the Army said they were satisfied with it. But they weren't satisfied as regards the bottom, because a scientist called Professor Bernal [an advisor at Combined Operations Headquarters] thought he'd found a peat bog. So in came Lieutenant Commander Willmott[1] with a COPP team, and borrowed myself and another officer called Harry Richards to take COPP swimmers to the area.

Had you ever met COPP people before?

No, never met them. Although I knew they existed, of course.

Did the COPP mission differ from the surveys?

Yes, in that we had to put them ashore at low water, not at high water. Aside from that it was the same format – MGB escort, and so forth. In my opinion Willmott made a mistake that night. He didn't look hard enough at the weather forecast. Because when the two swimmers, Major Scott-Bowden and Sergeant Ogden-Smith, went ashore the sea began to really get up. We put them ashore late on New Year's Eve, and waited. Every hour they would signal us. Then no signal. Bit of activity on shore – a few Very lights being fired. That didn't look too good.

Eventually we got a signal from the beach to pick them up. By this time the surf was quite something. So these poor devils, weighed down by augers and soil samples [carried in twelve 10in tubes worn on a bandolier] and measuring chains, had to swim out to us through this very heavy surf. We couldn't go in any closer or we'd have overturned. Two very strong young men, but they came up absolutely exhausted. We hauled them back on board, and by this time it was New Year's Day, of course. 'Happy New Year', they said. I know Willmott was pushed for time, and wanted to get it done, but he could easily have lost those two men.

And they couldn't leave anything behind on the beach, because that would have given the game away.

Actually, they did lose an auger. In the surf. They were very apologetic, but they couldn't help it – it just came adrift. Apparently it was found by a Frenchman walking on the beach, who hid it for the rest of the war. He put two and two together, and realised what was happening. It could just as easily have been found by a German patrol. Anyway, they didn't pick up on it.

So we came back, the samples were declared satisfactory, so the survey was then complete. We then idled our time away until D-Day, since our work was done, really.

A few weeks before D-Day the CO said 'I haven't seen young Waters recently'. And there were smiles all round, you know, and they said 'Oh, you'll find him in the chart room'.

---

1. Nigel Willmott was the head and founder of the Combined Operations Pilotage Parties, whose members were trained to reconnoitre potential landing beaches and to bring back samples for analysis.

Working in the chart room was a young Wren who would become Aubrey's wife in 1949.

How did you come to be working at Tormentor?

Gwladys: My family had been on the sea for generations, but in the Merchant Navy. My brother, my father and my grandfathers on both sides all followed in the tradition. If I'd been a boy I probably would have, too. Although I was in a reserved occupation I felt I might still be called up, and I wanted to go where I liked rather than where I was sent, so I joined the Women's Royal Naval Service. And they sent me to Warsash.

What job did you do in the chart room?

When I was having my interview I was asked what my present job was, which was as a tracer in a drawing office. So their eyes lit up, and they said 'Ah! Chart corrector'. So that was it. I had no idea what a chart corrector was. So I went to Portsmouth, and was drafted to HMS *Tormentor,* to the chart room there. The base had a resident Navigating Officer, and I was his assistant.

I used to get signals from the Admiralty on a daily basis – hourly, sometimes. And once a week we used to get the latest 'Notices to Mariners' and 'Fleet Notices to Mariners', which were printed pamphlets, and gave the corrections for all around the country. We kept more detailed charts of the South Coast, obviously, because that was our area.

What kind of information was being corrected?

Oh, alterations to swept channels; minefields; wrecks; all corrected by hand. I corrected the master charts in the chart room, and then the Flotillas had their own sets, which they corrected from mine. They would come in to get the up-to-date information.

Aubrey: On D-Day, for example, she would have been plotting all these buoys, and wondering what was happening.

Gwladys: I was! I plotted the one in the centre, the 'Z' buoy. And I thought 'What on earth is that buoy doing in the middle of the Channel, there?'. And as the day went on I could see the swept channels, and 'Piccadilly Circus' [the circular meeting point for the assault convoys] as they called it, with all these things coming in.

How much did you know about the survey work which had been going on?

Just snippets, really. We very rarely discussed your work, did we?

Aubrey: Well, no. It was very hush-hush.

Gwladys: I knew that they were taking soundings, and this sort of thing. But whenever they were out, people just used to say, 'Oh, they've gone on an exercise', you know.

Aubrey: I was at a dance at Fareham during our operations, and I was dancing with this Wren from Fort Southwick. I asked what she did, and she said she was a Wren plotter – she plotted the movements of ships in the Channel. And she asked what I did, so I said I was in landing craft, and mentioned the number – LCP(SY) 292. She said 'Ah! I know what *you* do on dark nights!'. It seems they would plot us as far as the point where we left the MGBs, but no further. So even they didn't know exactly which part of the coast we were going to.

Did you work shifts in the chart room?

Gwladys: No, same every day. But I do mean every day. I was the only Wren on the base that worked on a Sunday. It was just one of those jobs where you had to be there all the time. But the others, like the Wrens in the pay office, they finished for the week and went off on weekend leave. My block at the base was absolutely deserted on a Sunday.

What about spare time?

Well, we had records, you know. There were very few live performances. A few ENSA shows. Occasionally ones by base personnel. One of the officers, 'Ben' Franklin, used to do poetry readings with musical interludes.

Aubrey: Every now and then we could go to concerts, at Southampton or Portsmouth.

Gwladys: Of course, it was difficult. I was busy . . . he was busy . . .

Aubrey: And I was fond of listening to music on my little wireless. I remember some steward accidentally knocked it over and broke the old-fashioned valves, and when I mentioned this to Patricia Mountbatten, who was also a Wren at the base, she said 'My father's going to America shortly – let me have the valve numbers'. And about three months later they came! So I was back in operation again.

She was a nice person. I didn't know Lord Louis, of course; only when he came to the base to give us a talk, or something. But I admired him. I'm a firm believer that great men often have great faults. He *had* great faults – like showing off, and so on – but he was the right man at the right time. He was a fighter, and that's what Churchill wanted.

Where did the two of you live on the base?

Gwladys: About eight houses made up the 'Wrennery'. The main one was 'Hamble Meads'.

Aubrey: Similarly, they put all of us from the 712th LCP(SY) Flotilla in a house by ourselves, quite separate from anybody else. And of course the base itself was sealed before D-Day anyway.

So you both enjoyed your time at Tormentor?

Gwladys: Oh yes.

Aubrey: It was a great adventure. I was interested in it, technically, you see. I became a civil engineer after the war, which I'd *wanted* to be before it, only my parents couldn't afford to send me to college. So to be quite honest, I grabbed every opportunity I had in the Navy to better myself. And I went on to college after the war, as a mature student.

So, along came D-Day. This time our Flotilla's job was to guide in the various assault groups – some to GOLD, some to JUNO and some to SWORD. My boat and Ken Scott's were the two assigned to the JUNO landing area. His was sunk – he crashed into another landing craft. Then as soon as the beachheads had been established I was transferred to SWORD, to become hydrographic surveyor for the SWORD area. This would've been about 9.00am on D-Day morning. I still have my original log book, from Normandy [shows me the page for 6 June 1944].

When did you have the time to write this up?

Oh, at the end of each day.

And were you required to do this?

Well, yes and no. You were *encouraged* to do it. But you only noted important incidents in your own landing area, of course. Most of the time I was marking wrecks. Another, bigger task was to 'plant' one of the breakwaters of old ships, intended to give some measure of protection until the completion of the British and American Mulberry harbours further along the coast.

There had to be a point, an awkward point, where the British-held coastline ended and the German-held coastline started. That was SWORD. We were shelled there all the time, which wasn't very nice. In fact I lost one of my seamen at SWORD – the only person our Flotilla lost in the whole operation. SWORD wasn't considered to be the main landing area; more a sideshow, really. Frank Berncastle stayed at the next area along, JUNO, as its hydrographic surveyor.

How difficult was it, getting the blockships into position?

This is where I have a confession to make. When you're a young officer . . . well, you make mistakes, don't you? My job was to plant nine ships of varying sizes. Six merchantmen, two old cruisers – HMS *Durban* and the Dutch *Sumatra* – and an old French battleship, the *Courbet*.

Unfortunately the *Courbet* was late in arriving – in fact two or three days late. All the others had come except for her. So the key ship, the biggest one, wasn't there. We did what we could, but it was an awkward job, sinking the other eight ships while leaving a gap for this *Courbet,* which was more than 550ft long.

Eventually along came the *Courbet*. She was plonked in position . . . and there was a gap of 40ft. Red faces all round. But apparently the feeling was 'Oh well, RNVR – what can you expect?'.

The Army Captain who was responsible for unloading DUKWs said to me in all innocence one day 'You Navy people think of everything. Leaving a gap for my "Ducks" so they don't have to go all the way round the breakwater'! Ultimately they got a very small ship over from Britain, and filled it in.

One of the merchantmen we planted was the *Empire Tamar,* whose superstructure we took over as our living quarters. We could then tie our boats up at night and get some sleep in comparative safety.

After this point the Flotilla was dispersed. Some of us were ordered to the Far East, but two volunteers were asked for to continue working with the Army in Holland and so on, protecting its seaward flank. They made it clear the volunteers were in for a dangerous time. But I never liked hot weather, so I said right, I'm volunteering for that.

This was about September 1944.

After an exhilarating pursuit across France and Belgium, the Allied armies were finding their lengthening supply lines a problem.

The Mulberry harbours were now a long way behind the front. The Army were desperate for supplies, and the Germans had made sure that no deep-water ports were available, either by hanging on to them or by making sure they were wrecked before they were captured.

The ideal port would've been Antwerp in Belgium [captured, virtually undamaged, by British tanks at the start of September], but access to that was blocked because the Germans still held the long channel connecting it with the sea.

The First Canadian Army was engaged in clearing both banks of this channel, but at its seaward end the Dutch island of Walcheren, well garrisoned and bristling with heavy gun batteries, could only be taken by amphibious assault.

This is Walcheren [unrolls chart], at the entrance to the West Scheldt, the channel leading to Antwerp. Antwerp is down here. To open up the channel, it was decided to mount assaults on Walcheren from Ostend and Breskens [themselves only recently captured], with the aim of opening up Antwerp to the sea.

This was the end of October now. I was in England at the time, so mine and another boat – the remaining two from the Flotilla – were sent for, and we crossed over to Ostend during a gale. *Terrible* journey. Once there, we were told 'Right, the day after tomorrow we're going to invade Walcheren at two points; the first here [indicates location on the chart] at Flushing, and the second here [indicates again] at Westkapelle, on the west coast'. The Flushing assault was to go in just before first light; the Westkapelle one four hours later. I was to lead the Westkapelle assault.

So your assault was to be in daylight.

That's right. In daylight. I said I didn't fancy that at all, but I was told there was no alternative, so that was that.

But anyway, at 4.00pm on the afternoon before the attacks – I'll remember this all my life – I was sent for by no less a personage than Admiral Ramsay [the British Admiral Sir Bertram Ramsay, the Allied Naval commander in Normandy].

'There's been a change of plan', he said. 'The landing craft that we've got at Breskens, ready to assault Flushing in the early hours of the morning, haven't got a navigator. We've found a navigator to do your job, so I want you to do the Flushing job instead'.

My face was wreathed in smiles! Actually this was considered to be the more hazardous of the two assaults, because Flushing was very heavily defended; but it was in the dark, that was the point. So I said 'Right, Sir. When do I leave?'.

What was Ramsay like?

A straight talker. Everyone in the Navy knew him as the man who'd masterminded the Dunkirk evacuation. Soon after this episode I'm talking about now, when I met him, he was killed in a plane crash. That would've been in January 1945. Tragic.

Anyway, we had to leave immediately. We heard engines just off Zeebrugge, where the Germans were thought to be busy evacuating, so we drifted, engines off, being very quiet, until whatever it was had gone. Then we started up again, and slipped into the West Scheldt to Breskens harbour.

There was a sentry there who had the thickest accent I've ever heard. In fact, so thick that I thought at first he was a German! Turned out he was from Glasgow. He challenged us of course, and we answered him back. We eventually established he was from the 52nd (Lowland) Division. He was friendly, anyway.

By the time we arrived at Breskens it would've been about 11.00pm. We were briefed, by a Navy Captain and an officer from No 4 Commando, that we were to leave Breskens at 4.45am. I worked all night on the navigation and the timings, because I didn't know the Scheldt at all. I'd never been there before. But I soon realised that with the current that was running there – 4 or 5 knots of current – I'd need a lot more than an hour for the crossing. The landing craft, LCAs, were very slow. So I eventually persuaded them to leave at 4.30am; not much of a difference, but just enough.

The force Aubrey was shepherding, which consisted of No 4 Commando and part of No 10 Commando, was to assault Flushing at 5.45am on Wednesday 1 November 1944. Part of the 52nd (Lowland) Division would land behind them.

Four hours later, at 9.45am, the Westkapelle landing would be carried out by Nos 41 (Royal Marine), 47 (Royal Marine) and 48 (Royal Marine) Commandos, plus a further portion of No 10 Commando.

We'd got as far as here [indicates on the chart] when all hell was let loose by our own artillery, massed on dry land behind us. Hundreds of guns. Quite a few rounds started splashing short, all around. At the last minute the firing lifted, and we dashed in.

Despite the fact that I'd never seen Flushing, my brief was to find the right beach. Which I managed, because of a distinctive windmill. The Commandos scrambled ashore, and within ten minutes they'd got sufficient men there to overcome the immediate resistance on shore. Just a few hundred men, but enough to get that vital toehold on shore. The follow-up force from the 52nd (Lowland) Division could then come ashore and expand the beachhead, which eventually linked up with the landing at Westkapelle.

The marker boat at Westkapelle was shelled straight away and destroyed – so that would've been me. I wasn't afraid of many things, but I didn't like the idea of making that run. Because I knew that in my wooden boat I wouldn't stand much of a chance.

Air support was hampered by the November weather, and while artillery fire from the Army was able to assist the assault on

Flushing, few guns had the range to hit Westkapelle, on the seaward side of the island. The assault here was aided primarily by the Royal Navy, using landing craft backed up from a distance by the 15in guns of the monitors HMS *Erebus* and HMS *Roberts* and the battleship HMS *Warspite*.

As at Elba, there were numerous short-range duels between the landing craft and the shore batteries. Losses among the landing craft were heavy, and included the only two examples of the brand new Landing Craft, Gun (Medium).

Canadian cameraman *Ken Dougan* had a rather different job to do at Westkapelle.

My amphibious experience came as a total surprise. I was a cine cameraman working with the 4th Canadian Armoured Brigade, and had just finished some coverage of their fighting near the Scheldt estuary. I was told to report, along with Sergeant Lloyd Millon, to our HQ, and found out that we were on our way to Ostend. When we reported to Operations there was tight security, and we were confined to barracks awaiting some kind of briefing. All we *did* know was that we were now with the Royal Marine Commandos. This alone made me wonder what was the target, since it likely involved an amphibious operation.

We had our briefing, and found out it was Westkapelle. The RAF were to blast holes in the dyke around Walcheren, flooding the island, and they would also knock out the concrete gun emplacements. RN ships were to shell any remaining guns, all leading to easier access for our landings.

During the night I boarded a Royal Navy landing craft which had three LVT troop carriers aboard. I was in the rear corner of the first one with my motion picture camera, mounted on a tripod. The lenses just cleared the sides of the LVT and the landing craft. This was my location for the invasion.

The LVT – or Landing Vehicle, Tracked – was another new American design, which could land over much rougher terrain than a DUKW. Initial production had been directed towards the Pacific, where the LVT quickly became an indispensable part of operations.

When dawn appeared we were still a long distance from land. I could hear heavy guns firing, which turned out to be HMS *Warspite* firing salvoes toward the German gun emplacements at Westkapelle. I filmed some scenes of the shelling as we passed the area.

We could now see land ahead, and about the same time heavy-duty mortar fire started exploding all around us . . . we'd come within range. The group of Marines I was with had their Adjutant in charge of them, and he told us to keep down until we were told to disembark. We continued on through the mortar fire, eventually coming within range of small arms fire, which pinged off the sides of the craft. I did hear a tremendous explosion during this time, and I believe it was a direct hit by a heavy shell or a mortar on one of our landing craft.

We passed through German fire of all calibres, and our Adjutant warned us again not to put our heads up. No one did. Our craft ran ashore in the area of the dyke break [just to the south of Westkapelle], and we were the first LVT off the ramp. We headed for higher ground, but our vehicle ran onto an obstruction, which caused one tread to spin in the air. We were sitting ducks amid the exchanges of gunfire between the Marines and the enemy, so we abandoned 'ship' and made a run for shelter in some bombed-out buildings.

I decided to go north, following the Marines clearing out concrete gun emplacements that were still active, even after all the bombing. I filmed until my 400ft of 35mm was used up, canned it, made my notes as best I could, and took the film to an RN craft that was trying to get off to return to Ostend. That was 'news coverage done' for me.

Of course, the original plan was for me to return, as the operation wasn't expected to be lengthy. How wrong that was! The weather was probably as bad an enemy as the Germans. High winds, driving rain and cold temperatures made just existing miserable. I ended up being a 'gofer' . . . guarding POWs, or assisting with First Aid and helping the injured. Eventually the weather calmed enough to allow landing craft to come ashore, and some personnel plus the wounded were taken aboard for return to our start point.

As a final touch, when our craft arrived in darkness off the entrance to Ostend harbour, the town was being bombed by German aircraft! A rare venture for the Luftwaffe. We sat offshore till all was quiet, then docked.

It wasn't until much later that I learned the Westkapelle operation had been a success, but had taken a high toll in both personnel and equipment.

Meanwhile, as the beachheads at Flushing and Westkapelle struggled to link up, a third battle was being fought in the east of the island, where a narrow causeway connected it to the mainland.

Here infantryman *John Regan* was among those preparing to make their second amphibious crossing in a week.

We'd crossed the West Scheldt a few days before, to help the 2nd Canadian Division clear South Beveland, up to the causeway where it joined Walcheren. The use of Antwerp was being denied us because Jerry was clinging to these lower reaches, and the port was urgently required by the Allies. Our supplies were still being hauled up by road all the way from Normandy. Our crossing of the Scheldt was in darkness, and aboard tracked craft called Buffaloes [one of the names given by the British to the LVT. In Italy it was known as the Fantail].

Had you ever been in an LVT before the attack on South Beveland?

No, this was our first time. We'd moved up from Hulst to Terneuzen, where Royal Engineers were bulldozing a large section out of the dyke to allow the

Buffaloes through the gap and into the water. This was all done in darkness.

Had you been trained in amphibious warfare?

No, no training for an assault from the sea. Our Division had been trained in mountain warfare in the Cairngorms, though. That was very useful in Holland.

Did they issue you with a lifejacket or anything?

No. Maybe because of the weight of arms and equipment we were already carrying it might've been just another hazard. But many of my comrades did drown, due to fear or panic.

Did you stand during the crossing, or sit?

Oh, standing room only. Huddled like cattle.

And what was going through your mind?

Trying to figure out what was in store for us, if we reached the shore. And also wondering about the safety of my younger brother, who was in another Buffalo with part of 'C' Company of the Battalion – 5th Battalion, Highland Light Infantry.

Listening to the engine purring away above the sound of the sea lapping against the side of the Buffalo. Darkness, except for flashes of gunfire and tracers, with the ping of rifle or machine gun fire against the structure; silently staring into the helmet of the man in front, awaiting the moment when they'd lower the ramp and in no uncertain manner tell us to 'Go! Go! Go!'.

We weren't the first craft to arrive at Amber Beach, after the 5-mile crossing from Terneuzen. Previous craft had obviously met with mishaps one way or another, and were damaged, burning or partially sunk some distance short of the dyke.

Did the LVT drive up onto the far shore?

No, it couldn't get close enough due to anti-invasion devices, like steel beams and barricades. And the damaged and burning craft. The ramp was lowered to a level position, to allow us to get out and wade ashore across a sea of mud. That was very difficult, wading through mud waist high, with rifles, Brens and PIATs held clear. And then over the dyke. We knew we had to get on the beach, over the dyke, and away from the vehicle as quickly as possible. Fortunately we managed that part OK, and found ourselves in an orchard.

The opposition wasn't as strong as expected – although Jerry mortars and snipers gave us a bit of trouble – until we moved further inland to take our first objective. Then Jerry withdrew onto Walcheren and concentrated on denying us the use of the causeway. This was a narrow strip of land, 1200yds long by 40yds wide, water on both sides, linking South Beveland to Walcheren.

With the help of rocket-firing Typhoons from the RAF, the Canadians and the 1st Battalion, Glasgow Highlanders obtained a bridgehead over the causeway, but a heavy price had to be paid for the privilege. Further attacks gained nothing, and it was decided they should hold onto what they already had, while we crossed 2 miles further south to cause a distraction.

This Sloe Channel crossing was different from the Scheldt. This time the craft used were small collapsible canvas boats, which gave us no problems with assembly, although we were fortunate to have the Royal Engineers handy to assist. Thank God it was less than a mile to the other side, much of it wading through mud again. In the first phase of the assault, two companies from another battalion were ferried across. Once again mud delayed progress, Schu mines [German anti-personnel mines with a plywood or heavy cardboard casing, making them very difficult to detect] took their toll, and the opposition soon had them pinned down. It wasn't till dusk that they were reinforced by elements of our Battalion, but when darkness fell it allowed the necessary troops to flow more freely over the crossing. By this time Flushing and Westkapelle had been captured, so Middelburg [the principal town, in the centre of the island] was now within our sights.

How bad was the flooding caused by the pre-assault bombing of the dykes?

Oh, most of Walcheren was like a lake. And of course a number of local civilians, and cattle on the farms, had lost their lives by drowning. We just had to try and find the shallow parts. But remember it was the same for the enemy.

The German commander, General Daser, must've known that his command was disintegrating, because he despatched a message to assemble all ranks for an official surrender. The Jerry troops were marched into the main square in Middelburg as prisoners, obviously glad to be out of it.

Not so for us; we still had a long way to go – all the way to Bremen, via crossings of the Rhine and the Dortmund-Ems Canal.

By the time the island was declared secure on 8 November 1944, Royal Navy minesweepers were already at work in the West Scheldt. The first three merchantmen docked safely at Antwerp on 26 November, and the first full convoy arrived two days later. In December, their work done, the Mulberry landing piers at Arromanches began to be dismantled.

On 8 May 1945 the Allies were at last able to celebrate victory in Europe, and to turn their full attention to the war in the Pacific.

Semper Fi: the US Marine Corps at Guadalcanal

The United States Marine Corps, with its motto of *Semper Fidelis*, ('Always Loyal') was almost exclusively concerned with the Pacific campaigns. From the outset, despite America's 'Germany first' policy, the aggressive Japanese advances in this theatre made a completely passive defence impossible. Force had to be met with force, first in New Guinea – which the Japanese reached in March 1942 – and then in the neighbouring Solomon Islands.

In May 1942, while the British were seizing the northern tip of Madagascar, the Japanese experienced the first real check to their expansion. An attempt to complete the conquest of New Guinea by taking the main Allied base at Port Moresby – only an hour and a half's flying time from the Australian mainland – was blocked by an American carrier force at the Battle of the Coral Sea.

The following month, far away to the north, a more powerful invasion of Midway Atoll in the Hawaiian chain was also ambushed. The Americans, who had broken the Japanese naval codes and been able to position their ships accordingly, sank five of their opponents' precious carriers in the two battles, and damaged a sixth. Their own losses were two carriers sunk.

Regardless of this shift in the balance of naval air power, however, the Japanese continued to apply pressure in the South Pacific, where their troops could operate under the protection of land-based aircraft. While the Australians, with growing American help, fought to hold on to New Guinea, plans were drawn up for an American counterattack in the Solomons, where the Japanese were busily building a new forward air base on the island of Guadalcanal.

The US 1st Marine Division, already on its way to New Zealand for training, was ordered to conduct America's first amphibious invasion of the war, aimed at taking this prize before it could become operational. D-Day was set for Friday, 7 August 1942 – three months before the landings in North Africa.

John McCarthy was one of the Division's young Marines.

I'd signed up just before Pearl Harbor, and in fact on December 7, 1941 I was on a train heading for boot camp at Parris Island, South Carolina [the Marine Corps recruit depot on the East Coast]. Our training was very good. Most of our officers were old hands – China Station, and even World War One. Our NCOs were the same, so we had the right people to whip us into Marines.

Even so, I only just qualified with my rifle – every Marine is a rifleman first – but after a time in combat I became quite expert, and when I came home I could drop a pigeon in flight. I *had* to learn, in order to stay alive. My rifle at the time of Guadalcanal was the old 1903 Springfield bolt action. They didn't have any of the new Garands to give us. My first encounter with the Garand was in the hands of an Army National Guard unit they managed to sneak in to reinforce us. The new rifles sure helped their firepower.

We'd never heard of Guadalcanal before we landed. The evening before it'd come over the ship's PA, but we still didn't know where it was. The initial landing was a snap. It was what happened next that was like opening up the gates of Hell.

> Prior to the landing, the commander of the Navy carriers providing air cover had announced that he was not prepared to hazard his ships for longer than two days. Even though the Marines quickly took possession of the Guadalcanal airstrip, renaming it Henderson Field after a Marine Corps aviator, this impossibly short deadline meant they could unload only a portion of their supplies and equipment.

They made a point of telling us to unload the ships fast. Well, that was a laugh, with the Jap Navy coming at us and Jap planes overhead. We did manage to unload plenty of ammo, but you can't eat that.

> On D+2 the carrier force withdrew. Left without air cover, the transports had no option but to follow, taking with them much of the Division's food and even some of its men.

We did get twenty days' rations off the ship, but that was all the food we had, and when that ran out we used what little the Japs had left behind – mainly rice and barley.

Our belts didn't have notches, so we never really noticed how thin we were getting. But when we eventually left Guadalcanal and we tried to board the ship by cargo nets, so many men fell in the water that they had to put down the Captain's ladder. We were all very weak. I was down to 99lbs when I left on December 12, 1942. Lack of food, dysentery . . . I had malaria twenty-seven times in six years, and also dengue fever.

After nearly sixty years I'm still haunted by that island. I'm reminded of it every day when I walk or stand, like many of the boys. And we *were* boys then.

I was only eighteen, and I wasn't the youngest, because some of them had lied about their age to be there.

But I'm still proud of being a Marine.

Sharing the same privations as the Marines were US Navy corpsmen like *John Richter.*

I served from the day of the assault – August 7, 1942 – to December 15, 1942 as a Pharmacist's Mate 3rd Class with the 11th Marines [the Divisional artillery regiment], 1st Marine Division, Fleet Marine Force. You see, the Marines were subject to the Navy Department's authority, and the Navy supplied them with medical personnel. So Navy corpsmen and doctors trained and fought alongside the Marines, and wore Marine uniform.

I was assigned to a 75mm gun mounted on a half track, as sole corpsman for a crew of Marines. Our half track crew ranged from around eighteen to twenty-four years of age. I was nineteen. It was led by Shorty, our 'ageing' Corporal, who characteristically carried his rifle over the back of his neck like the Kentucky mountaineer he was.

Prior to our landing on Guadalcanal the half track crew had already been subjected to reduced rations on board the ss *Ericsson* – a commercial ship under charter. Insufficient food supplies had been taken on board for the trip from California to New Zealand. We were limited to two meals per day, and often a 'meal' consisted only of soup and bread. An average loss of weight of between 16 and 23lbs was documented for many of the troops. The time span from arrival in Wellington, New Zealand to final landing on the 'Canal was too short to reverse this, so you see we were quite lean and mean from day one on the island – our stomachs were already partially programmed to accept the dieting that loomed ahead.

Upon arrival in Wellington on the 'low calorie' *Ericsson,* we transferred to the uss *Hunter Liggett.* The troops were granted liberty to visit the city. Not caring to go ashore, I was hoping one of the men would bring back something filling to quiet down my grumbling stomach. Much later that night I received a wake up call from my shipmate Tom Richardson as I slept on the very top of the four-high tier of bunks. Climbing the dizzy heights, he handed me this mangled package, hot and greasy, unceremoniously wrapped in the local newspaper. My introduction to fish and chips.

After sailing for a practice landing at Koro in the Fiji Islands – declared 'a complete bust' by General Vandegrift [Major General Alexander Vandegrift, USMC, commanding the 1st Marine Division] – we finally arrived off the northern coast of Guadalcanal on August 7, 1942. The *Hunter Liggett* was one of fifteen attack transports which anchored off Red Beach [the only landing beach selected on Guadalcanal] and proceeded to disembark.

The Marines descended the rope cargo nets hung over the side of the ship's hull into waiting Higgins boats, offloaded from the ship for the assault. The Higgins boats were manned by US Coast Guard men experienced in handling small craft. The Coast Guard, of course, had come under command of the USN for the duration of the war.

The landing was carried out in daylight, as was to become standard practice in the Pacific.

Were you always able to tell where you were on the island?
No. We were at four or five different positions in the four-month period on the island, and except for our main position in a coconut grove bordering the coastline in the Lunga area, and our position at the mouth of the Matanikau River – east bank – we did find it difficult becoming orientated. We were close enough in the Lunga area for our returning planes to skim over our heads on their approach to landing at Henderson Field.

At our other isolated positions we couldn't actually pinpoint just *where* we were. Only the top brass really knew what was going on. We 'peons' never knew that many a time we came close to losing the island to the Japs, but like the saying goes, ignorance is bliss.

In the waters around Guadalcanal the Americans generally had the upper hand during the hours of daylight, and the Japanese at night. Both sides struggled to feed in a trickle of reinforcements and supplies, but neither could establish a decisive superiority over their opponents.

Whenever the Jap Navy's attention was diverted to our ships at sea and away from us on the beach, the action could be witnessed undisturbed. At times close enough in daylight to see ships laying down smoke screens, and at night to observe the blasts of naval guns and on occasion the resulting fireball of an exploding ship. All this sitting – we were too fatigued to watch standing – on a long wooden plank brought near the water's edge to furnish dry seating on the '50 yard line'. From there we sat witness to these deadly games, always praying the last ball of fire was one of *their* ships, and not one of ours.

The Marines tormented one another with rumours of the arrival of relief, et cetera, so being Navy I was looked upon as Honest John, who would tell it straight. I used the area around my shelter half 'sick bay' as the focal point for poker playing, swapping stories, and so on, to help ease the increasing strain of almost daily bombing, naval shelling and visits from 'Pistol Pete' [the mobile artillery with which the Japanese harassed the Marine positions].

Once, our newly-relocated defense position was completely levelled by an enemy air raid, blowing me out of my shallow foxhole, and causing haemorrhaging and temporary deafness in my right ear. It also wounded one of gutsiest and most physically powerful Marines. While tending to him, the wounded Marine whispered to me 'Doc . . . I think I *did it* in my pants'. I had to reassure him that under similar circumstances this'd happen most of the time. And besides, no one in the crew would ever know. The tension suddenly eased from his face, and we had him transported to a medical facility.

Being responsible for the health of the gun crew, and all of us being on drastically reduced food rations, I was desperate to supplement in some way our sparse, dull diet. One day a member of our crew was assigned to a truck detail transporting precious dwindling food from the supply depot to outlying units. After strong urging I finally persuaded him to toss something extra tasty and stomach-filling from the truck the next time it passed our bivouac.

As darkness fell and the truck went by, off flew a large can, which came to rest within our perimeter, in the middle of a coconut grove. Setting it aside, we decided to tantalize ourselves by not checking its contents. Later that night we figured it was time for some goodies. Aided by partial moonlight – strict blackout was in effect – I was given the honor of reading its contents. The answer? 'Shredded coconut'. Obviously they picked a budding comedian for that truck detail.

On the 'Canal a corpsman's task extended slightly beyond the obvious one of attending to physical wounds. I felt in time my main focus became one of Chaplain/Morale Officer/Psychiatrist. But most of my medical ministerings involved the treatment of diarrhea, dehydration and fatigue, and the dispensing of the much detested anti-malarial Atabrine tablets. I admonished the men to keep as dry as possible. In that clammy, steaming jungle this of course brought the snide retort 'Yeah. Right. Sure'.

Being more or less isolated with our mobile 75mm gun, I had to make do with limited medical supplies, most of which were carried in an empty Jap gas mask case.

What kind of medical supplies?

Mainly First Aid items, ranging from simple band-aids to morphine sulfate ready-to-use tubes with a sterile needle attached, for extreme pain. The ready-to-use tubes were about so long [about 6cm], with a squeezable plastic tube full of morphine sulfate solution, and a sterile needle ready attached, protected by a plastic cover. The administering procedure was: one – coat the area with alcohol; two – remove the plastic cover from the needle; three – push a sterile seal breaker down [inside the needle] until it pierced the seal holding back the morphine sulfate solution; four – remove the seal breaker; five – squeeze tube slightly until a single drop exited the tip of the needle; six – thrust the needle into the deltoid muscle of the patient's shoulder; seven – squeeze the tube until the required amount of solution'd been administered, and eight – remove needle!

Sulfa powder was an item at that time to be sprinkled on open wounds. Rashes – mostly fungus and heat rash – were treated with Calamine lotion, coughs with Terpin Hydrate. APC capsules – Aspirin/Phenacetin/Caffeine – were considered an old trusty standby for just about all ailments known to man, mainly for their placebo effect! Symptoms of malaria and other conditions that couldn't be handled properly in our isolated position were referred to the Regimental sick bay back in the 'rear'.

As if there *was* a 'rear' on an island like Guadalcanal.

The smaller islands of Tulagi and Gavutu-Tanambogo,[1] on the other side of the stretch of water soon to be nicknamed 'Ironbottom Sound' because of the number of ships lost in it, were also selected for invasion on 7 August 1942.

One of the units committed to the fight for Tulagi was a regiment of the 2nd Marine Division, taking the place of one missing from the 1st on detached duty.

Ray Schneider belonged to it.

I'd joined the United States Marine Corps Reserve in May 1940 – Company 'C', 9th Battalion, USMCR. We had boot training initially, and qualified with the 1903 Springfield. Had some bayonet drills, and an introduction to the BAR [Browning Automatic Rifle] and the .45 caliber pistol. Threw a bunch of dummy hand grenades. Learned how to follow orders, keep our equipment and clothes clean, and perform the basic close order drill.

Joining the Reserves was a way to earn a few Dollars, since we were still coming out of the throes of the great Depression. It wouldn't interfere with my regular job – or so I thought!

I'd finished High School in January of 1939. My father was a building and wood flooring contractor, and I'd worked with him weekends and vacation periods while I was in school, so I was qualified as a carpenter and as a floorlayer and finisher by the time I graduated. I was studying a correspondence course in Electrical Engineering in 1940, but had to put the schooling on the back burner when they called us to active duty.

On 15 October 1940 the Reservists of all twenty-three Marine Corps Reserve Battalions – including Ray's 9th – were ordered to report for active service. Although the USA was technically still at peace, conscription had been introduced the previous month, and the part-time Marines were being called out to assist the Regulars.

Ray, whose training had so far consisted of two weeks at camp and about six weekends at his local civic center, found himself on his way to the Marine Corps base at San Diego.

We arrived in San Diego on November 10 – the birthday of the Marine Corps. We put up some six-man tents on the west side of the parade ground, installed wooden slat floors, and moved in.

This is where we got the rest of our boot training. We had a young First Lieutenant that took us in tow. He gave us comprehensive training on the .30 and .50 caliber machine guns, until we could break them down and reassemble them blindfolded. I still know what a 'belt feed lever stud cam groove' is.

---

1. Gavutu and Tanambogo were linked to one another by a causeway.

He also got us acquainted with the Thompson sub machine gun, our two mortars, the grenade launcher, and the 37mm anti-tank gun.

The Fleet Marine Force was meanwhile undergoing a complete reorganisation, with the Reserve battalions being broken up and their personnel integrated into other units.

Ray was sent to the newly-reactivated 2nd Marines, one of the regiments formed to expand the existing pair of FMF brigades into full divisions – the first in the history of the Corps.

I was sent off to Radio School, and when I came back it was to the HQ of the 2nd Battalion, 2nd Marines,[2] of the new 2nd Marine Division. They had enough radio men, so they put me in the Telephone Section. I eventually ended up as the NCO in charge of the Battalion message center.

Reserve Marines made up much of the 2nd Marine Division. In addition to the 2nd Marines, we also filled out the ranks of the 6th Marines, who went to Iceland [in July 1941, to free its British garrison for other duties] and the 8th Marines, who went to protect Samoa after Pearl Harbor. There were very few Regulars around, so the Reserves took up the slack. We learned real quick.

They kept us mean, lean and tough; long marches – one for 50 miles – and many practice landings around La Jolla and San Diego. You can't simulate the real thing, but we went through the motions.

Then came the attack on Pearl Harbor. I recall it vividly, because I was CQ [in Charge of Quarters] that Sunday, December 7. We were at Camp Elliott, San Diego, and had just requalified with the '03. I'd met our new Sergeant Major, and instantly had my first 'run in' with him. I had the message center set up in the office – the message center consisted of a field desk and a switchboard, and we had lines to all the Companies, to Regiment, et cetera. In any event, he wanted me out of there. I went and checked with the CO, so the Sergeant Major was ticked off at me for going over his head.

That Sunday they hit Pearl Harbor there were three of us in our area – the Sergeant Major, me, and a young Lieutenant. We were in the Lieutenant's office in the barracks listening to the radio when we heard the news. We discussed the situation and decided we should have the ammunition out, but neither of them could find the key to the ammunition bunker. I volunteered to break the lock off with a wrecking bar. The Sergeant Major almost had a fit, but the Lieutenant said 'Let's go get it!', so once again I rubbed his fur the wrong way.

Rumours of a Japanese attack on the American mainland were rife, and the San Diego Marines were hastily deployed to anti-invasion positions.

---

2. As with US Army infantry regiments, USMC marine infantry regiments were each composed of three battalions.

US Marines at Betio, November 1943. Nowhere on Tarawa atoll was higher than 10ft above sea level. (Imperial War Museum: EW10802)

US Marines boarding an LCVP at Bougainville, November 1943. The 'war dog' (right) was used by patrols and guard details. (Imperial War Museum: NYF11373)

US Army troops using a flamethrower on New Georgia, 1943. (Imperial War Museum: NYF9923)

US Army stretcher bearers on Attu in the Aleutians, 1943. (Imperial War Museum: OEM5433)

US Marine Corps burial at sea, Saipan, June 1944. (Imperial War Museum: NYF30296)

Above: LVTs coming ashore on Tinian, July 1944. (Imperial War Museum: NYF34788)

Right: Under air attack, Mindoro 1944. (Imperial War Museum: NYF52691)

LSTs (top right) dwarfed by Mount Suribachi, Iwo Jima, 1945. (Imperial War Museum: NYF58685)

Kamikaze. (Imperial War Museum: NYF70679)

We were spaced out along the coast from the Mexican border to as far north as Oceanside. But in about six days the Navy, Coast Guard and Army Air Forces were patrolling the entire West Coast, and they brought us back to camp, where training resumed.

We were assigned to a ship called the *President Hayes*, and made more practice landings.

Like the British the year before, the Americans had been expanding their amphibious capability during 1941 by taking over suitable civilian vessels. A passenger ship converted to carry troops, together with the landing craft to put them ashore, was designated an Auxiliary, Personnel – or AP. A ship primarily to carry cargo was designated an Auxiliary, Cargo – or AK.

At the time of Pearl Harbor the USS *President Hayes*, which in British service would have been called an LSI(L), was just completing her conversion into an AP.

We were filling our ranks rapidly, and soon found ourselves up to strength and outfitted with the best they had to offer – although that mostly meant leftovers from World War One. Then one day the *President Hayes* started out from San Diego and never turned back.

The 2nd Marines were on their way to join the 1st Marine Division's assault on the Solomon Islands.

The sailors had another surprise for us when we crossed the Equator. They called us up topside in small groups and shaved our heads. The uniform for the event was bare feet and shorts only. Then they ran us down the port side, washing us along with salt water hoses, and whacking us with belts along the way. They stopped us just short of the end of the quarterdeck and put blindfolds on all of us, but not until we'd seen a gangplank going over the side and a man being prodded up the short ladder to get over the rail and onto it.

They lined us all up along a bulkhead and led us forward one at a time. You were told to open your mouth and take a bite, and they shoved a raw fish in your mouth. Then they spun you round and round to disorient you, took you to the ladder and made you walk the plank. They said 'No diving – jump in and come up swimming'. They'd also painted us from head to toe.

In fact they'd rigged a large piece of canvas into a frame and had only about 3ft of water in it, so you got to watch people trying to swim after they jumped in, which was funny. Trying to get the paint off with salt water showers and salt water soap was less funny.

Having survived the traditional 'Crossing the Line' ceremony, the 2nd Marines prepared for their part in the forthcoming operation.

Our Battalion was in reserve, so we didn't go ashore until August 8 [D+1]. In the meantime we lay in Ironbottom Sound, between Guadalcanal and Tulagi, and were there when about thirty Jap torpedo planes came in for a daylight raid. They only hit one transport, and the Marines were off her. The Navy beached her to salvage what she had in her holds. The Japs lost quite a few planes. The ship that was beached [the USS *George F Elliott*] caught fire and burned all day long on August 8, and into the early morning of August 9. With her burning in the background she made perfect silhouettes of all the other ships.

We were called onto Tulagi just after the air raid. I'll never forget the multitude of tropical fish swimming around our feet as we walked in about 1ft of water to the beach. How beautiful they were – every color in the spectrum. And at the same time a Navy bomber was strafing and bombing a tiny island just a stone's throw from Tulagi . . . Quite a contrast.

The minute we set foot on the beach a sniper saw us and, 'Ping', we heard a sound we'd become very familiar with. Almost to the point where we ignored it. They rarely hit anything they were shooting at, especially when they were tied up in trees.

We started down a path along the water's edge, and experienced a strong putrid odour. I at first thought someone had left a can of dead worms on the beach from a bit of fishing. It turned out to be a dead Jap officer that'd been hit by Navy shellfire and blown to bits. I've always regretted passing up a pair of binoculars laying there, and a beautiful sword. Two things stopped me – bits of flesh were stuck on both articles, and they could've been booby-trapped.

It was that night, just past 1.00am on the morning of August 9, that the Japs came in and sank a lot of our ships. We actually had an unobstructed view of the battle. Many of the ships had fired starshells, and with low rainclouds and the transport *Elliott* blazing in the background, it was lit up like a huge stadium.

A Japanese cruiser force had managed to approach the area undetected, and once loose in the anchorage it proceeded to sink a succession of Allied warships which crossed its path. Had the Japanese pushed further into Ironbottom Sound they would undoubtedly have massacred the landing ships as well, but in fact their commander decided to break off the action.

We lost three cruisers that night – the *Astoria*, the *Vincennes* and the *Quincy* – and the Australians lost HMAS *Canberra*. We watched them from the beach on Tulagi. They also damaged the *Chicago* and several other ships. It was a terrible thing to be witnessing, and forty-one years later I realized what an impression it'd made on me when my wife and I visited the Australian War Memorial in 1983. On a wall there they have a record of all the men that lost their lives aboard the *Canberra* that night, and I cried all through their museum. I hadn't done that since I was a little kid. Our surviving ships sailed away. We got a message from the *President Hayes* that they were under way and leaving the area.

We'd made our landing with only light packs and one day's supply of food and ammunition, so we got pretty desperate for food. We remembered that we'd pushed two large sacks of mixed grain off the end of the government dock, so I volunteered to dive down with a line and have the people on the dock pull them up. We split those bags out and dumped the grain on a couple of ponchos to let it dry out. It grew thousands of grub worms, and little black and red bugs, which we eventually ended up eating.

While the battle over on Guadalcanal continued to grow in intensity, operations on Tulagi and the adjacent, much larger, Florida Island remained confined to consolidation and patrol work.

One day we had two fourteen-man patrols in a Higgins boat. They dropped our patrol off on Florida at what had been a British mission, where they had a little dock running out into deep water. The other patrol went off to Mandoliana [another small island] looking for a seaplane base occupied by 'Washing Machine Charlie', who would arrive each night around midnight, spray the area with machine gun fire, and drop a small bomb.

The patrol I was with was looking for stragglers. Neither patrol saw one Jap in four days. We figured any that *were* there had been transported to Guadalcanal to bolster their forces there. We set up a bivouac area on the porch of the mission, and were delighted to find papaya trees all round the building, adding the fruit to our rations.

A young native boy about ten years old had been over behind a tree watching us set up, and he finally got over his shyness and came closer to us. He had open sores all over his body. Our corpsman dressed them, and he scooted back into the jungle.

In a short while we had about two dozen people with the same problem, and an older man that spoke some pidgin English. His name was Old Ben, and he asked if we could help them, which we did. The corpsman swabbed their sores, and we cut up a clean undershirt for bandages. I just happened to have one in my pack that I was going to use as a towel, because it was too hot to wear. When they were all taken care of, Old Ben said the Chief had invited us to visit their village the next day.

The area had been under a British colonial administration until the arrival of the Japanese earlier in the year, and many islanders had initially welcomed a change from white rule. Since then, however, the Japanese had established such a reputation for brutality that the vast majority of the local population had sided with the Allies again.

The next morning Old Ben was waiting, and eight of us left to go to the village. They took us through the Chief's grass house, and out onto a veranda where we could see much of the activity going on in the village. Someone brought us green coconuts so we could drink the milk.

One of our party flipped a cigarette butt out near a youngster in the yard, and he picked it up and walked around smoking it like an old man. A woman, perhaps his mother, came over and talked to him, and he put it in her lips. She took a puff on it, and he took it back and puffed on it a couple more times and then gave it to her, and she walked away puffing on it.

They'd prepared a feast for us – chicken, a form of poi, green onions, lettuce, tomatoes, bananas cooked in papaya juice and green coconut milk. A real delight. We ate till we couldn't hold any more.

Old Ben came over and said their warriors had made up a dance for us, and not to be afraid, they wouldn't hurt us. The warriors chanted and danced toward us with their spears, and turned just before they made contact. When they'd stopped, they wanted us to do something to entertain them in return, so the Lieutenant put us through a bit of Marine Corps close order drill. We had a memorable four days with them.

On another patrol we were all out of water, and had many thirsty hours ahead of us until we could get near a river. We came upon a waterhole about 12ft in diameter, and in it was a dead, thoroughly putrefied Jap. He fell apart when the corpsman tried to pull him out of the water. He was full of maggots and little worms, and terribly smelly. We scooped out water, strained it through some gauze and filled our canteens, and then the corpsman added Iodine to them. You could taste Iodine for weeks after that.

Control of Henderson Field gave the Marines an advantage during the day, but their supply convoys still had to run the gauntlet of Japanese surface ships, bombers and submarines. At night, when American air power was less of a threat, the Japanese brought in fresh troops and supplies of their own.

We had another memorable event while we were on Tulagi. The Navy cargo ship USS *Bellatrix* came in and anchored in Tulagi harbour, and they sent me and Eugene Wilson on board to handle ship-to-shore communications. It was past noon, so we weren't concerned about air raids, but Washing Machine Charlie or his equal came in out of a clear blue sky and dropped a bomb, just missing the fantail.

We were under way in a matter of minutes, justifiably – the ship was a floating bomb. The holds were full of bombs and ammunition they needed badly on Guadalcanal, and all the decks were covered with hundreds of drums of aviation gasoline. One tracer bullet into a drum would've set it off.

After many hours of evasive manoeuvring, the *Bellatrix* returned to complete unloading the following day.

The Skipper got orders to turn us around and get back and get unloaded, even if he had to float it off. As soon as we arrived back offshore, a formation of high altitude bombers dropped their whole load on us. It just wasn't our time!

We got our part of the cargo unloaded, and the *Bellatrix* on her way to Guadalcanal. We also came off there with about thirty loaves of bread in a pillow case, as a treat for the men on the beach.

On 29 October Ray's battalion was ferried across Ironbottom Sound to strengthen the Marine beachhead on Guadalcanal, which was under constant attack by land, sea and air.

We had an air raid by about two dozen Jap bombers every day. These would drop their loads on Henderson Field, or any ships that might be in the area. They'd be accompanied by fighters that could climb faster than any of ours, but they still couldn't outfight our 'Cactus Air Force' [the Army, Navy and Marine Corps air units flown in to operate from Henderson Field. 'Cactus' was the original codename for Guadalcanal]. If we weren't on the move we could tune in to the planes' frequencies and have a ringside seat at the daily dogfights. Hollywood could never reproduce what we saw overhead.

Every time we moved our lines we each had to dig a new foxhole, because the Jap Navy had a free hand to blast us whenever they had a notion to. The Japs also harassed us with their knee mortars,[3] which were light enough for one man to handle. Of course someone else had to carry the shells for them. Pistol Pete got into the act on occasions, especially when we were moving our lines, or warding off Jap assaults.

Most of us became fatalists, and figured it just didn't have our name on it if we walked away from a fire fight, or a shelling or bombing. We soon learned not to cluster or get in groups, in order to present a small target. We learned to do without clean, fresh water and to drink some you wouldn't normally consider drinking. Thirst is far less tolerable than hunger.

We never changed our clothes, in fact there were only two times I had my clothes off in about six months. Ordinary things like toothpaste or brushes, toilet paper – or paper of any kind – and soap would've been nice.

The mosquitoes were a constant problem, day and night. And malaria didn't get you off a patrol or a spell in the front line. 102 or 103 degree fevers were common. The food – when we could get it – was poor. We were pretty skinny by the end. To add to the problem of an inadequate diet, about 90 per cent of the men had violent dysentery, which debilitated them further. Some of them almost died from it.

We had very little sleep. The Japs seemed to prefer night encounters, unless they could ambush us on our daytime patrols. The Jap Navy ran up and down

---

3. 50mm grenade dischargers, capable of firing high explosive, smoke or flares. The nickname came from the curved base plate, which led the Americans to believe the weapon was steadied against the firer's leg.

blasting away at targets, and were always trying to reinforce their ground troops.

> The seas around Guadalcanal were the scene of six full scale battles, and dozens of smaller engagements. Japanese and American naval losses were roughly comparable, but while the Americans could afford such losses, knowing their massive industrial capacity would more than replace them, the Japanese could not.
>
> Gradually the Americans began to choke off the flow of Japanese reinforcements, while their own strength on the islands continued to grow.

In January 1943 we were replaced by the 6th Marines.

We passed the word to our outposts to secure their gear and head back to the beach as soon as the replacements arrived. All but one of our outposts got the message – a Squad from 'H' Company had become disconnected by phone. I volunteered to go out and give them the word.

I followed the telephone line out toward the outpost, and met a man coming toward me that I recognized from my old Reserve Battalion. It was his Squad that I was looking for. He was carrying a shoe with a foot and part of an ankle in it, and he was understandably all shook up. We had a quick funeral for the remains. This was the first time our paths had crossed since we'd landed almost six months before. His whole Squad had been killed by one of our own mortar shells.

We continued together toward the beach, and came across another man from our Reserve Battalion, also from our home town, coming in with the 6th Marines. Finally we got aboard the same ship that'd brought us there, the *President Hayes*. We had to climb up nets to get back aboard, and standing at the top of the net was a guy from my graduating class at High School! Just a brief encounter at the top of the net, and I never saw him again. I continued down to our troop quarters and found a soft, safe sack and slept most of the way to New Zealand.

> On 1 February 1943 the *President Hayes*, together with other APs which carried their own landing craft, was formally redesignated an Auxiliary, Personnel, Attack – or APA. Similarly equipped cargo ships were reclassified as AKAs.
>
> The six-month Guadalcanal campaign ended on 7 February, with the evacuation by destroyer of the remaining Japanese. The 2nd Marines were by then enjoying a period of rest near Wellington, on the North Island of New Zealand, but Ray found his personal situation anything but restful.

I had three men I couldn't get along with – my Company commander, the Battalion Sergeant Major from before, and a Technical Sergeant. Each one was a separate tale of woe.

The Company commander was a politician. He promoted a friend of his that'd only been in the service twelve weeks, and passed over seven men that were starting their second year. I told him we never had to put up with that before, and the men wouldn't like it.

The Sergeant Major was used to having the last word and never taking no for an answer. We argued every day for eight months.

The Tech Sergeant had me on many dirty or risky jobs.

As soon as I could, I went in the office and asked to be transferred. I was told to forget it; they wouldn't be transferring anyone. Then, about five months after we got to New Zealand, and out of a clear blue sky, the Tech Sergeant came running in to ask me if I still wanted that transfer. I had to pack and be on a truck in ten minutes or I'd miss my chance!

My new unit, the Tank Battalion [part of the establishment of each Marine Division], didn't even know I was coming. Then when I went into Wellington and was having a beer, the doctor from my old Battalion came up and shook hands, and said 'You have to buy me a drink, Sergeant'. I said 'Nothing personal, but I can't drink with officers, Doctor Welte', and he replied 'You've a field commission coming. I'll see you in the morning for a physical exam, but you're as healthy as the rest of us'!

I asked if it was going to follow me to the Tank Battalion. He didn't know I'd been shipped over there. This Tech Sergeant had shanghaied me out of my old outfit because if I'd stayed there I would've been senior to him and the Sergeant Major! Doctor Welte called the CO of the Tank Battalion the next day, and he called me in and said he'd send me wherever I wanted to go as soon as my service records caught up with me. But someone had pigeon-holed them, and they didn't catch up with me until after our next operation. That probably saved my life, because otherwise I'd have been a junior officer with a Platoon of men, and at Tarawa those guys took heavy casualties.

While the 2nd Marine Division had been training in New Zealand, the Allied leaders had been mapping out a strategy for the Pacific war. The British, after some persuasion, had agreed that sufficient resources were now available for an American thrust through the Marshall Islands, as well as New Guinea and the Solomons. Because the Marshalls were currently outside the range of their land-based air power, however, the Americans decided that two closer coral atolls – Makin and Tarawa, in the Gilbert Islands – should be the first targets of this Central Pacific drive. D-Day for both assaults was set as Saturday 20 November 1943.

The focus of resistance in Makin Atoll was the island of Butaritari, which was captured with relative ease by part of the US

Army's 27th Infantry Division. But at Tarawa, where the main Japanese garrison and the vital airfield lay on the island of Betio, the defences proved far more formidable. The whole of the 2nd Marine Division had to be used to overcome them.

Tarawa is one of those nightmares that never should've happened. Everything that *could* go wrong, went wrong at Tarawa. The landing was delayed waiting for our air support to come in and bomb the bunkers and seawalls, and we lost the element of surprise.

The coordination and timing essential to an amphibious operation started to unravel. Worse was to follow.

Betio Island lay on a shelf of coral, the depth of water over which was known to be unpredictable. The initial landing waves were able to negotiate this obstacle because they were carried in LVTs,[4] but the subsequent waves, attempting to land from ordinary LCVPs, grounded on the coral while still well short of the beach. Their Marines had no option but to wade the several hundred yards to the shore, under murderous machine gun and artillery fire all the way.

Ray's old unit, the 2nd Battalion, 2nd Marines, were assaulting Red 2, the central of the three landing beaches used on the first day.

Some men had as much as a quarter of a mile to swim and bob up and down to get to the beach, and they not only had fire from the seawall, but enfilade fire from several machine gun nests in a beached ship to their right, and under and on top of a long pier to their left. Our landing craft hit the reef and got hung up, so the Japs had another sitting duck for target practice. We couldn't wade ashore because we had a radio jeep.

I had gone in as an observer, to see how effective the tanks were going to be, but by the time I got up on the pier, only two were still working. That was early in the morning when we started floating on the high tide of the second day. I got ashore at the end of the long pier [which separated Beach Red 2 from its neighbour on the left, Red 3], and had to wade in where Bill Hawkins [First Lieutenant William D Hawkins, one of two members of the 2nd Marines to win the Medal of Honor on Betio] had burnt a few sections of it closer to the beach.

The coxswain got us to the pier, then took a load of wounded out to the ships and came back later with supplies for the men on the island – water, medical supplies, ammunition and some field rations. I spent the rest of my

---

4. Makin and Tarawa were the first battles in which massed LVTs were used to land the assault troops. Previously these vehicles had been viewed more as stores carriers.

time working on and off the pier. I had no other assignment, so I helped with handling the incoming supplies and loading wounded, and acted as a runner on one occasion.

It took the Marines until D+3 to secure the tiny island, by which time most of the Japanese garrison had fought to the death.

I don't remember eating or sleeping until it was all over. I ate on my way back to our ship, and almost threw up. I reached over the side to wash out my messkit, and saw a shark with part of a body. Back on the ship I found a place to sleep, and staring at me was a bottle of Scotch whisky. The name on the pack was an officer that'd been killed in one of the tanks, so I toasted him and chug-a-lugged a good amount out of the bottle. When I came to, the corpsmen had found me and pumped my stomach, and we were on our way to Hawaii.

In addition to the 1st and 2nd Marine Divisions with which America had entered the war, a series of further units were now being readied for combat, as the expansion of the Marine Corps gathered pace.

Frank Hall's regiment was raised as part of a new 3rd Marine Division.

Our Regiment, the 21st Marines, was formed in 1942, starting with a small cadre of men transferred from the 6th Marines.

At the time the battle for Guadalcanal was raging we were still being organized at New River, North Carolina – later called Camp Lejeune. We were getting useful feedback from the 1st Marine Division on how the Japanese fought in the jungle. For example, we had to revise what the handbook told us about setting out guards at night in front of the line, where they would walk a post. Using the cover of the dense jungle, the Japanese would silently ambush these sentries and cut their throats. So if we were putting out sentries at night, there should be two or three guys together in a foxhole, with one awake at all times, and no walking. In fact, after that, no one ever got out of his foxhole at night.

We were in the swamps near the coast. It rained most of the time, and the mosquitoes were huge and plentiful. We learned to operate in Squads – twelve men at that time – and they designated me as a scout.

Did that involve special training?

No, there was no individual training as a scout where I was separated from the others. We just learned how to handle our specific roles on the job, mostly in Squad-sized maneuvers. As a Squad, we learned how to keep far enough apart so one grenade, mortar shell or burst from an automatic weapon wouldn't get more than one of us. We learned to walk along in silence, and we learned to spot likely places for ambushes. I took it all pretty seriously. Of the ninety guys in the Regiment in my position leading patrols, eighty-seven were later killed or wounded. I wasn't scratched. It took a Jap artillery shell to do that. We learned how to read a compass, how to knock out pillboxes and machine gun positions by leapfrogging as a Squad, and how to dig in for the night. At one point they put us in foxholes and drove tanks over us, so we'd get the feel of it.

Mostly our training taught us how to operate as a team and to respect one another. Whereas a good part of our morale and motivation in battle came from the pride we had as Marines, 'the World's best', another big factor was not letting our buddies down.

We'd been training with bolt-action Springfield '03s, but were now issued the new semi-automatic M1 Garand rifle. We also fired the BAR – Browning Automatic Rifle – as well as the .30 caliber machine gun and the Thompson submachine gun.

In December 1942 we went by train from North Carolina to Camp Elliott, just outside of San Diego. For the next few weeks we started the first of many six-week training and conditioning cycles that continued throughout the war. The first day we'd go on a 3-mile hike, then each day the distance would be increased, until by the end of the first week we'd be hiking 20 miles a day.

All through the war, every time we came out of combat we would rest a couple of days, then start the six-week conditioning cycle; learn how to dig foxholes all over again, and in lieu of boats, run out into the surf with full gear, turn around and in Squad formation hit the beach, run inland, and dig in.

Then in early January 1943 we were moved to Camp Pendleton, about 50 miles north [on the coast between San Diego and Los Angeles]. This time there was no train. We walked. At Pendleton we did a lot of camping out in eight-man pyramidal tents in the hills. We ran obstacle courses, especially at night. Then we'd clean up, change our clothes and go out on liberty to Oceanside, the nearest town. I remember one night it was raining and we had to crawl through the mud under barbed wire and through slit trenches while they fired machine guns with live ammunition over our heads and threw practice grenades at us. When we were dismissed that night, a couple of guys and I, covered from head to toe with mud, walked into the barracks and right into the shower – rifles, helmets, packs and all.

We arrived on Guadalcanal [now transformed into a staging base for further expansion up the Solomons chain] in July 1943, and became acclimated to the heat and humidity. We practiced jungle fighting there for a few months until we left for Bougainville in November.

Was it spelled out to you what the Division's role would be on Bougainville?

Yes, they briefed us very well. We knew exactly what our mission was, and generally what the timetable was. Bougainville was the largest of the Solomon Islands, about 130 miles long by about 30 miles wide, with a chain of mountains running lengthwise.

If we built an airfield there, our bombers and fighters could support General Douglas MacArthur's [US and Commonwealth] forces over in New

Guinea, and also hit north at Rabaul in New Britain [the principal remaining Japanese base in the South West Pacific].

Our job was to land on the beach, push inland to form a semi-circle about 10 miles deep, then make sure the Japanese kept off the backs of the Seabees while they built the airstrip.

The Japanese had about 40,000 troops on Bougainville, so they initially outnumbered us more than two to one. But I don't believe there were any more Marines to spare. The 1st Marine Division was in Australia, pretty well devastated from their battle for Guadalcanal – a lot of malaria and dysentery. In December 1943 they were going to land on New Britain [at the opposite end of the island from Rabaul] in an operation similar to ours. While we were on Bougainville the 2nd Marine Division landed on Tarawa, so they weren't available either, and a little later the recently formed 4th Marine Division landed in the Marshall Islands. At the time of our landing on Bougainville there were no 5th or 6th Marine Divisions.

We came up from Guadalcanal in an APD [Auxiliary, Personnel, High Speed] – an old four-stack destroyer converted to a high-speed transport. Like some of our rations, she'd been made for World War One.

The Americans shrewdly avoided the well-defended part of the island, and went ashore instead at Empress Augusta Bay on the west coast, taking the Japanese by surprise. D-Day for the operation was Monday 1 November 1943.

The 3rd and 9th Marines landed on D-Day, with Frank's regiment joining them a few days later.

We saw no Japs, because the 3rd and 9th Marines had already wiped out all resistance on the beach and on the two little islands just offshore, Puruata and Torokina. The 9th Marines had landed on the left and the 3rd Marines on the right, where they'd met twenty-five pillboxes on Cape Torokina containing machine guns, artillery and a force of Japs who fought to the bitter end. Our naval gunfire had knocked out only three pillboxes of the twenty-five before they landed, so they'd had a very bloody time wiping them out one by one. During the landing, Jap Zero fighters had shot up the landing craft, the transports, and the Marines on the beach.

We didn't know about all this. All we knew was the 3rd and 9th Marines seemed to have done a nice job clearing the way. We saw no Zeros, no Japanese Navy or troops, and figured this invasion was a snap. We soon found out otherwise.

We weren't enchanted with our first look at Bougainville, especially this swamp in the Empress Augusta Bay area. The trail leading inland was impassable for trucks and jeeps because it was a sea of mud, and LVTs were requested to carry supplies up to the front. As we proceeded up the trail we passed men from the 9th Marines and the Raiders[5] coming back from the front lines. Some were carrying wounded buddies. From the dark and haggard looks on their faces, we could see they weren't happy. Even though they were being relieved for a little rest there wasn't a smile anywhere to be seen, and they didn't say anything.

We continued another couple of miles up the trail, then we stopped. 'E' Company, which was leading, had gotten surprised by an ambush and was cut off from the rest of the Battalion. The Lieutenant led our Platoon, with the First Squad first – meaning me as scout – up the trail a little ways, until we got to a few guys from 'E' Company who showed us where the Japanese ambush was, and where they thought the rest of their Company were.

We left the trail to the right, and in single file we made a big semi-circle around 'E' Company and cut back to the trail. Then we each turned left, and slowly closed the circle, sneaking very quietly and slowly in a skirmish line, searching for the Marines and the Japanese.

I was crawling along through very thick bushes with my bayonet mounted on my rifle, listening to snapping sounds. When a twig fell off a bush right next to my head, I decided the snapping sounds were the sound of bullets passing by. I stopped crawling, to see where the Jap sniper was. A Marine crawled up from my right rear, and no sooner had he got in front of me where I was about to crawl than he was shot in the head. I still couldn't spot the Jap, because their snipers were usually so well hidden that they only fired exactly where their rifles were pointed. If they swung the rifle around, we'd see them, so unless you walked where they were aiming, they couldn't hit you.

So I crawled around this guy, and continued on until I reached the trail. The Japanese in the ambush had seen us encircling them, and had sneaked away before we could close the trap. I came across a few wounded Marines, and got them a corpsman – a Navy medic who looked like a Marine, dressed like a Marine, and was right with us no matter where we went. They used to wear Red Cross armbands until the Japanese used them for targets. That was my first real action. The first time, but not the last, that I was shot at.

That night we formed a perimeter, dug in and spent the night listening to our artillery pounding away outside our circle. The 12th Marines, our Divisional artillery regiment, were excellent. They kept dropping rounds within 10 yards or so outside our positions, and the only time anybody on our side got hurt was from a tree burst.

Most nights we simply settled down, because once it was dark we didn't light a match, we didn't talk above a whisper, and we positively did *not* leave our foxholes. Anyone walking around after dark got shot, because he'd be Japanese. They got very brave at night, and would try to infiltrate our lines and quietly cut a few throats.

We could see nothing, but we'd hear all kinds of strange sounds – birds, bugs – and swear it was the Japanese signalling to each other. At the start this

---

5. The USMC had begun raising commando units called Marine Raider Battalions during 1942. The 2nd and 3rd Marine Raider Battalions were attached to the 3rd Marine Division for the Bougainville operation.

made the guys edgy, so all along the line people'd be opening up with rifles, BARs, even machine guns. Every time someone opened up we'd think the Japs were attacking. One section of the line would spook the next, and around and around it'd go. We'd spend the whole night like this, shooting at every sound. If we hadn't been Marines, I'd have said we were scared silly.

We found out that every unit goes through something like this when they're first in combat in the jungle. Later, on other nights, we'd hear sounds of shooting in the distance, and would shake our heads in scorn and say 'Boots . . . !'.

About dawn one morning we woke with a shake; the ground was moving around, and the trees were swaying. We decided it must be an earthquake. But before we could make up our minds whether to stay in our foxhole and maybe have a tree fall and bury us, or jump out and maybe get shot by a Jap, the shaking stopped. A few trees already weakened by mortar fire did fall, but not on us. As the daylight got brighter and we could see across to the mountains, the biggest one [the 8650ft volcanic cone of Mount Bagana] had smoke coming out of it. We got a little spooked, what with the jungle, the earthquake, and now a volcano. All we needed was for King Kong to show up.

Most of the Japanese were on the other side of those mountains, so they had a big problem trying to get their artillery and other heavy equipment to our side of the island. For three or four days we had a forward observer from the 12th Marines way up a tall banyan tree right near our foxhole. He had a pair of field glasses, and was watching some Japs about 7 miles away carrying a big artillery piece through a mountain pass on their backs. The gun was broken down into several pieces. We could hear him on his field telephone reporting their progress. Finally we heard him say 'They're digging in and assembling the gun', and give their map coordinates.

After he saw where his shells had landed he gave new coordinates, then hollered 'Fire for effect!'. We heard the whomp, whomp of about ten shells exploding, then he reported they'd blown up the gun. We all cheered, and when he climbed down we told him we liked the way he'd waited until the Japs had done all that work before he destroyed the gun. We invited him to come back any time!

Every day we'd go out on five- or six-man reconnaissance patrols to cover the jungle right in front of our position, to make sure the Japanese weren't massing for a surprise attack. Our Colonel didn't like surprises. Since I was a scout, I'd lead the way while we looked for Japs. We'd hike out 2 or 3 miles in one direction, take a left turn for another couple of miles, then left again to return. We'd make this big triangle using a compass, and make notes as to where we'd located Japanese. We came across small groups at times, but they didn't see us. Other patrols were ambushed, but we were lucky; we always saw them before they saw us.

It was a lot easier to follow a trail, and the other guys let me know this after our first patrol. But after they heard our buddies in 'E' Company and 'G' Company had got all shot up when they followed trails, they didn't complain.

I saw my job as to find out where the Japs were and to get back alive, so we never followed a trail. The Japs loved to wait alongside of trails wherever there was a sharp bend, a small hill to climb, or a little stream to cross – any kind of natural barrier which would distract us.

Can you describe a patrol?

Well, for example, on the morning of the earthquake Mike, our Sergeant, told us to hike 3 miles out toward the mountains on a compass azimuth of 95 degrees, then turn left for 2 miles at 350 degrees, then left again at 225 degrees. We each had a compass, so in case we got in a firefight and got separated, we could find our way back. As usual, we were looking for any large groups of Japs to see if they were gathering for a surprise attack.

We climbed through the barbed wire and went down the hill, and walked in single file through the jungle. Louie the Lip was second scout, so he was about 5 yards behind me. Behind him was Mike, then Tony with his BAR, with Gunner Budell bringing up the rear, all about the same distance apart. You had to stay close enough to see the guy in front, yet far enough apart so we didn't all get hit by the same Nambu machine gun or grenade.

You walked silently, keeping about 10 to 20yds away from any trail. Nobody in the patrol said anything. You used hand signals. I lined up my compass for 95 degrees and drew a bead on a tall tree about 100 yards away. When we reached the big tree, I took out my compass and did the same thing again. Mike double-checked with his. He'd delegated Gunner to count paces, so we'd have an idea when we'd gone 3 miles. The jungle was pretty thick, and what with weaving around trees and bushes and over dead logs, it wasn't easy to keep track of our direction or the distance we'd travelled.

I had my machete in my left hand, and a Browning Automatic Rifle in my right. I was supposed to carry a Garand, but I soon learnt that, being out in front and all, having an automatic weapon that could get off twenty rounds with one squeeze of the trigger was much better insurance than an eight-round Garand which fired one shot at a time. So after we landed, I picked up a BAR no longer needed by its original owner. Except for the BAR, that day we were travelling light. All I had with me was my cartridge belt with two canteens of water and a First Aid kit, a bandolier with six magazines of ammunition, and a couple of grenades. Oh yes – I'd also have a D ration in my pocket.

The D ration, developed to take the place of a normal meal for emergencies, consisted of a 4oz chocolate bar with an unusually high melting point. The principal ingredients were plain chocolate, sugar, skimmed milk powder, cocoa fat, oat flour and artificial flavouring.

It didn't taste very good, but you could survive on it.

After about two hours we reached the 3 mile point, and took ten. We'd no sooner started forward again than we came to a stream, and I could see what might be a good spot for an ambush about 30yds upstream. On our side a path met the stream, and a big tree was laying in the water, blocking the way. The path continued on the other side, and passed right by a little hill covered with very dense underbrush. I motioned for our guys to hold up, and Louie and I went downstream so we could cross out of sight of anybody who might be waiting at the log. We made a big circle and came up beside the path as it continued toward the mountains. Sure enough, we could see two Japs peering over a mound watching the tree trunk in the stream, while about fifteen more lounged around eating their fish heads. We couldn't be sure of the exact number because of the density of the bushes, but fifteen was enough for us.

Louie and I very cautiously sneaked away and rejoined the rest of the guys. Mike marked the spot on his map. Nothing much happened during the rest of the patrol, but in a couple of places we spotted evidence of recent occupation by forty or fifty soldiers.

Our patrols kept them off balance.

Not all the troops to hold the beachhead came from the Marine Corps, however. The US Army's 37th Infantry Division joined the Marines after an exhausting campaign of its own on New Georgia, another of the Solomon Islands.

Charles Henne was an officer in the 148th Infantry Regiment, the first of the 37th's units to arrive on Bougainville.

Preliminary to the Empress Augusta Bay landing, on October 27, the 8th Brigade of the 3rd New Zealand Division had been landed on Mono Island [off Bougainville's south coast].

My Battalion – the 3rd Battalion, 148th Infantry – boarded the USS *Fuller* a Company at a time, starting at 2.00pm on Saturday November 6, 1943. Embarkation lasted throughout the afternoon.

Approaching the *Fuller* in boats, the ship looked like all the others of the same class. When my boat pulled broadside to a cargo net, designated men pulled the dangling net into the boat and up we went. Going over the rail, we were greeted by the familiar faces from 'C' Battery, 140th Field Artillery Battalion, who'd boarded earlier. They were expected, for we were loading as a Battalion Combat Team[6] and 'C' Battery was the artillery component. It gave me a good feeling to have them with us, for on New Georgia we'd had no direct fire support of any kind. The third component, also aboard, was a Platoon from 'C' Company, 117th Engineer Battalion. I wasn't sure what the Engineers could or would do for us, but their presence rounded out the Team according to the book.

All APAs – attack transports – looked much alike. Their troop spaces looked alike, were organized alike, and one and all they were hot and stuffy. So hot and stuffy that when all troops were aboard and the men were released to

---

6. An infantry battalion plus attached units, in the same way that a Regiment Combat
   Team was a regiment plus attached units.

move to fresh air topside, only a few ever remained in the holds. The *Fuller* was relatively clean, but she had the usual transport stink. To my nose, all transports stunk alike – something like an abused bivouac spiced with the smell of salt water and crude oil.

While the first shift to eat was being called to dinner, the transports upped anchor. Dark came quickly, and the Boatswain twittered his pipe and announced 'The smoking lamp is out!'. Denied smokes, most men headed for their bunks, worn out by a long day of waiting.

Sunday November 7 was like any other day aboard ship; the days of the month had no meaning unless orders directed something to be done on a particular day at a particular time. November 8 had meaning, because that would see us ashore on Bougainville. But shipboard routine slowed a bit on Sunday, and time was reserved for Church services for those who wished to attend. I never attended Church; I'd long since become convinced that our Bible thumpers couldn't read any better than I could.

In my Company, as the day progressed, men not tied up by details found time to go topside. There they played cards, rolled dice, or leaned on a rail to watch the ocean roll by the ship. It was fascinating to watch the purple water form a deep curl around the bow of the ship, and then become a wake of white fluorescence. Drawing interest and comment were flying fish that skipped and skittered as the ship sliced through their schools. Also drawing attention were distant islands, showing as smudges on the northern horizon. Flying fish were a fleeting novelty, but the guessing game about the identity of the islands lasted as long as they could be seen. Some swore we were seeing Vella Lavella [secured in October 1943, in the last part of the New Georgia campaign], and one insistent trooper claimed one of the islands was Kolombangara [also secured in October]. Obviously my eyesight wasn't as good.

The night of November 7/8 was a short one. Veterans tried to get some shuteye. The sleepless rookies waited for daylight, but at the same time wanted to hold on to the night. Like many others, they were frightened, but had no idea what was scaring them. I knew their apprehension stemmed from not knowing what lay ahead of us, but it was always that way.

Stand To came early, an hour before dawn. It was announced by Non Coms shouting the men out of their sacks into queues for breakfast. A favored few led the chow line to wash down the not-so-savory transport chow with strong coffee. These were those selected to man gun stations on deck. After eating breakfast the men, like well-drilled automatons, filed back to the troop compartments. There they readied themselves and their loads to move to boat stations.

At dawn the first waves were called topside. We could make out the shapes of other ships, and those at the landing nets on the port side of the *Fuller* were the first to glimpse Bougainville through the mist. We knew that the Marines were ashore, and that Jap planes had been raiding the beachhead daily, so raids were expected during our landing.

Typically, pre-invasion briefings gave travel brochure type rundowns on an objective area, and Bougainville was no exception. From the briefings, we understood we were to land on a big island with interior mountains. We knew less about Jap dispositions, only that most of them were in the south near Kahili or in the north on Buka Island. Empress Augusta Bay, the only indentation on Bougainville's western coast, was located approximately half way between these Jap centers of strength. The distance to Rabaul was about 220 miles. This placed our beachhead well within the range of Jap planes based there.

As the rising sun stripped away the mist, the tip of Mount Bagana appeared. As the mist cleared, other high mountains and foothills could be seen. To the eye, except the summit of the big mountain, all of it was covered with jungle. From high on the mountainsides, the jungle rolled downward in a continuous green carpet to a narrow beach. At first, the beach was more perceived than seen.

Only the volcanic mountains and the earthquakes presented a new dimension to us. Not new were the crocodiles in the rivers, the top canopy formed by mahogany and banyan trees, the dense undergrowth, the swamps, the mud, the torrential rain and the malarial mosquitoes. Bougainville was like New Georgia, only a lot bigger.

As the day brightened, the beach became visible. It didn't look like much. It was steep, narrow, colored dirty grey, and swept by rolling surf. It was also congested – clogged with Marine trucks, bulldozers and stacks of supplies. In contrast, the water alongside the *Fuller* was crystal clear. Its depths were crowded with fish quickly identified as barracuda. When this became known, more than one man questioned whether they would attack a man in the water. They received mixed answers, but the barracuda weren't active. They appeared content to lie log-like, undisturbed by the hubbub overhead. The island, the beach, and the barracuda were pushed out of mind when the swabbies lowered the *Fuller's* LCVPs over the side into the water.

When in the water, individual boats held away from the ship until called to net stations. On order, four men at a time threw a leg over the rail, grasped a vertical strand of the cargo net draped below them and climbed swiftly down. The descent was accompanied by bitching and cussing, especially when someone planted his boondockers on the head of a man lower on the net.

The swells were not dangerously high, but high enough to create testy moments for those caught on an upswing or a drop of the boat out of phase with the rise and fall of the ship. Caught on a rising net, you had to decide whether to hang on or jump. But the disembarkation went smoothly, and no one got an unscheduled dip in the briny. As boats were loaded, they pulled away and made quick time to the beach, where they dropped ramps. Some made it to the beach with dry feet, others with boots full of salt water. Once there, the men were shouted across the beach and into the brush fringe, which separated the narrow beach from a knee-deep swamp. When empty, the landing craft returned to the ship to shuttle more men ashore.

After several such round trips, the only men left aboard were members of the unloading detail, composed of men from each of our Companies and 'C' Battery – all under my nominal command.

The *Fuller*'s boats returned and took on loads of cargo, then turned for shore and disappeared into the chaotic confusion of the beach. When they didn't return, the Captain of the *Fuller* summoned me and demanded to know what the Army'd done with them. It rankled to be chewed out by a swabbie officer, and he surely knew that I had no control over his damned LCVPs. Not having communication with the beach, I told him if he could get me a boat, I'd go ashore and find out.

At the net station I found a landing craft that was shore bound, and it didn't take me long to reach the beach. I got lucky, for we dropped ramp at the spot where our Battalion's unloading detail was waiting. They too wanted to know where the boats were.

I searched out the Navy Beachmaster, and when I found him, I learned that he too was looking for the *Fuller*'s boats. While talking to him, one of his men spoke up, recalling that he'd seen a bunch of them at the north end of the beach, just sitting waiting. We made a quick trip up the beach. They had to be the *Fuller*'s.

They were. We learned that when one of them had gone to the wrong beach the others, sheep-like, had followed. Now the problem was either to move the landing craft or move the waiting unloading detail. The Beachmaster decided to move the landing craft. While he was issuing orders to the coxswains, the air raid klaxons sounded.

I'd just rejoined our beach detail when the first Jap planes – a mixture of Zeros and Bettys – powered overhead. The Zero was the standard Jap fighter plane. The Betty[7] was a twin-engined medium bomber. A Navy officer standing nearby with a radio told me that fifty Jap planes had been sighted coming in. Our fighters had bounced them and split off about half, but this left twenty-five or more to be dealt with by the anti-aircraft artillery on the ships and on the beach.

The Japs came in low and zipped overhead heading for the ships, so we got a close look at them. The ships had been alerted, and the gunners were standing to their guns. As soon as the Japs came within range all guns that could be brought to bear opened up. Jap planes began to fall, but undeterred by by the heavy ack-ack fire the pilots made repeated runs on the ships. Then they suddenly pulled away, to disappear to the north west. When they were gone, beach operations resumed.

While talking to the Beachmaster I could hear artillery off in the distance, and I realized that the swabbies I'd just met were also discussing the battle sounds. I was told that the shelling was a preparation fired to support a Marine counterattack against a bunch of Japs a couple of miles up the beach. I recognized American artillery, in this instance Marine artillery. I didn't hear any small arms fire; the battle was too distant. When the artillery tapered off and quit I assumed that the situation was well in hand.

---

7. The system of aircraft designations used by the Japanese was particularly arcane, so their planes were given easily-remembered reporting names by the Allies.

The only incident on the beach was caused by a not-so-bright Marine cradling a .30 caliber machine gun, who couldn't have had an easier target than a P-40 [US Army fighter] flying low overhead. No doubt the pilot hoped to escape friendly fire, but the gun-happy Marine hosed his plane from propeller hub to tail.

The plane's engine began smoking and lost power, and the pilot took to the water on the land side of Puruata Island. Fished out of the drink unhurt, the pilot, flaming mad, hitched a ride to the 148th's part of the beach demanding the son of a bitch who'd shot him down.

The Marine was long gone into the bush by the time he reached our section of the beach, but the persistent pilot trolled the area for an hour before giving up. I'd been within yards of the shooter, but to me one Marine looks much like all the others. I was able to tell the pilot that the Marine was big, and wide between the eyes. My description was of little help, for it described a lot of Marines.

With the *Fuller*'s landing craft found and under control of the Beachmaster, I returned to the ship to report to the Captain. Back on board, I climbed to the bridge, saluted and told him that someone had led his boats to the wrong beach. I then volunteered that I thought by now the Navy should've learned how to control its boats.

The Captain, not being accustomed to being addressed that way by a mere Army Captain, took umbrage and demanded my name, rank and serial number. However, he never reported the incident – or if he did, no one gave it any attention. I never heard another word about it.

Walking aft through a dozen or more enlisted swabbies, it was obvious they were scared. They were decked out in their funny steel helmets, and as a group were the most nervous sailors I saw any time during the war. They desperately wanted to sail away from Bougainville, and to hell with unloading the ship.

During the raid the Japs had hit the ship three times with bombs, and made a near-miss with a fourth. Lieutenant Hawkins, my Assistant Unloading Officer, told me six men from the 140th Field Artillery Battalion had been wounded, but none seriously. They were being cared for by the ship's medical corpsmen and were in two of the officers' cabins. Their names were unfamiliar to me, but I visited them, verifying what Lieutenant Hawkins had told me. Next, I wanted to see the bomb damage.

One bomb had hit the fantail 5in gun, ricocheting off the gun tube. As it came to rest, men from the gun crew ran to it and tipped it over the side. Another bomb had dropped into Hatch No 7, where it exploded killing several sailors and wounding the men from the 140th. That bomb caused the most damage, and the greatest number of personnel casualties. The third bomb was another dud. It fell into No 6 Hatch, landed on a stack of cargo with a thunderous crash and scared the bejazzus out of everyone down there. If it'd detonated it would have killed them all. After a few minutes of shocked immobility, cool heads took over. They rigged a sling, and used a boom to lift the thing topside and swing it outboard to drop it into the water. The fourth bomb had landed in the water alongside the ship. Its explosion lifted the ship and then dropped her. The sick bay was riddled, and hot searing fragments set mattresses and other flammables burning. When I arrived on the scene smoke was still drifting up gangways and mattresses were smouldering in the water alongside, but a damage control party had everything under control.

When assured that all was well with our men on the *Fuller*, and wanting to put some distance between myself and the glowering Captain, I told Lieutenant Hawkins that the detail was his and that I was going ashore, not to return.

Once ashore, I found that our unloading detail was staying ahead of the incoming landing craft. They were quickly unloading them, giving them a short turnaround time. But daylight was fading, and the Navy suspended unloading, pulled anchor and departed for safer water. When this word was passed to the Beachmaster, he sent a man to let me know that there'd be no more boats that day, but unloading would be resumed the next day.

When released by the Beachmaster, our unloading detail was on its own. After finding my Company, 'M' Company, I reported to the Battalion commander to inform him that unloading had been suspended, but I said nothing about my confrontation with the Skipper of the *Fuller*. I then returned to my own Company to get on with the business of running the outfit.

The Marines intermingled with us thought we were their relief. 'We're beachhead troops, amphibious specialists . . . '. Now that the Army had arrived, they would be leaving. This was news to me; and they were to be disappointed, because they had to wait until late December to be relieved by an Army division. Of course, Marine Corps hype claims that six Marine divisions swept the Pacific clean of Japs. There was a familiar Army answer to this, but the newspaper weenies never picked it up. It ran 'A typical Marine squad consists of two shooting, two rooting, two talking, and two taking pictures'.

A couple of our loudmouths appointed themselves as spokesmen. Mouthing off, they gave the Marines every provocation to start an inter-service fistfight, but the Marines gave way and put some distance between themselves and their enemy, those unappreciative Army types.

The next morning our ship returned to complete unloading. When this had been completed our unloading detail on the *Fuller* came ashore, and when all the men had been accounted for, we pushed our way through the Marines and out of the swamp, to higher ground inland.

> Since the role of the landing force was not, on this occasion, to clear the island, the vulnerable American perimeter required fixed defences.

On the new line the Battalion was supplied with saws and axes to build log bunkers, bulwarked with a few sandbags. The real labor went into clearing fire lanes, particularly for machine guns.

After we'd made a couple more short moves inland, word was passed that the Battalion hadn't been advancing aimlessly – its moves were expanding the beachhead by phase lines. The rest of our Divisional Headquarters and the 129th RCT landed five days after us, and the Division took over responsibility for the whole left half of the expanding beachhead. Another six days later the 145th RCT and final Division elements arrived, and once more the beachhead expanded. The 145th moved up into the line between the 129th – on our right – and the 3rd Marine Division, which was defending the right half of the beachhead. Again, the front line units dug in, repeating the construction of foxholes, slit trenches and gun positions that'd been built along preceding defense lines.

The final move came after Thanksgiving. On the final line the construction of permanent pillboxes, bunkers and gun positions was given priority. Splinterproof shelters, like on the 'Canal, were required for everyone. Sandbags were used in great numbers to cover the tops of bunkers and pillboxes. In addition, the men made use of the abundant vines and brush to weave revetments. Most of the sandbags were used to thicken roofs; woven revetments were used to secure the walls of communications trenches and fortifications.

The final line was indelibly marked with two double-apron barbed wire fences that spanned the front. Inside the wire was a long row of pillboxes grouped in Platoon strongpoints. The outer double-apron was installed first. Next, where possible, laterals and traverses were built to steer attacking Japs into machine gun fire.

When the outer fence was completed, we went to work installing the inside one. The inside barbed wire fence was separated from the outside fence by an average of 20yds. The space in between, by design, was for sowing anti-personnel mines. Both the inside fence and the outside fence were garnished with noisemakers and booby-traps. The last job was clear-cutting the interior areas of the Battalion sector to remove possible hiding places for intruding Japs.

The promised anti-personnel mines, received late in December, turned out to be the infamous 'Bouncing Betty'. The Betty was a wicked looking device that when tripped threw its killer charge upward to shoulder height. It was so sensitive that the slightest increase or release of tension on the trip wires would cause it to fire, and it wasn't selective; it killed both foe and friend. They were so dangerous they were never removed. They may still be there, exploding one by one.

When needed we could also call on artillery support, and on planes based on New Georgia. Later, when the Bougainville strips became operational, air support was based on the island and the response times were shortened.

When the kitchens started operating, hot chow and lots of good coffee boosted morale. Daily, the cooks fed us hot meals. Two meals a day were B rations, but the noon meal, whether prepared by the cooks or by the men themselves, was a C ration meal.

B rations were the closest approximation in the field to normal peacetime garrison food, but with tinned equivalents taking the place of perishables like fresh meat and milk.

C rations came entirely in tins – two tins per man per meal. One tin contained the main course and the other contained items like crackers, coffee, sugar and confectionery.

Our own 117th Engineer Battalion, using bulldozers, worked to scrape out jeep roads and to gradually improve them to carry heavier loads.

Japanese nighttime raids still managed to get through the anti-aircraft defenses to hit the beachhead. The attacks were a costly nuisance, changing nothing, but the Japs were persistent. During November the Division endured ninety-two air alerts. A popular target of the Jap bombers was Puruata Island, which was used as a transshipment point and was packed with stacked supplies.

On the plus side, mail was catching up. During December several shipments of mail were received, all a month or two months old. But the men in the line knew very little about what was happening elsewhere on the island, or elsewhere in the Pacific.

A Different Kind of Scared:
Kwajalein Atoll

Distances in the Pacific were vast. Over 1000 miles separated the men fighting on Bougainville from their colleagues on Tarawa, and more than 3000 miles lay between Tarawa and the most northerly of the island groups fought over during 1943, the Aleutians.

The Japanese had established outposts on two of these fog-shrouded islands, Attu and Kiska, back in June 1942. Although an enemy presence in the Aleutians posed no real threat to the rest of Alaska or the Pacific Northwest, American pride was undoubtedly stung by their occupation of US soil, and as soon as the resources became available a task force was assembled to retake the islands, starting with Attu.

The landing force, which consisted of most of the US Army's 7th Infantry Division plus some attached units, expected to overcome resistance in a matter of days.

Lawrence Jensen arrived on D+8, to find the Japanese still partly in control of the island.

On April 1, 1943, two months after graduating from Officer Candidate School, I was assigned to the 78th Coast Artillery Regiment (Anti-Aircraft) at Fort Ord, California [near Monterey]. Two weeks later we boarded a ship and sailed out of San Francisco. We had no idea where we were going, but we were issued foul weather gear – high-topped boots, and waterproof outerwear. The Division we were attached to, the 7th Infantry Division, had just had desert training! I hadn't really thought about leaving the States. I was just going where I was ordered.

The ship stopped at Dutch Harbor [the American base on Unalaska Island, further along the Aleutian chain in the direction of the mainland], but I didn't go ashore. After we sailed again the officers were given topographical maps of the island of Attu – our destination. On the way our convoy passed Kiska, where the Japanese Navy had minisubs, but there was no contact as we passed.

The ship I was on didn't take part in the landings. We went ashore after the beaches were secure, at the cheerfully-named Massacre Bay [on the south side of the island] on May 19, 1943. We went over the side, going down on netting to the landing craft below for the trip to shore. The temperature on Attu was about 40 degrees Fahrenheit, and it was foggy. No trees. All tundra.

The ground was mushy. I heard the men in battle were getting frozen feet; they probably didn't have time to take their boots off, to let their feet dry out. We had mess tents, but we ate where we could. In the field with no access to the mess station, we ate K rations [developed as a lighter weight alternative to C rations, and widely preferred to them].

On May 23 I was put in charge of forty-nine men, and reported to the 7th Infantry Division command post for a five-day morgue detail. We carried dead Americans and Japanese to a processing station for disposition. We had no vehicles, as the island wasn't suitable for them, so we had to use two rifles and a GI blanket as makeshift stretchers. The Chaplain would tell us where the bodies were, and we would get them to the processing station. We had no paperwork to do ourselves. After morgue duty, we bivouacked at the Division command post.

Before dawn on May 29 I was awakened by gunfire and shouting. I grabbed my carbine and helmet, and left my tent, looking for a place to hole up. When it became light enough to see, I noticed a Japanese soldier trying to get into one of the CP tents, so I put a couple of slugs into him. He was the only one I shot.

I eventually found a foxhole, raising myself up just enough to see and have my gun at the ready. While looking in the direction of a gunfire flash, I felt my right arm go limp. It felt like being stabbed with a red-hot knife, it stung so. I hunkered down and hoped I wouldn't bleed to death. I knew where the First Aid station was – probably 50 to 100yds away from me – but it wasn't light enough to see my way.

I don't know how long I waited. My blood didn't feel like it was running; the cold evidently slowed its flow. It finally became light and the gunfire died down to sporadic shots. Before I left my foxhole, I looked in on those on either side; the men weren't moving, so I assumed them dead.

I crawled and walked as low as possible to the First Aid station. The attendants had me lie down on a stretcher, put Sulfa powder on my wound, then dressed it. My wool shirt was bloody. The notebook listing my detail's names that I kept in my shirt pocket was also stained with blood. I still have the notebook.

The next thing I remember is awakening aboard a tracked personnel carrier, and myself and the other injured men being taken aboard a Navy cargo ship for treatment. I don't remember receiving anesthetic – I felt the surgeon scraping and cleaning the wound. It felt like he hit every nerve . . . He had to cut deep in order to get all of the gravel out. I'd been hit by a bullet that'd ricocheted off a rock, just missing my jugular vein.

The cargo ship stopped at Dutch Harbor to transfer the injured to a ship bound for the States, which turned out to be the same one I'd taken to Attu. While being carried aboard I recognized the steward who earlier had wished I could go back with them after anchoring off Attu. I said to him 'You got your wish!'.

He responded 'Not this way'.

Saul Stein was fortunate not to be caught up in the same banzai charge.

I was a Battalion Surgeon for the 78th Coast Artillery Regiment (Anti-Aircraft), attached to the 7th Infantry Division for this particular campaign. Some of our Batteries had landed at Red Beach, near Holtz Bay on the northern side of the island, while the main force had landed at Massacre Bay in the south. D-Day had been Tuesday May 11, 1943, and the struggle for the island was being hampered by fog, cold, and an unseen enemy, well entrenched in the mountainous terrain.

We were unable to communicate with the Batteries at Holtz Bay, so on D+17 Major Defusco our senior Medical Corps officer requested that we attempt to make contact in person, and directed me and Sergeant Hearn to do so. So on May 28 we left the safety of our encampment for the first time. It was a 7-mile trek through rugged terrain. As we left the pass, where already a trail had been created, we saw the tents of a 7th Infantry Division medical detachment and a detachment from the 50th Engineer Regiment. Then for the next 5 miles we saw nary a soul, until we reached the familiar faces of our men at Holtz Bay. We decided to return that same day, and arrived back at camp around 8.00pm.

Neither Saul nor his Sergeant had been armed during their walk to Holtz Bay and back, and both believed that the Japanese had been safely penned into a corner of the island.

That night, however, the Japanese garrison found a gaping hole in the American line, and a banzai charge swept through the shocked hospital and engineer encampments.

We retired exhausted after our hike, only to be awakened at 4.00am by terrific gunfire. The Japanese with their last 800 men had made a surprise attack, and were devastating the very areas we'd been so casually walking through!

It was a bloody battle against Japanese who refused to surrender in spite of the odds, but it was their last throw, and hardly any of them remained after this final counterattack. Many of them were killed in the banzai charge; many others killed themselves with grenades rather than surrender. They also killed their own wounded. This was our first exposure to this suicide, or 'kamikaze' mentality, which was to make them such formidable opponents. After these harrowing events, we secured the island easily.

Attu cost us 549 Americans dead and 1148 wounded, as well as about 2100 casualties due to the cold and to trench foot. We had no serious trench foot cases in the 78th due to the previous lectures by all of our officers on the importance of changing socks several times daily, and the fact that since we didn't do much infantry duty, we had ample opportunity to act on the advice.

After the battle was over we remained in our tent city for about two months, before a supply ship brought in a quantity of Quonset huts. Our chief problem was then one of boredom. The only one who was very busy with the routines of his profession was Dr Wasserman, our dentist. Our sick calls were basically minor. We never had to use the facilities of the 7th Infantry Division's hospital, and we were never called upon to help out there, although we visited them frequently.

Time passed eternally slowly, and to combat boredom and declining morale we developed programs of physical activity. But this seemed inadequate, and so I volunteered to develop High School programs for the enlisted men. We obtained textbooks for English, Mathematics, Literature, History, and my favorite, which I taught – Psychology.

After Attu, the assault on Kiska was set for Sunday 15 August 1943. The 7th Infantry Division was heavily reinforced for this second operation, to give the landing force more than twice the manpower used on Attu. Among the reinforcements were a number of Canadian units. When this force stormed ashore, however, it found that the Japanese had quietly evacuated their entire garrison, leaving the island undefended.

With the Aleutians cleared, the 7th Infantry Division prepared to move south, to join the Central Pacific drive. The next objectives here were the Marshall Islands, where the major centres of resistance at the northern and southern ends of Kwajalein Atoll were to be assaulted simultaneously. The 7th Infantry Division was allocated the southern assault, against Kwajalein Island. The northern assault, against the twin islands of Roi and Namur,[1] was to be conducted by the new 4th Marine Division. D-Day for both assaults would be Monday 31 January 1944.

Learning from their mistakes at Tarawa, the Americans were this time prepared to sacrifice surprise in order to carry out lengthier and more effective bombardments. Exact replicas of the pillboxes and other defences encountered on Betio were constructed on the Hawaiian island of Kahoolawe, so that the bombardment ships could practise on them. The number and scale of the planned air strikes were also increased.

Finally, the plans for both Roi-Namur and Kwajalein involved spending the first day capturing several of the smaller islands nearby. Artillery would then be set ashore on these to support the main assaults, which would go in on D+1.

---

1. Linked, like Gavutu and Tanambogo in the Solomons, by a permanent causeway.

Most of the transports assigned to the Roi-Namur landings were brand new, with untried crews. *Henry Torres* retains vivid memories of this, his first operation.

Our first invasion was the Marshall Islands, Roi-Namur. The first time I went in, my first invasion, I was scared to death. It was a different kind of scared than you would get at home, you know. I think I drank a gallon of water going in to the beach. Seeing all the explosions . . . It was really something for a young kid who'd never been away from home.

We had over thirty landing craft aboard the ship. Four crewmen to each landing craft, which was a bow hook man, a signalman, a motor machinist – which I was – and a coxswain. And each LCVP like ours carried thirty-six troops. The ship had loaded up with troops from the 4th Marine Division at San Diego. They'd drop us over the side, and we'd go to the stern of the ship and we'd circle round until they called us in and loaded us up.

All these troops were in this small LCVP, and they were all looking over the gunwales as we were going in to the beach. And the closer we got to the beach, the further down they got. So by the time we hit the beach it looked like an empty boat!

I had all these gauges on the motors, you know – temperature gauge, and all this and that. Well, I just stuck tape over them so I couldn't see them. Less worry that way. All you're worried about is hitting that beach and coming back alive.

We went in, and the first thing I saw was they had a Jap they were going to interrogate, and they were walking him along the beach. One foot was blown off. And they sat him on an ammunition box, and they were interrogating him.

After we'd dumped our troops off we went back to the ship, and loaded up with other stuff. They lowered everything in nets when they loaded it in the landing craft. So we went back with a bunch of radios and stuff like that. They motioned to us to come to the beach, and on that occasion we hit the beach hard, and all the cargo shifted forward toward the ramp.

When we backed off the beach, pretty soon water was coming in from somewhere . . . So we looked around for a ship to get to before we sank, and we got to an LST, who lowered down a handy billy [a small petrol-driven pump] to pump this water out. We started pumping, but it wasn't enough; it just couldn't handle the water.

So from there we went to a cargo ship, which had a crane that could hook onto us and pull us aboard. So we got alongside and they lowered the boom, and I hooked onto this big hook, and just as I hooked on our boat sank. They hoisted us aboard this cargo ship and dried us off.

And there was a Marine there, he had a string of Jap ears, like a necklace. These little brown ears. You can talk about atrocities the Japs committed, but I thought that was pretty damn bad, to see all these little brown ears round that guy's neck. I said to him 'Are those real?'. And he says 'Yeah!', and he put one in his mouth and pulled on it.

Anyway, after we got our boat all squared away they lowered us back down, and we floated around. Because our ships would leave at sundown and go out and rendezvous somewhere else. And if you weren't back at your ship, you were just out of luck. You sat there or you went round in circles. Whatever you had to do to stay out there.

The Navy was understandably sensitive about the air and submarine threat. There were never enough destroyers to screen the Fleet, and during the seizure of Makin the previous November the Army casualties ashore had been dwarfed by the Navy casualties afloat.

Most of the latter had been sustained when the escort carrier USS *Liscome Bay*, flagship of the Air Support Group, had been torpedoed by the Japanese submarine *I-175*. An unlucky hit in the bomb store had caused the *Liscome Bay* to blow up, with the loss of 644 lives. Bitter recriminations followed between the two services, with the Navy accusing the Army of being dilatory in its operations on the island. The *I-175* was herself sunk on 5 February 1944, while stalking another carrier group in the Marshalls.

We'd get so many Marine casualties that we'd take a boatload in, and bring a boatload off. There was one time I brought a young kid off. He was probably seventeen years old. I was twenty-one when I went in. And this kid, he was shell-shocked. You can't *believe* how much a person who's shell shocked will shake. Just shaking, all the time.

I also had guys die in my arms. They'd turn cold real, real quick. Body would just turn ice cold, seemed like seconds after they died.

The ships'd get so darned full of casualties. I can remember our ship had a doctor from New York, and a little country doctor. Of course the big shot, he had the operating table and all that good stuff down there on the ship, and the country doctor was up there towards the bow. He just had a little table there, and he'd operate on these different guys, the Marines.

I happened to be standing there when he was operating on a Marine who'd got a mortar fin in his back. And it was in so far they had to get it out through his stomach. I was there watching them, and then he got that scalpel, and he started cutting that belly . . . And that's when I started getting sick. I thought 'Oh man, I gotta get the hell out of here . . . '. But they did get that mortar fin out of this guy, and he had that for a souvenir. He had it hanging on his bunk in the sick bay.

Usually when we'd go in to the beach we'd go in there line abreast. The officer'd be right in the middle, and he'd have the radio. But us guys out on the end of the line abreast, we didn't have any information, other than his signals. He'd give you a signal for line abreast, or V formation, and stuff like that.

One such officer was *John Ferrill,* who served as a Small Boat Officer in the Boat Group of an APA from September 1943 until May 1945.

Despite being interviewed for our preferences, almost every man out of our class of 850 received orders for the Amphibious Force. So after two weeks' leave, which I spent in New York, I took the train to Little Creek, Virginia. There were other servicemen in the car who I was able to pass the time away with. Fortunately I had a Pullman ticket, and slept in a bed rather than sitting up. The trip lasted all night.

The next day, July 16, 1943, we arrived in Norfolk. It was unusually warm, and in my dress blues I was really perspiring. I didn't know where I was, and asked for directions. The people spoke with a unique accent, which made it difficult for me to understand. However, I was told that Little Creek was on the outskirts of Norfolk. There was a trolley car that took me out to the end of Granby Street, where I caught a cab.

The amphibious base was new – only twelve months old [work on it had commenced in July 1942, a few weeks after construction work had begun at Solomons, Maryland on the first such base] – and it had a primitive look about it. As I proceeded on foot into the base I remember passing row on row of Quonset huts, which were being used as officers' quarters.

I decided to catch the shuttle bus to the administration building, which was the location of the Officer of the Deck. On boarding the bus I saw a friend of mine from College, who was dressed in the officers' khaki work uniform. He told me he was getting ready to be assigned to a Boat Group aboard ship, and that he'd just returned from advanced amphibious training at Fort Pierce [on the Atlantic coast of Florida, where a third base had just been opened]. All in all, he said the training was quite rigorous. There was very little time for liberty or relaxation.

On arriving at the administration building I reported to the OOD. My orders were stamped, and I was directed to report to Training Flotilla 1, which was located in the Quonset hut area. The administration building was also a temporary wooden structure. There appeared to be no permanent buildings on the base.

On leaving the administration building I remember stepping into a mud hole accidentally and going up to my waist in it. I scraped it off as best I could, but my blues were 'totalled'. Fortunately they were my old ones which I wore in Midshipmen's School. This was the last time I ever had this sort of accident while at Little Creek!

On reporting to the Flotilla headquarters, I was assigned to a Quonset hut. I also paid my mess bill and was issued a 'meal ticket' for that particular month. My hut was empty at the time – the other occupants were out in the boats, training. I was told that each officer was responsible for maintaining his own space – in other words, his bunk and the area around it. Once a week bed linen was changed and mattresses were aired. The huts were inspected on Saturday by the Flotilla commander. This was followed by a personnel inspection, likewise by the Flotilla commander.

At dinner time I went over to the mess hall, also a temporary wooden building. The food, which was both plentiful and good, was served to the officer trainees cafeteria style, but the base staff sat on a stage and were individually served their food by mess attendants and stewards. The Mess Officer had been manager of one of the major hotels in Chicago. He ran a very good mess. After dinner I wandered back to the Quonset hut, wrote some letters and turned in for the night.

I woke to the call of Reveille at 6.00am on the bugle, went to the mess hall for breakfast and returned to the hut to shave and shower. At 8.00am, as directed, I went to the parade ground and fell in with the other officers. We were then introduced to our Flotilla commander and his staff.

The Flotilla commander was a Lieutenant Junior Grade – soon promoted to Lieutenant – whose nickname was 'Dutch'. He was definitely a leader type. Very alert, articulate and likeable. His Flotilla was divided into three Boat Groups. My Boat Group commander was a Southerner, 'Hap'. He was also a Lieutenant Junior Grade, and somewhat older than the Flotilla commander. I struck it off well with both of them. Our instructors were two Boatswains – one a 'jack-me-hearty', full of bluster and jowls, and the other a very quiet, almost retiring man who was very patient and thorough. Both men really knew their profession.

Each day we were out learning how to handle the 36ft LCVP – the Landing Craft, Vehicle and Personnel. We'd usually take a lunch with us so we wouldn't have to return from sea, and we did this until each of us had mastered the handling of the boat in fairly calm waters.

We then spent some time landing and retracting the LCVPs. There were usually a couple of LCP(L)s standing by as salvage boats in case any of the LCVPs broached, in other words turned broadside to the beach while in the process of retracting. When salvage boats weren't available we also used our own LCVPs. This involved the bow hook man heaving a line over to the broached boat. This heaving line was made fast to a manila hawser or wire rope, which was then used to pull the boat off the beach. As soon as their sterns were waterborne the crews of the broached boats would start their engines and back out into the surf. Care had to be taken not to get the tow line fouled up in their propellers, and the towing boat, if not handled properly, could also broach. Fortunately this didn't happen during the course of our training.

At night we went to lectures on amphibious warfare. Officers who were veterans of Guadalcanal and the North African campaign gave us lectures on tactics, and the employment of landing craft in a typical amphibious operation. Each of the phases were covered, such as the pre-assault phase, when the beaches were cleared for landing by minesweepers and UDT [Underwater Demolition Team] frogmen; supporting air operations; gunfire support by bombardment ships; the assault phase, when the boats were launched, to proceed to the beach via the 'Line of Departure', and the troops and equipment were disembarked; the logistic phase, when cargo was discharged; salvage operations, such as retrieving disabled craft from the beach, and the retirement phase, once a beachhead was established.

We also had classes in things like radio communications, semaphore and Morse code, and practiced using small arms. We would go for target practice at Camp Bradford, which was adjacent to Little Creek. I became fairly proficient with the .45 caliber pistol, but was a terrible rifle marksman. One of the Marine instructors told me 'Sir, you couldn't hit a bull in the ass with a bass fiddle!' when my final scores were interpreted.

During this time we were given a much more intensive physical, and also had to have psychological testing. The psychiatrist interviewed us individually and gave us the Rorschach ink-spot test, and asked us such personal questions as whether or not we masturbated. I must've been OK, because I passed. One of the other officers obviously wasn't, because he'd begun behaving strangely. The Boat Group commander blew his top and had him restricted to quarters when his behaviour got the attention of the Flotilla commander. He was sent over to the sick bay, and we never saw him again. I later learned that he'd been medically discharged from the Navy.

Was this just an isolated incident, or did you know of other cases where the stress got to people?

No, I knew of other cases. The best known was Rear-Admiral Don Moon, which was a real tragedy. He saw some pretty rough going during the early part of the war, and evidently the pressure was too much for him.

> Moon served as a destroyer squadron commander on Arctic convoys and in the North African landings, and then as Naval commander for the UTAH assault in Normandy. Shortly after being nominated for a similar responsibility in the Mediterranean, this time for the Camel sector during the smaller landings in the South of France, he committed suicide.

One day the Flotilla commander called me aside in the mess hall and said 'Ferrill, you're our new assistant Boat Group commander. We've a big job ahead of us. I want Hap and you to get a Group ready for advanced training in Fort Pierce, Florida in a month'.

At this point we were introduced to our men. There were about fifty men in our Boat Group, most of them very young, and they'd never worked together before as a team. We immediately started training under simulated operational conditions. We would head out each day at 8.00am to an area off the Virginia Capes, near the Cape Henry lighthouse, where there were excellent surf conditions and it was generally unobstructed for miles. There we would circle round a mock-up of a ship, fitted with debarkation nets over the side, and practice coming alongside, tying up and casting off, as though troops were embarking. We'd then head out to sea and form boat waves. On a signal from the Flotilla commander we would hit the beach, simulate the discharging of troops onto it, and then retract and return to the mock-up.

At night we would meet with our Flotilla commander and discuss the day's exercise. Errors were pointed out in a constructive manner and corrective actions recommended. One of the hardest things to do was to get the crews to keep their lifejackets on in the sweltering Virginia sun. Later we were to find out in landings against the Japanese that the lifejackets also provided invaluable protection against shrapnel.

Finally our 'OR' inspection came off quite well, and we were pronounced 'operationally ready'. We were then put on hold to await orders, which were delayed in coming. It was now mid-September 1943, and I began getting restless because the status of our Boat Group was still undetermined. One night over in the officers' club I had too many beers and let it be known to all present that I was tired of sitting on my butt all day waiting for the top brass to decide what to do with us. I further added that I was anxious to get to sea because my younger brother Bill had enlisted in the Marine Corps, and I didn't want him to beat me out there.

The next morning an officer asked me if I was still anxious to go to sea. I said yes, and he told me over breakfast that his wife was ill and that if he could get someone to take his place, he could stay at Little Creek until she recovered. I told him I'd do it. I had a set of emergency orders within about half an hour, and went over to my quarters, packed my bags and said goodbye. I then reported in officially, orders in hand, to my new Boat Group.

What happened to the officer you'd traded places with?

My old Flotilla commander later wrote me and said that he and his wife were out on the dance floor that Saturday night, and she looked anything but sick. So I guess when he saw what was in store for him he just got cold feet, and decided he didn't want any part of it.

At 2.00pm we mustered on the parade ground, and I met my new enlisted boat crew, some of whom I'm still in touch with. I learned we were going aboard the USS *Elmore* as her Boat Group. The *Elmore*, which was a newly commissioned ship, was docked at the commercial piers along the Elizabeth River in Norfolk. She was a C-3 Maritime Commission cargo vessel[2] that'd been converted into an attack transport, or APA. She'd been laid down by the Ingalls Shipbuilding Corporation in Pascagoula, Mississippi as the SS *Sea Panther*, but soon transferred to the Navy and converted for amphibious use as the APA-42. APA of course stood for Auxiliary, Personnel, Attack.

She was fitted with yard and stay type booms and associated deck machinery that enabled her to handle cargo and equipment. She had two 10-ton booms forward and a large 20-ton one aft. She was also fitted with davits to pick up and lower the landing craft that were located amidships. All in all she was a very impressive ship to an Ensign of only three months' Naval service.

Our time of arrival was about 6.00pm, so the evening meal was finished. However, after presenting our orders to the OOD we were taken to the

2. The United States Maritime Commission had been formed during the inter-war period to subsidise the ailing American Merchant Marine and to rejuvinate its ageing fleet. It used three standard cargo ship designs – the C-1, C-2 and C-3. The C-3 was the largest.

wardroom and fed the leftovers. The Chaplain, who was the Mess Treasurer, immediately collected the month's mess bill from each of us. Meanwhile our enlisted men were being fed and berthed.

Our quarters on the ship lay way down in the troop officers' quarters on 'B' Deck – the second deck below the Main Deck. Actually these were the same as the enlisted quarters. We initially had to make up our own bunks and take turns cleaning the compartment, as well as the heads and showers, but later stewards were assigned to take care of us.

The only Regular officer on board was the CO, Commander Drayton Harrison, USN. He was a graduate of the US Naval Academy, and his early service had been in submarines. Prior to taking command of the *Elmore* he'd been the CO of the USS *Pleiades,* a Navy cargo ship in the North Atlantic. He was regarded as a 'character' because he was very eccentric. Some people felt that this was attributable to either too much time in submarines, or too much time in the North Atlantic, or both. He also had a little cocker spaniel dog named Cheerio who went to sea with him. I found him a very good Commanding Officer despite his eccentricities.

The Executive Officer, Commander Frank Wauchope, USNR, was ex-Merchant Marine, as were most of the key ship's officers. Both he and his brother had gone to sea at an early age, and both were highly regarded in the Merchant Marine. Both held Reserve commissions, and as soon as the National Emergency arose they were called up into the Navy. At this time, Frank's brother [Captain G M Wauchope, USNR] was Commanding Officer of our sister ship the USS *Du Page.* Frank Wauchope was a very good seaman, but I feel he was disgruntled because he didn't have his own command as did his brother. Neither of them spoke to each other. Consequently he was very difficult and hard to get along with, and he had no patience with junior officers.

The Chief Engineer was a Lieutenant Commander, USNR. Another Merchant Marine officer, he'd been Chief Engineer in several ships running from the West Coast to the Hawaiian Islands and South Seas. Frankly, he was an old and tired man who wasn't going to go any further in the Navy, and who spent most of his time in the wardroom drinking coffee or in his bunk sleeping. The Captain later got rid of him. The Navigator was also a Lieutenant Commander, USNR. He'd likewise been in the Merchant Marine, having sailed for the American President Lines. He was a very good officer. The Gunnery Officer was a Lieutenant, USNR. He was a World War One Reservist, and a real piece of work. In civilian life he'd been an Assistant District Attorney for the City of New York. He was a vicious SOB, who did everything he could to ingratiate himself with the Captain and Executive Officer, while being hell on junior officers. He was responsible for several of them getting passed over for promotion. The enlisted men also hated him. I made it a point to keep on his good side.

The first thing we did before the *Elmore* actually started training was to pick up our boats from the Naval supply depot. We travelled there in a bus, and sailed the boats back to the ship. Then we took on stores and ammunition.

Barges with ammunition were sent out to the ship at anchor from the Naval ammunition depot, and despite some chaos, things came off without mishap.

The ship then went over to the fuel piers and took on 'Bunker C' – oil fuel for the main boilers – and lubricating oil for the auxiliary machinery. We also took on feed water for the boilers. The ordinary water in the mains had too high a mineral content and too many impurities to be usable in the ship's boilers. At sea feed water had to be produced from sea water using the ship's evaporators.

For the next month we conducted individual ship's exercises off Virginia Beach and the Capes. These mainly consisted of lowering the boats and later retrieving them. At first this process took far too long, so we drilled and drilled until we got the time down. We also made several in-surf landings on the beach, and practiced some gunnery exercises which simulated high level bombing and torpedo runs. Target towing was provided by the Naval Air Station at Oceana, adjacent to Virginia Beach.

Then as part of a Transport Division [a unit usually consisting of three or four APAs and an AKA, and able to lift a Regimental Combat Team] we practiced steaming in formation. We executed column movements and turns. We also practiced zig-zagging and other evasive maneuvers. Above all, the Transport Division practiced landing with the boats from all of the ships acting in concert. Although we didn't take troops aboard, we staged several landings up and down the Atlantic coast.

In October 1943 we received word that we were to redeploy to the West Coast. Most of the married officers sent their wives home to their parents or in-laws. Others told them to proceed to San Diego, while the ship headed for the Panama Canal via the Windward Passage. Since there was a threat from German U-boats we were given a destroyer escort screen, and we zig-zagged all the way down to Cuba.

Off Cuba a simulated air attack was conducted by planes from the US base at Guantanamo Bay. We had a serious mishap during this exercise. The director for the British pom-pom guns was out of synchronization with them, so when firing commenced, several shots went into the bridge of the USS *Wayne*, the APA behind us. Fortunately there were no casualties.

We arrived at Colon on the Caribbean coast of Panama in the late afternoon. The entire evening was spent in transit through the canal. I was fortunate enough to be on watch as the ship went through the locks. When we arrived at Panama City on the Pacific coast, the ships tied up there for part of a day. I spent most of my time at the Army PX [Post Exchange. The American equivalent of the British NAAFI], where I was able to buy gifts for my parents and some work khakis for myself. Everyone else seemed to be trying to get as much liquor and sex as time permitted. A Pharmacist's Mate came back drunk and went down to sick bay, where the duty doctor, a Lieutenant Junior Grade, told him to go to his bunk. He refused and the matter escalated, ending up with him assaulting the doctor. He was then taken into custody by the Master at Arms and put in the ship's brig until he sobered up. He was later given a court martial and reduced in rate.

The *Elmore* then left Panama City for San Diego, via some heavy weather in the Gulf of Tehuantepec, off southern Mexico. The ships arrived at San Diego in mid-November, and some of the wives and girlfriends met us at the pier.

Except for a trip to the Naval shipyard in San Pedro, just south of Los Angeles, the ship was intensively involved in training with the 4th Marine Division. We took their troops aboard and conducted several full scale landings at a place called Aliso Canyon near Oceanside, and on San Clemente Island about 70 miles west of San Diego. All of these came off very well. We were then organized into a Task Force under Rear-Admiral Richard Conolly [back in the Pacific after having commanded the Naval force for the JOSS landing area in Sicily].

We spent Christmas and New Year in San Diego, and then on January 13, 1944 the entire Task Force [less the Landing Ships, Tank carrying the 4th Marine Division's LVTs, and their escorts, which had left a few days earlier] sailed for the fleet anchorage at Lahaina Roads in Hawaii, led by the command ship USS *Appalachian*. By this time everyone had a pretty good idea that we were going into action, because we were combat loaded with a battalion of Marines from the 4th Marine Division. After getting under way again from Lahaina Roads we were told that we would attack the Marshall Islands, in the Central Pacific. These islands had belonged to Germany until the end of World War One, when they were mandated to Japan. The Japanese had fortified them heavily, and now held them with a large combat-ready garrison.

The *Elmore* was part of the assault force assigned to the islands of Roi and Namur in Kwajalein Atoll. To the south another assault force with the 7th Infantry Division was assigned to take the island of Kwajalein. The 7th was an Army Division, which had previously seen action in the Aleutian Islands campaign, including landings on Attu and Kiska. The 4th Marine Division, being newly formed, had not as yet seen action. En route to the Marshall Islands from Hawaii there was a general mood of anticipation, almost excitement, that at long last we were going to see the action most of us had been training for for over six months.

I was assigned as a Wave Guide commander during the assault on Namur. My responsibilities were to take my boat up to the Line of Transfer, which was just a little beyond the Line of Departure [5000yds from shore]. At the Line of Transfer I would transfer the troops from the LCVPs in my wave to Landing Vehicles, Tracked – usually called LVTs, or 'amtracs' ['amphibian tractors'] – which would be waiting there. The amtracs had been carried to Roi-Namur in LSTs, which were also part of the assault force.

There was to be a long association between these two types, but it was not without its problems. For example, the lift normally used to move vehicles between the upper deck and tank deck of an LST proved to be slightly too small for the latest LVT models. A wooden ramp had to be hastily built on each lift to tilt the LVTs upwards, thus shortening their length and allowing them to squeeze through.

The transfer had to be delayed because the LVTs were slow in arriving. They'd been used to capture the approach islands – needed to force a passage into the lagoon, and for the Marines to place their artillery on – the day before, and most of them were low on fuel.

> With the smaller islands now in American hands, the assault could be directed against the inner, lagoon, side of Roi and Namur – as had been done at Tarawa.

When the LVTs *did* arrive I was able to effect the transfer smoothly and without any fire from the enemy ashore. Fenders were put over the side of each boat in order to cushion the impact when the LVT came alongside. The Marines were required to climb over the boat gunwales and step across onto the LVTs.

Did you stop to accomplish the transfers?

No, we remained under way. Low throttle was used to maintain steerage way and control of the boat. Also, the engines had to be in operation for the bilge pumps to function, because they ran directly off the boat engines. Obviously we tried to choose fairly smooth water for these transfers.

After discharging the troops, I headed back to the *Elmore* and picked up a load of high octane gas, which we were told was critically needed on the beach because the LVTs were out of fuel. The load consisted of several 55-gallon drums, which filled the boat.

While lying off the beach, waiting to deliver this fuel to the fuel dump which had been set up, I noticed that we had a fire on top of one of the drums! Fortunately we were able to get to it right away, and myself and the bow hook smothered it. We learned that this particular drum had a perforation on the top which had caused a leak. It'd probably been damaged in handling by the deck crew aboard the *Elmore*. During the process of putting the fire out I was burned in the face, and developed some blistering around my lips.

When we were called in to the beach and offloaded the high octane at the gasoline dump, I reported the leaky drum to the Beachmaster, and he called a Pharmacist's Mate over. He immediately put some ointment on the area affected. We then went back to the *Elmore* and began picking up loads of medical supplies, ammunition, rations, water, diesel fuel and equipment, and bringing them to the beach.

As the day wore on, the heat became intense and the blisters worsened. But as we were also bringing some of the serious casualties on the beach back to the *Elmore* for a surgical team to perform operations on them, my problem seemed pretty insignificant by comparison.

When Namur was in US hands [as was officially announced at 2.18pm on D+2, Roi having fallen before dark on D+1] I returned with my boat crew to the *Elmore* on receipt of a recall by the Task Force commander. We were taken aboard, and after securing my boat as well as the others assigned to me, I reported to sick bay.

There my burns were treated, and they placed me on the sick list while the ship retired from the assault area and headed south. Although I was able to walk around and do the administrative aspects of my job – crypto watch in the cryptographic shack, censoring mail, preparing correspondence – I wasn't allowed to be exposed to the sun in any way. This meant that I was taken off the deck watch list, for OOD on the bridge. This made a couple of the other officers angry because they thought I was using my condition to get out of work. As soon as I heard their feelings on the matter, I asked to be put back on the watch list. Since we were short of watchkeepers, I was assigned to the watches from 8.00pm to midnight and 4.00am to 8.00am, so I wouldn't have to be exposed to sunlight. This seemed to placate the complainers.

When the ship crossed the Equator my burns, though greatly improved, still kept me on the sick list. The initiation of crewmen who hadn't 'Crossed the Line' was held, and the Boatswain was King Neptune. I wasn't permitted to participate, but did get to watch it. The Gunnery Officer seemed to be the person who took the biggest beating in the initiation. The crew despised him because he was really a mean and overbearing officer.

When under stress to this day my face, particularly the area around my lips and nose, suffers some discoloration. My doctor has told me that this is related to the earlier burns incident, but isn't in any way serious. It hasn't happened as much since I've been on blood pressure medication.

My wife Ruthie also notices it when I drink too much booze . . .

Organised resistance on Kwajalein Island ended on D+4, and the next few days saw the Japanese outposts in the other parts of the atoll being mopped up. A reserve landing force, unused at Kwajalein, then advanced a further 326 miles to take another strategically placed atoll – Eniwetok.

With American air power firmly established in the Marshalls, its remaining Japanese bases could be left to wither on the vine. US planes could simply neutralise the bypassed islands by cutting them off from supply and subjecting them to regular harassment.

The same strategy was meanwhile being applied in the South West Pacific, where the Japanese stronghold of Rabaul was under regular air attack. On 12 March 1944 the American Chiefs of Staff ordered that the Central Pacific drive should press on, skirting the great Japanese anchorage at Truk, already damaged by bombing, and striking directly at the islands of Saipan, Tinian and Guam in the southern Marianas. From airfields on these, American land-based bombers would be able to reach the mainland of Japan.

ELEVEN

Returning: Guam and the Philippines

D-Day on Saipan was set for Thursday 15 June 1944. Their time on the island is a far from happy memory for most of the men in the landing force. Casualties during the three and a half weeks of fighting were heavy – over four times those on Tarawa – and relations between the Marine Corps and the Army were seriously damaged when Marine Lieutenant General Holland McTyeire Smith, better known by his colourful nickname of 'Howlin' Mad', sacked one of his Army subordinates.

Out at sea, however, the Americans had more to celebrate. On D+4 the Japanese surface fleet, which had not attempted to intervene in the Gilberts and Marshalls, finally challenged the American drive, precipitating the Battle of the Philippine Sea. The Japanese had assembled a formidable strike force of nine carriers. But the Americans now had fifteen, and the Japanese air attacks on them were slaughtered in what became known as the 'Great Marianas Turkey Shoot'. The Japanese lost three carriers, two of them to US submarines, and the Americans were left in complete control of the seas around the islands.

Such was the ferocity of the fighting ashore on Saipan that it was feared the landing force, which consisted of the 2nd and 4th Marine Divisions and the Army's 27th Infantry Division, might not be able to cope. The landing on Guam scheduled for 18 June was accordingly shelved, and the Guam landing force was kept aboard ship, ready to reinforce Saipan.

Shadow Nelson's APA was one of the transports involved.

Although destined for Guam, we were designated a floating reserve for Saipan. For ten days the Task Force maneuvred off the islands, and at night we would sit on deck and watch as the sky over Saipan was lit up from the shelling.

Then we returned to Eniwetok for logistics. One man of the ship's company drowned while swimming off one of the islands there, and was buried locally.

On July 17 we got under way for Guam again.

Organised resistance on Saipan had finally ended on 9 July, and W-Day – the new date for the assault on Guam – had been set for

Friday 21 July. Part of the delay had been to allow time for the Marine landing force to be strengthened by the addition of some Army units.

The new plan called for the landing of the 3rd Marine Division, the 1st Provisional Marine Brigade[1] and part of the Army's 77th Infantry Division on W-Day, followed by the rest of the Army division on W+2.

As on Saipan the assaults would take place on the western side of the island, with the 3rd Marine Division landing to the north of Apra harbour, and the other units to the south.

From July 21 to July 25 the ship was in the transport area. The battalion from the 3rd Marine Division we were carrying was debarked for the assault, followed by their cargo. Once again we approached an enemy beach, and again saw the devastation of the trees and surrounding growth, with the now familiar sights and odours.

No matter how many invasions you have, the fear is constantly with you.

Unlike the previous landings, Guam had a much greater distance from the waterline to the dunes and cover, maybe 30yds through machine gun and mortar fire. Once the troops *did* reach cover, the mortar fire was directed at the boats.

I was squatting low between the two machine gun mounts when a mortar hit our boat. It hit the port rear corner, not 3ft from me, sending shrapnel like a fountain over my head and onto the men in the forward part of the boat. One seaman and a couple of the troops were hit. I was hit next to my spine, but it didn't break the skin, only made a knot. An officer also received a minor scratch. The boat immediately began taking on water. Two other boats were ordered alongside of us, one on each side, and we were tied to them to keep us afloat while they took us back to our ship. There we were hoisted aboard for repairs. Within two hours we were back in the water and continuing our duties.

Our wounded seaman, Nance, was replaced with another seaman to be bow hook. As is often the case, several stories were about as to our fate, from being dead to all degrees of being wounded. We were very lucky.

169 Marine casualties were received from the beach, 12 of whom died and were buried at sea, and 92 of whom were later transferred to the hospital ships USS *Rixey* and USS *Solace*.

On July 25, with the remaining Marine casualties still aboard, we got under way. While at sea, as usual after an engagement, the crew spent the days cleaning, and bringing the ship back to 'ship shape'. The period of August 23

---

1. This consisted of two Marine regiments – the newly reformed 4th Marines and the previously independent 22nd Marines – and was shortly to become the basis of another new Marine division. The 4th Marines had absorbed the Marine Raider battalions, whose time was judged to have passed.

to August 31 was spent in the Solomons, training with units of the 1st Marine
Division for the invasion of Peleliu.

Organised resistance had ceased on Guam on 11 August, and
Tinian, invaded by the 2nd and 4th Marine Divisions from nearby
Saipan on 24 July, had officially fallen on 1 August. Fighting still
continued long after these dates, however, as individual Japanese
were painstakingly winkled out of their places of concealment.

Peleliu marked the start of the next phase of operations, during
which the Central Pacific drive and MacArthur's advance up the
coast of New Guinea prepared to combine, with the object of
retaking the Philippines.

There had been much debate over whether this was the right
course of action, and similar disagreements over the need to take
Peleliu and Angaur as first steps. However, the majority of the
American commanders agreed that the two islands, at the
southern end of the Palau group, would have to be taken if
MacArthur's flank was to be protected.

The veteran 1st Marine Division was given the task of seizing
Peleliu, beginning on D-Day, Friday 15 September 1944. Angaur
would be assaulted by most of the Army's untried 81st Infantry
Division two days later.

Finally we were under way for Peleliu, in the southern Palau Islands. The ship
hove to in the transport area, and the various elements of the 1st Marine
Division aboard were landed with their cargo and equipment. Heavy mortar
fire was encountered all along the reef, which constantly hampered the
unloading phase.

LVTs would meet us at the edge of the coral and we would transfer our
loads to them by hand, but once a channel was blasted open we could pass
through to the beach. Though that created another traffic problem. Boats
entering had to wait until the departing boats were out, et cetera . . .

One time we were on the beach when the tide went out, and were left high
and dry, so we decided that we'd leave the boat until the tide came back in.
The new seaman – newly from the States – that replaced Nance was so
frightened that he wouldn't leave, remembering his orders of remaining in
his boat.

Things were 'hot and heavy' on the front, so some young Second Lieutenant
decided to grab a bunch of us sailors and send us to the airfield [the reason
for the island's significance to both sides] to help out. He handed out rifles,
loaded us onto a truck and we were on our way. There was much activity about,
but the front was well beyond the airfield, so we felt relatively safe.

I saw a burned-out Jap Zero by the trees, and as I drew closer I realized the
pilot had tried to get airborne, but his plane had been hit and set on fire,

running into the shrubs by the wooded area. He had jumped out ablaze, and had landed on a burnt sapling, driving it through him. I saw in the plane a radio which would make a great souvenir, and proceeded to get it.

A couple of other sailors and I then wandered across the airfield, and seeing a pillbox thought we could find something of interest inside. A Marine stopped us and first threw a hand grenade in. It's good he did, as inside we found a dead Jap with a machine gun pointed at the entrance! Of course, the grenade had destroyed anything of interest we might have wanted.

As we were looking about, the Japs began a counterattack, sending mortars and machine gun fire all around us. The Marine suggested we stay in the pillbox for protection, but being on the far side of the airfield from the shore, my fear told me to get back. So I lit out for the beach at a hard run. As I moved, I began seeing bullets hit the runway around me. From this point on I believe I could've outrun the fastest man alive. Reaching the beach, I fell into the closest shell hole I could find.

I saw four men running with a poncho with my boatmate in it. He was screaming that his legs hurt, but he no longer had legs. A shell had hit our boat, and our frightened seaman was there to be hit. He died within a few minutes.

While still in the shell hole a couple of Marines jumped in with me, and at one point one tried to light a cigarette, but his hand was shaking so badly the matches wouldn't stay lit. I found that amusing, and the sight took my mind off my own fear for a moment.

25 September, D+10 on Peleliu, was *Bob Naughton*'s twentieth birthday.

I guess Peleliu stays with me mostly because it was so bloody. I'd never seen so many casualties. I thought Guam was bad, but this one was far and above Guam.

There was a coral reef that ringed the island, so we would wait until Marine LVTs – Landing Vehicles, Tracked – could take boat loads of Marines and transport them over the reef and into a shallow lagoon, and then to the beach. Eventually Underwater Demolition Teams came in and blew holes in the reef. The Japanese are a lot of things, but they're not stupid. They simply zeroed in on the holes in the reef with their deadly mortar and artillery fire. The only time in my Navy career that I disobeyed a direct order was at Peleliu. I didn't mind the idea of giving my life for my country, but I'd be damned if I was going to let some stupid officer without an ounce of common sense throw it away. I tried to tell him that the reef hole was being blasted to pieces, and that I'd go in after the barrage lifted. He would have none of that. He used his bull horn to tell me that I was to pick up casualties on my return trip. I tried to tell him if I went in then he was giving the Japs four *more* casualties, *and* he would lose a boat, which were getting scarce enough by this time. He told me that it was an order, and it was only when I threatened to blow his fucking head off that he got the message. Luckily the Navy then brought the big guns of the battleships into action. After a couple of salvoes the mortar barrage lifted, and I got my boat on the beach. I picked up casualties, six of them, pretty badly hit, and delivered them to hospital ships, or to ships designated as hospital ships.

On one of my later trips that day I had more casualties, and after I backed off the beach, I shoved the throttle forward and nothing happened. The boat just sat there. After the motor machinist looked at the engine, he declared there was nothing wrong with it. But the stern sheet had about ten holes in it, and all our fuel was leaking out. From the way the wood was chewed up, it must've been a heavy caliber machine gun that did the damage. I had to be towed back to my ship and hoisted aboard. Fortunately our ship was a designated hospital ship, and the casualties were able to get much needed medical attention. The repair crew broke all existing records in replacing my fuel tanks, which had holes the size of silver dollars in them. I was relaxing in the mess hall, having a cup of good Navy coffee, when I heard the immortal words 'Will the coxswain of Boat 19 lay up to the boat deck! You are holding up the war!'.

Another incident which I'll never forget happened on my birthday – because I remarked to one of the boat crew, a guy by the name of Stevens, 'What a hell of a way to spend your birthday . . . '. It was my twentieth; September 25, 1944. My boat had drifted free of the pack of boats gathered at the holes in the reef. I had three netloads of cloverleaf canisters of 105mm ammunition for the artillery, and an LVT had tied up to us to get the ammunition. You see, the Beachmaster had taken to sending amtracs out to the boat clusters to get priority cargo, namely ammunition and medical supplies, as well as food and fresh water.

One of the Marines from the LVT noticed a huge splash off to our left. The next splash was closer, and one of the Marines wondered out loud if they could be shooting at us? The next splash left no doubt. I shoved the throttle forward and dragged the LVT to where I thought it was safe. That shore gun was persistent, though. It tracked us, and the splashes kept getting closer. Those cloverleaves of ammunition were now the weight of a cottonball. I never saw ammunition unloaded so fast. The next splash was close enough that we didn't even bother to untie the lines that joined us. We both just gave it full throttle and parted the lines as though they'd been cut with a knife!

Did you envy the rest of the crew, who could stay out in the transport area while you made these dangerous runs to the beach?

I think the boat crews had a feeling of not being appreciated, yes. It was the boats that caught all the flak, and while we were getting the mortar, machine gun and artillery fire, the boys back on the ship were catching all the action through binoculars. Hence we dubbed them the 'binocular warriors'.

Of course all that would change at Leyte, where we'd get a new word in our vocabulary – Kamikaze. Now the binocular warriors would find out what it was all about. We had four or five kamikaze attacks at Leyte. We fired an awful lot of ammunition at them, but were never awarded credit for shooting any of them down. I don't see how that could be possible anyway, in that maelstrom. Some of them were *very* close.

How did you become a landing craft coxswain?

When we entered initial small boat training we were divided into groups of four, because a single boat crew was made up of a coxswain, two seamen and a motor machinist. The selection of coxswain for this stage seemed pretty much a random choice by the training supervisor – usually a Boatswain's Mate or Chief Boatswain's Mate. If the person chosen proved to be an inept boat handler, another person was selected and the former coxswain was relegated to a seaman's job.

When we entered training it was as Seamen Second Class. Upon completion of training, the entire class was upgraded to Seaman First Class. This initial small boat training was at a place called Coronado [where work on an amphibious training base for the West Coast had begun in July 1943], at San Diego, California.

As for my contingent, we went up the California coast about 50 miles to a Marine Corps base called Camp Pendleton, for advanced training. Here we were all given a chance to display our boat handling skills in a surf. Some fellows made their coxswain's stripe, but not all. Then, after eight weeks of intensive training, night landings included, we were sent up the California coast even further, to a place called Fort Ord. My God, what a surf! It could really damage boats and personnel, if you didn't keep your eye on what you were doing. After a further month of this training we were deemed ready. We were given ten days' leave and then loaded aboard a Dutch motor vessel called the MV *Bloemfontein*, which after a twenty-two day voyage deposited us at Guadalcanal.

The first boats we'd trained on were rampless LCP(L)s, which had a sharp prow. The troops jumped over the sides of the boat to disembark. Later came the LCV – Landing Craft, Vehicle. These had a ramp, but the coxswain stood up on the stern sheet of the boat with only a flimsy railing around him to keep him from being washed overboard in a heavy surf. Our examples of the LCP(L) and the LCV were powered by Hall-Scott gasoline engines, which proved to be not very seaworthy, as they were always dying on us. The steering mechanism was a small replica of a ship's helm. Very difficult to control in a heavy or running sea.

Then came the newer LCVPs – Landing Craft, Vehicle and Personnel. They were greatly improved, and the coxswain was inside the boat, which meant much less exposure of him both to the elements and to enemy fire. Two major improvements were the new engines, which were Gray marine diesels with a lot more oomph, and the addition of two .30 caliber machine guns mounted on rings at the rear of the boat. These rings permitted the horizontal and vertical tracking of the guns. Steering was accomplished with an automobile-type steering wheel, drive by a shovel-handled throttle within easy reach of the coxswain. The throttle was pushed forward to go forward, and pulled back to go backwards. A simple twist of the shovel handle gave you more speed; all the way to wide open, the same for reverse. The response was almost instantaneous.

I made coxswain on Guadalcanal. Up to this point, none of us had ever been aboard ship as part of an attack transport's crew. Attack transports, or APAs – APA stood for Auxiliary, Personnel, Attack – carried anywhere from thirty to forty landing craft. We had thirty-six. Thirty-two LCVPs and four LCMs. An LCM – Landing Craft, Mechanized – could take one tank like a Sherman, or a big artillery piece. An LCVP could carry thirty-six fully equipped troops, or a jeep, or a light artillery piece. None of the first APAs were built as such. They were all former merchantmen; passenger/cargo ships.

The LCM was much larger than an LCVP, and had two Gray marine diesels with shovel-handled throttles. The coxswain was positioned on the stern sheet, in a steel housing with slits so he could see where he was going.

Boat crews were separate and distinct from normal ship's company. Once assigned to a boat, the crew of that boat was yours forevermore, except by promotion, transfer, discharge or death. Whichever came first.

On D-Day your boat was put in the water unloaded. A Boat Control Officer told you to get into the port or starboard circles, formed aft of the ship, off the port and starboard quarters. When all the landing craft were turning in circles aft of the ship, a Control Officer would hold up a huge sign which designated the hatch you were to bring your boat to. A '1' meant No 1 Hatch, and so on through No 5. If a troop net was over the side of the ship it meant you were taking troops; if not, you were taking cargo – ammunition, medical supplies, gasoline, et cetera. Usually the first boats called were for troops. All hatches were rigged for troop debarkation. Once a boat was loaded, she was sent forward of the ship to form another circle. When the circle was complete you'd be signalled to form line abreast, and to proceed to the Line of Departure. Throttled down, you would wait for a signal to go; then it was a full throttle rush toward the beach. After the third or fourth wave of boats into the beach, this circling went by the board, and everything was catch as catch can.

As for life aboard between invasions, they managed to keep us busy. However, no matter how busy, the thought was always in the back of your mind – what if I never get home? Thousands of guys my age were dying for these islands.

The war seemed endless. When would it ever be over?

Al Sakavich was also to see far more of Peleliu than he would have wished.

At the time of our graduation we were very excited, because there was a rumor that our entire class was going to be sent to Aviation Electrician's School for advanced training. It was not to be. The US had begun its slow island-hopping advance to dislodge the Japanese from the Pacific, and we were shortly informed that electricians were badly needed in the Navy's Amphibious Forces. So I travelled by public bus, train, and Navy bus to the Amphibious Training Base at Solomons, Maryland, where I was assigned to the training crew of the *LCT 513*.

Each LCT was powered by three Gray marine diesel engines, and also had two Hercules diesel powered one-kilowatt generators. On the forward bulkhead of the engine room there was a large switchboard, which was the central power control. The back of the switchboard carried two large 'hot' copper bus bars and all the cartridge fuses of various sizes. The switchboard was offset from the bulkhead by about 20in. To avoid touching the bus bars was especially tricky when we were in the Pacific. The temperature in the engine room, with the heat from the running engines and the radiated heat from the metal deck above, had one sweating like a horse, and the wet body is especially conductive for electricity. It reminds me of the old joke: How do porcupines make love? Very carefully!

All the engines were cooled with sea water, and each of the diesels was fitted with a large tube-like filter to filter out sand and coral pieces that might be stirred up when making a beach landing. As I recall, the overall external measurements of the plastic tubes were about 18in long and about 9 or 10in in diameter. Inside each transparent tube was a perforated metal tube which acted as the filter and could be removed for cleaning. The generators were also water-cooled in a similar manner. However, each had a connection to a separate tank of sea water as well. To keep a generator operating when the LCT was beached for unloading, its cooling system was switched from external sea water to the cooling tank. This provided several hours of cooling for the generator. Of course, when beached, the main diesels were shut off.

My interest was strictly in the generators; the diesels were serviced by the Motor Machinist's Mates. About the only new thing I had to learn was how to transfer generating power from one generator to the other without shut down. Under normal conditions only one generator was operating. To service the running generator, it was necessary to start up the other one and get it up to speed. Then, employing side-by-side rheostats on the main switchboard, and with both generators running in parallel, the generating power of the second generator was increased to the usual level, while simultaneously reducing the generating power of the first generator to zero. Then the first generator was shut off so that it could be serviced. It was a tricky procedure, somewhat akin to learning how to drive an automobile with a standard transmission, clutch and stick shift.

Unless there was an electrical repair of some kind that had to be made, my time was spent in general maintenance and housekeeping. This didn't take all of my time, so the Boatswain always felt free to involve me in projects such as chipping rust and paint from various surfaces, and repainting.

The permanent crew of which I was to be a part began to assemble. Our first Skipper, Mr Lieberman, was a prince of a fellow. Unfortunately it turned out that he suffered from chronic seasickness. Even when the LCT was tied to the dock there was a slight motion from passing boat wakes. When Mr Lieberman climbed to the conning tower, that slight motion would make him ill. He was soon relieved of command and assigned to land duty. Our next Skipper was a former violin teacher with, as it turned out, a slight similarity to Nero.

We all left Solomons on March 24, 1944, bound for the Naval Station at Algiers, Louisiana, where we were to await the arrival of our very own LCT. Algiers was a station for the repair and refitting of ships, and it was also the place to which LCTs were floated down the Mississippi from shipyards in the North, to pick up crews. The LCTs were then loaded [complete, as deck cargo] aboard LSTs for their trips to the Pacific war zone.

We spent four weeks at Algiers, digging ditches and carrying out other make-work projects. Fortunately there were frequent liberties to the city of New Orleans – a fascinating place. Then we boarded the new *LST 661* to await the imminent arrival of our LCT. In essence we became part of the LST crew, carrying out duties of various kinds as assigned. Electrical duties were miscellaneous and minor, and I was frequently assigned to engine room watch.

Our own *LCT 858* was finally brought down the river and lashed to the side of the LST. Our crew went aboard and began the task of unpacking, cleaning and installing all of the various pieces of equipment. In addition, everything had to be secured to withstand the launching of the LCT that was eventually to take place. For example, the propeller shafts had to be disconnected from the diesel engines.

In the meantime, work began on the construction of a double framework of timbers, one on top of the other, on the deck of the LST. A very heavy layer of grease was applied to the top of the timbers making up the lower framework. A layer of canvas was then installed on top of the greased timbers. Then the matching upper framework was lowered into place. Both frames were then securely chained to the deck of the LST. I didn't realize this until much later, but a thin heaving line – about the thickness of a clothes line at home – was also installed as a 'trigger'.

On April 29 a huge crane lifted *LCT 858* out of the water and slowly carried her over to the LST before carefully lowering her onto the timber framework. The LCT was then chained into place.

LST 661, with the *LCT 858* aboard, left for a shakedown cruise early in May. We sailed from New Orleans to the tip of Florida, where we anchored offshore for thirteen days while all equipment was tested and tuned. We weren't given liberty, and heard that this had been discontinued because of bitter protests from the local community. It seems the pregnancy rate in the area had skyrocketed since the arrival of the Navy, and they were very unhappy about it! We left on May 20, bound for Gulfport, Mississippi, where we *were* granted liberty. On our return to New Orleans we were given permission to draw virtually anything we desired from the Naval Supply Depot on the base.

We left on June 2, 1944, bound for the Panama Canal, and encountered a storm in the Caribbean that had the LST rocking something fierce. I was so fortunate not to become seasick, as some of the others did. We arrived at the Panama Canal on June 12, and suffered a tragedy shortly after passing through the locks. Coupled with the tropical heat, the heat from the huge LST diesels turned the engine room into an incredible hot box. One's clothing would be soaked with perspiration after only a few minutes there. In the engine room, a catwalk paralleled the large propeller shafts. A Fireman First Class, a young man in his early twenties, had the late watch in the engine room. It was so hot that he'd opened his shirt and pulled his shirt tails out of his dungarees. He was found dead the next morning. As the scene was reconstructed, it appeared that he'd leaned over one of the propeller shafts for some reason. The shaft had caught a shirt tail and pulled him over . . . After the appropriate ceremonies, his body was removed at Balboa, Panama.

We arrived in San Diego on June 25. I don't recall anything very eventful that happened there, except that when I went on liberty I learned to my disgust that, at age nineteen, I couldn't buy beer.

We arrived in Pearl Harbor on July 12. It was a sobering experience to view the scars of the Japanese attack, which were still readily visible. We left Pearl on July 16, bound for Guadalcanal in the Solomon Islands. We left Guadalcanal again on September 4. In retrospect, I suspect that our group of landing ships and craft left earlier than other Task Force components because we were so slow. After we were under way, we were told that we were part of the force which was going to invade the Palau Islands, the gateway to the Philippines. Specifically, the Marines were scheduled to invade Peleliu and the Army was going to fight ashore on Angaur, a neighboring island. We were to be part of the Peleliu effort.

The invasion of Peleliu took place on September 15, 1944. Of course, our LCT was still sitting aboard the LST. To prepare for launching, our crew had secured everything aboard the craft. We then returned to the LST and stood by while launching efforts took place. All of the chains attaching the LCT and the double framework beneath it to the LST were removed, as was the railing on the starboard side of the LST. Lines were attached to the bow and stern of the LCT, and to the front of the top part of the framework. Fuel and water were transferred to the starboard tanks of the LST, causing the ship to list about 12 to 15 degrees. Remember the 'trigger' line I mentioned earlier? After everything was clear, the Boatswain used an axe to cut that line and the entire top framework slowly slid off the LST, launching the LCT. The launching framework was then pulled away from the LCT, and our crew boarded the *858* to hurriedly prepare her to move into the invasion. The propeller shafts were connected to the diesels, and they and the generators were started. Then we cast off the lines and moved away from the LST. The entire launching operation took surprisingly little time.

We then moved to a cargo ship where five Sherman tanks were loaded aboard us, and we headed for the beach. I remember that we passed about a half mile or so from the stern of the battleship USS *Pennsylvania*, and just as we passed she let loose a broadside. The shock wave from the blast practically lifted our LCT out of the water, tanks and all, and the helmsman had to fight the wheel to get the craft turned back in the proper direction.

We were later told that we were in the eighth wave. Japanese mortar shells were soon splashing around us in an attempt to stop the landing of the tanks and amtracs, thus isolating the infantry on the beaches.

There were numerous coral protrusions just below the surface. Our LCT had to maneuver in as close as possible, sort of parking on the coral outcroppings. We were in close enough so that the tanks, with waterproofed hatches and with long exhaust extensions above them, were able to splash into the water and move ashore.

After disgorging our tanks, there were a few scary moments when a mortar shell landed on one side of us. Shortly thereafter, a second shell landed on the other side. Our engines were thrown into full reverse and I began dragging in the anchor. We'd moved only about two or three lengths when the third shell landed – right where we'd been only a few moments earlier.

But other than stray bullets from snipers, and the occasional mortar shell, we weren't directly involved in life-threatening action. We began shuttling in supplies of all types. At first it was huge slings of ammunition, followed later by innumerable types of other supplies.

The nights were scary. All the ships and landing craft had to stay far enough offshore to avoid broaching and becoming impaled on the coral reefs. Of course, no exterior lights were permitted. Every once in a while a flare would go off, illuminating the beach with a silvery, ghostly brightness.

Ashore, the Marines were having a tough time of it. The Japs were dug in and the toll of invading troops was heavy. Running along the interior of the island was a group of low hills and ridges, and here the Japs had built their defenses in a warren of caves that were difficult to neutralize. As we came in to deliver supplies, floating bodies of Marines were everywhere. Earlier, I told you about the filtration system on our diesels. We learned that the filters had to be cleaned much more often – of waterlogged flesh. Obviously the propellers of the landing craft which were darting about had shredded some of the corpses. In retrospect I find it incredible that we were able to disconnect our emotions from the horror of the situation, and just clean the filters in a matter-of-fact way.

As we plodded our way back and forth from the supply ships, we noticed the hospital ships which were anchored some distance from the island. As we were going by, I remember watching the crews washing down the blood and gore from their decks.

As I mentioned earlier, the 1st Marine Division had invaded Peleliu and the Army had invaded the nearby island of Angaur. We were told that the Japs used Angaur as a source for phosphates. In any case, the Army met with relatively less resistance than the Marines were encountering on Peleliu, and were able to provide desperately needed reinforcements for them later.

I've done some reading about the invasion of Peleliu, and I learned a great deal that I didn't know – including the fact that the invasion was totally unnecessary.

An eleventh-hour discussion had in fact been held on whether to continue with the operation, after the Japanese had reacted only feebly to a series of carrier strikes begun against the Philippines on D-6. The landings had gone ahead.

Organised resistance on Angaur ended on 21 October, but the bloody slogging match on Peleliu dragged on until 27 November. By that time the Americans had already been ashore in the Philippines for over a month, establishing themselves on the island of Leyte without any of the planned bomber support from the Palaus.

The Philippines, like Guam, had been American territory before the war, and there were emotional as well as practical reasons for wishing to liberate the islands. Their reconquest had originally been scheduled to start in December 1944, but due to the suspicion that Japanese air power might be a spent force – which had prompted the last-minute discussions about Peleliu and Angaur – the timetable had been advanced by two whole months. Intermediate operations had been cancelled, and the assault on Leyte, in the central Philippines, by the US Sixth Army had been brought forward to October.

To begin the assault, a Ranger battalion had been used to clear the islands in Leyte Gulf; then on A-Day – Friday 20 October 1944 – the US Army's 7th and 24th Infantry Divisions, the 1st Cavalry Division[2] and most of the 96th Infantry Division had been landed on Leyte itself. Little opposition had been encountered on the beaches, because the Japanese had learned the lesson of previous preliminary bombardments, but inland they had defended as tenaciously as expected. Their attempts to intervene at sea, by beginning a series of surface and carrier actions known collectively as the Battle for Leyte Gulf, had resulted only in their Navy being finally and decisively crushed.

On 15 December the Sixth Army had gone on to establish a foothold on Mindoro, closer still to the main island of Luzon. Operations to clear Leyte and Mindoro had then been handed over to the US Eighth Army, while the Sixth prepared for the assault on Luzon, scheduled for Tuesday 9 January 1945.

On 9 January, S-Day, a landing force consisting of most of the US Army's 6th, 37th, 40th and 43rd Infantry Divisions was put ashore in the north west of Luzon. The remainder of each division was held back as a floating reserve. The discovery of false beaches just offshore, which caused the LSTs to ground too early, caused delays in the unloading of vehicles and supplies even more serious than those experienced in Sicily in July 1943, but

---

2. For all practical purposes an infantry division, but retaining the cavalry nomenclature of its various units. One of these was the 7th Cavalry, George Armstrong Custer's old regiment.

luckily the Japanese had again chosen not to contest the beaches.

Inland, however, progress was slow, despite the fact that the Sixth Army eventually expanded to the equivalent of over eleven divisions. To aid the push southwards towards the major port of Manila, a series of additional landings further down the west coast were quickly planned and executed using some of the build-up units. The first two of these landings, on 29 and 30 January, brought in the 38th Infantry Division and part of the 24th Infantry Division. The third, on 31 January, involved most of the 11th Airborne Division.

Irwin Stahl took part in this third landing, at Nasugbu, south of Manila.

My Company – Company 'C', 1st Battalion, 187th Glider Infantry Regiment – was relieved from combat on Leyte, and sent for rest and recuperation on the beach.

Late in January we were told to prepare for a seaborne invasion. The 11th Airborne was a small Division. At full strength it had 8200 men [compared with the 14,037 in one of the US Army's normal infantry divisions]. The 187th and 188th Glider Infantry Regiments consisted of only two Battalions each, though the 511th Parachute Infantry Regiment had three Battalions, and their Companies had larger tables of organization than we did. In any event the 511th didn't accompany us. They joined us later by parachute.

Company 'C' provided about ninety-five men to the invasion force. Each Battalion in the 187th and 188th had three Rifle Companies and a Headquarters Company. The Headquarters Company had a Heavy Weapons Section, but only with things like .50 caliber machine guns and 81mm mortars.

This meant that the glider units were light on firepower as well as small in size – an inevitable result of being tailored for air portability. The crowded airfields on Leyte and Mindoro, however, could not accommodate the gliders and tugs needed to fly them in, so they had to be landed by sea.

In due course we were loaded onto LCI(L)s, and we were accompanied on our trip from Leyte by destroyers. The 1st Battalion of the 187th, which included Company 'C', was the reserve unit for the invasion force, so I was in the last wave ashore and had a great view of the invasion. Of course, I was only a Pfc [Private First Class], so I was looking from the bottom up.

Two destroyers shelled the shore from a position between the LCI(L)s and the beach. Once they made a high speed run, and dropped depth charges. A cruiser shelled the shore from behind us. This bombardment kept up for about half an hour.

When the first of the LCI(L)s were a few hundred yards from the beach, eight P-38 Lightnings appeared. The first airplane strafed the beach, the second dropped a bomb, the third strafed, the fourth dropped a bomb, and so on. Each plane carried two bombs, and they continued in this order until all the bombs had been dropped. Minutes later my LCI(L) was on the shore, and I was off and running to shelter of some kind past the sand of the beach. Apparently there was no resistance on the beach, and only minor firefights inland.

I later learned that this was a feint to try to draw some Jap soldiers away from the main invasion force, which was still well north of the Philippines capital, Manila. The site of our invasion was Nasugbu, a little town about 55 miles south of the capital.

There was so little reaction from the Japs that we kept going, and later joined by the 511th [which parachuted in, albeit in three separate lifts because of aircraft shortages] we participated in the attack on Manila, but from the south.

On 12 February, while the 11th Airborne Division was engaged in heavy fighting around the runways at Nichols Field, on the southern outskirts of Manila, contact was made with the rest of the Sixth Army pushing down from the north.

While much of the Army turned its attention to the Japanese garrison now trapped in the city, the 11th Airborne was given a new task.

In cooperation with the local Filipino guerrillas, it would launch a raid deep into Japanese territory to rescue the inmates of the internment camp at Los Banos, south east of the capital.

Part of the attack force would advance overland, part would be dropped by parachute, and part, since Los Banos lay on the shore of a huge lake known as the Laguna de Bay, would come ashore in LVTs. The parachutists would be flown in from Nichols Field, which the Division had just taken.

Several hundred of the internees were British, among them *Lewis Watty*.

I was always an early riser in Camp, and as usual had awakened at 6.00am, bathed, and thereafter had lit a fire and was cooking up a small pan of rice for breakfast – 60 grams, or about three heaped tablespoons full, which was half my day's allowance. At 7.00am sharp I heard the roar of planes overhead, but as that had been a daily occurrence for weeks past I didn't attach particular importance to it. I did, however, stroll out of my quarters to have a look, and passing almost over the Camp to the east were nine large transport planes. They were unusually low and flying slowly. Even as I watched, the first parachute dropped out, and in a matter of what seemed to be seconds the sky appeared to be full of parachutes. I discovered later that the actual number of troops dropped was 123, but that number of parachutes all in the air at once looks like a great deal more. What a roar went up from the Camp. One could hear the cheers swelling in volume as more and more internees dashed out of their quarters to watch. The day of deliverance was with us at last. We had waited for it for over three years. At times we had almost despaired of it ever arriving, but here it was at last, and arriving in a form that no one had anticipated.

Then from the western boundary of the Camp came the sound of rifle and machine gun fire. This I learned later was from the Filipino guerrillas who during the previous few days had infiltrated into the area, and were timed to operate against the Japanese guards on the western boundary of the camp simultaneously with the dropping of the paratroops on the eastern boundary.

In a matter of minutes rifle and machine gun fire was general all round the Camp, and soon it was inside, as the Japanese troops retreated into the Camp, using our barracks buildings as shelter.

Guerrilla troops were all over the place. They seemed to rise out of the ground, and I can vouch for the fact that they showed no mercy. In addition to rifles they all carried bolos – long, heavy knives which were the beloved weapon of the Filipino – and they made sure with their bolos that any Japanese they shot had gone to meet their ancestors. I saw one Japanese bolt into one of the large drainage pipes that went through the Camp. Unfortunately for him he was spotted by a guerrilla, who with a grin dashed up to the pipe and threw a hand grenade in after him. I can understand the Filipinos' hatred of the Japanese in view of the treatment the Japanese handed out while they were in full control of the Philippines.

At 7.10am I saw my first American soldier on the ground. He was a great big blond boy, and he came strolling – I can think of no better word – up to the boundary fence close to my quarters, calmly cut the barbed wire and walked into Camp. He came up between my quarters and Barracks 12. We were all taking what cover was available from flying bullets, but when we saw him we forgot bullets, danger and everything else and dashed out cheering. I never saw a man look so embarrassed. He was carrying a Tommy gun, and he looked at us all with a sheepish grin as if he'd been caught doing something wrong. All he could say was 'Good morning, folks'. I had to laugh. It was just too wonderful a situation for words.

However, he wasn't sheepish when he got down to business. I asked him if he needed help or information, and he asked me where was the Japanese office. I pointed to Barracks 3 and 4, which lay adjacent to Barracks 11 and 12. He glanced around, then said to the men from Barracks 11 and 12 'You folks have been here long enough. Suppose you leave these quarters to me for a minute'. Then as an afterthought he added 'Maybe you better take cover; there's liable to be some shootin' around here'. He was right. There was 'some shootin', and he did most of it. He whistled up about twenty guerrillas and they attacked Barracks 3 and 4 through Barracks 11 and 12. It was a pretty piece of work, and lasted about fifteen minutes, in which time the entire Commandant's staff, including the Commandant himself, were accounted for and the barracks set afire over them. No prisoners were taken, and I may say that remark applies to the whole operation against the Camp.

Shortly after 7.00am the first amphibian troop carriers reached the Camp. There were forty-seven in all. They knew exactly where to go. The first half dozen wheeled around to the hospital and commenced evacuating the sick at once. The remainder lined up on the baseball field adjoining the Camp, after smashing their way through the boundary fence. I was sent for by the Commanding Officer, and had to make a decidedly unpleasant journey from my quarters to the hospital. The American soldier who came for me seemed to think nothing of it, and all the way along was asking me questions about how the Japanese had treated us. We passed close to the Commandant's office right while the scrapping was at its worst. I ventured to remark that it was a bit dangerous, but the soldier dismissed the whole affair by pointing out airily that the Japs were too busy to take any notice of us. I hoped they were, and was exceedingly thankful when we reached the shelter of the hospital.

The officer in charge of operations informed me that the Camp must be completely evacuated by 9.00am. He anticipated heavy fighting in the area if he had to stay longer, as there were considerable numbers of Japanese in the near vicinity. I had to instruct the whole Camp to file along to the baseball field and into the amtracs, and they would move off for the lake as they filled up.

So, with a few helpers, I got the instructions to all the barracks, and I must say I was agreeably surprised at the orderly way in which people turned out. There was no time to pack anything. People just grabbed one or two essentials and off they went. They didn't bother to ask questions. All they knew was that the amtracs meant safety and liberty, and with bullets flying around the average person makes for safety with very little urging. Furthermore several of the barracks were already on fire, which helped to speed people's actions. I had had a small bag packed for just such an emergency for over a week, so when I'd made sure all the barracks had been notified I streaked back to my quarters, grabbed my bag, and bolted for the amtracs.

We were fired on once en route to the lake by a few snipers in the trees on the roadside. One internee was wounded, but a burst from one of our machine guns and from a couple of amtracs immediately ahead seemed to deal with the situation. Anyway we had no further trouble.

When we reached the lakeside the amtracs took to the water in a long line, and we churned our way across the lake, the last one reaching the [American controlled] shore at about 12.30. After dropping us on the shore the amtracs returned across the lake to pick up the paratroopers who had remained behind to do a bit of mopping up and to protect our retreat in case the Japanese managed to bring up reinforcements. From the beach we were taken in ambulances and trucks to Muntinlupa. As soon as we arrived we were given hot soup and a light meal. What a joy it was. Our troubles were at an end.

The rescue operations were a triumph of organisation and split-second timing. All was well that ended well, and the perfection of organisation continued after our arrival at Muntinlupa. We were all assigned to quarters from already-prepared lists. We were fed, given cigarettes, matches and clothes, hospitalised where necessary, dosed with vitamins, and special diets were arranged for bad cases with an absolute minimum of trouble. We were even given two sheets of writing paper in order to write to our nearest relatives, and we were assured that if the letter was posted that night it would be in America in four days or in England in ten days.

Later that evening the paratroops who had rescued us returned to camp. What a reception we gave them. How young they all looked, and what splendid physical specimens. I spoke to several of them. To them the day's operation was just another job done in cleaning up the Japs. I heard a story from one of their officers. A day or two before our rescue their Commanding Officer had called the men together and said to them 'Boys, there are 2000 civilians – men, women and kids – in Los Banos Camp. They are our own folks, and they are going to be slaughtered if we don't do something about it. Let's go and get them out'. So they came and got us out from behind the Jap lines. One young lad said to me 'It was easy!'. Perhaps it *was* easy, but it was only perfect organisation, splendid equipment, and above all, wonderful boys that made it easy.

I must conclude with one final story which illustrates the casual way the paratroops treated their work. I watched one lad attack a sentry post with five sentries posted in it. He stalked the post from the shelter of a barracks building until he reached within about 20yds. Then he unhitched a hand grenade from his belt, and calmly and deliberately stood up and lobbed it into the post. Then he moved at lightning speed. It seemed to me he was in the middle of the post almost simultaneously with the explosion of the hand grenade. I heard the roar of his Tommy gun, and in a matter of seconds he came strolling back. He joined a group of internees who were crouching under a bank, and his first remark was 'Any chance of a cup of coffee around here?'.

TWELVE

Backwaters: the Burma Campaign

While the Americans were pushing back the Japanese in the Philippines, the British were doing the same in Burma.

Paul Roessler's LCT was one of those sent to operate among the inland waterways and mangrove swamps of the Burmese coast.

I arrived at Cocanada [on the east coast of India] in a blazing mid day temperature, and walked with my suitcases across a sandy plain towards some huts in the distance. On the way I met a man dressed only in shorts and shoes, who asked me where I was heading. I said that I was looking for *LCT 2435*. He replied that he was Lieutenant Curran, the Captain, and invited me to follow him to the officers' mess for a drink. Then we walked to a nearby canal where his landing craft was tied up. He called on some crew members to get my bags aboard, and showed me the uppermost bunk in the cabin I was to share with him. I was the second in command, commonly known as the First Lieutenant, or even more commonly by the crew as 'Jimmy the One'.

Our craft was armed with two 20mm anti-aircraft Oerlikon cannons; we also had rocket launchers which fired miles of piano wire into the sky to entrap aircraft. At least that was the theory. Apart from that we possessed two rifles, two submachine guns and two different sized pistols. One was a Colt .45, and the other a .38 Smith & Wesson.

The *2435* was there to practise beach landings with amphibious Valentine tanks [a type long superseded at home by the DD Sherman]. These were expected to 'swim' ashore once launched off our craft's ramp. The practices took place at an artificial island on a sandbar off the coast, but despite all the practice I never saw them in action, and I concluded that they weren't considered successful enough.

The only relaxation we had there, apart from evenings drinking in the mess, was to watch the local fishermen and their families enjoying some entertainment. This consisted of making silhouettes on a white sheet strung up on poles, by dancing about on the other side in the light of a wood fire. There was music on crude wooden instruments to accompany the native dancers.

Some weeks later we received orders to sail for Calcutta, north of us, to join the rest of our Flotilla. The *2435* was an LCT Mk5, and the bolted-together construction of the vessel was put to the test severely on the voyage up the east coast. After a few days chugging along, a monsoon storm blew up, and we were caught in the middle of it. Hurricane force winds and raging seas battered the superstructure. Being a landing craft we were flat bottomed, with a very shallow draught. The bows kept getting picked up by giant waves and smashed down again. It was quite frightening to see our front end whipping up and down like a rubber stick! Some of the bolted sections became loose, and we had to get a motor mechanic to stay in the double bottom tanks for hours to tighten the bolts up. I can remember that when the storm started we were off the port of Vizagapatam. We had our engines going at emergency full ahead, but when dawn broke we found that we were still in the same position. The force of wind and tide had combined to overcome our forward motion, so that we hadn't moved ahead for many hours. Both the Skipper and I got bruised, because we had to take turns on watch, wedging our bodies between the coaming on the bridge and the compass binnacle in order to stay on our feet.

It was during this voyage that I came to appreciate the seamanship and tough qualities of the Skipper. The crew, which consisted mainly of youngsters like me under twenty years old, worshipped him. But he was a strict disciplinarian and brooked no nonsense from those he commanded. For example, at Cocanada, when our signaller was insolent, the Skipper ordered two Petty Officers to take him ashore and put him in the cells there. They marched him away, and we never saw that defaulter again. It was small wonder that the Captain was held in awe. He was a man of few words, smiling only rarely and chainsmoking cigarettes. Everyone on board had great faith in his capabilities.

The epic trip ended when we arrived off the mouth of the River Hooghly, and then sailed up it to reach the sprawling docks in Calcutta. We took a taxi to a Chinese restaurant for a welcome meal ashore. The vehicle was an old American open-topped saloon car, its paint and leather upholstery bleached by the sun. Our driver was a bearded Sikh – most taxi drivers seemed to be Sikhs. At the restaurant we shared a table with an old salt who'd become a Royal Naval Reserve officer. In the daytime we went sightseeing in the city centre. Monkeys scrambled about in the trees along the boulevards.

It was in Calcutta Docks that black rats first got on board by climbing along the mooring ropes. They hid and bred in spaces below the decks, or above the deckheads. When switching the cabin light on at night we would see rats' eyes glinting before they scuttled away. Once I awoke with a rat in my hair. Thereafter I rigged up a bedsheet to prevent a recurrence. Cockroaches swarmed everywhere, and would drown themselves in our opened tins of milk.

Most of our Flotilla's craft had seen service in the Mediterranean before going to India, and nearly all were becoming unseaworthy with leaks and weakened joints. It was decided that they should be drydocked for the necessary repairs. That meant having temporarily to live ashore somewhere. The crew went into barracks. Officers were offered the choice between hotels or private accommodation. The civilian billets were owned by British Colonial Officers who were willing to open their homes to us as a sort of war effort. The Skipper and I decided to try this, and our hosts were the Civil Commissioner of Police and his wife. They had no children, and were looked after by six servants, who also cared for us. The style of life was a great eye-opener for me.

Breakfast was served early and a truck collected us daily to go down to the docks to supervise the work there. We returned the same way each evening. On arrival home there would be a hot bath drawn ready for us. Clothes were left on the floor after undressing. A freshly-ironed set was laid out on the bed and the soiled ones removed for washing.

Dinner was a fairly elaborate affair, for which we donned evening dress – including white jacket, black trousers and a red cummerbund around the waist. A beautifully-appointed table would be laid out with silverware and porcelain, and small finger bowls of water for rinsing hands after handling fruit. All salad leaves, tomatoes and fruit had to be swilled around in a big bowl of water mixed with Potassium Permanganate. That acted as a disinfectant, which was most necessary in a country that was anything but hygienic. After dinner, which was served up by a 'bearer' under a Sikh chief servant, we often went to one of the typically British clubs, to talk, drink and dance. Weekends saw us sunbathing and bathing in the club pools.

Tea was usually taken in the garden under a tree. The servants brought the necessary furniture out from the house and then carried out our meal. Once, a snake charmer was invited to do a demonstration for us while we had tea. He had a basket of cobras, which rose up and swayed when he played his pipe to charm them. At a certain moment he pretended that he could produce a snake from the air. No doubt one was hidden up his sleeve, and with a quick gesture he threw the cobra at our hostess' feet. She was most alarmed, and the charmer was bundled lock, stock and barrel into the street for his stupidity.

It was now November 1944, and a signal arrived ordering us to report to the docks with our crews at midnight. We heard that an Admiral was on his way to address us about the Army's situation on the Burma front. The Japanese were still in occupation there, having thrown out the British as they'd done in Malaya, Singapore and Hong Kong. At the rendezvous, a large dockside godown [warehouse], we were told that some 31-ton Sherman tanks were to be transported to Burma, where they were required urgently. Although our LCTs were quite unseaworthy, we were asked to de-dock, store ship, load the Army personnel with their tanks, and to sail next morning across the Bay of Bengal.

Our Mk5s were only designed for coastal navigation and were definitely unsuitable for ocean crossings. However, orders were orders in wartime. After a fever of activity we left the Hooghly River and made for point in the estuary. There we met an armed trawler of the Royal Indian Navy, which was to act as our escort.

All went well with our Flotilla for a day or so. Then another monsoon storm blew up. One of our sister craft began to get into difficulties. Water had got into her fuel tanks, and the engines stopped. The trawler escort took her in tow, but the LCT began to sink, and her tow was therefore slipped. All vessels were ordered to close up to the scene, which we did, just in time to observe the crew abandoning ship. They all jumped overboard except the Skipper, Jock Hall. He was a dour, 6ft Scot, and was intent on saving his ship's log and signal book. As his craft sank underneath him we could see that he'd become trapped under the canvas sun awning over the bridge. Miraculously, though, as the waves slid over his head the craft turned on her side and the four Shermans she was carrying broke through the side coamings and sank. With 124 tons of weight gone, the crippled vessel lurched back above the waves, still held up by the air in her double bottom bilges.

Jock Hall was still on the bridge, gasping for breath. We moved up to the LCT's stern and tied a rope to it, holding our bows close in and urging him to jump aboard us. However, he was in a state of shock, and all he could think of doing was running up and down to his cabin to rescue the crockery! Our Skipper ordered him to leave under threat of slipping the rope, because our bows were getting damaged crashing up and down in the waves and hitting his vessel. Reluctantly he then leapt over the gap to join us.

Meanwhile his crew members were either swimming around bawling for help or floating unconscious on the surface of the sea. We threw some lifebuoys overboard towards the survivors. Another member of the Flotilla moved near and picked up a few of the swimmers. I tied a heaving line round my waist and jumped onto the catwalk running along the hull just above the water. From that position I managed to haul two men up alongside me. They got badly scraped by the barnacles on the hull, but were otherwise not seriously hurt. All the rescued crewmen revived quite quickly, although shocked and with water in their lungs. After a final count up, we found everyone had been saved.

The problem then arose of what to do with the stricken LCT, which was drifting half submerged. It was decided to try to sink her by gunfire. But although the trawler fired 4in shells at her and we pumped away with our Oerlikon cannons, the wretched craft wouldn't sink. Other craft joined in with *their* guns, and several hours later we were able to witness her demise as she sank out of sight.

The next day our own craft, *LCT 2435*, began to ship water in the high seas that were still running. Our engine room began to flood and our pumps couldn't cope with the volume of water. In the dark hours next evening the trawler sent a rowing boat over to us carrying a large manual pump. That helped us to bale out faster. We also used an auxiliary petrol-driven pump. Unfortunately that exploded when the Chief Motor Mechanic was operating it, burning his chest, back and arms. There's a snapshot in my album showing him swathed in the bandages that I dressed his wounds with. He recovered from these injuries within a few weeks.

The sea began to rise up and down in a great swell, in which we started to roll heavily from side to side. It was then that we made a worrying discovery. In our haste to sail from Calcutta we'd omitted to load the chains and bottlescrews [tensioning gear] which were normally used to tie down vehicles to the deck. After a while the craft's motion was such that the Sherman tanks we were transporting began to slide violently back and forth. It was a terrifying sight. These situations often bring out the best in men, and some of the crew immediately volunteered to crawl in between the heavy tanks to wedge them tight with dozens of boxes of tinned food from the stores below. The work was highly dangerous, and they risked getting crushed without warning. In the end everything was prevented from moving, but we'd taken on a sharp list to one side. The deck on the listing side was under water.

The tank crews were Indians, with British officers. They formed part of the 19th (King George V's Own) Lancers, an Indian cavalry regiment. Some of them were Sikhs from the Punjab up near Afghanistan. They'd never seen the sea before, let alone sailed on it, and they were most afraid. We gave them orders to stay up on deck lest we should sink. Like me they were very seasick, and looked green under their brown skins. We had no wish to capsize in those shark-infested waters, and we therefore stayed up all night pumping out floodwater. On one occasion I collapsed with sickness and fatigue, but I recovered quickly and carried on with my turns at watchkeeping on the bridge.

At long last we reached the coast of Burma, and headed for the port of Teknaf.

Teknaf was the last harbour on the Indian side of the border. The area had seen much heavy fighting, and was now the jumping-off point for a renewed offensive to push the Japanese back southwards.

After limping into the port we managed to beach on a sandbank to land the tanks and repair our craft. The soldiers in Teknaf had been there for months, living through a monsoon season in little slit trenches, with rubber capes over the top for a bit of protection from the torrential rain.

Then began what became known as the Third Arakan campaign, named after that stretch of the Burmese coast. While this coastal campaign was going on, the main British Fourteenth Army was advancing down the centre of Burma, under the command of Lieutenant General Sir Bill Slim – a man who'd risen from the ranks. The Fourteenth was known as the 'Forgotten Army', because it was far from Britain and tended to get consideration only after the demands of the European and Mediterranean theatres had been satisfied.

Sometimes our forces had to be supplied by air drops. I recall seeing showers of coloured parachutes falling out of Dakota aircraft, each chute carrying a drum packed with stores and ammunition.

We were by then in December 1944, and on the 27 and 28 December we made two reconnaissance landings further south in Japanese-held territory, during which we put some self-propelled Priest field guns ashore. They were on caterpillar chassis, and could fire shells on the move, like a tank. That operation was to test the defences prior to a major assault to be made at the start of 1945.

The major assault, scheduled for 18 February 1945, was to be against Akyab, further down the coast from Teknaf. When it was revealed that the Japanese had begun to withdraw, however, the date was brought forward to 3 January.

When we got there we found that the enemy had fled, except for a few soldiers our troops captured. We ferried the prisoners back to the [Teknaf] peninsula for interrogation. They were bedraggled and demoralised, because in the Japanese Army tradition it was a disgrace to be made a prisoner and not to die for their Emperor. We noticed that as infantrymen they wore rubber-soled canvas boots, with a separation for the big toe.

We then spent several days transporting stores from the peninsula to Akyab.

Before the war, Akyab had been Burma's third port, with a population of over 36,000.

Indian sapper regiments were using elephants to haul logs from the jungle, in order to repair the broken jetties. These had been left damaged since the Japs had invaded Burma. Like so many towns we were to see afterwards in Burma, Malaya and Indonesia, it surprised us to see things left in ruins. Grass grew in the streets, and buildings remained unrepaired.

During this period of operations we worked night and day, taking it in turns to snatch a little sleep whenever possible. The non-stop work in the tropical heat sometimes overcame our normal resistance to fatigue. An example of this was when my friend Doug Smallbone got overtired and, as he walked along the catwalk of his craft, just fell into the sea in a trance. This wasn't noticed for half an hour, but when he was nowhere to be found on board, the craft turned round and steered a reciprocal course. Being dark at the time didn't help the search. It was like looking for a needle in a haystack, but by an amazing stroke of luck he was spotted in the beam of the signalling lamp being used to scan the water. After being picked up he told us what a shattering experience it'd been, watching the convoy disappear into the distance and believing that there was no chance of any rescue.

Apart from the hazards of exhaustion we sometimes succumbed to annoying illnesses such as boils, carbuncles and ulcers on the skin, as well as bouts of food poisoning. Most such problems I treated on our craft, with the meagre means at my disposal, from the First Aid box we kept. On one never-to-be-forgotten occasion the whole ship's company, and the men on other craft too, went down with water poisoning. We'd received a signal saying that a certain water boat was carrying a polluted cargo, and either we were to discharge any water we'd tanked up with from her, or we must treat it with cleansing tablets. We *had* no tablets, and anyway, we'd already been drinking the tainted water for several days. The net result was that our skins broke into big yellow water blisters all over our bodies. On bursting, the sores just wouldn't heal up. Everyone had to stop shaving, and we all grew beards. We painted ourselves with a lotion called Gentian Violet, which gave us the appearance of Stone Age Britons! Eventually we linked up with a larger ship carrying a Naval surgeon. He provided some sort of ointment to spread on the sores, and gradually, over a period of a month, our skins healed up. It'd been a very trying illness, due to our salty perspiration irritating the sores.

At the best of times most of us suffered from 'prickly heat'. This was a pricking sensation on the skin. When leaning back in a chair, contact with the upholstery gave one a shivering convulsion. There was absolutely no effective treatment. It had to be ignored by using mind over matter.

A short time later I missed the dramatic first day's action at a place called the Myebon Peninsula. I'd taken the opportunity of a lift on a MGB back to Chittagong to collect stores; especially, as I recall, some toilet rolls. Although I was only away for two days, in my absence the Flotilla was ordered to land tanks and the 3rd Commando Brigade at Myebon. When I returned the Flotilla was lying offshore, and I heard the story. The earlier reconnaissance had reported that no enemy was present. However, as the craft headed for the beach they were caught in a crossfire by Jap soldiers hiding on an island and in the jungle ashore at the landing zone. Apparently it was chaotic. The beach was mined, and the first Beachmaster stepped on one and was blown up. Despite the problems, the tanks and troops fought their way up the beach and inland.

When I rejoined my craft that second day of the landings, the Royal Air Force was dive bombing the jungle fringes. We had instructions to collect drums of aviation fuel from a merchant ship and land them for future use of spotter planes, if an airstrip could be built. It was hair-raising to have to carry such a volatile cargo in the middle of a battle.

The Commando Brigade had been landed at Myebon to cut off the Japanese retreat, but because of the unexpectedly fierce resistance it had been unable to push inland to the vital north-south road, and a further landing was hastily arranged.

Following that spell in action we were selected for a special operation. We were required to slip up various rivers and chaungs [creeks] under cover of darkness, to a place called Kangaw. We had to get through Japanese-occupied areas of jungle without the enemy realising what we were up to. Our particular job was to transport soldiers from a mountain artillery regiment and their fifty mules. Each mule carried pieces of their guns on its back – one a barrel, another a wheel, yet another the ammunition boxes, and so on.

On the way we saw the wrecks of Japanese gunboats. Eventually we got to the landing site and met some British soldiers there. They'd been engaged in a fierce battle, and we were told there were about 1000 dead Japanese troops in the fields behind the landing strip on the edge of the river. The Skipper wanted to go and see them, but he tripped over a branch on the shore and broke his ankle! We had to get him back aboard and give him a shot of Morphine from a throwaway injection pack. I signalled the senior craft to explain that we needed him to be transported to a hospital ship. A boat took him away, but first brought Jock Hall to take over as Captain. He was spare, having of course lost his own craft in the crossing of the Bay of Bengal.

We had an anxious time trying to navigate back to Myebon, because neither of us had been on watch to follow the route to Kangaw. We'd managed to reach an inland lake that we recognised, when a catastrophe occurred. Weeds had got into our engine cooling filters and blocked them, and the main engines and generators cut out. We knew that having lost electric power we couldn't use our capstan, but nevertheless we couldn't risk drifting ashore, so we had no alternative but to drop our anchor, not knowing how we'd be able to get it up again.

We assumed that the Japanese were in the area, and thus expected to be attacked. All day we waited on tenterhooks. A small spotter plane flew over. It was one of ours, but although we fired a flare into the sky it didn't see us.

We were still there at dusk. Luckily, though, just at that point we heard the chug-chug of another boat and saw the familiar silhouette of an infantry landing craft. We explained our predicament by signal lamp, and the other craft came alongside. They hauled up our anchor using their capstan, and then set off with us tied up to them.

After getting back to the temporary base we beached so as to clean out our filters. It'd been a harrowing experience, and one we didn't wish to have to repeat.

Some days later we were anchored in a lagoon with several sister craft under the command of a Royal Indian Navy sloop. It was a lovely sunny, peaceful day and we had nearly 200 tons of petrol and ammunition on board. Suddenly all hell let loose. The Japanese had managed to get some heavy guns into the hills above us. They fired into the lagoon, and with their first salvo hit the stern of the sloop, blowing it off. I remember seeing the splashes of the shells landing in the water, blowing up plumes of spray, followed by the sound of them exploding. No one waited for orders. Anchors were hauled up in record time, and craft then sailed around in circles to confuse the enemy gunners. The sloop commenced firing shells into the hills, and after a while silence fell. We moved downsteam and re-anchored!

At the end of the long months of the coastal campaign some of the Flotilla went on as far as Rangoon [the Burmese capital, retaken in May 1945]. Others, including us, were ordered back to India, where we left our LCTs. We never saw them again.

They'd served us well, but were unfit for further service.

Des Crowden was one of the Commandos who fought at Myebon and Kangaw, having arrived in India a year earlier.

I went to India in 4 Troop, No 5 Commando, as a Sergeant. I was with No 5 Commando for four and a half years, and managed to reach the dizzy heights of RSM. My Troop leader when I joined became CO, so no doubt that helped. Since then I've always looked on five as my lucky number, though I still haven't won the National Lottery!

We were part of the 3rd Commando Brigade, which had two Army Commandos, No 1 and No 5; and two Royal Marine Commandos, No 42 and

No 44. There were four Commando Brigades formed – two in the UK, one which fought in the Mediterranean; and my lot, who went to the Far East.

On the way out we'd been dive-bombed in the Mediterranean. The Brigade was in two troopships – us and 44 in one, and 1 and 42 in the other. The other ship was hit; not badly. Only killed one man. He was in the toilet, hit by a piece of flying metal. But they had to go into Alexandria to get the ship repaired, so we arrived well ahead of them. A Dutch Troop from No 10 Commando was also attached to the Brigade for a time.

In March 1944 Des and the rest of No 5 Commando had their first taste of fighting the Japanese, when they and No 44 (Royal Marine) Commando were ordered to mount an operation south of Teknaf. The intention was to distract Japanese attention from the main front, which it was hoped might be pushed south, away from the Indian frontier.

You always dug in in a 'box' [position for all-round defence]. Because you never knew which way the Japs would come. They were very doughty enemies. They never knew when to give up. It was a disgrace for them to withdraw, you see. And if they were killed for the Emperor, they felt their name would be revered.

They had one or two little goes at us. But the annoying thing was their artillery, which would shell us from the hills. When there was no firing going on you'd go into the trees with your mess tin and some water out of your water bottle, and make some tea. Then when you were making it they'd inevitably start shelling again, and you'd rush back to your trench. When you got back to your mess tin it'd be full of dirt. Which was most disappointing.

I was on a patrol which the CO took out. We went inland, up this hill, and suddenly all these Japs appeared. They were heading away from the fighting, but for some reason or other we weren't allowed to fire. Maybe we were just too badly outnumbered. But there were mules and everything; I'm sure we could've had a real field day. But we didn't reveal our presence.

The next night another patrol went out, and just at the same time they were setting out, the Japs decided to attack us. They were on three sides of the box, and our lads walked right into them . . . One poor chap was screaming. He was a very good boxer. He had over a dozen bullet wounds, and he was out there all night, screaming . . .

Of course we couldn't leave the box. But we got him in next morning, and he lived. We all stood-to at daylight, and I could see this order being passed round the box. And it ended up with me. I was to take two or three men and go out and pick up our dead. Which wasn't very pleasant. And of course by the time we got out there some of the bodies were stiffening up; their limbs were crooked, and they looked quite ghastly. We had this young kid who was absolutely brilliant academically; he was one of the bodies. And when we tried to lift him up to bury him, he kind of fell apart.

Another good friend of mine was badly wounded, but luckily the Navy came in and got him off the beach. He'd gone down to the beach to pick up stores from the Navy. They got him out to a ship, and then to a hospital ship. Saved his life.

Eventually it was decided we should pull out. But how were we going to pull out? We were under continuous shellfire. Well, then two dive bombers turned up – American built Vultee Vengeance dive bombers. They had a crew of two, and the poor gunner sat with his back to the pilot. So imagine what that's like, hurtling earthwards and not seeing where you're going. Or perhaps that's better! So as they blasted the place, we moved out. I think they must've hit some guns, because no shells followed us.

And then it was decided that my bloody Troop, 4 Troop, should cover the withdrawal of the others. Somebody produced two bottles of rum. We'd seen some Burmese, who'd warned us that the Japanese were coming after us. About 3.00am the bushes started rustling. So we all cocked our weapons, ready. You learned the lesson quite early on that you kept absolutely silent all the time, and never gave your position away. Because they would shout to you 'Come on, Tommee. Come and fight!'. You kept silent. And you saw the yellow of their eyes before you fired. Anyway, it turned out that all the movement was just cattle. So everybody breathed a sigh of relief. Lucky nobody had fired. Bloody cattle.

When you came out of action the first thing was to have a little service, in remembrance of those killed and wounded. And then you needed replacements, which came out to you.

While we were out of the fighting, the Japs started pushing through into India, much further north. We knew that if they got a big foothold in India there'd be trouble, because there were a lot of sympathetic nationalist Indians, many of whom went across to the Japs. Very tricky.

So they sent us up there a reinforcements. On the way up, trains were coming the other way, full of wounded.

This was a last desperate gamble by the Japanese, aimed at encircling and destroying the divisions facing them in the Imphal area. Their attack, however, was beaten off by the Fourteenth Army, and the Commandos found themselves with little to do except to mount patrols.

We got up to the railhead at Silchar in Assam [west of Imphal], but found that we'd 'missed the boat'. We were too late. So we went into tents there. By this time the monsoon had started, and the river rose 12ft. Livestock was floating past! We had to dig deep trenches round our tents.

We made our own beds out of bamboo. You got four bits about that long for the corners, banged them in, cut a notch in them. Then fixed on two long pieces of bamboo for the sides and two short bits at each end, filled it up with more bamboo, and that was your bed. Quite comfortable, too.

We also used bamboo when we were in boxes. We put stakes in front of us, so if the Japs charged, they'd be impaled by the bamboo. We were looking forward to hearing the Japs say 'Dash!'.

We were ordered to send patrols into the hills, in case any remaining parties of Japs filtered round. I took several patrols out. On one of them we were based in this beautiful little village, on top of a hill – as they tended to be. They had their own Christian Church, because of the efforts of a missionary who'd previously spent a lot of time with them. So we were made very welcome. They didn't want the Japs, that's for sure.

There was one hut larger than the others, and we slept in there. We used to go out on little probing patrols during the day. And go to Church, which we thought we needed. We eventually ran low on food, so I decided that we'd have to go out and shoot a couple of monkeys. Of course we didn't like doing it, but we found some in a tree, and we shot a black one and a golden one. We took them back to the hill tribesmen, and they cooked them for us over an open fire – in a hut with no chimney! It was like eating pieces of leather. One chap refused to eat it, but the rest of us managed. It tided us over until it was time for me to take the patrol back. The Japs never turned up.

On our way back we were getting near this small town that we had to go through to rejoin the Commando, when we found ourselves on the wrong side of a river. Luckily an Indian was walking along the far bank, and he had an umbrella. He knew English, so I shouted across to him could we borrow it, and I explained what for. Then I swam across and got it, brought it back, and we put our gear in the inverted umbrella and ferried it across. And, seeing how hungry we were, this chap then took us home and cooked us a chicken curry, which tasted like the best we'd ever had in our lives.

So we made it safely back to Silchar. Then we heard the Brigade was moving to what is now Sri Lanka – Ceylon then. I was to be in the advance party, so we got on this train at Silchar, to travel back down the whole length of India. What a trip. It took a whole week, with meals at various points along the way. I used to sit on the steps and watch India go by. Fantastic. When we got down there we started getting this camp ready, which was just off the beach, in a coconut grove.

Then eventually it was action time again. The Japs were then on the turn. Our blokes had won a hell of a fight at Imphal and Kohima, and now we were pushing them back in the Arakan too. The first landing they planned for us was Akyab Island, very close to the mainland. We landed there [on Wednesday 3 January 1945] to find the Japs had withdrawn. Fortunately.

We came across an enormous paddy field by the airstrip [the principal objective of the landing] full of damaged Japanese planes. We did get one luxury there – somebody arrived with some tins of self-heating cocoa. The only ones we ever saw.

And then we came back, got on board ship again, and went down the coast to a place called Myebon, which was being subjected to the most savage Air Force and Naval attack. You could see the whole shore vibrating, you know, as they hit it.

And then [on Friday 12 January] the landing craft went in. The whole Brigade. People had gone in overnight to clear the underwater obstacles, but that still left a great expanse of mud to cross. We just had to wade ashore through this sticky mud, with mines going off on the beach. If the Japs had still been dug in along the shoreline they'd have wiped us out.

Once ashore, the Commandos began clearing the Myebon peninsula, against stubborn resistance.

They decided to call in more support from the RAF. Well, unlike in Europe you didn't get it in the next five minutes, you had to wait till the next day. But then these planes came in, and cleared the problem, and we moved forward another little bit.

The Japanese delaying tactics were, however, successful in keeping open the north-south road the Commandos were trying to sever. It was in an attempt to sidestep this resistance that the Commandos handed over Myebon to part of the 25th Indian Division and re-embarked for Kangaw, ready to make another assault landing on Monday 22 January.

Our third landing in three weeks was up a chaung, a minor river. So we got in these landing craft and we went up this chaung; 27 miles I think it was [Myebon to Kangaw was 8 miles by the direct – and guarded – route up the Myebon River, but the indirect – and unguarded – route via the Thegyan River and Daingbon Chaung which the landing force actually followed was 27 miles]. We came to another sandy beach; still tidal, you know. Where we landed, and pushed inland to take a hill feature codenamed 'Brighton', 170ft high. In fact afterwards it was better known as Hill 170. We had to try and dig in, which was very hard because of the rocky soil; but we knew it was absolutely necessary to dig in. With Jap artillery around, the thing was always to dig a big hole and get down it.

Having dug in, the next thing to do was to have a cup of tea. So I went down to a bomb crater for some water. There were a lot of these bomb craters nearby. And a dead Burmese woman and child, obviously hit by the bombing.

We had these little solidified rounds of fuel, which didn't show any smoke and hardly any flame when lit, so they were ideal for these occasions. Put my tea in, stirred it up, drank it . . . and found it was salt water.

The Commandos soon had other things to worry about, as the Japanese launched counterattacks of increasing ferocity in an effort to save their units further north from being cut off.

That was the start of a ten day battle there, which was, if not *the* most savage, then certainly *one* of the most savage Commando actions of the war. The Japs managed to get a foothold on one end of the hill, and this officer, who'd only been with us six weeks, come from Blighty, he was picking up weapons that mortally-wounded people had dropped, and using them till the mags ran out, and then picking up another one. But eventually they got him.

The RAF came in, Hurribombers [Hawker Hurricane fighters equipped for the ground attack role] dropping bombs on the Japanese. At one point I looked up and I thought 'Why a leaflet raid?'. The Japs wouldn't take any notice of leaflets. But it was one of our Hurricanes, that'd been hit and exploded. Just falling. Fluttering down in bits.

The medical people were doing major operations, including amputations, right on the hill. Just behind canvas, you know. From the Casualty Clearing Station they had to get them down the chaung to the sea, and onto a hospital ship.

And this went on and on. Jap bodies were piling up all around us. On the last night my Troop was up the sharp end in a very tight box. Almost shoulder to shoulder. Waiting for the Japs to charge. We lost a lot of people again when they did.

But the crazy thing was, the post continued to arrive. The Navy always got the post to us! So when you weren't fighting you'd have a big pile of letters for your Troop, and go through it, 'Oh, Christ, he's dead', put it underneath. Take out your own, and then pass it on.

When I was out in India I took a correspondence course in Advertising and Journalism, which helped me get a job when I got home. This was with one of the big correspondence course firms, who had offices in Bombay. And some papers for me to do arrived at Kangaw. Now, I've got a tidy mind. I've got to do things immediately. So in a quiet moment I scrounged some khaki paper from the orderly room – when I say orderly room, they just come in with a tin box, with the records in, because in a military unit every day an officer is deputed to write down everything that happens. When you get out of action it's typed up, and copies are sent here, there and everywhere. So, I got this khaki paper, and wrote my answers on it. And then got some bamboo, because I didn't have any pins or anything, and skewered it to keep it together. God knows what they thought when they saw it. Then I gave it to the orderly room, and they got it away for me.

Then came the last morning in the front line, after which Indian troops were going to come in to relieve us. Our Sergeant Major got shot in the stomach. Somebody dragged him out, badly wounded. Other people were getting killed around me. I crawled forward to a body. We'd had a big intake of policemen at one time, and this was one of them. He had a little hole in one side, but when I turned him over he had a great big hole in the other. Dead, of course.

I was told to take my Section forward to clear the hill again. So we advanced, only to find that the Japs had broken. I saw four of them carrying another one, probably an officer, and I emptied a full Tommy gun magazine at them, but I don't know whether I hit them, because they were just disappearing.

One of the people we found alive was a Naval officer, with a dead Jap lying on top of him. When I spoke to him he said he'd been wounded, dropped in the trench, and a live Jap had jumped in with him. He ended up a dead Jap. And this was the officer who directed the gunfire support. Believe it or not he said he'd done the same job for us in Madagascar, nearly three years before.

We also had tank support at Hill 170 [from the Shermans of the 19th (King George V's Own) Lancers, the regiment Paul Roessler had helped ferry across the Bay of Bengal]. Had a job to get them ashore, but they were very useful. One of them was knocked out by a Jap with a bangalore torpedo – a steel tube full of explosive – strapped to him. Just jumped on it and blew himself up. Killed the whole crew.

I found one live Jap, who I made come out and sit down. He was lucky none of our chaps shot him, because we detested the bloody Japs. I mean, I had a friend out there who came from the Midlands, and as he was lying wounded a Jap officer – or a Warrant Officer, because NCOs and Warrant Officers carried swords as well – lopped his head off.

We hated the bastards.

But by then they'd run, and the medics sorted out the wounded.

Later that morning we were relieved by an Indian infantry battalion, and we went straight out to a paddy field and held a service on the spot.

The increasing freedom to carry out such landings on the Burmese coast was an indication of the shifting balance of power at sea, where Japanese fortunes continued to decline and British ones to revive.

With Germany nearing defeat, the British had also begun to consider how their surplus naval strength in Europe might be usefully employed. The obvious answer was to add it to the great American effort in the Pacific.

While some Americans resented what they saw as an attempt to encroach on 'their' theatre, others foresaw the bitter struggles yet to come, and welcomed the newcomers' contribution, however modest.

Richard Meaby served aboard one of the LSI(L)s sent to help with the never-ending task of moving men and supplies.

I'd joined the Royal Marines as a Second Lieutenant in September 1938, at the Royal Marines Barracks, Stonehouse, Plymouth. After service in big ships I was sent in December 1943 to HMS *Northney*, a shore station at Hayling Island, to start training with landing craft. The first course was in signalling and learning Morse and semaphore. This was followed by navigation, and later in the month we started boat work. This lasted till February 1944, when we moved to Clacton-on-Sea. Here we went out in LCP(R)s [the ramped versions of the LCP(L)], having worked with LCMs at *Northney*. We first started using LCAs in March, and I joined a Flotilla soon after for exercises with the Army.

Later I went on a course in Glasgow where we had various exercises in different landing craft.

I eventually joined the new Landing Ship, Infantry (Large) HMS *Lamont* at Glasgow on 26 July 1944. She was due to carry eighteen LCAs from the 558th Flotilla, commanded by Captain W C Curtis, RM. On 30 July we anchored off Greenock and collected our LCAs at Rosneath, and hoisted them on board. We left for New York on 3 August. I was busy sorting out Confidential Books, and also had to keep watches while at sea. We arrived at New York on 14 August, and left again on 18 August to join the American forces in the Pacific. We stopped at Charleston, South Carolina and took the LCAs on exercise, but there was no shore leave.

The crews of the LCAs were mainly employed in keeping the craft clean and doing maintenance work on the engines, but they also attended lectures on seamanship and navigation. They were of course responsible for looking after their part of the ship, and as Marines they also provided guards when required.

The *Lamont* arrived at Panama on 27 August, and the LCAs were lowered to allow them to follow the ship through the Canal during the night, arriving in the Pacific Ocean at 5.00am the following morning. The next day we took the craft to Panama City and were able to go ashore. Some drill exercises were carried out, and we went by train back to Colon, on the Caribbean side of the Isthmus of Panama, on 3 September. There we took part in a pistol shoot against some local teams. On 9 September for three days the ship was evacuated so that she could be fumigated, and we lived ashore in an American camp.

We eventually left on 17 September and the craft were finally hoisted back aboard after following the ship out. Our next stop was at the Society Islands, crossing the Equator on 23 September. We arrived at Bora Bora on 2 October, leaving the next day for the New Hebrides, and crossing the International Date Line on 7 October, when Saturday instantly became Sunday. On 9 October a man fell overboard, but we picked him up in an LCA.

We arrived at the New Hebrides on 12 October, and spent the evening of 18 October at a New Zealand mess. The next day we took the craft on an exercise in the morning, and the day after that we left for Milne Bay [at the south eastern tip of New Guinea].

We went out in the craft while the ship took on oil, and on 29 October we left for Cape Gloucester in New Britain, arriving the next day.

The western end of New Britain, including Cape Gloucester – the scene of an assault landing by the US 1st Marine Division in December 1943 – was now garrisoned by the US 40th Infantry Division. The Japanese remained in control of Rabaul, at the opposite end of the island.

Since all available US divisions were required for the Philippines, however, Australian units were in the process of taking over these beachheads on New Britain, Bougainville and elsewhere.

On the last day of the month we had a landing exercise with HMS *Empire Arquebus*, another new LSI(L), at Cape Gloucester. We received our first mail from home, and I heard of my sister's engagement and my brother's injuries in Normandy. On 2 November we tested our W/T sets and had an exercise with some of the American troops on the island.

On 9 November the monsoon started, and there was trouble hoisting in the LCAs. Some Americans came on board and we took them out in the craft. The Americans in general thought our LCAs were very unsuitable for the heavy surf of the Pacific. As if to emphasise this, there were further exercises on 12 November, and half the craft broached-to when landing on the beach.

We returned to Milne Bay on 20 November, and left for Australia next day carrying Australian troops. We arrived at Cairns, Queensland on 23 November, and more Australian troops came on board. On a subsequent exercise one craft sank and one was damaged. I went on leave on 6 December, and stayed at an Australian Army camp. However, on returning to Cairns the next day we found the ship had unexpectedly left for New Guinea!

On 11 December I and the two other officers who'd been on leave flew in a Mariner flying boat to Port Moresby, the capital of New Guinea, and the next day we flew on by Dakota to Finschhafen, over the Owen Stanley Mountains, where we rejoined the ship. We sailed from there on 14 December for Morotai.

Morotai, north west of New Guinea, had been invaded at the same time as Peleliu, and for the same reasons. Unlike Peleliu, however, no attempt had been made to secure all of it. The American garrison – the 31st Infantry Division – held only enough of the island to safeguard the strategic airfields.

The airfields and American camps were only a short distance from the Japs, but we saw no action. On 21 December we sailed for Hollandia [on the northern coast of New Guinea], and spent the time at sea at Defence Stations, arriving on Christmas Eve to find the LSI(L) HMS *Glenearn* in the harbour. After spending Christmas there we sailed for Milne Bay and Brisbane, collecting some more craft at the former. We reached Brisbane on 2 January 1945, and then went into dry dock.

On 24 January we took on board American troops and sailed to Manus in the Admiralty Islands [to the north of New Guinea; secured as a useful anchorage in the Spring of 1944]. We arrived there on 31 January and offloaded some of the Americans by LCA. Then on to Hollandia to offload the remainder. Further troops were then brought from Oro Bay [in eastern New Guinea] to Hollandia.

After two days of craft exercises we left in a convoy to the Philippines, arriving at Leyte on 20 February. On 21 February we had signal exercises, and the next day we had to send two craft to rescue a third one which'd become beached the night before. We left Leyte on 24 February in a convoy to Manus, and in very rough weather during the voyage we lost another LCA.

I was keeping regular watches, and when we arrived at Manus on 2 March I had to collect some more Confidential Books. We spent some days in harbour, with me busy on the tobacco and mineral accounts which were coming up for audit, and with the CBs for muster. In addition I was appointed Boats Officer, which involved helping to supply boats for the Fleet, which arrived in harbour on 7 March.

The force which arrived to join the *Lamont* on 7 March consisted of four Royal Navy carriers, escorted by two modern battleships and a bevy of cruisers and destroyers.

This, the main body of the new British Pacific Fleet, had been sent to operate under American orders for the remaining, climactic, battles of 1945.

THIRTEEN

Setting Sun: Iwo Jima and the Japanese Surrender

The return of American air and naval power to the Philippines had cut the Japanese Empire in two. But in the absence of any signal that the Japanese might be willing to surrender, the advance towards their home islands continued.

The two big groupings of American forces which had come together to take the Philippines now separated again. MacArthur's units, which had fought their way up from New Guinea and the Solomons, concentrated on subduing the rest of the Philippine archipelago. Those under Fleet Admiral Chester Nimitz, which had carried out the Central Pacific drive, turned north with orders to seize Iwo Jima as a staging post for air operations, and Okinawa as the final step before Japan.

Monday 19 February 1945 was chosen as D-Day for Iwo Jima, and the US 3rd, 4th and 5th Marine Divisions were assigned the task of securing the heavily-fortified 8 square mile island.

Joe Hoban shared the views of many Marines on seeing it for the first time.

It was an ugly piece of land no one would want as a gift. We awoke one morning and there it was, standing out against the skyline like an abandoned hunk of the Moon that'd fallen out of the sky.

We'd had reports about Iwo Jima, and there was an argument among the top brass about the ability of any landing force to take it away from the Japanese, who'd been fortifying it for years. Iwo Jima's claim to importance was its geographic position and the airstrips, which had radar equipment that was picking up B-29s on the bomb route to Japan.

The Boeing B-29 Superfortress was the USAAF's new heavy bomber, with the range to hit Japan from bases in China and on Saipan, Tinian and Guam.

Iwo Jima's location, 625 miles from the Superfortress bases in the Marianas and 660 miles from Tokyo, made it perfect for both sides. The Japanese were using it to harass the bombers. Once safely in American hands, US fighters could be based there to escort the Superfortresses to and from their targets, and damaged planes would be able to land.

Our Division was to serve as a reserve for the 4th and 5th Marine Divisions. The Marine Corps had put its reputation on the line on this one, and both sides were geared to go for all the marbles. No quarter would be given or asked.

The shelling by the huge fleet of ships that was standing offshore, which had been going on for days, was putting the final touches to the softening-up process.

Parts of our Division were ordered to go ashore the second day of the invasion, after the terrible losses the 4th and 5th had taken on the first day. The sea wouldn't allow our guys to land. They came back to our ship after a day in the choppy water. Many were seasick, and all were very tired.

I overheard the Navy officers discussing the possibility that the landing force might be pulled out because of the losses that'd been sustained. But the decision for our Division to go in the next day and relieve the pressure on the 4th and 5th was made. With more shelling of the new Japanese positions that'd been spotted, it appeared it wouldn't be too difficult for our Division to move in and get the operation back on schedule.

The 3rd Marine Division began landing on D+2, but the whole of its strength was never in fact committed. Much to the anger of the hard-pressed men ashore, one of its regiments – the 3rd Marines – was held in floating reserve during the entire battle, because of concerns about overcrowding in the beachhead.

The rest of the Division moved into the centre of the American line, with the 5th Marine Division on its left and the 4th Marine Division on its right.

The sea had some chop to it, but except for the chill in the air and the roar of gunfire overhead, anybody could've made the trip. We needed few instructions. There were a few rookies in the Platoon, but it was definitely a veteran Division. We were as trained and capable as any force of Marines ever assembled. We were going to take this two-bit piece of real estate in a few days, and move on.

The ground, or better to say the ash, was evident after the first few quick steps ashore. I was used to seeing beautiful beaches, and this wasn't in that category. The trouble with our footing was a small problem compared to the disaster the tanks had suffered trying to get traction. They were like so many ducks in a barrel to the Japanese gunners, and only served as artillery markers for the Japanese to zero in on the infantry. The Navy ships kept the bulk of the Japanese guns down with constant covering fire, or it would've been impossible to hold even the small foothold we had.

We were told to get some rest, as night was closing in fast. Our job of keeping control of a nearby airstrip [the southernmost of the three on the island] would wait; the wind and rain were our enemy at the moment.

The next day the reasons for the slight advance across the island became apparent. I hadn't seen such numbers of dead Marines before without seeing a lot of dead Japanese. Although we were an engineer outfit, our Platoon was assigned the job of getting wounded off the front.

The noon of February 23 [D+4], someone mentioned an American flag had been raised on Mount Suribachi, the ugly looking hill to the south of our position at the end of the airstrip. The important thing was that it was one less direction to worry about getting a mortar shell.

Others were not so dismissive. The original flag raising was restaged in the afternoon with a much larger Stars and Stripes obtained from the *LST 779*, and the photograph of the event taken by Joe Rosenthal of the Associated Press has become the single most enduring image of the Pacific War.

The island was very narrow between the only landing places possible for an invasion force the size of ours. Turning north and moving toward the gradually rising hills under heavy fire, at times from three directions, would surely not take more than three more days. It was about 2 miles as I could see, so why should it take any longer than that?

The Japanese would prove just as determined – that if they were to die, they would take as many of us with them as they could. They weren't going to give up their lives cheaply in mindless attacks, as some of the Japanese units on other islands had done. They did their job. It was up to us to do ours as quickly as possible.

We were in a three-day rotation system, which meant we were on front line support for three days and would be pulled back a few hundred yards for three days, to less pressure-type jobs.

It was late one afternoon when we got a message delivered by Sergeant Cage that an infantry unit was expecting an attack that night, and could we come up to their line and pick up four wounded. 'You, you and you' became volunteers, and I asked for, and got, a few of the new men in our outfit to go with me to make up a party of eight. I decided for some stupid reason not to take weapons, in the hope we could beat the darkness if we moved faster.

It was a mistake, and I knew it as soon as we got to the front and an officer told me we had to take *eight* men not four. I asked if any of them could walk, and enough of them got on their feet to make it possible to move the rest of them on stretchers. The trip back was much slower than I'd ever made with wounded, and our situation went really bad when we were fired on by a machine gun at close range. The shell holes that pockmarked the area were a blessing. Rafalowsky, one of the new men from Philly, pulled out a .45 and told me he'd carried it in spite of what we'd decided about not carrying any dead weight. I had to stop him when he went to go to the top of the shell hole to fire back at the machine gun. I knew that would've been a bad move, because I figured they'd have attacked us if they'd known we only had a .45 among such a large group.

We sent one man back to the front because we felt he had a better chance going that way for help. He made it, and through a field telephone got the message to our Platoon. We sweated it out for about a half hour. The Japanese hadn't moved any closer to us, and were playing possum.

The sound and sight of Marines coming to our rescue made up for the foul-up I might've avoided. We were treated like heroes, but I felt like a dunce.

In addition to shells and bullets, combat fatigue was to take its toll of the Marines. Experience and apparent toughness were no defence against its effects.

We got an emergency call from an infantry unit that'd been hit by a burst of artillery fire. We rushed out there as quickly as we could, and started bringing in the wounded to a cave that we'd found earlier and which'd been set up as a field hospital. A doctor and a couple of corpsmen were working in there, and our job was to get the wounded into the cave quickly for treatment.

We'd made several trips in and out of the cave when I noticed that Sergeant Cage was sitting against the wall, and sitting next to him was our Warrant Officer, who'd been wounded on Guam and had had to be forced to leave the line for treatment. As I looked closer, I could see the Warrant's eyes were glazed. He appeared to look straight ahead, yet didn't react to people walking by him or to anything around him. Sergeant Cage was gently trying to give him a drink, but the fluid just ran down the Warrant's chin.

Another time a Marine called Phipps was sitting with a couple of guys when I joined them. I sat on the ground, resting my back on the rise of the hill, and lit up a cigarette as I stretched my legs forward. I picked up my canteen and was completely relaxed. The conversation was of no consequence, which was nice for a change. I noticed while we were shooting the breeze that Phipps had a hand grenade. He would pull the pin out of it until there was only a short length left to hold the handle that would start the countdown for the explosion. It distracted me, but we were all experienced with grenades, and I had no reason to suspect Phipps wouldn't push the pin back into place. Instead he released the handle and threw the grenade toward me, and said 'Here, catch'.

I was gone from that spot about the time it hit the ground. The grenade went off with a 'pop'. They all had been in on the joke of taking the powder out of the body of the grenade. They thought I was too tense, so they wanted to change the pace a little. I was glad Phipps hadn't gone off his nut. I was hoping I wouldn't go off mine.

As on Peleliu, the Japanese defenders had created a labyrinth of interlocking strongpoints, bunkers and caves which defied bombardment and could only be taken at great cost by Marines on the ground.

A Marine called Frank was on his way back to his machine gun outpost with his mess gear in one hand and canteen cup of coffee in the other hand when a Japanese soldier staggered out of a cave opening. Frank left his food in mid air and was running the few steps necessary to reach his rifle, shouting as if he was in the midst of a full-blown banzai attack! Before he reached his rifle, the laughter from the other two guys in the gun crew rose above Frank's screams. The 'charging' Japanese soldier was a little, bewildered old man who was as frightened as Frank.

Frank scared him so bad he went back to the edge of the cave entrance and had to be coaxed out with offers of water and food. It must've been days since the old man had eaten, yet he was too frightened to take our food. A couple of us drank out of canteens and bit on the food so he'd know it was OK. You could guess the fear he had was that we would kill him. It took us some time to calm him as we waited for him to be taken to Headquarters for questioning.

Cave sealing was escalated, and we were given two squads of replacement infantry to guard us while we worked with the explosives. It gave us the chance to set our weapons on the ground and make the best use of our time, tools and talent. The infantry's job was to fan out and protect us from any snipers or surprise attack. We put our whole attention on working our pinch bars and preparing the holes for the charges.

After about fifteen minutes, one of the guys looked up and hollered 'Where's the infantry?'. We all looked up, and couldn't see one of our guards. We dropped our tools and picked up our rifles. Fortunately there were only three directions the infantry 'boots' could've gone. We spotted them in a few minutes. They'd found a cave that had a bunch of Japanese dead, and some of their possessions, spread out in front of it. They were going through that junk looking for souvenirs. We all hollered, almost in unison, for them to halt. We were chewing pretty hard on them for leaving us unguarded, and when one of the guys checked the junk for booby traps and found two in the area, we *really* got on their case. We checked all the junk while we were there just in case other guys would do the same thing these young infantrymen had done.

The Marines on the front pressed the Japanese so hard they had to stay down more and more each day. I was there when a loudspeaker tried several times to talk the Japanese in a cave into giving up. They were completely surrounded. I think one Japanese soldier came out, and he didn't surrender. We sealed the cave entrances. I didn't like to calculate how many men we sealed in caves, but we did try to give them a chance to surrender.

I preferred my times with the wounded, because it gave one a feeling of helping to extend life.

Burying the Japanese dead was one of the jobs that no one liked doing. The climate was quite cool, so it wasn't the problem that it was on Guam. We worked in teams of about ten men each. I had some replacements with me, and asked them to tell me if they happened upon any Marines. It wasn't difficult work. Few bodies had to be moved very far, because the ground was so pockmarked with holes from artillery shells. It was just a matter of backfilling after pushing the bodies into the holes.

We found a few Marines in careful searching of small crevices and in the brush that cropped up occasionally. The big surprise I got one day was when I was called over to check a Marine for Graves Registration and found him to be a friend of mine. There was no doubt it was him. He had gotten killed while carrying a wounded man near the Sulphur Mine [in the centre of the island] a couple of weeks back. The survivors of that incident couldn't remember exactly where they'd left him, but they said he'd been hit by machine gun bullets, and he was dead for sure. They got out with only one more man being hit, and were too shook up to be questioned too much at the time. A trio of us guys spent the better part of three days looking for him, but the snipers in that area were having a field day picking off stray Marines. The visibility was very poor because of the steam-like vapors coming from the Sulphur Mine, so a sniper could move in and out of the shadows with ease. We were finally forced to abandon our search because we were only risking lives based on what we guessed was confused information.

As soon as I got back to my unit I told Sergeant Romero who I'd found, and he knew we'd bunked in the same tent on Guam, so I was a perfect witness. He checked with Graves Registration and found, by odd chance, that there'd been another man with the same name reported buried. With three Marine Divisions on Iwo and with so many dead to handle, the mistake was easily understood.

Another buddy, L I Morgan, got shot in the lower back, but I was told he would be OK. It had been close to a month since we landed on the island, and the end was near.

The Marines had gradually worked their way to the northern tip of the island, and the last organised resistance was extinguished on 26 March, D+35.

When we finally got the official secure message there was no sense of real joy. The price could not be justified. Never was the utter stupidity of war more evident.

We left for home. It was a beautiful Easter Day – April 1, 1945 – when we arrived back on Guam. I had never seen this view of Guam. It was really a striking sight from the sea. The green was such a contrast to the ugly blacks and greys of Iwo. It was good to be alive. Even the news of the start of the invasion of Okinawa on the same day as we returned to Guam couldn't dampen the feeling.

23,203 Marines had been reported as killed, wounded or missing.

Such heavy casualties to take a tiny island like Iwo Jima added fuel to the debate within the American armed forces on whether chemical munitions should have been used.

Poison gas had been employed widely in the First World War, and the United States maintained stocks for the purposes of deterrence and retaliation. Soldiers from the US Army's Chemical Warfare Service, like *Hyman Justman*, were trained and equipped to operate in a chemical environment.

In my basic training of March 1944, our training officers told us that: one, the US Army Air Forces could've bombed Tarawa Atoll in the Gilbert Islands with Mustard Gas bombs; and two, that twenty-four hours afterwards we could've captured Tarawa without any casualties. We wouldn't have needed to fire another weapon.

We were told that our 4.2in chemical mortars could fire gas shells, and we were trained in decontamination of Mustard Gas. This entailed wearing an impregnated suit, a gas mask, and chalking the soles of your shoes with an impregnation crayon. Also, you used a shovel to take an anti-gas mixture from a pail and put it on the ground, or on leaves of bushes – wherever you saw the Mustard liquid.[1] Our mission was to go ahead of the infantry and to decontaminate an area so that they could proceed. We trained with real gas, of course. This was at Camp Sibert, Alabama.

There were, however, equally valid arguments against the use of gas, and Roosevelt was personally opposed to it on moral grounds. The United States therefore limited its use of chemical weapons to incendiaries like Napalm – first dropped during 1944 – and White Phosphorus. The latter, although officially a means of laying smoke screens, could also inflict horrific burns if fired directly onto enemy positions.

In training we were told to put mud on burns from White Phosphorus, to block the oxygen in the air from causing it to burn.

At Camp Sibert my Platoon Sergeant had been in combat with the US 1st Infantry Division in the Mediterranean Theater. He told us his 4.2in mortars would fire White Phosphorus on dug-in Nazi troops. This would cause them to run out of their holes and withdraw to another position because of the burning WP. This practice was continued in rapid succession, and it wreaked devastation.

For the majority of the time, though, the units equipped with the 4.2in chemical mortar found themselves firing high explosive in support of the infantry.

---

1. 'Mustard Gas' actually covers a family of noxious compounds, all of which exist as oily brown or amber liquids in their natural state.

After training I was assigned to the 91st Chemical Mortar Company (Motorized), and on the morning of April 1, 1945 we participated in the landings on Okinawa. We were at that time attached to the US 7th Infantry Division, which was part of the new US Tenth Army.

> The Tenth Army's landings on 1 April involved putting ashore two USMC and two Army divisions – the 1st and 6th Marine Divisions and the 7th and 96th Infantry Divisions – on either side of Hagushi, on the west coast. The 2nd Marine Division was meanwhile staging a diversion off the east coast, boating its troops and only pulling back from making a real landing at the last moment.
>
> The smaller islands to the south west of the Hagushi beaches had already been captured by the Army's 77th Infantry Division, and a Field Artillery Group of two 155mm 'Long Tom' battalions emplaced to support the landings.
>
> A further division, the Army's 27th Infantry Division, would arrive a few days later.

We'd sailed from Leyte to Okinawa aboard the *LST 795*. We slept topside on mattresses which were laid on top of 5-gallon gasoline cans, and we had about 27in clearance from the mattresses to the bottom of the hull of a landing craft being carried above us.

On the morning of Sunday, April 1 [designated L-Day] we made our landing on the Hagushi beaches of Okinawa. My amtrac had two air-cooled .30 caliber machine guns in front and one air-cooled .30 on each side. I sat on top of the left side after we exited the *LST 795* through her open bow doors. We formed up with the rest of the Amphibian Tractor Battalion until a Naval officer, in a Higgins boat, stood up and lifted up his arm and shouted 'Army, go on in!'. We passed a battleship on our left, with orange flames belching from her big guns.

I still have a list of my clothing and equipment for the assault: 'Green fatigue uniform; one pair of shoes; khaki wool knit cap, to be worn under helmet liner in cool weather; green fatigue cap for warm weather; two pairs of lightweight socks; two pairs of undershorts; two undershirts; one very thin wool 'jungle' sweater, to be worn on a cool night; an M1 semi-automatic carbine, caliber .30; five magazines, each containing fifteen rounds of .30 caliber, for the carbine; two canteens filled with water; two webbing cartridge holders for the magazines, one of which we pulled over the wood stock of the carbine for immediate access; one trench knife and holder; one First Aid pouch; one new style gas mask; one bag with straps, for clothing, food, et cetera, carried on the back with the straps over the shoulders and under the armpits; one webbing belt with eyeholes to attach magazine holders, First Aid pouch and knife holder; identification tags – dog tags – worn around the neck; Atabrine tablets as a prophylactic for malaria; canvas tent shelter half, with pegs to anchor it to the ground; poncho; steel helmet with plastic liner'.

As our amtracs approached the beach we could see the high stone seawall extending along the entire shore. At intervals the combat engineers and the Naval gunfire had made large holes in this for our amphibious tractors to go through. We exited our amtrac from its rear ramp, pulling our ammunition and mortar carts.[2] A few enemy shells came over us, causing the entire Squad of eight men to dive into one foxhole. On our right flank a Rifle Company was in a prone position on the beach. They got up and moved off, inland. Upon the order we too moved inland. I was pulling an ammunition cart. We got to Kadena Airfield and dug in about 20 to 25yds behind a Rifle Company.

One of the reasons for choosing the Hagushi beaches in preference to the more sheltered ones on the east coast had been that two airfields – at Kadena and Yontan – would be placed within easy reach of the Army and Marines respectively. Both were captured almost unopposed, as the bulk of the Japanese defenders had again been pulled well back from the beaches.

The second day we advanced across the island right to its other side, still without opposition. Here on the east coast the vegetation resembled that of Southern California.

The third day our motorized vehicles came ashore. Thereafter we no longer needed to pull our mortars and ammunition around, and instead loaded them onto our weapons carriers and trucks.

Having secured the centre of the island, the landing force fanned out northwards and southwards. The main Japanese garrison was found in the south, where conditions were ideal for a protracted defence.

As we went further south the island had miniature pine trees which grew to 3ft or 4ft in height, except where the hills and ridges had been denuded by our aerial bombardment and Navy gunfire. The trees were beautiful, especially at dawn. We didn't see any more of them after we advanced past Skyline Ridge and the massive Hill 178 [features in the path of the 7th Infantry Division, on the left of the American advance].

I was sent on one occasion to a nearby Rifle Company of the 17th Infantry. Here I was just below the top of a hill, and could see over it and look at the panoramic view of the terrain. I saw a succession of hills and ridges in

---

2. Hand carts were necessary because of the considerable weight of the 4.2in chemical mortar. Each weapon broke down into three pieces – the barrel, which weighed 105lbs, the mount, which weighed 53lbs, and the base plate, which weighed 175lbs.

proximity to one another, including the towering Conical Hill dominating the east coast and Highway 13.

This enemy line – the Shuri Line – was one of the strongest Japanese positions encountered so far in the Pacific.

The Japanese garrison was also unusually well supplied with artillery, although still outgunned by the lavish fire support available to the Tenth Army

We had to keep firing even when enemy artillery and mortars had us zeroed in.

Normally we mortar crews never saw our targets, and fired on instructions from our Forward Observers. Each man knew his job and did it without drill commands. My job was to unload the ammunition, prepare the ignition device protruding from the rear of the projectile, and hand it on to be dropped down the barrel, firing the mortar.

The 7th Infantry Division was relieved for ten days, and thereafter returned to the line. We got one day's rest and then on May 11 we went to the west side of the island to join the 6th Marine Division [newly committed in the south after clearing the north of the island], which we supported for the remainder of the campaign.

The west coast had splendid views of the East China Sea. We could gaze upon small islets offshore, like scenes in oriental paintings. Southward, our advance took us to firing positions where we could see the city of Naha. Actually we could look *through* the entire city, because there were only a few buildings still standing.

Two or three times we had a hot meal our rear-echelon cooks prepared and delivered to us. This occurred when we were firing for the 22nd Marines, from the 6th Marine Division. However, this was discontinued and not resumed, because it attracted enemy artillery and mortar fire. Thus C rations comprised our food. Everything we ate was shipped to us. I didn't see any indigenous fresh food except that grown in the gardens of Okinawan families.

Did you see many civilians?

Not until the later stages of the campaign, when there was a mass exodus from their caves and hiding places. The young women were carrying babies in their arms. US interpreters and Japanese prisoners had been coaxing them, and I think they'd realized that we wouldn't kill them, and that their island would inevitably be under US control before long.

In April and May the days were mainly warm and the nights were cool, but some days were cool enough to wear a wool shirt and a field jacket. These, and a wool blanket, had been issued to us once we got to the island. At nights we needed the wool blanket to keep our backs warm during guard duty. By June we didn't need the field jacket.

Bruce Matthew was an infantryman in another of the US divisions. Okinawa was the fifth Japanese-controlled island on which he had landed, the first having been Guam.

At Eniwetok the ships sat baking in the hot July sun, so they allowed us to go swimming by hanging cargo nets over the side. We were having a great time until Portuguese Men o' War moved into our area. You should've seen the guys climbing over one another to get up the nets and out of the water! I didn't hear of anyone getting stung, so all was well that ended well.

We finally left Eniwetok on July 17 [1944], heading directly for our rendezvous with the Japs. As we neared our destination, weapons were test fired, ammunition and grenades were issued and conferences were stepped up in tempo. We sighted Guam early in the morning of July 21; that is, we could see the dark outline of the island against the flashes of the Navy guns raking the shore. Everyone was up and about on deck that morning, as most of us were too nervous to sleep. We watched as dawn broke and we could see our objective for the first time. The beaches were clouded in smoke from the exploding shells, and Navy planes were dropping their bombs on suspected installations. At 8.30am the 1st Provisional Marine Brigade went ashore first, I assume because they'd seen combat before and we were green troops. Pretty soon, however, it was our Regiment's turn to hit the beach.

When I'd become company clerk of 'H' Company, I'd assumed that I would accompany my Company command post wherever it went. But all the company clerks and other regimental clerks were instead assigned to one Section, known as the 305th Personnel Section, under the command of Captain Clesson M Duke. Therefore when 'H' Company was called to the boats in mid-morning, I didn't go with them. Instead I was assigned to the unloading detail, handling supplies and ammunition.

Working in the steel hold of our ship at mid day was like working inside an oven. Of course, the topside crews had to switch with the hold crews to give them a breather. Fortunately for us Japanese air power in the islands had been eliminated, so there was no worry about being strafed.

Since mid-morning the Navy had been bringing Marine casualties to our ship for medical treatment, and the medical people on board were tired out from the workload and the heat. Therefore we were summoned from the unloading detail to act as medical transcribers for the doctors who were operating. No matter that we had no medical training; they said 'Just write down what it sounds like'. I did pretty well until the second operation, when they dug a bullet out of a Marine's back. Between his screams, the smell of the operating room and the heat, I soon had to be relieved by someone else. So it was back to the unloading detail.

By the time we'd finished our work it was late afternoon, and then we loaded our gear and weapons and headed down the nets to the landing craft. We didn't meet much enemy fire because the action had moved inland, but an occasional sniper would ping away at us. Our craft couldn't cross the reef, so we unloaded into the water and waded ashore. It was becoming dusk after we got ashore, so we dug in for the night, right on the beach. Fortunately there were no counterattacks against us during the early hours [although there were further inland], but we didn't get much sleep because we fully expected the Japs to try it.

Next morning, after a tin can breakfast, we formed up on either side of the beach road and headed north until we reached our assigned area on the high ground overlooking the Orote Peninsula. On the way we saw our first Jap soldier being brought in as a prisoner by a Marine. After the build up we'd gotten about the 'fierce Jap enemy' we'd expected a sort of super-soldier. Instead, here was this scrawny, bow-legged person who didn't look the least bit intimidating.

We reached our area after an hour or so, and began to dig in. We'd been working about a half hour when a Warrant Officer who'd been down at a stream below our position came running up yelling 'Japs!'. Seems he'd come face to face with a Japanese soldier who'd been down at the stream getting water. I dropped my entrenching tool and grabbed my rifle, just in time to see someone running through the high elephant grass below my hole. I fired a whole clip in the vicinity of the movement and it stopped. I reloaded and went down to flush that person out, but there was a terrific explosion. At first I thought he was grenading me, but the explosion had been too far away for that. Pressing on, I found this man lying face down in the dirt, dead. He had chosen to lie on a grenade rather than surrender to me. I searched him for a Japanese flag and other identification but found nothing. Strangely, I didn't feel much emotion over the incident, just a little sadness that this man would rather die than surrender to me.

After an uneventful night in our foxholes, we had cold rations again for breakfast and set to work putting up a large tent where we'd be doing our clerking. I had the service record of every man in the Company, and made entries in their records as information came in from the field. Morning Reports were submitted indicating who was on sick call, who had been wounded and who had been killed. In addition, we were called upon to do duties outside our realm, such as acting as messengers, carrying supplies, guarding supply depots or anything else they couldn't spare an infantryman for.

Our days settled into routine and our nights were spent in our foxholes listening for enemy noises. The usual order was not to fire unless you were attacked, because firing would give our positions away.

Dengue fever and dysentery then struck our Section, and that meant there were a lot of sick people. In fact, so many became sick that your fever had to be 104 degrees before you could be hospitalized. At this time word came back to me that my original assignment, 'G' Company, 307th Infantry, had been in action and my old Platoon had been ambushed. My two friends from training camp, Mike Maugeri and Allen Ludlow, were among those slain.

As the campaign progressed in our favor, we saw less and less of the Japs because they were being forced to the north of the island. Pretty soon I was reunited with those in my Company who'd survived. Naturally, the combat soldier liked to razz his company clerk because we weren't front line troops, but it was done in good nature and I never took any personal offense.

We then moved back onto the Orote Peninsula itself and set up new quarters, without foxholes, and tried to live a more normal lifestyle. There were still patrols to pick up Jap stragglers, and there was still some fighting, but basically as far as we were concerned the battle was over. We now slept in tents, had hot meals, got to wash more frequently and were able to get our ration of beer.

Also, we were able to get USO entertainment, and the star of our show was blonde bombshell Betty Hutton [famous for her roles in a number of hit film musicals]. Of course, our radios picked up 'Tokyo Rose', who gave us our fill of good old American jive along with her zany reports that we were losing the war.

We spent the remainder of August, all of September and most of October on Guam, helping the Chamorro people rebuild their island and their lives. At the same time we received some replacements, got more shots and contemplated our next move, which they said would be to a rest camp in New Caledonia.

We weren't combat loaded this time, and left equipment on Guam which would be replaced from the large supply depot on New Caledonia. It was nice to know that we'd be offloading on an island where we wouldn't have to face the Japs.

However, fate caught up with us four days short of New Caledonia, when orders came via the ship's radio to change course and sail to Manus Island. We sat there for two days and got in some swimming, sunbathing and beer drinking at the facility on the island. But all good things must end, and we finally received new orders to proceed to Leyte Island in the Philippines. It appeared that the battle for Leyte had bogged down, and we were to go in and assist the effort.

So it was that we arrived on Thanksgiving Day on the east coast of Leyte. Fortunately for us the beach had been secured by the original assault forces the previous month, so there was no enemy to face. It was just as well, because we weren't combat loaded, and were not well equipped. We waded ashore in pouring rain and began to set up on the beach at a town called Tarragona. There was no air activity because of the inclement weather, which helped our unloading efforts. However, that came to an end a couple of days later when the Japs landed near our position.

In the early hours of 27 November three Japanese aircraft carrying troops and demolition charges crashlanded at various points on the eastern side of Leyte. Many of the Japanese were killed, and the survivors were scattered into the jungle without accomplishing their mission of destroying the airfields in the area.

Our days were taken up with routine patrols and assisting the other divisions whatever way we could. Finally the brass came up with the idea of an end run. Our Division [the 77th Infantry Divison] would re-board transports and be landed on the west coast of the island, behind enemy lines.

On December 6 we boarded a ragtag fleet of LCI(L)s, LSMs[3] and LSTs, and convoyed by a few destroyers we started our trip through enemy waters to the back side of Leyte Island. The next morning [Thursday 7 December 1944] – the third anniversary of Pearl Harbor – at 7.07am, we landed at Deposito, to face little opposition. I guess the Japs were busy elsewhere and didn't expect us to land in their backyard.

The approaches to Ormoc [the main Japanese supply base on Leyte] were swampy rice paddies and open fields, which they'd zeroed in with artillery and small arms fire. It appeared the only way open to us was a frontal attack. As usual our artillery first softened up the defenses with heavy barrages, and the Navy also got in on the act. Soon the town was a blazing inferno of exploding ammunition and gasoline dumps, and black smoke hung everywhere.

Once the enemy had been killed or had evacuated the town, the mopping up continued.

The Division then pushed north up the Ormoc valley, where it joined hands with the US 1st Cavalry Division coming south.

Minus our 1st Battalion, the 305th Infantry now started westward along the road toward Palompon [the last Japanese port]. Although we were travelling along a road, the bridges had all been blown and the rivers had steep banks and very muddy bottoms. On Christmas Day, Douglas MacArthur called the island of Leyte secured. His message was more for the morale of the civilian population back home than it was for the GIs in the field. That day our 1st Battalion made another amphibious end run, and took Palompon.

December 26 on Leyte coincided with December 25 in the States due to the International Date Line, so the Division commander decreed that every soldier would get the traditional turkey dinner on that day.

Patrols of Company size continued to operate throughout the area and to find pockets of Japs from twenty to sixty men in size, which we continued to annihilate. The 305th Personnel Section set up headquarters at San Miguel [where the 305th had linked up with its end run force on New Year's Eve, reuniting the Regiment], and life became more stabilized.

By January 15, 1945 I thought life had become so boring that I volunteered as an armed guard on a motor convoy travelling the road we'd just captured. Going out, the passage was uneventful. However, coming back west we were ambushed by an estimated company of the enemy. They'd prepared well, and allowed the lead tank and our personnel carrier to cross the first bridge, then blew it up. The bridge at the other end of the convoy was then blown, trapping the convoy between the two blown bridges. Their machine guns were placed so that they enfiladed the top and bottom of the convoy. A

---

3. The LSM – Landing Ship, Medium – was basically an LCT with improved seakeeping qualities. The design was originally to have been called the LCT Mk7 (the Mk6 having simply been a double-ended variant of the Mk5).

grenade attack knocked out some of the trucks, setting them afire. I had crawled under the truck in back of our personnel carrier and when it caught on fire, the guys at the side of the road called to us to get out because the truck was carrying ammunition and could go up at any time. As we crawled out from under the truck and ran to the sanctuary of an embankment, the guy in front of me stopped short. When I rolled him over, he was stitched up the front from running into the machine gun fire. Lady Luck was still with me. We laid in a ditch until it started to get dusk and the guys in the tank said they were leaving. Not wanting to wait for the Japs to come down in the dark and kill me, I grabbed my rifle, ran to the tank and hopped on. They geared it up and we ran for home. Later I learned the Japs had come down and burned the trucks carrying mail, PX supplies and ammunition, in addition to stealing half a dozen .50 caliber machine guns.

We were now relieved by another infantry division, the Americal,[4] and sent back to Tarragona, where we'd landed on November 23. We thought we'd done a good job and would be entitled to an extended rest period. However, that wasn't on the cards for us, and soon we were being issued the new combat boot to replace our old shoes and leggings, plus new weaponry and clothing, and replacements for items that'd gone missing during the campaign just finished.

The only thing different this time was that we knew beforehand where we were going next. The objective this time was the Kerama Retto group, just off the island of Okinawa, in the Ryukyus. The Ryukyus were known as 'the Dragon's Tail', because they formed a string of islands running all the way from Formosa to Japan itself.

The small cluster of islands making up the Kerama Retto surrounded a decent anchorage, which the Navy felt it would need to shelter its damaged ships, and to allow for easier replenishment.

Five separate islands were attacked during the first day of the operation, Monday 26 March 1945.

Aboard ship, life was pretty much like it'd been on previous movements, with studies of the objectives ahead and battle plan information, plus the usual debarkation drills. On March 26 [L-6 for Okinawa] we arrived in the Ryukyus. The Navy, being there first, were bombarding the islands to be invaded with their usual abandon. Different units had different objectives on different islands, because there were so many of them. A large number of suicide boats were discovered and destroyed, plus the garrisons there to prevent just that.

By March 31 all these islands were secured and our operation was

---

4. 'Americal' was a contraction of 'American troops on New Caledonia', where the
   Division had been formed in May 1942.

ended. We were now reboated, and put out to sea on April 2, but not before the kamikazes caught us. One came in on my ship, the USS *Chilton*, and tried to dive into us, but the Navy gunners threw him off track, so that he merely tore off our radio antenna and crashed into the ocean. The USS *Henrico*, our Regimental flagship, wasn't so lucky. She took a kamikaze right in the superstructure, killing our Regimental CO Colonel Tanzola, most of his staff, and the ship's Captain. We put out to sea to escape any further raids.

The first deliberate kamikaze attacks, with suicide pilots diving their planes onto ships, had come during the invasion of Leyte in October 1944. The number and severity of the attacks were much greater off Okinawa, however, and so were the losses inflicted.

As the ships carrying the 77th Infantry Division manoeuvred in these dangerous waters, word arrived of the sudden death of Franklin Delano Roosevelt, and the swearing in of Harry Truman as the new President of the United States.

We sailed around in leisurely circles off the coast, preparing ourselves for the next landing – on the island of Ie Shima [just off the Motobu Peninsula, in north western Okinawa].

With our Navy escorts blasting away at the shoreline you would wonder how anything or anyone could possibly survive. However, we knew from previous operations that the enemy was always waiting, regardless of how much we shelled and bombed them. The mountain of Iegusugu which dominated the island was lost from sight in the smoke and dust. After the shelling it was time for us again to climb down into our landing craft and head for the beach. Our destination was the south side of the island, just past the middle. We landed unopposed [on Monday 16 April 1945] with the exception of sporadic sniper fire, and moved on past the airfield on the island. Finally heavy machine gun fire opened up, so we knew this wasn't going to be a cakewalk. In addition to the gunfire we had to be very careful because the Japs had mined the place very heavily using aerial bombs, buried and wired to each other. When we ran across such a situation we called on the demolition guys to come in and defuse them. Unfortunately for all their training one team set off a minefield, and six of them disappeared.

News reached us next day that the famous war correspondent Ernie Pyle [already a veteran of numerous amphibious landings in North Africa and Europe] was with our Regimental command post, observing the war at first hand. We all respected him because he was the infantryman's kind of correspondent, who got down and dirty with us. On the morning of April 18, Ernie Pyle was out and about scouting around with Colonel Coolidge [the new CO] when a Jap machine gun opened up on them. They left their jeep and took cover in a roadside ditch, where Pyle evidently poked his head up, and took a round in the temple. Although we were used to death and buddies being killed, this event really saddened us. I didn't know it at the time, but April 18 would find me a casualty too.

That night we were bivouacked in our holes in the usual perimeter fashion, and there was a 2.5 ton truck parked inside our defense. Somehow or other a Jap soldier loaded down with explosives got inside the perimeter, and the only ones able to fire were six of us down at the bottom. The other guys were directly opposite each other so couldn't fire because of the danger of hitting each other. Well, one or more of us hit this Jap and he went up like Mount Vesuvius, spraying the area with his cargo and himself. At dawn we took stock, and I found I'd been hit in the right wrist with grenade fragments. By the time we discovered this the blood had already congealed, so I just went about my duties as usual, thankful the wound wasn't more serious.

The next few days were spent fighting on and around Iegusugu and Ie Town, with heavy casualties on both sides. Evidently the only way we were going to get off the island was to kill them all, and that was what we set out to do.

By April 27 we'd mopped up most of the resistance, and we now had hordes of civilians surrendering to us. At first they were afraid because the soldiers had convinced them that we were barbarians and would torture and kill them, but after humane treatment they volunteered to go back and convince others that they wouldn't be harmed.

Most of the 77th Infantry Division was then despatched to Okinawa, but Bruce and part of the 305th Infantry remained behind for a short time.

We enjoyed a week of relative quiet on Ie Shima before we were ordered to enter the fray on the big island – a battle completely different from our jungle warfare and small island campaigns. On May 6 we began to load our gear on an LST for transport to Okinawa. The Japs did their best to keep us from completing our task by constant air raids. However, early the next morning we shoved off for our new endeavor. Later that day we landed on Okinawa at a secure site, and boarded trucks for our trip inland to an assembly area in the central part of the island. That same day, we moved into combat positions to relieve those who'd been doing the fighting.

There was little doubt in our minds that we were going to have a tough time ahead of us. That first night we took heavy enemy mortar and artillery fire in our sector, and there were attempts at infiltration during the night. The next few days saw the usual advance against stubborn resistance. Our main problem seemed to be that the Japs held most of the high places, and were able to direct mortar and artillery fire from their vantage points.

Moving southward we approached the outer limits of Shuri, where the enemy fire from machine gun nests and tanks grew heavier. Some of our battalions had been so depleted by casualties that they were only at half strength. I guess the brass had to find some way to knock the Japs off balance, so it was decided that we'd launch a night attack against them. As far as we knew, this was the first time that American troops on Okinawa had done this. We did catch the Nips off guard, because they'd been taught that we would never attack at night, but as usual they were able to regroup and fight back. A few nights later we did it again. Finally on May 21 we were relieved and moved back to a rest area where we could clean our equipment and weapons [heavy rain having turned the battlefield into a quagmire].

While we were bivouacked we still had to be aware of the possibility of Jap stragglers penetrating our area, so every night about dusk we would reconnoitre our area. One night another soldier, our Lieutenant and I were making a sweep on a hilly area when a machine gun opened up on us. Fortunately no one was hurt. Lo and behold it was an American Seabee outfit, and the kid on the gun said he'd thought we were Japs. Our Lieutenant went to lodge a complaint, while the Seabees crowded around us and asked the usual question in the service, namely where we were from. I stated I was from Paterson, New Jersey, and they said they had a guy from Paterson, named Pryor, and went to get him. When he arrived I didn't know him, but I did know his brother, who lived about six or seven blocks from my home. This Seabee asked if I could stay and visit, but I had to get back on the hill for my guard duty. The next morning I asked my CO if I could visit this kid, and he said OK as long as he knew where I was in case they had to move out fast. So, off to the Seabee camp I went, and was I ever surprised. They had pyramidal tents with wooden floors; cots with air mattresses and mosquito netting; a laundry; hot showers; a screened-in mess hall where you sat at a table to eat . . . and they also had cold beer. I spent the day with those guys and they couldn't do enough for me, but the next day we pulled out and I never saw them again.

Back at the war we found that replacements had come in, and these 'greenies' had to be taught hard and fast. To replace lost Noncoms, it was nothing to go from Pfc to Sergeant in one day.

While we'd been resting the Marines had taken Shuri Castle, much to our relief. This didn't meant that we would get off scot-free, because there were still many hills and enemy strongpoints before we were done. From the end of May through the end of June it was the same old pursue and destroy.

After a year of fighting the little yellow bastards we found we'd become just as ruthless as they were. It was no longer a horrible thing to seal pockets of them forever in some Okinawan cave, or to burn twenty or thirty at a clip with flamethrowers. It even got to the point where we'd shoot them even if they were offering to surrender. Too many times they'd appear to surrender, only to use a grenade to kill themselves and you. It boiled down to the age-old urge to survive.

After the fall of Shuri American progress began to quicken, aided by an end run by part of the 6th Marine Division.

The Japanese were still fighting, however, and on 18 June the commander of the Tenth Army, Lieutenant General Simon

Buckner, was killed as he observed the advance. Major General
Roy Geiger, USMC was promoted to Lieutenant General and
appointed as his replacement – the first time a Marine had
commanded so large a force.

Organised resistance on Okinawa was declared over on 21
June, although as usual a considerable amount of mopping up
remained to be done. Kamikaze attacks against the ships offshore
continued until the end of July.

As the combat divisions began to move out, huge numbers of
construction troops laboured to build more airfields, ready for
the next campaign.

Few were under any illusions as to what this would involve.

We sailed away on July 1, making it three months and six days since we'd
invaded the Ryukyu Islands.

Germany had surrendered while we were on Okinawa and we were glad for
the guys in Europe, but we knew that our fight was far from being over, and
the only place left was Japan itself.

The US Sixth Army's plan for invading Kyushu, the southernmost
of the four main islands of Japan, was based on the same formula
employed at Okinawa.

On X-5 some of the offshore islands would be seized by the US
40th Infantry Division and an independent regiment, in order to
provide radar sites and anchorages. X-Day would then see
landings by the 2nd and 3rd Marine Divisions, the 25th, 33rd and
43rd Infantry Divisions and the 1st Cavalry Division, using three
distinct landing areas at the southern end of Kyushu. The 5th
Marine Division, Americal Division, 41st Infantry Division and
another independent regiment would be in floating reserve.

The ships carrying a further two divisions, the Army's 81st and
98th Infantry Divisions, would stage diversions off Shikoku from
X-2 until X-Day, and then be ready to land their troops wherever
they were required.

Bruce and the rest of the 77th Infantry Division would arrive
shortly afterwards, followed on X+22 by the 11th Airborne
Division.

As early as 25 May, the date for X-Day had been set as Thursday
1 November 1945. Most of the assault units were in the
Philippines, where the 77th was now heading.

Aboard our LST, leaving Okinawa, rumours were flying thick and fast as to
where we were headed. Some of the more ludicrous suggestions were that we

were going back to Hawaii, or even that we were going to be rotated back to the United States, and that we'd be replaced with troops from the European Theater.

Nevertheless, life on board the LST was easy and the only rule aboard ship was that the Navy personnel ate first, the Army second. So one day, being the chowhound that I was, I was close to the front of the Army personnel, and one of the last sailors going through the chow lines said to the cook 'Jesus Christ, cherry pie again!'. So I leaned over and said to the cook 'If he doesn't want his, I'll have his and mine'. It just goes to show you how spoiled some services got.

Finally we arrived at our destination – Cebu, another Philippine island pretty much like all the other islands we'd been to. The big difference here was that we didn't have to invade, although there'd been some enemy activity by remnants of the Japanese Army. We'd been assigned to a nice area right near the beach, although there was the usual landscaping and digging of rain troughs outside each pyramidal tent area. Native labor was secured to help in the erection of various buildings, including a Regimental theater called the Doogan Theater after Pfc Theodore Doogan from my Company, who'd been awarded the Silver Star for gallantry in action. There were movies and talent shows performed in the theater most every night.

In addition, the GI has ways of finding his own recreation and one was to buy native booze. The natives made it from coconuts, and it was far more potent than the beer we got from the Army, so there were some occasions of drunkenness. However, it wasn't all fun and games on Cebu. We still had training schedules to adhere to, and Non Commissioned Officer's classes were instituted. There was still a war on, and we had to be ready for whatever lay ahead. Rumours were rampant that we were going to invade Japan, and many of us felt that casualties would be so heavy that a lot of us wouldn't survive.

> The objective of the Kyushu operation would be to capture enough of the island to ensure the use of Kagoshima Bay and the numerous airfield sites in the south.
>
> With these in American hands, preparations could be made for a landing on Honshu, the largest of the home islands. The first of the extra divisions needed for Honshu had already left Europe on their way to the Pacific.

Then one evening at a movie at the Doogan Theater, the film stopped, and the Chaplain came onto the stage to announce the war was over.

The place went wild, and guys were hugging each other and clapping one another on the back. The movie was no longer of interest.

I went back to my Company area and we decided to have a celebration, so we gathered together all the native booze we could lay our hands on, and packets of powdered lemonade, and our CO brought us a bottle of Scotch. All these were mixed together and valiantly disposed of to the tune of 'I'll be home for Christmas'. Needless to say, the next morning was one glorious hangover for all concerned.

The United States had secretly developed the first nuclear weapons, and the dropping of two of these – on Hiroshima on 6 August and Nagasaki on 9 August[5] – by Superfortresses from Tinian had finally induced the Japanese to surrender.

But our hopes of being sent home for discharge were dashed when we found out we'd be going to Japan after all, as occupation troops. There was lots of grumbling because those of us who'd survived combat felt we should be allowed to go home, and that those who hadn't seen combat should be used as occupiers. Of course, our feelings didn't count for much with the brass, and finally we reboated for our sea voyage to Japan. We watched the lazy, tropical island of Cebu fade in the distance and headed for the second largest and most northern of the main islands of Japan, Hokkaido.

Peter Norcock was one of the first Allied servicemen to step ashore on Japanese soil, as the Royal Marine officer leading a landing party.

On the morning of 15 August, when offensive operations were suspended in light of the Japanese announcement that they were ready to surrender, his ship – the battleship HMS *King George V* — was steaming off Tokyo.

We suddenly got the news that the Japanese had given in, and that their surrender would be signed on board the USS *Missouri* [flagship of the American fleet with which the *King George V* was sailing] at the Yokosuka Naval Base in Tokyo Bay.

A regiment from the US 6th Marine Division was despatched from Guam the same day, ready to secure the base and the entrance to the bay. The ships already off the Japanese coast also organised a landing force from their own Marines and Naval personnel.

I was sent for by Vice-Admiral Sir Bernard Rawlings [flying his flag aboard the *King George V*], and in consultation with the Captain told to take half my detachment plus some Marines from two of our cruisers, and to embark in three American APDs – fast transports. The island of Azuma, close to the position where the *Missouri* would anchor, was to be occupied by a British force to be landed two or three days prior to the surrender being signed.

The landing force had to be a bit of a compromise, because the Marines manned a large part of the armament of the three ships, and no Captain

---

5. Nagasaki was in fact the secondary target, and was bombed because the primary target
   – Kokura – was completely obscured by cloud on the day of the mission.

would willingly give up much of his firepower in case the Japs decided to have a last fling.

So, a few days later, we were transferred while under way, in US landing craft, to the three APDs – the USS *Barr*, USS *Pavlic* and USS *Sims*. All this taking place with a typhoon approaching. My ship, the *Barr*, seemed very small compared with the *KGV*, and oh how one missed the stately pitch and roll of the battleship in rough weather!

From 20 August to 26 August we manoeuvred to avoid the typhoon, and then on 28 August I and an American liaison officer were transferred, for a conference, to an HQ ship where the American Marine element of the landing force was embarked. This time the transfer was made at speed. A stout rope was made fast to the APD and then passed to the HQ ship. One was then pulled across sitting on a thing like a swing seat, just holding onto the side ropes. There were twenty American sailors there to keep the rope in tension, so that should the two ships heel towards each other, they could pull like mad to keep the rope taut. The sea was still very rough, and we were steaming at about 15 knots. The American went first, and when half way over the ships heeled towards each other suddenly. This took the twenty sailors by surprise and allowed the rope to go slack, and I saw the unfortunate liaison officer drop like a stone into the water. Then of course the ships came upright and he shot like a yo-yo into the air. Luckily he held on. Had he let go – and one wasn't strapped in, in any way – I think he'd have been lost, as we weren't wearing lifejackets.

By the time it was my turn the twenty sailors had been backed up by ten more, and I had a very easy crossing. But at the conference I found my mind constantly thinking of the return journey, which in fact was uneventful for us both.

On Thursday 30 August 1945, armed to the teeth, we were duly landed on the island of Azuma. There was no trouble, and the Jap Naval officer who surrendered the island was taken to the mainland with about six others. We were left to explore and guard the island, so that *Missouri* when she anchored was safe at least from that quarter. The American Marines occupied other strategic points on the mainland.

The Japanese surrender was signed on 2 September.

Azuma was a fascinating place to explore – a warren of underground tunnels and stores, with generating plants, machinery for pumping oil, and stocks of every type of hardware. My HQ was billeted in a hut near the oiling pier. All the huts and heads were in a filthy state, and a large number of rats occupied the hut with us. To overcome the heads problem I had a canvas screen erected at the end of the pier, and an ammunition box cut to size and placed over a hole.

During our time on the island I arranged for everyone to have some form of souvenir from the underground stores. Nothing valuable, but something to remember Azuma by, like a glass with the Jap Naval crest on it. Having done this the tunnels were padlocked and guarded. As it was, within twenty-four hours of having turned over the island to the Americans at the end of our stay, objects such as binoculars were being sold ashore. It was difficult for the troops to see that what we'd done was correct, when comparing a glass with saleable items worth a lot of money!

We returned on board for a couple of days, *KGV* having now anchored in the harbour, and then we changed into ceremonial rig and, preceded by the band, the detachment marched through Yokohama to take over the British Consulate. In the thirty-one years I did in the Marines, I must've done dozens of Ceremonial Guards, but this was the only one where I made sure every man had a pocketful of ammunition. Happily this proved entirely unnecessary. One realised very early on that the discipline of the Japanese, military and civilian, was excellent. If the Emperor told you to die for your country you did so; in this case he'd said 'No more fighting'. To my limited knowledge they obeyed this to the letter.

We then returned on board, packed a few things and motored to Tokyo, where the British Embassy was turned over to me by its caretaker from the Swiss Legation, who'd lived there with his Japanese wife during the war. Nothing was damaged; the Rolls Royce was in the garage, the visitors' book open at the signature of the last visitor prior to hostilities.

Another little bit of history. In 1864, some eighty-one years before, my paternal grandfather, then a Lieutenant, had landed at Yokohama with the Royal Marine battalion sent there to guard the interests of the European community during a period of disturbances in the country. Later that year he carried the Plymouth Division Colour into action at the storming of the Japanese stockade at Shimonoseki. The day I joined Plymouth in 1930, the Mess Corporal, one Corporal Turver, took me to see it.

You're obviously proud of your heritage.

Yes, I am. I was born in a Marine barracks. My father was a Marine. My grandfather was a Marine. My step-great-grandfather was a Marine, and I married the daughter of a Marine officer.

But heritage is a funny thing. People's memories can be so short.

My last job was as Director of the Royal Marine Forces Volunteer Reserve, which involved visiting lots of places and meeting lots of people. And I remember somebody saying to me 'Oh, you're a Marine. What instrument do you play?'.

They'd seen the band on parade, and that was their sole knowledge of what the Marines did.

Sometimes I wonder if people really know anything about their own history.